A Tale Blazed
Through Heaven

*Imitation and Invention
in the Golden Age of Spain*

OLIVER J. NOBLE WOOD

OXFORD

UNIVERSITY PRESS

Great Clarendon Street, Oxford, OX2 6DP,
United Kingdom

Oxford University Press is a department of the University of Oxford.
It furthers the University's objective of excellence in research, scholarship,
and education by publishing worldwide. Oxford is a registered trade mark of
Oxford University Press in the UK and in certain other countries

First Edition published in 2014
Impression: 1

Published in the United States of America by Oxford University Press
198 Madison Avenue, New York, NY 10016, United States of America

British Library Cataloguing in Publication Data
Data available

Library of Congress Control Number: 2014935636

ISBN 978–0–19–870735–6

Printed and bound by
CPI Group (UK) Ltd, Croydon, CR0 4YY

Preface

It is hoped that this book will prove of interest to students and specialists not only in the literature and culture of early modern Spain but also in cognate subjects. To this end, some contextual information on the main poets and painters discussed in this study is given at the start of each new chapter/section. This information is designed with a view to being useful to non-specialists without being overly intrusive to readers already well acquainted with the figures under examination.

Throughout this study, I have followed the spelling, punctuation, and accentuation of the editions cited. Translations into English of titles and quotations from foreign-language works cited in the main text are provided except in cases where the meaning of such titles/quotations is obvious, or made such by their immediate context. All translations are mine, unless otherwise acknowledged in an accompanying footnote, and are given in brackets immediately after the first appearance of each title/quotation. In the cases of the titles of some works of art, the translations given are not literal but rather the accepted English versions.

This book would not have been possible without the input and support provided by many individuals and organizations over the past decade. I would like to thank my friends and (former) colleagues in Oxford and Nottingham, the staff at the Taylor Institution Library, and the three anonymous readers for OUP (whose comments and suggestions helped to eliminate some of the more egregious errors and infelicities). I owe particular debts of gratitude to Colin Thompson, who supervised, with his characteristic blend of the comic and the serious, the DPhil thesis on which this book is based; Jeremy Lawrance and Bernard McGuirk, whose contrasting but complementary *modi operandi* made my time in Nottingham so profitable; and Dominic Moran and Jonathan Thacker, whose good-fellowship has helped me to stay (reasonably) sane since taking up my current post. I am also grateful to Hertford College for a generous contribution to the cost of the illustrations. This book is dedicated to my parents, Ann and Philip, whose love and encouragement over the past thirty-four years have been unwavering.

ONW
Hertford College, Oxford

15 April 2014

Contents

List of Illustrations

Abbreviations and Conventions

AEA	*Archivo español de arte*
Aut.	*Diccionario de autoridades*, Biblioteca Románica Hispánica: Diccionarios, 3, 3 vols. (Madrid: Gredos, 1979)
BCC	Biblioteca Capitular y Colombina
BHS	*Bulletin of Hispanic Studies*
BSS	*Bulletin of Spanish Studies*
CC	Clásicos Castalia
CEEH	Centro de Estudios Europa Hispánica
Cov.	Sebastián de Covarrubias, *Tesoro de la lengua castellana o española*, ed. Ignacio Arellano and Rafael Zafra, Biblioteca Áurea Hispánica, 21 (Madrid: Iberoamericana, 2006 [1611])
CSIC	Consejo Superior de Investigaciones Científicas
CTSA	Colección Támesis Serie A
HR	*Hispanic Review*
LCL	Loeb Classical Library
Lex.	José Luis Alonso Hernández, *Léxico del marginalismo del Siglo de Oro*, Acta Salmanticensia: Filosofía y Letras, 99 (Salamanca: Universidad de Salamanca, 1976)
LH	Letras Hispánicas
MHRA	Modern Humanities Research Association
MLR	*Modern Language Review*
MSPS	Manchester Spanish & Portuguese Studies
RAH	Real Academia de la Historia
TWAS	Twayne's World Author Series

The poems of Quevedo are identified according to the numeration in Francisco de Quevedo, *Obra poética*, ed. José Manuel Blecua, 4 vols. (Madrid: Castalia, 1969–81), and given in the form Q513, Q825, etc.

Introduction

In his burlesque ode 'A son lict' [To his Bed] (1550), 'Prince of Poets'
Pierre de Ronsard suggests that anyone who has seen Mars and Venus
cavorting in bed, 'dans un tableau portraits tous nus' [captured stark naked
in a painting], will be able to picture what he and his mistress get up to
in their spare time.[1] In a painting dating from the same year (Fig. 1), the
Venetian artist Jacopo Tintoretto presents an equally playful handling of
a different, yet related, scene. Venus reclines naked on a bed, as her husband Vulcan carefully lifts the sheet that maintains her modesty to check
for signs of infidelity. She has, it seems, narrowly avoided being caught *in
flagrante delicto*, for her lover Mars, identified by his helmet and armour,
can be seen peeking out from under a nearby table. Forced to take evasive
action by what the viewer must assume was the untimely return of Venus's
husband, Mars now waits for the appropriate moment to flee or perhaps
even rejoin his lover. Though at present Vulcan seems oblivious to Mars's
presence, a small dog standing at the foot of the bed barks at Mars and thus
threatens to give the lovers' game away.

What do Ronsard's poem and Tintoretto's painting share in common?
One answer is that both present humorous treatments of a well-known
mythological tale: the story of an affair between Venus, goddess of love and
beauty, and Mars, god of war, and the lovers' eventual capture and public
shaming at the hands of Vulcan, god of fire and the forge. Whilst Ronsard
draws an amusing comparison between his own sexual practices and those
of the classical gods to introduce an erudite allusion to carnal embrace
(the next allusion, this time to the rhythmic movements of the bed's headboard, is rather less subtle), Tintoretto presents an innovative reworking
of an episode from the same narrative to offer a light-hearted meditation on the theme of cuckoldry. The contemporary reader or viewer might
be indignant at such frivolous treatments of one of the most salacious
classical tales, but, in each case, the audience is included in the conspir-
acy, and thus made to side with the lovers against the hapless husband

---

[1] Pierre de Ronsard, *Les quatre premiers livres des Odes de Pierre de Ronsard* (Paris: Guillaume Cavellart, 1550), fols. 71^v–2^r (Livre II, Ode 27).

Fig. 1. Jacopo Tintoretto, *Venus, Vulcan, and Mars, c.*1550. Oil on canvas.

(conspicuous by his absence in Ronsard's poem). Both the French poet and the Italian painter create worlds in which stories of the gods and their affairs (in both senses of the word) may be read (or viewed) and enjoyed rather than merely consulted as learned authorities or repositories of moral lessons. They do so by poking gentle fun at the gods, stripping them of their divine authority, and suggesting or showing that they are subject to the same desires, instincts, and foibles as mere humans.

Significantly, both Ronsard and, to a greater extent, Tintoretto succeed in reframing aspects of this celebrated tale. The latter offers a new take on the recumbent Venus, a tradition stretching back through Titian to Giorgione, by including a series of playful details that strike a chord with the mythological episode: the jealous husband, complete with lame leg, checking his wife's groin for signs of recent sexual activity; the armed lover cowering under the table; the barking dog, a reflection of fidelity to its master (providing an ironic contrast with the unfaithful Venus); the sleeping Cupid, the offspring of a previous tryst, blissfully unaware of his parents' predicament; and the mirror (Mars's shield?) on the back wall, which may have given the lovers advance warning of Vulcan's arrival.[2]

---

[2] On this suggestion, given by Jean de Meun, *Roman de la Rose*, 18061–70, see Carla Lord, 'Tintoretto and the *Roman de la Rose*', *Journal of the Warburg and Courtauld Institutes*, 33 (1970), 315–17.

Notably, Tintoretto surprises his audience by depicting the opposite of what they might anticipate: those familiar with the tale's principal classical sources—as we shall see, Homer, *Odyssey*, VIII.266–369, and Ovid, *Metamorphoses*, IV.169–89—would expect to find Vulcan with the upper hand, trapping Mars and Venus in his net, flinging open the doors of heaven, and exposing the lovers to the *Schadenfreude* of their peers. Here, however, the tale is turned inside out. Vulcan continues to be the one deceived, and, for the time being at least, the affair remains secret. The only difference is that now the audience is in on it too.

As Jean Seznec observes in his influential work on classical mythology in early modern Europe, 'the knowledge of mythology became so diffused [in the Renaissance] that it took on the character of a veritable invasion'.[3] The period from the late fifteenth century to the end of the seventeenth saw the publication across Western Europe of innumerable editions and translations of classical works, of commentaries on canonical Graeco-Roman texts, and of manuals designed to aid individuals in their understanding of specific classical tales. Whilst, on the one hand, this invasion gave poets and painters a rich storehouse of mythological narratives from which to draw, on the other it meant that all but the most obscure classical tales were already well known to prospective audiences. What, therefore, was the point in telling or illustrating tales that everyone already knew? How could poets and painters outstrip their predecessors and contemporaries? If imitation was an end in itself, what scope was there for originality and invention? Were there advantages to knowing that one's audience would already be familiar with the tale one was telling? The invasion described by Seznec posed all these questions and more to poets and painters in the sixteenth and seventeenth centuries. Ronsard's ode and Tintoretto's painting embody just two of the many different ways in which such questions could be answered.

Like many classical tales, the story of Mars, Venus, and Vulcan left an indelible mark on the early modern European imagination. Whilst by no means the most frequently imitated of the storehouse's tales, it was nevertheless a popular subject in almost every Renaissance art form, literary or visual, liberal or mechanical: poetry, prose, and drama; painting, sculpture, and tapestries; woodcuts, engravings, and book illustrations; coins, medals, and bronze reliefs; stonework, cabinetry, and door panelling; and decorative schemes for bedrooms, bathrooms, and reception rooms. One need look no further than the middle decades of the sixteenth century

---

[3] Jean Seznec, *The Survival of the Pagan Gods: The Mythological Tradition and its Place in Renaissance Humanism and Art*, trans. Barbara F. Sessions, Bollingen Series, 38 (New York: Pantheon, 1953), 219.

Fig. 2. Guglielmo della Porta, *Mars and Venus Trapped by Vulcan*, *c*.1555. Gilt bronze.

for further examples of its influence. The Lombard sculptor and architect Guglielmo della Porta captures several scenes from the tale, including Mars's courtship of Venus (centre background), Apollo's visit to the forge (left middle ground), and the lovers' imprisonment at the hands of Vulcan (centre and right foreground), in a miniature gilt-bronze relief dating from the mid-1550s (Fig. 2). A series of scenes from the tale is also the subject of a celebrated set of mid-sixteenth-century Flemish tapestries that had a profound influence on English tapestry design in the following century.[4] The tale was especially popular in Renaissance and Baroque painting, with artists across Western Europe turning to the union of Mars and Venus (Titian, Veronese, Rubens, Guercino, Poussin, etc.) and Vulcan's imprisonment and unveiling of the lovers (Martin van Heemskerck, Frans Floris, Joachim Wtewael, Hendrick de Clerck, Luca Giordano, etc.) for subjects and sources of inspiration.

---

[4] See Ella S. Siple, 'A Flemish Set of Venus and Vulcan Tapestries. I: Their Origin and Design', *Burlington Magazine*, 73 (1938), 212–21; and 'A Flemish Set of Venus and Vulcan Tapestries. II: Their Influence on English Tapestry Design', *Burlington Magazine*, 74 (1939), 268–79.

The tale also left its mark on the culture of the Iberian Peninsula, providing a source of inspiration for poets, playwrights, prose writers, and painters throughout the Golden Age of Spain—the period from 1526, the year in which Juan Boscán and Garcilaso de la Vega, Spain's first Renaissance poets, began to experiment with Italianate subjects and forms, to 1681, the year of the death of Pedro Calderón de la Barca, the last great writer of the Spanish Baroque. Allusions to the tale are found in some of the most famous works of Golden Age prose fiction. The net that Vulcan forges to catch Mars and Venus often serves, for instance, as a synecdoche for an invisible, unbreakable, and inescapable trap. In Mateo Alemán's monumental picaresque novel, *Guzmán de Alfarache* (1599/1604), a sermon-like digression on *engaño* [deceit], in II.i.3, begins with a description of it as 'una red sutilísima, en cuya comparación fue hecha de maromas la que fingen los poetas que fabricó Vulcano contra el adúltero' [a very fine net, in comparison with which the one that poets claim Vulcan forged against the adulterer was made of thick ropes].[5] Vulcan's net is surpassed by *engaño*: if Mars and Venus fell into the trap set for them by Vulcan, what chance do mere mortals stand in a world of ubiquitous deceit? Another example is seen in *Don Quijote*, II.58: when Cervantes's knight-errant becomes entangled in a green net stretched between trees, he boasts that, even if it were 'más fuert[e] que aquella con que el celoso dios de los herreros enredó a Venus y a Marte' [stronger than the one with which the jealous smith-god ensnared Venus and Mars], he would break it with the utmost ease, as if it were made out of 'juncos marinos o . . . hilachas de algodón' [rushes or . . . cotton thread]. The absurdity of this claim, and of the implied parallel between Don Quixote and Mars, is underscored when it is revealed moments later that the net was set by two country girls in order to 'engañar los simples pajarillos' [trick silly little birds].[6]

Though the tale represents an inherently dramatic subject, its emphasis on adultery, nudity, and public shaming poses obvious problems in terms of theatrical decorum. Nevertheless, it still inspired a number of dramatic

---

[5] Mateo Alemán, *Guzmán de Alfarache*, ed. José María Micó, LH, 86–7, 2 vols. (Madrid: Cátedra, 2003), ii. 63. The association of Vulcan's net with *engaño* is common in the literature of the period; see e.g. Lupercio Leonardo de Argensola's sonnet that begins 'Sin duda que esta red de hierro dura', in *Rimas de Lupercio, i del Dotor Bartolomé Leonardo de Argensola* (Zaragoza: Hospital Real, 1634), 24.

[6] Miguel de Cervantes, *Don Quijote de la Mancha*, ed. Francisco Rico (Madrid: Alfaguara, 2004), 990. This is the second time that an incongruous parallel is established between Don Quixote and Mars: in I.21, when Cervantes's knight discovers that half of Mambrino's helmet is missing, he counters Sancho Panza's observation that it looks like a barber's basin by stating that he will have it repaired so that 'no le haga ventaja, ni aun le llegue, la que hizo y forjó el dios de las herrerías para el dios de las batallas' [it will not be surpassed, or even equalled, by the one that the smith-god forged for the god of war] (p. 190).

works in the Golden Age, from *comedias* to shorter forms of theatre such as *loas, entremeses, bailes,* and *mojigangas*.[7] To my knowledge, no full-length play on the subject written in the Golden Age survives today, but there is evidence to suggest that such plays did exist. In his account of the elaborate court festivities held in Lerma in October 1617, Pedro de Herrera recalls a performance of a play entitled *El adulterio de Marte y Venus* [The Adultery of Mars and Venus], thought to have been written by Lope de Vega, the greatest playwright of the age, together with an anonymous *mojiganga* mocking it.[8] On 11 February 1619 a play by the little-known Valencian dramatist Vicente Esquerdo entitled *Marte y Venus en París* [Mars and Venus in Paris] was performed in the Salón de Cortes in Valencia's Palacio de la Generalitat.[9] Francisco Bernardo de Quirós's miscellany *Aventuras de don Fruela* [Don Fruela's Adventures] (1656) features a burlesque *baile* which sees Mars begin his affair with Venus by disguising himself as a wild boar and killing her previous lover Adonis.[10] References to the tale were also included in works on other subjects. In Tirso de Molina's *La mujer que manda en casa* [The Woman Who Gives Orders at Home], a play on the Old Testament figure of Jezebel, Jezabel [*sic*] counters her servant Criselia's warning against adultery by citing the example of Venus's affair with Mars. The brief discussion of the tale that follows in lines 404–29 ends when Criselia draws a prophetic contrast between her mistress, a mortal queen, and Venus, an immortal goddess, who ' . . . se pudo infamar | pero no perder la vida' [could lose her honour but not her life] (lines 422–3).[11]

The biggest mark, however, was left on the poetry and painting of the period. In the poetry of the sixteenth and seventeenth centuries Mars, Venus, and Vulcan appear in a wide range of contexts. As individuals, they are often introduced as embodiments of military might, female beauty, and divine artistry, respectively. The lovers Mars and Venus frequently

---

[7] For a brief introduction to these various forms, see Jonathan Thacker, *A Companion to Golden Age Theatre*, CTSA: Monografías, 235 (Woodbridge: Tamesis, 2007), 152–62.

[8] See Manuel Cornejo, 'Lope de Vega y las fiestas de Lerma de 1617: la teatralización de «las fiestas de Castilla» en *Lo que pasa en una tarde*', *Mélanges de la Casa de Velázquez*, 37 (2007), 179–98.

[9] Henri Mérimée, *Spectacles et comédiens à Valencia (1580–1630)* (Toulouse: Edouard Privat, 1913), 74.

[10] Francisco Bernardo de Quirós, *Obras de don Francisco Bernardo de Quiros. Alguacil propietario de la casa, y corte de su magestad. Y aventuras de don Fruela* (Madrid: Melchor Sánchez, 1656), fols. 29ᵛ–31ʳ. For more on this work, see Ignacio Arellano Ayuso, 'Paradigmas burlescos en *Las aventuras de Don Fruela*, de Francisco Bernardo de Quirós, enciclopedia jocosa del Siglo de Oro', *Monteagudo*, NS 9 (2004), 109–26.

[11] Tirso de Molina, *La mujer que manda en casa*, ed. Dawn L. Smith (London: Tamesis, 1984), 78–9. On the role of Mars and Venus in another of Tirso's plays, see Everett W. Hesse and William C. McCrary, 'The Mars–Venus Struggle in Tirso's *El Aquiles*', *BHS* 33 (1956), 138–51.

appear together in conjunction with the age-old metaphor of love as war, the trials and tribulations of the soldier-lover, and/or the theme of the educative or pacifying power of love. Bringing all three gods together, the tale of Mars, Venus, and Vulcan addresses a wide variety of themes and motifs, including: love, lust, and adultery; honour and social reputation; dishonour, cuckoldry, and revenge; envy and jealousy; deceit and deception; secrecy and spectacle; and justice, judgement, and punishment. From Garcilaso on, Golden Age poets drew on these and other associations to a number of ends. In the second half of the period several poets indulged in long narrative retellings, adopting a range of tones, perspectives, and attitudes to the tale inherited from Homer and Ovid. On the painting side, it is a question not of quantity but of quality. The only extant Golden Age paintings on the tale are by the period's most revered artist, Diego Velázquez, who turned to scenes inspired by it in two of his most famous and enigmatic works.

This book presents the first detailed study of poetic and pictorial representations of the tale of Mars, Venus, and Vulcan in the Golden Age of Spain. It complements existing monographic studies dedicated to the treatment of other mythological tales in the literature of the period, such as those of Orpheus, Phaethon, Hero and Leander, Icarus, Apollo and Daphne, Adonis, Iphis and Anaxarete, and Cupid and Psyche.[12] It builds on José Cebrián García's study of the Sevillian poet and playwright Juan de la Cueva's poem 'Los amores de Marte y Venus' [The Loves of Mars and Venus], going beyond the limited scope of Cebrián García's monograph by engaging in detailed analysis of a wide range of literary and visual works.[13] The main body comprises five chapters. The first chapter begins with a discussion of the principal classical sources of the tale of Mars, Venus, and Vulcan, as found in the Greek writers Homer and Lucian and the Latin poets Ovid and Reposianus. After briefly sketching out a number

---

[12] Pablo Cabañas, *El mito de Orfeo en la literatura española* (Madrid: CSIC, 1948); Antonio Gallego Morell, *El mito de Faetón en la literatura española* (Madrid: CSIC, 1961); Francisca Moya del Baño, *El tema de Hero y Leandro en la literatura española* (Murcia: Publicaciones de la Universidad de Murcia, 1966); John H. Turner, *The Myth of Icarus in Spanish Renaissance Poetry*, CTSA: Monografías, 56 (London: Tamesis, 1976); Mary E. Barnard, *The Myth of Apollo and Daphne from Ovid to Quevedo: Love, Agon, and the Grotesque* (Durham, NC: Duke University Press, 1987); José Cebrián García, *El mito de Adonis en la poesía de la Edad de Oro* (Barcelona: Promociones y Publicaciones Universitarias, 1988); Vicente Cristóbal, *Mujer y piedra. El mito de Anaxárete en la literatura española* (Huelva: Servicio de Publicaciones de la Universidad de Huelva, 2002); and Francisco Javier Escobar Borrego, *El mito de Psique y Cupido en la poesía española del siglo XVI*, Literatura, 65 (Seville: Universidad de Sevilla, 2002).

[13] José Cebrián García, *La fábula de Marte y Venus de Juan de la Cueva. Significación y sentido* (Seville: Secretariado de Publicaciones, 1986).

of classical, medieval, and Renaissance interpretations of the tale—from Plato and Aristotle to Ficino and Scaliger—the opening chapter then proceeds to a discussion of the role played by vernacular translations, iconographical and mythographical handbooks, and illustrated editions of Ovid's *Metamorphoses* in the dissemination of the tale (and readings of it) in sixteenth- and seventeenth-century Spain. Establishing points of reference with which later tellings can be compared and contrasted, this assessment of the tale's classical sources and their reception in the Golden Age functions as an indispensable backdrop against which the rest of the study stands. As this chapter shows, Golden Age poets and painters had at their disposal a vast array of different tellings, readings, and illustrations of the tale. Knowledge of these—and of the various details, emphases, and perspectives offered by them—is essential for a proper understanding of each poet's or painter's use of the source material available to them, of the relationship between imitation and invention, and of the development of representations of the tale in the Spanish Golden Age.

The next three chapters offer a broadly chronological examination of poetic treatments of the tale between the mid-1520s and the mid-1670s. These chapters analyse poems in a wide range of forms (*canción*, sonnet, *tercetos, octavas reales, romance*, etc.) by both canonical writers of the stature of Garcilaso, Luis de Góngora, and Lope de Vega and lesser-known figures such as Juan de la Cueva, Salvador Jacinto Polo de Medina, and Miguel de Barrios.[14] In contrast to other classical tales, such as those of Phaethon, Hero and Leander, and Venus and Adonis, the story of Mars, Venus, and Vulcan is not the subject of extended poetic treatment in Spain in the sixteenth century. Chapter 2 thus analyses the function of explicit references and/or veiled allusions to the tale in works on other subjects by Garcilaso, Diego Hurtado de Mendoza, Francisco de Aldana, and Góngora. In particular, this chapter shows how poets from successive generations of Golden Age writers exploit classical allusions to create mythological subtexts that either reinforce or, conversely, undermine the surface meanings of poems otherwise unconnected with the tale. In each case, readers must spot the references and use their knowledge of different tellings and interpretations of the tale to establish the relevance of the references to the poem as a whole. As we shall see, the above poets employ allusions to the tale of Mars, Venus, and Vulcan to a wide range of effects: to convey in memorable ways some of the trials and tribulations associated with love;

---

[14] For an introduction to the various verse forms discussed in this study, see the 'Note on Versification' in Arthur Terry (ed.), *An Anthology of Spanish Poetry, 1500–1700*, vol. II: *1580–1700* (Oxford: Pergamon, 1965–8), ii. pp. xlvii–li; and 'Appendix 1: Verse Forms' in Thacker, *A Companion to Golden Age Theatre*, 179–85.

to present innovative imitations or continuations of classical or Italian Renaissance works; to refresh Petrarchan and Neoplatonic topoi; and to make a mark on the contemporary literary stage by parodying works by rival poets. This chapter also introduces a number of details and motifs that are developed, reworked, or subverted in the later tellings analysed in the chapters that follow.

Chapter 3 considers two long mock-heroic treatments of the tale from the first quarter of the seventeenth century. The first half of the chapter examines the first extensive narrative poem in the Golden Age to focus on the tale of Mars, Venus, and Vulcan, Cueva's 'Los amores de Marte y Venus' (1604). This poem combines and expands on a wide range of previous tellings, and, at over a thousand lines long, represents a significant amplification of the tale. The second half of the chapter analyses Lope's treatment of the tale in 'La rosa blanca' [The White Rose], an eclectic poem published in *La Circe* [Circe] (1624) and dedicated to the daughter of Philip IV's first minister, the future Count-Duke of Olivares. Here, the tale of Mars, Venus, and Vulcan forms part of a biography of Venus that splices together various different stories featuring the Roman goddess of love and beauty. Focusing on the relationship between imitation and invention, this chapter discusses the use of forms and structures associated with epic poetry; the inclusion of original backstories and continuations; and the incorporation of details drawn from commonplace books, iconographical handbooks, and vernacular translations of Homer and Ovid. It also looks at the influence on both poems of contemporary theatre, considering the role and function of dramatic motifs; the emphasis on honour, jealousy, and revenge; and the ways in which certain changes and additions made by the two poets serve to draw out the theatrical qualities inherent in the tale. Finally, this chapter argues that the two poems represent a halfway house, simultaneously looking backwards to the types of Petrarchan and Neoplatonic topoi prevalent in sixteenth-century treatments of the tale and forwards to the unequivocally burlesque tellings that would become popular in subsequent decades.

Chapter 4 turns to the rise and development of the mythological burlesque, analysing *romances* (i.e. popular ballads) by five lesser-known writers active in or around the second and third quarters of the seventeenth century: Alonso de Castillo Solórzano, Salvador Jacinto Polo de Medina, Alberto Díez y Foncalda, Miguel de Barrios, and Jerónimo Durán de Salcedo. For the most part, these five writers have been dismissed as servile imitators of Góngora and/or Francisco de Quevedo—the Scylla and Charybdis of seventeenth-century Spanish poetry—and, as a result, the ballads examined in this chapter have received little or no critical

attention.[15] The five poems are significant, however, in view of the light
they shed not only on the development of representations of the tale under
consideration but also on the wider phenomenon of the mythological burlesque, the legacy of Góngora and Quevedo and the interplay between
culto and *conceptista* styles (long seen as the two dominant styles of Baroque
poetry), and the overall state of late seventeenth-century Spanish poetry.[16]
Paying special attention to the longer, more elaborate, and more complex
tellings by Castillo Solórzano, Barrios, and, in particular, Polo de Medina,
this chapter discusses some of the ways in which the above poets adapt the
basic narrative and develop humorous details from earlier tellings to draw
out the rich comic potential inherent in the tale. Starting with a detailed
examination of the portrayal of the tale's three main protagonists (now
transformed into a ruffian, a prostitute, and a cuckold) and their extensive
supporting cast, it shows how these poets refresh a well-known classical
tale by exploiting a wide range of forms of humour (wit, parody, satire,
farce, grotesque, etc.), by developing complex linguistic and conceptual
play, and by taking to their logical extremes certain motifs and characteristics present in earlier tellings.

Together, Chapters 2–4 chart a general movement—though by no
means a straightforward, linear progression (as we shall see, many of the
elements that come to the fore with the rise of the mythological burlesque
can be found in embryonic form in earlier tellings)—towards realism with
regard to the representation of the pagan gods and their affairs; subversion
of Petrarchan and Neoplatonic commonplaces; linguistic play and conceptual difficulty; the usage of underworld slang (*germanía*) as a means
of poetic expression; and the development of self-conscious references to
contemporary artistic trends, traditions, and polemics. It is against this
backdrop that Velázquez's paintings of the tale's main protagonists stand.
The fifth and final chapter therefore analyses in detail two of his most
celebrated mythological paintings: *La fragua de Vulcano* [The Forge of
Vulcan] (1630), a work unquestionably based on the tale of Mars, Venus,
and Vulcan; and *Marte* [Mars] (*c.*1640), a work whose subject and context are more open to debate. It also touches briefly on the *Venus del espejo*
[Venus at her Mirror] (*c.*1648), a portrait of Venus otherwise unconnected
with the tale in question. This chapter considers how these paintings relate

[15] The analogy is borrowed from Dámaso Alonso, 'Escila y Caribdis de la literatura
española', in *Estudios y ensayos gongorinos*, 2nd edn. (Madrid: Gredos, 1960), 11–28 (p. 11).
[16] For useful introductions to these two much-debated styles, see Andrée Collard, *Nueva
poesía. Conceptismo, culteranismo en la crítica española* (Madrid: Castalia, 1967); and Arthur
Terry, 'Theory and Practice', in *Seventeenth-Century Spanish Poetry: The Power of Artifice*
(Cambridge: Cambridge University Press, 1993), 35–64 (esp. pp. 52–64).

to some of the poems analysed in earlier chapters, how they alter once more the audience's perceptions of the gods and the tale under examination, and how they develop specific aspects of the general movement outlined above.

It shows how, like many of the poets discussed in the first four chapters, Velázquez combines and reworks a range of sources, poetic and pictorial, to create innovative depictions of both the tale's protagonists and specific scenes or elements from the Homeric and Ovidian narratives. It argues that at the heart of his enigmatic portraits of the gods lie ambiguity, a blurring of the boundaries between the comic and the serious, a tension between the world of everyday reality and the world of the pagan divinities, and a requirement for the viewer to become an active participant in the process of reception and interpretation.

As its title suggests, the emphasis throughout this study is on the relationship between imitation and invention, between what poets and painters take from the storehouse stocked by their predecessors and what they add to it for their followers. Anchored in close analysis of individual primary texts, the five chapters look at how poets and painters breathed new life into the same well-known mythological tale, examining some of the ways in which the story of Mars, Venus, and Vulcan was disguised, developed, expanded, mocked, combined with or played off against different subjects, or otherwise modified in order to pique the interest of successive generations of readers and viewers. Each chapter discusses what particular changes and shifts in emphasis reveal about the tale itself, specific tellings, the aims and intentions of individual poets and painters, and the wider context of the literary and visual culture of early modern Spain. In the process, each chapter will give proof of both the 'multilayered, polyvalent nature of classical mythology' in the Golden Age of Spain and the flexibility and multifaceted nature of the specific tale under examination—'a tale blazed through heaven' of 'how unawares | Venus and Mars [were] taken in Vulcan's snares'.[17]

---

[17] Isabel Torres, 'Introduction: *Con pretensión de Fénix*', in Isabel Torres (ed.), *Rewriting Classical Mythology in the Hispanic Baroque*, CTSA: Monografías, 233 (London: Tamesis, 2007), 1–16 (p. 12). The final quotation, like the title of this book, is adapted from the opening lines of an account of the story of Mars, Venus, and Vulcan in an early seventeenth-century translation of Ovid's *Ars Amatoria* attributed to Thomas Heywood. See *Loves Schoole: Publii Ovidii Nasonis de arte amandi, Or, The Art of Loue* (Amsterdam: Nicolas Jansz Visscher, [n.d.]), 54; and, for a modern edition, *Thomas Heywood's 'Art of Love': The First Complete English Translation of Ovid's 'Ars Amatoria'*, ed. Michael L. Stapleton (Ann Arbor, Mich.: University of Michigan Press, 2000), 95.

1

Mythological Sources: Classical Texts, Renaissance Contexts

In short, Virgil mentions this story, Ovid translates it, Plutarch commends it, and Scaliger censures it.[1]

HOMER

The story of Mars (Ares), Venus (Aphrodite), and Vulcan (Hephaestus) is first told in Homer, *Odyssey*, VIII.266–369. At the start of Book VIII the Phaeacian king, Alcinous, invites Odysseus to a lavish banquet, which is followed by a pentathlon comprising running, wrestling, jumping, throwing, and boxing. When Odysseus at first declines to take part in the games, the Phaeacian Euryalus, who is compared to Ares when first introduced, questions Odysseus's athletic prowess. The wanderer is stung into action by Euryalus's insolence. Inspired by Minerva, he hurls a discus that is much heavier than those used by the Phaeacians considerably farther than any of his competitors, before launching into a fierce rebuttal of Euryalus's accusations. To defuse the situation, Alcinous calls upon the blind bard Demodocus to strike up song. Having earlier reduced Odysseus to tears of anguish with his account of Odysseus's quarrel with Achilles (VIII.62–103), the bard now reduces him to tears of joy with the song of Ares and Aphrodite:

> Meantime the bard, alternate to the strings,
> The loves of Mars and Cytherea sings;
> How the stern god, enamor'd with her charms,
> Clasp'd the gay panting goddess in his arms,
> By bribes seduced; and how the sun, whose eye
> Views the broad heavens, disclosed the lawless joy.

---

[1] The epigraph to this chapter is taken from Alexander Pope's annotations in Homer, *The Odyssey of Homer*, trans. Alexander Pope, Elijah Fenton, and William Broome, 5 vols. (London: Bernard Lintot, 1725–6), ii. 211. The English translations of Homer that follow, both here and in subsequent chapters, are taken from this work.

The lovers' affair is already well established by the time that the all-seeing sun-god witnesses it. When Apollo informs him of his wife's infidelity, 'vindictive Vulcan flies [to his black forge]', where he fashions an invisible and unbreakable net from fine links of steel. The smith-god then sets the net around his marriage bed before feigning departure for his island home of Lemnos. When the lovers seize what seems to be an ideal opportunity to renew their affair, they are immediately ensnared:

> Down rush'd the toils, inwrapping as they lay
> The careless lovers in their wanton play:
> In vain they strive; th' entangling snares deny
> (Inextricably firm) the power to fly.

Prompted once more by Apollo, Hephaestus returns home, catches the lovers *in flagrante*, and then calls out to Zeus (Jupiter) and the other gods of Olympus, entreating them to come down from the heavens to witness the shocking sight of the lovers' entrapment, and refusing to release the lovers until Zeus has returned the dowry. Significantly, only the male gods descend, breaking into uproarious laughter as soon as they see their peers' predicament:

> Meanwhile the gods the dome of Vulcan throng;
> Apollo comes, and Neptune comes along;
> With these gay Hermes trod the starry plain;
> But modesty withheld the goddess train.
> All heaven beholds, imprison'd as they lie,
> And unextinguish'd laughter shakes the sky.

Further laughter ensues as Apollo and Hermes (Mercury) then share a scabrous joke about Ares's good fortune:

> 'Would'st thou enchain'd like Mars, O Hermes, lie,
> And bear the shame like Mars, to share the joy?'
> 'O envied shame! (the smiling youth rejoin'd);
> Add thrice the chains, and thrice more firmly bind;
> Gaze all ye gods, and every goddess gaze,
> Yet eager would I bless the sweet disgrace.'

The one spectator left unamused is Poseidon (Neptune), who intervenes and negotiates the lovers' freedom. When Hephaestus sets them free, on the understanding that Poseidon will pay Ares's damages if the warrior-god fails to return the bride-price himself, Ares heads immediately for Thrace while Aphrodite flees to Paphos, where she is bathed, anointed, and clothed by her attendants, the Three Graces:

To the soft Cyprian shores the goddess moves,
To visit Paphos and her blooming groves,
Where to the Power an hundred altars rise,
And breathing odors scent the balmy skies;
Conceal'd she bathes in consecrated bowers,
The Graces unguents shed, ambrosial showers,
Unguents that charm the gods! she last assumes
Her wondrous robes; and full the goddess blooms.
　　Thus sung the bard: Ulysses hears with joy,
And loud applauses rend the vaulted sky.

And so ends Demodocus's song of Ares and Aphrodite.

On the surface, the main aim of the tale is to entertain the Phaeacians and their guest, and thus dissolve the growing tension between Odysseus and Euryalus. The song's humour is based on the inappropriateness of the marriage between Aphrodite and Hephaestus, one 'virtually unattested elsewhere'.[2] The response of the gods to the sight of the lovers' entrapment presents a memorable instance of *Schadenfreude*: the male gods laugh in mockery of their fellow gods, who are trapped in an embarrassing situation.[3] The audience can appreciate the visual comedy of the scene, imagining the lovers struggling in vain to maintain their dignity, at the same time as enjoying the verbal comedy of the dialogue between Apollo and Hermes. Demodocus adopts a humorous style to compound the light-hearted treatment of daily life on Olympus. When describing the net, for example, he employs the '(not) even + hyperbole' motif to suggest that it is so fine as to be invisible even to the gods, ironic given that Ares and Aphrodite will soon fail to see the trap that is set for them. The digression reaches beyond the light humour found elsewhere in the narrative into the realm of lewdness: mirth surrounds the issue of adultery ($\mu o\iota\chi\epsilon\acute{\iota}a$).[4] Like both Helen and Clytemnestra, Aphrodite engages in an extramarital affair; the potential consequences of a husband's absence (i.e. the threat of $\mu o\iota\chi\epsilon\acute{\iota}a$), the need to punish adultery, and the question of compensation due to the aggrieved party are all explored (in the main narrative, Alcinous calls on Euryalus to make a formal apology and offering to Odysseus). Unlike them, however, she is immortal; at the end of the tale her divine authority is swiftly restored. Whilst the gods are humanized, and made

---

[2] Ingrid E. Holmberg, 'Hephaistos and Spiders' Webs', *Phoenix*, 57 (2003), 1–17 (p. 2).
[3] On the laughter of the gods within the 'context of early Greek shame-culture', see Christopher G. Brown, 'Ares, Aphrodite, and the Laughter of the Gods', *Phoenix*, 43 (1989), 283–93.
[4] For a detailed examination of $\mu o\iota\chi\epsilon\acute{\iota}a$, see Maureen J. Alden, 'The Resonances of the Song of Ares and Aphrodite', *Mnemosyne*, 50 (1997), 513–29.

to act as if they were mortal men and women, '[they] can always reassert their divinity, show their superiority to men, and retire from the realm of suffering and passion into their blessedness'.[5]

OVID

Given its focus on love, lust, and sexual intrigue, it is not surprising that of the three canonical Augustan poets it was Ovid on whose imagination the song of Ares and Aphrodite left the greatest mark.[6] Ovid reworks the song on two separate occasions. In *Ars Amatoria* [The Art of Love], ii.561–92, the story is introduced to support the argument that a lover gains nothing by establishing the infidelity of his beloved, since she simply becomes more openly instead of stealthily unfaithful: 'Crescit amor prensis; ubi par fortuna duorum est, | In causa damni perstat uterque sui' [Detection fans the flame of passion; where two have shared misfortune, each persists in the cause of his/her own fall] (559–60). Potential lovers should take heed of a tale that is notorious amongst the gods: 'Fabula narratur toto notissima caelo, | Mulciberis capti Marsque Venusque dolis' [There is a story, most famous over all of heaven, of Mars and Venus caught by Mulciber's guile] (561–2).[7] In the lines that follow Ovid outlines the bare bones of the narrative, pausing only on occasion to develop some of the tale's comic potential. Whereas little attention is paid to the construction of the net, Vulcan's appeal to the gods, or the process by which the episode is resolved, we hear how Venus was repulsed by her husband's calloused hands and how she would laugh at his deformed legs and imitate his limp when alone with Mars (567–70). An element of more salacious humour is introduced when the Sun is reproached for his actions: had he kept quiet, he too would have been granted his privilege by Venus, who would, after all, have

---

[5] Jasper Griffin, *Homer on Life and Death* (Oxford: Clarendon Press, 1980), 201. This brief introduction is indebted to the editor's notes in Homer, *Odyssey, Books VI–VIII*, ed. Alexander F. Garvie, Cambridge Greek and Latin Classics (Cambridge: Cambridge University Press, 1994), 293–312; and Irene de Jong, *A Narratological Commentary on the Odyssey* (Cambridge: Cambridge University Press, 2001), 206–9. For further discussion of this passage, see Bruce K. Braswell, 'The Song of Ares and Aphrodite: Theme and Relevance to *Odyssey* 8', *Hermes*, 110 (1982), 129–37.

[6] The tale is not present in Horace and is mentioned only in passing by Virgil, in *Georgics*, iv.345–6: 'inter quas curam Clymene narrabat inanem | Volcani Martisque dolos et dulcia furta' [Among these Clymene was telling of Vulcan's baffled care, of the wiles and stolen joys of Mars] (*Virgil*, trans. H. Rushton Fairclough, LCL, 2 vols. (Cambridge, Mass.: Harvard University Press, 1916–18), i. 220–1).

[7] 'Mulciber' (> *mulceo*) was a title given to Vulcan because of his—or his fire's—ability to soften iron.

been well equipped to buy his silence (575–6). The concluding lines of the passage in question focus on Vulcan:

> Hoc tibi pro facto, Vulcane: quod ante tegebant,
>   Liberius faciunt, ut pudor omnis abest:
> Saepe tamen demens stulte fecisse fateris,
>   Teque ferunt artis paenituisse tuae. (589–92)

[This is what you get for your pains, Vulcan: the affair they once kept dark they carry on openly, now that all shame is gone: yet often dost thou confess that thou didst act stupidly, madman, and they say thou hast repented of thine skill.][8]

Vulcan is offered as an example of how not to behave. Intriguingly, it is suggested that the smith was left to rue his own artistic talent: had he not been so skilled, he would not have been endowed with the means by which to ensnare the lovers and thus publicize his own dishonour. The humour associated with the episode serves to reinforce the advice given on the art of love: men should not think of using such traps, for they rarely achieve the desired effect.[9]

A more well-known recasting of Demodocus's song is found in *Metamorphoses*, IV.169–89. The start of Book IV sees the introduction of the daughters of Minyas and their impious rejection of the cult of Bacchus. Rather than celebrating his feast-day, Alcithoe, Arsippe, and Leuconoe choose instead to spend the day indoors, spinning and telling each other stories in order to pass the time. Embedded within this frame are the stories of Pyramus and Thisbe (IV.55–168), Apollo and Clytie (IV.169–284), and Salmacis and Hermaphroditus (IV.285–388). When Alcithoe finishes her account of the tale of Pyramus and Thisbe, Leuconoe turns the spotlight onto the figure of Apollo. By way of introduction to the tale of Apollo and the sea-nymph Clytie, she recounts the story of Mars, Venus, and Vulcan. Given, as will become evident, its importance in the Golden Age, it is worth citing this version of the tale in full:

> hunc quoque, siderea qui temperat omnia luce,
> cepit amor Solem: Solis referemus amores.
> primus adulterium Veneris cum Marte putatur
> hic vidisse deus; videt hic deus omnia primus.
> indoluit facto Iunonigenaeque marito

---

[8] The text and translations, with minor corrections and emendations, are taken from Ovid, *The Art of Love and Other Poems*, trans. John H. Mozley, rev. George P. Goold, LCL (Cambridge, Mass.: Harvard University Press, 1979), 104–7.

[9] For a line-by-line analysis of this passage, see Markus Janka, *Ovid Ars Amatoria: Buch 2 Kommentar* (Heidelberg: Universitätsverlag C. Winter, 1997), 404–20.

furta tori furtique locum monstravit, at illi
et mens et quod opus fabrilis dextra tenebat
excidit: extemplo graciles ex aere catenas
retiaque et laqueos, quae lumina fallere possent,
elimat. non illud opus tenuissima vincant
stamina, non summo quae pendet aranea tigno;
utque levis tactus momentaque parva sequantur
efficit, et lecto circumdata collocat arte.
ut venere torum coniunx et adulter in unum,
arte viri vinclisque nova ratione paratis
in mediis ambo deprensi amplexibus haerent.
Lemnius extemplo valvas patefecit eburnas
inmisitque deos; illi iacuere ligati
turpiter, atque aliquis de dis non tristibus optat
sic fieri turpis; superi risere, diuque
haec fuit in toto notissima fabula caelo. (iv.169–89)

[Even the Sun, who with his central light guides all the stars, has felt the
power of love. The Sun's loves we will relate. This god was first, 'tis said, to
see the shame of Mars and Venus; this god sees all things first. Shocked at
the sight, he revealed her sin to the goddess' husband, Vulcan, Juno's son,
and where it was committed. Then Vulcan's mind reeled and the work upon
which he was engaged fell from his hands. Straightway he fashioned a net of
fine links of bronze, so thin that they would escape detection of the eye. Not
the finest threads of wool would surpass that work; no, not the web which
the spider lets down from the ceiling beam. He made the web in such a way
that it would yield to the slightest touch, the least movement, and then he
spread it deftly over the couch. Now when the goddess and her paramour
had come thither, by the husband's art and by the net so cunningly prepared
they were both caught and held fast in each other's arms. Straightway Vulcan,
the Lemnian, opened wide the ivory doors and invited in the other gods.
There lay the two tied together, disgracefully, and some one of the merry gods
prayed that he might be so disgraced. The gods laughed, and for a long time
this story was the talk of heaven.][10]

Given that the tale does not feature any kind of metamorphosis, it is
perhaps not surprising that this telling should take up just twenty-one
lines in Ovid's famous collection of shape-changing myths. The tale is told
chronologically, but all direct speech, ornament, and evaluation is left out.
Here, Ovid's emphasis is on the agency of the sun-god, Vulcan's response to
Apollo's message, and the artistry involved in the forging of the net. While

---

[10] The text and translations, with minor corrections and emendations, are taken from
Ovid, *Metamorphoses*, trans. Frank Justus Miller, LCL, 2 vols. (Cambridge, Mass.: Harvard
University Press, 1971), i. 191.

the Homeric tale ends on the drawn-out, solemn note of Poseidon's guarantee of redress, Ovid's cursory ending focuses on the note of laughter and
notoriety produced. There is no mention of Vulcan's appeal to the gods,
no negotiation over the lovers' freedom, and no restoration of their divine
dignity. Whereas the most famous of the Homeric love stories concludes on
a note of equilibrium between the merry and the solemn, between the salacious and the moral, Ovid underlines the impression of farce by refusing
to restore the compensatory aspect of the lovers' ideal roles. Mars and Venus
are stripped of their divinity, limited to human behaviour, and subjected to
ridicule. There is an oblique allusion to the exchange between Apollo and
Mercury, but no reference to any response of displeasure or shock: ' . . . su-
peri risere, diuque | haec fuit in toto notissima fabula caelo.' After this rela-
tively light-hearted interlude, the spotlight then turns to focus on the figure
of Apollo, soon punished by a merciless Venus for his part in her shaming.[11]

LUCIAN

In the second of Ovid's two tellings the lovers' peers seem utterly unper-
turbed by their strife: ' . . . illi iacuere ligati | turpiter, atque aliquis de
dis non tristibus optat | sic fieri turpis.' If imprisonment in Vulcan's net
means lying naked in the arms of Venus, then the unnamed onlooker of
the *Metamorphoses* would happily swap places with Mars. In the *Ars Amatoria* one witness jokingly addresses Mars about the weight of his current
burden: 'hic aliquis ridens "in me, fortissime Mavors, | si tibi sunt oneri,
vincula transfer!" ait' [Then someone laughs and says, 'Most valiant Mars,
if they burden you, transfer your chains to me!'] (585–6). In both tellings
Ovid thus alludes to a specific detail present in Homer's account, namely
the exchange between Apollo and Hermes, given above, which leads to
the latter declaring that he would willingly endure even greater imprisonment (i.e. three times as many chains bound three times as fast) and public
exposure (to both gods and goddesses) if it allowed him to lie naked at the
side of the beautiful Venus.

In his *Dialogues of the Gods*, a series of satirical dialogues exposing the
absurd and immoral lives of the gods of Antiquity, the second-century
AD Greek writer Lucian makes additions to this exchange, drawing out in
the process some of the comic potential inherent in Demodocus's song.
Dialogues XVII and XXI are both between Apollo and Hermes, the former

---

[11] For more on the second of Ovid's two tellings, see Victor Castellani, 'Two Divine
Scandals: Ovid *Met.* 2.680 ff. and 4.171 ff. and his Sources', *Transactions of the American
Philological Association*, 110 (1980), 37–50.

an exchange about Aphrodite's extramarital affair, the latter an account of her husband's revenge. In xvii Hermes immediately remarks upon the grotesque nature of the (mis-)match between Aphrodite, Queen of Beauty, and her crippled husband, who spends his days bent double over the forge, covered in soot and sweat. The gods proceed to comment on their own troubled love lives, Apollo bemoaning the loss of Daphne and Hyacinth, Hermes trying not to boast about his one-night stand with Aphrodite (which engendered Hermaphroditus). This leads them to discuss Aphrodite's latest affair, and their own envy of her new lover, Ares. Despite having been aware of the affair for some time, Hephaestus has chosen to hold his tongue because of the identity of his wife's new lover:

APOLLO. Do you think Hephaestus knows of this?

HERMES. Of course he does, but what can he do when he sees Ares is such a fine strapping young fellow, and a man of war? So he keeps quiet. But he's threatening to invent some sort of trap for them, and to catch them in a net on the bed.

At this stage the net is no more than an idea. *Dialogue* xvii thus paints a picture of Hephaestus as a knowing cuckold, a coward, but one whose behaviour accords with the advice given in the *Ars Amatoria*. In xxi the same story is approached from a different perspective, as Hermes gives Apollo an account of the lovers' capture in the smith's net—'the funniest thing [he] ever saw'. He describes how Ares tried at first to escape but then began to act the suppliant, and how Hephaestus stood over the lovers and laughed. Despite the ignominy suffered by the lovers (and the husband's apparent revenge), Hermes admits to being envious of Mars 'for having made a conquest of the fairest of the goddesses, and even for being a fellow-prisoner with her'. When Apollo expresses surprise at this, Hermes invites him to go and have a look (the lovers have not yet been freed), suggesting that he too will be overwhelmed with the desire to find himself—and thus, by extension, be found—in Ares's position.[12]

In other tellings, such as that found in *The Dream or The Cock*, Lucian includes the figure of Alectryon, a Greek youth charged by Ares with guarding the door during Ares's trysts with Aphrodite.[13] In this tale the cobbler Micyllus tells his interlocutor, his cockerel, the story of how, one night whilst on sentry duty, Alectryon fell asleep and failed to warn the lovers of the passing of Helios's chariot. As a result of the youth's negligence

[12] Translations are taken from Lucian, 'Dialogues of the Gods', in *Lucian*, trans. Austin M. Harmon, K. Kilburn, and M. D. MacLeod, LCL, 8 vols. (Cambridge, Mass.: Harvard University Press, 1913–67), vii. 239–353, esp. 320–3 (xvii, 'Hermes and Apollo') and 334–7 (xxi, 'Apollo and Hermes').

[13] *Lucian*, ii. 172–239 (esp. pp. 176–9).

the sun-god caught sight of the lovers lying in bed together, thus triggering the chain of events that led to their imprisonment by Hephaestus. By way of punishment Ares turned Alectryon (armour and all) into a cockerel (the youth's helmet becoming the cock's comb). From then on, as a form of apology to Ares, each morning the cockerel would crow to herald the imminent rising of the sun.

REPOSIANUS

The final source to be considered here is *De Concubitu Martis et Veneris* [On Mars and Venus Sleeping Together], a short epyllion in 182 hexameters by the minor Latin poet Reposianus. Little is known about Reposianus and, as a result, the poem's date is uncertain, with critical opinion ranging from the second to the sixth centuries AD.[14] In his study of the *De Concubitu* Ugo Zuccarelli splits Reposianus's most famous poem into two acts. The first of these acts (lines 1–130) is then subdivided into: an invocation (1–32); the setting of the scene in a forest (33–50); the introduction of first Cupid, the Graces, and Venus (51–73) and then Mars (74–95); and a description of the gods' lovemaking (96–110) and post-coital repose (111–30). The two main scenes in the second act (lines 131–182) relate to Apollo's discovery and revelation (131–56) and Vulcan's revenge (167–82).[15] Though it takes as its subject the tale of Mars, Venus, and Vulcan, the emphasis here—as both the poem's title and Zuccarelli's breakdown suggest—is not on Vulcan but on the lovers and their tryst, the latest in a long line of such encounters. Reposianus gives detailed descriptions of the scene, the lovers' respective preparations for the tryst, the act itself, the height of the lovers' passion, and its aftermath. Throughout, he draws attention to the role-reversal experienced by Mars, developing the metaphor of love as a form of warfare: 'semperque timendus | te timet' [he that should ever be feared fears you (i.e. Venus)] (15–16); and 'post proelia victor | victus amore . . .' [after his battles the vanquisher vanquished by love . . .] (77–8).[16]

Reposianus goes into far greater detail than any of his predecessors about the lovers' sexual encounter—before (Venus tying her hair up,

[14] On Reposianus, the dating of the *De Concubitu*, and the epyllion genre, see Jean Soubiran, 'Deux notes critiques au "Concubitus Martis et Veneris" de Reposianus', *Bollettino di Studi Latini*, 3 (1973), 93–5; Danuta Shanzer, *A Philosophical and Literary Commentary on Martianus Capella's 'De Nuptiis Philologiae et Mercurii' Book 1*, Classical Studies, 32 (Berkeley: University of California Press, 1986), 17–21; and Anna Maria Wasyl, *Genres Rediscovered: Studies in Latin Miniature Epic, Love Elegy, and Epigram of the Romano-Barbaric Age* (Krakow: Jagiellonian University Press, 2011), 16, n. 19.

[15] Reposianus, *Concubitus Martis et Veneris*, ed. and trans. Ugo Zuccarelli, Collana di studi classici, 12 (Naples: Libreria scientifica, 1972).

[16] Translations of Reposianus are taken from *Minor Latin Poets*, trans. J. Wight Duff and Arnold M. Duff, LCL (Cambridge, Mass.: Harvard University Press, 1978), 519–39.

Mars's disarming/disrobing, etc.), during (Venus's coquettish behaviour, Mars's wandering hands, etc.), and after (Venus's agitation, Mars's snoring, etc.). Significantly, he also changes important aspects of the original story. The principal change sees the setting switch from Vulcan's house to an idyllic forest. Indeed, much of the poem is given over to description of this *locus amoenus*, to the lovers' bower and bed of flowers. Cupid is also given a part to play in this telling, helping Venus to prepare for Mars's arrival, undressing Mars in preparation for sex, and then playing with Mars's weapons (decorating them with flowers, weighing up his lance, hiding in his helmet when Vulcan arrives, etc.) while the lovers recover from their exertions. Whilst Apollo is still responsible for informing Vulcan of his wife's affair, here, rather than visiting the smith's forge, he sheds light on the forest so that Vulcan can see the lovers for himself. Once Vulcan has forged the net, he then directly ensnares the lovers during their post-coital slumber (rather than setting a trap for them to fall into). Reposianus also introduces several details not present in the above tellings. Some of these details serve to introduce further elements of humour—or, as Montero Cartelle argues, to humanize the gods (e.g. Mars's snoring)—others playfully to rework or subvert aspects of earlier tellings (e.g. the suggestion that Mars could escape from the net but that love and fear of hurting Venus prevent him from doing so).[17] At the end of the poem Venus's indignation is tempered by the prospect of revenge against Apollo. Here, though, it will be wrought not through the amorous trials and tribulations of Apollo, as in the *Metamorphoses*, but through those of the sun-god's daughter Pasiphaë, who would give birth to the Minotaur after lusting for and mating with a bull (this last detail allowing for an oblique allusion to the horns of Vulcan's cuckoldry).

AN IMMORAL TALE?

Despite the lovers' capture, their apparent punishment for the crime of adultery, and the presence of gnomic utterances hinting at possible overarching moral concerns—one witness's asides to the effect that 'evil does not prosper' and that 'the slow one catches the quick one'—*Odyssey*, VIII.266–369 is one of the most controversial episodes in the Homeric poems.[18] Designed to provoke not serious reflection but laughter, the main purpose of Demodocus's song is that of entertainment (cf. the descriptions of the banquet of the gods and Thersites in the opening two books of the

---

[17] See the editor's comments in *Priapeos. Grafitos amatorios pompeyanos. La velada de la fiesta de Venus. El concúbito de Marte y Venus. Centón nupcial*, ed. and trans. Enrique Montero Cartelle, Biblioteca Clásica Gredos, 41 (Madrid: Gredos, 1981), 201.

[18] De Jong, *A Narratological Commentary*, 208.

Iliad). The tale poses a serious interpretative challenge, as anyone uncomfortable with its seemingly licentious and lubricious nature must, perforce, find a justification for its presence. Many classical philosophers reacted strongly against the interlude, arguing that the public spectacle represents an intolerable affront to divine decorum. Though he does not explicitly mention the tale of Mars, Venus, and Vulcan, the ancient Greek poet and philosopher Xenophanes of Colophon alludes to precisely this kind of story when criticizing such portrayals of the gods:

> Homer and Hesiod have attributed to the gods
> all sorts of things which are matters of reproach and censure among men:
> theft, adultery, and mutual deceit.[19]

Immoral and illicit deeds are, it is suggested, incompatible with divinity. In his *Republic* 390c, as part of his famous root-and-branch condemnation of poetry, Plato deems this specific episode inappropriate, observing that it should be censored for inculcating in the young the wrong attitudes and values. Like the tale of Hera's seduction of Zeus in *Iliad*, xiv.153–351, the story is morally unsound and has the potential to encourage a lack of self-control. An episode that shows the gods treating serious human issues, such as adultery, with humour and indiscretion should, therefore, be suppressed.[20]

If one rejects the oft-made claim that the interlude is un-Homeric, and thus accepts it as intrinsic to *Odyssey* viii, how does one account for the frivolous handling of serious issues, for the apparent breach of decorum, for the sudden descent from lofty epic to low comedy, and for the decidedly unflattering portrayal of several of the principal gods of the Greek pantheon?[21] Despite the fact that such qualities are all perfectly Homeric, these and other related questions were raised and addressed, either explicitly or implicitly, by a succession of classical and late classical writers and thinkers. Many, following the example of Xenophanes and Plato, condemn the episode and argue in favour of censorship and/or excision. Others, however, establish more favourable lines of interpretation. Accordingly, the tale is variously seen, for example, as evidence that soldiers incline to lust (Aristotle, *Politics*, 1269b); as an example of how discord (Ares) and love (Aphrodite) fuse to form perfect accord (Harmony) (Plutarch, *Moralia*, 370); as a demonstration of the interaction of fire

---

[19] Xenophanes of Colophon, 'Fragment 11', in *Fragments*, trans. James H. Lesher (Toronto: University of Toronto Press, 1992), 22–3.

[20] Plato, *Republic*, trans. Robin Waterfield, Oxford World's Classics (Oxford: Oxford University Press, 1993), 84–5.

[21] On the much-debated question of athetesis (i.e. the rejection of this passage as spurious), see e.g. Alden, 'Resonances', esp. 513–18.

(Hephaestus), metal (Ares), artistry (Aphrodite), and water (Poseidon) in the forge (Heraclitus, *Allegoriae Homericae*, 69); and as a warning against the Deadly Sin of Lust (Fulgentius, *Mythologiae*, 2.7).[22]

When discussing the tale derived from the song of Ares and Aphrodite, medieval and Renaissance writers faced the added challenge of reconciling pagan mythology with Christian practices and teachings. Whilst some writers, including, most notably Scaliger, continued to see it as fundamentally immoral, others adduced several of the aforementioned readings whilst also putting forward their own lines of interpretation.[23] Developments of Plato's and Aristotle's responses to the tale were particularly common amongst fifteenth- and sixteenth-century humanists and mythographers.[24] Those who held classical tales to be repositories of beneficial morals were faced with challenges similar to those outlined above. Building on the tradition of classical allegory, successive generations of philosophers, commentators, and translators interpreted the tale in various ingenious ways to correspond to particular moral, religious, physical, astrological, anthropomorphic, or pseudo-scientific concerns. Explanations based on the marriage of opposites, the principles of generation, the interplay of the four elements and/or the four humours, the process of working metal, the movement and conjunction of the planets, the pain and suffering brought by amours, and the juxtaposition of warm, naked flesh and cold, hard armour were all put forward in attempts to prove that a seemingly salacious episode actually encapsulated profound truths relating to man and his experience of and relationship to the world around him. As we shall see in later chapters, many of these interpretations, most notably the Neoplatonic readings put forward by Marsilio Ficino and León Hebreo, had a profound influence on tellings of the story in the Golden Age of Spain.

The shocking content and surface immorality of the tale marked it out as an obvious subject for allegorical exegesis, and it was precisely this interpretive stance that was adopted time and again throughout the course of the fourteenth, fifteenth, and sixteenth centuries. From the early fourteenth century on, the production and dissemination of 'moralized Ovids'

---

[22] Aristotle, *Politics*, trans. Harris Rackham, LCL (Cambridge, Mass.: Harvard University Press, 1932), 135; Plutarch, *Moralia*, trans. Frank C. Babbitt and others, LCL, 16 vols. (Cambridge, Mass.: Harvard University Press, 1927–76), v. 117; Heraclitus, *Homeric Problems*, ed. and trans. Donald A. Russell and David Konstan (Atlanta, Ga.: Society of Biblical Literature, 2005), 111; and Fulgentius, *Fulgentius the Mythographer*, trans. Leslie George Whitbread (Ohio: Ohio State University Press, 1971), 72–3.

[23] For Scaliger's argument that Demodocus's song is inferior to that of Iopas in *Aeneid*, 1.740–6, and thus indicative of Homer's inferiority to Virgil as an epic poet, see Julius Caesar Scaliger, *Poetices libri septem* ([Lyons]: Antoine Vincent, 1561), 216.

[24] See e.g. Mario Equicola, *Libro de natura de amore* (Venice: Lorenzo Lorio da Portes, 1525), fol. 63ᵛ; and Vincenzo Cartari, *Le imagini con la spositione de i dei de gliantichi* (Venice: Francesco Marcolini, 1556), fol. 78.

and scholastic compendia and commentaries on the *Metamorphoses*—most famously, Pierre Bersuire's *Ovidius Moralizatus* (*c*.1340), its anonymous vernacular counterpart, the *Ovide moralisé*, and the later commentaries of the Venetian humanist Raphael Regius—helped to tip the scales firmly in the favour of moral, ethical, and allegorical readings of this and other mythological tales.[25] The tales themselves were often drowned out by the sheer weight of accompanying materials. For example, in the *Ovide moralisé*, which in total stretched to almost 72,000 lines, the tale of Mars, Venus, and Vulcan is told in just over one hundred lines (iv.1268–1371). Over twice as many, however, are dedicated to the moralizing commentary on it (iv.1488–1755), with emphasis placed on the negative effects of amours, on the inability of 'riches ne sages ne poissans' [neither the rich, nor the wise, nor the powerful] (iv.1692) to withstand them, and, by way of conclusion, on the fact that 'la mauvese ardure' [immoral desire] (iv.1752) condemns individuals:

> a honte et a laidure,
> a mort et a perdicion
> a dampnable derision. (iv.1753–55)[26]

[to shame and disgrace, to death and perdition, to damnable derision.]

Interpretations became more and more convoluted, as commentators strove to account for and explain the significance of the tale's every last detail (e.g. the eruption of *Schadenfreude*, the roles of Poseidon and Alectryon, and the offspring resulting from the affair). By the early sixteenth century a rich allegorical tradition had thus been constructed around the tale, skewing the balance between the comic and the serious firmly in favour of the latter.

[25] Originally published in Venice in 1493, Regius's commentary was the first and most frequently printed Renaissance commentary on the *Metamorphoses*. Bersuire's work, which circulated in manuscript form after its completion in *c*.1340, was published in Paris in at least four editions between 1509 and 1521. Ann Moss contends that whereas Regius provided a guide for teachers in schools, Bersuire provided one for preachers in the pulpit. The emphasis throughout the latter's work is on moral and/or allegorical readings. Bersuire's summaries give the information required for each subsequent allegorization, but leave out a lot of detail. The focus is not on the tales themselves—little if any attention is paid to matters of language and style—but on the use that can be made of them (and on the ends to which they can be put). For more on Regius, Bersuire, and other commentators, see *Latin Commentaries on Ovid from the Renaissance*, ed. and trans. Ann Moss (Signal Mountain, Tenn.: Summertown, 1998).

[26] *Ovide moralisé. Poème du commencement du quatorzième siècle*, ed. Cornelis de Boer, 5 vols. (Amsterdam: Johannes Müller, 1915–38), ii. 39–49. For more on the *Ovide moralisé*, see Renate Blumenfeld-Kosinski, 'The Hermeneutics of the *Ovide moralisé*', in *Reading Myth: Classical Mythology and its Interpretation in Medieval French Literature* (Stanford: Stanford University Press, 1997), 90–136.

RENAISSANCE DISSEMINATION

In Spain—as in England, France, Germany, Italy, and the Low Countries—the sixteenth and seventeenth centuries saw a dramatic increase in the circulation of works by, or relating to, both well-known and recently rediscovered classical writers. The vogue for the translation of Greek and Latin texts into the European vernaculars inevitably led to the wider dissemination of the works of canonical writers such as Homer, Ovid, and Lucian.[27] Latin translations of the *Odyssey* had been available in print since the late fifteenth century, and by 1550 there were already at least seven different ones in circulation. The first complete translation into a major European vernacular appears to have been Simon Schaidenreisser's German prose translation of 1537. The *Odyssey* then appeared in Italian in 1573 (in a verse translation by Lodovico Dolce), French in 1604 (prose, Salomon Certon), and English in 1614–15 (verse, George Chapman). A Spanish translation was published at a comparatively early stage: the Segovian Gonzalo Pérez, secretary to Philip II, completed a translation of the first thirteen books in 1550, a full twenty-four-book translation in 1556, and finally a revised, now definitive, version, dedicated to the king, in 1562.[28] In the introducton Pérez claims to be a 'fiel interprete' [faithful interpreter]—those readers who know Greek will recognize the skill and effort he has put into the translation, whilst those who do not will be indebted to him for being able to read 'el mejor Poeta de los Griegos' [the best Greek poet].[29]

Given the extraordinarily wide dissemination of his work, the principal source of the tale for Golden Age poets and painters was, however, not Homer but Ovid. More specifically, it was the account found in the *Metamorphoses*, a work celebrated across Renaissance Europe as the

---

[27] For a standard reference work on translations of the classics into Spanish in the sixteenth and seventeenth centuries, see Theodore S. Beardsley, *Hispano-Classical Translations Printed Between 1482 and 1699* (Pittsburgh: Duquesne University Press, 1970).

[28] Gonzalo Pérez, *De la Ulyxea de Homero XIII libros, traduzidos de Griego en Romance Castellano por Gonçalo Pérez* (Salamanca: Andrea de Portonaris, 1550); *La Ulyxea de Homero, traduzida de Griego en lengua Castellana por el Secretario Gonçalo Pérez* (Antwerp: Juan Steelsio, 1556); and *La Ulyxea de Homero, traduzida de Griego en lengua Castellana por el Secretario Gonçalo Pérez. Nuevamente por el mesmo revista y emendada* (Venice: Francesco Rampazeto, 1562). All subsequent references are to the 1562 edition.

[29] *La Ulyxea*, fols *6ᵛ–*7ʳ. For more on translations of Homer, the question of the attribution of *La Ulyxea*, and the influence of Latin translations on Pérez's Spanish text, see Luis Arturo Guichart, 'La *Ulyxea* de Gonzalo Pérez y las traducciones latinas de Homero', in Barry Taylor and Alejandro Coroleu (eds.), *Latin and Vernacular in Renaissance Iberia, II: Translations and Adaptations*, Cañada Blanch Monographs, 8 (Manchester: MSPS, 2006), 49–72.

'poets' Bible'.[30] Whereas the fourteenth and fifteenth centuries had been marked by an interest in the ends to which Ovid's tales could be put, as exemplified by the *Ovidius Moralizatus* and the *Ovide moralisé*, the sixteenth century saw an explosion of interest in the tales themselves. The *Metamorphoses* circulated widely in both the original Latin and the major European vernaculars. The mid-sixteenth century saw the appearance in print of influential translations into German (Georg Wickram, 1545), Italian (Lodovico Dolce, 1553), French (François Habert, 1557), English (Arthur Golding, 1565–7), and Dutch (Johannes Florianus, 1566). Three complete Spanish translations were published before 1590. The first of these was a prose translation by Jorge de Bustamante. Though critical debate continues about both the dating of the *editio princeps* (*c.*1540) and the existence and identification of a number of ghost editions, there is no doubt that Bustamante's free prose translation, which went through a dozen or more editions in the following one hundred years, was the source of many people's knowledge of Ovid.[31] The ethical bent outlined in the previous section lives on in this translation: in his prologue Bustamante states that Ovid's tales contain 'escondida moralidad y provechosa doct-rina' [hidden morals and beneficial teaching], and that the ancients' goal 'no fue otro sino sólo mostrar a los hombres muchos avisos, y astucias, para más sabia y prudentemente vivir' [none other than simply to present men with many warnings and ruses, in order for them to live more wisely and prudently].[32]

The second complete translation, published in Salamanca in 1580 and later re-edited in Burgos in 1609, was by Antonio Pérez Sigler. This trans-lation, 'en verso suelto y octava rima' [blank verse and octaves], is much more faithful to Ovid than that of Bustamante. Significantly, however, at the end of each book Pérez Sigler also includes explanations of the allegor-ical sense of each tale. Many of these are translated almost word for word from those by Giuseppe Horologgi incorporated into several editions of Giovanni Anguillara's Italian translation from 1560 on. The allegory asso-ciated with the tale of Mars, Venus, and Vulcan draws on many aspects of the tradition outlined above. Once more, even relatively minor details are

---

[30] The epithet is taken from the title of *La Bible des poètes* (Paris: Antoine Vérard, 1493), an illustrated edition of the *Ovide moralisé* published by Colard Mansion in Bruges in 1484. See Marie-France Viel, 'La *Bible des poètes*: une réécriture rhétorique des *Métamorphoses* d'Ovide', *Tangence*, 74 (2004), 25–44.

[31] José María de Cossío, *Fábulas mitológicas en España* (Madrid: Espasa Calpe, 1952), 42.

[32] Jorge de Bustamante, *Las Transformaciones de Ovidio en lengua española* (Antwerp: Pedro Bellero, 1595), fol. a7.

accounted for, as seen in the following explanation of Venus's subsequent hatred of Apollo and his offspring:

> Que Venus tenga después odio a la progenie del Sol que descubrió sus amores, no es otra cosa sino que aquel apetito desenfrenado del coitu, es enemigo de la prudencia y juicio, conociendo que éstos con sus advertencias le quitan gran parte del placer: por lo cual se dice que las mujeres quieren más en este acto el amante bobo e insensato que sabio y prudente.[33]

[It is easy to explain why Venus should subsequently hate the offspring of the Sun, who made her affair public: the uncontrolled appetite for coitus is the enemy of prudence and judgement, knowing that these take away much of its pleasure with their warnings. For this reason it is said that, when it comes to this act, women prefer stupid and foolish lovers to wise and prudent ones.]

The final translation, this time entirely in *octavas*, was that of Pedro Sánchez de Viana, printed in Valladolid in 1589.[34] Published together in an accompanying volume of *Anotaciones*, Sánchez de Viana's commentaries synthesize a wide range of previous allegorical interpretations of Ovid's tales. In his discussion of the tale under examination, he develops even more detailed explanations than Pérez Sigler, accounting for different elements drawn from competing tellings of the story, including Vulcan's lameness, the presence of Apollo, Mercury, and Neptune, the birth of Cupid, and the role of Alectryon.[35]

---

[33] Antonio Pérez Sigler, *Los XV libros de los Metamorfoseos de el excellente Poeta Latino Ovidio* (Salamanca: Juan Perier, 1580), fols. 100^r–1^r. For Horologgi's allegories, see e.g. Giovanni Andrea dell' Anguillara, *Le metamorfosi di Ovidio, ridotte da Giovanni Andrea dell' Anguillara in ottava rima con le annotazioni di messer Giuseppe Orologgi* (Venice: Francesco de' Franceschi, 1571).

[34] Pedro Sánchez de Viana, *Las Transformaciones de Ovidio* (Valladolid: Diego Fernández de Córdoba, 1589); and *Anotaciones sobre los Quince libros de las Transformaciones de Ovidio* (Valladolid: Diego Fernández de Córdoba, 1589).

[35] *Anotaciones*, fols. 81^v–3^v. For a fourth, but incomplete, translation, see *Del Metamorphoseos de Ovidio en Otava rima traduzido por Felipe Mey. Siete Libros* (Tarragona: [n. pub.], 1586). On these translations, and for other notable contributions to the study of the reception of Ovid in the Renaissance, see Rudolph Schevill, 'The *Metamorphoses* Retold in Spanish', in *Ovid and the Renascence in Spain* (Berkeley: University of California Press, 1913), 143–98; Cossío, *Fábulas mitológicas*, 38–56; Charles Martindale (ed.), *Ovid Renewed: Ovidian Influences on Literature and Art from the Middle Ages to the Twentieth Century* (Cambridge: Cambridge University Press, 1988); Philip Hardie (ed.), *The Cambridge Companion to Ovid* (Cambridge: Cambridge University Press, 2002), esp. the essays in Part 3: Reception (pp. 249–367); Barry Taylor and Alejandro Coroleu (eds.), *Latin and Vernacular in Renaissance Spain, III: Ovid from the Middle Ages to the Baroque,* MSPS, 18 (Manchester: MSPS, 2008); Peter Knox (ed.), *A Companion to Ovid*, Blackwell Companions to the Ancient World (Oxford: Blackwell, 2009), esp. the essays in Part V: Literary Receptions (pp. 395–484); John C. Parrack, 'Mythography and the Artifice of Annotation: Sánchez de Viana's *Metamorphoses* (and Ovid)', in Frederick A. de Armas (ed.), *Ovid in the Age of Cervantes* (Toronto: University of Toronto Press, 2010), 20–36; and Katharina Volk, *Ovid*, Blackwell Introductions to the Classical World (Chichester: Wiley-Blackwell, 2010).

As with Homer, the principal works of Lucian were also translated into both Latin and the major European vernaculars. Erasmus and Thomas More had worked on translations into Latin of a number of works by Lucian in the first decade of the sixteenth century. These translations, published for the first time in Paris in 1506 (and again, with Latin translations of seven more works by Lucian, in 1514), helped shape many of the Latin editions of the dialogues that date from the mid-sixteenth century. From that point on there also appeared several important translations of Lucian's works into Spanish, including, most notably, the *Diálogos de Luciano* of 1550, attributed to Francisco de Enzinas (complete with the 'Diálogo del Gallo'), Francisco de Herrera Maldonado's *Luciano español* of 1621 (also featuring 'El Gallo'), and Sancho Bravo de Lagunas's *Discurso de Luciano* of 1626.[36] By far the least well known of the four writers discussed above was, and still is, Reposianus; as a result, little is known about the reception and dissemination of the *De Concubitu*. The existence of a number of seventeenth-century copies of the *Codex Salmasianus*, the single extant source for the poem, suggests, however, that it was probably in circulation, albeit only on a limited scale, in Renaissance and Baroque Europe.[37]

ICONOGRAPHICAL HANDBOOKS

As noted in the Introduction, iconographical or mythographical manuals and encyclopedias also circulated widely in Renaissance Europe. The first and most influential of these was Giovanni Boccaccio's *De Genealogia Deorum Gentilium* (1360/74), an attempt, as the title suggests, at a comprehensive genealogy of the pagan gods. After the first printed edition was published in Venice in 1472, large numbers of editions of Boccaccio's manual appeared in Latin and vernacular translations, including Spanish, over the course of

[36] On the reception of Lucianic satire in the Renaissance, see Christopher Robinson, *Lucian and his Influence in Europe* (London: Duckworth, 1979); and David Marsh, *Lucian and the Latins: Humor and Humanism in the Early Renaissance* (Ann Arbor, Mich.: University of Michigan Press, 1998). On Lucian and the Spanish Golden Age, see Antonio Vives Coll, *Luciano de Samosata en España (1500–1700)* (Valladolid: Sever-Cuesta, 1959); Michael O. Zappala, *Lucian of Samosata in the Two Hesperias: An Essay in Literary and Cultural Translation* (Potomac, Md.: Scripta Humanistica, 1990); Alejandro Coroleu, 'El *Momo* de Leon Battista Alberti: una contribución al estudio de la fortuna de Luciano en España', *Cuadernos de Filología Española: Estudios Latinos*, 7 (1994), 177–83; and Antonio Azaustre Galiana, 'Las obras retóricas de Luciano de Samosata en la literatura española de los siglos XVI y XVII', in Ángel A. González, Juan Casas Rigall, and José Manuel González Herrán (eds.), *Homenaje a Benito Varela Jácome* (Santiago de Compostela: Universidade de Santiago de Compostela, 2001), 35–55.

[37] On the transmission of the poems contained in the *Codex Salmasianus*, see Loriano Zurli, *Apographa Salmasiana. Sulla trasmissione di 'Anthologia Salmasiana' tra Sei e Settecento*, Spudasmata, Band 96 (Hildesheim: Georg Olms, 2004).

the next two centuries. In the sixteenth century several scholars followed in Boccaccio's footsteps by producing handbooks, commonplace books, and miscellanies dedicated to classical and mythological subjects. These included Domenico Nani Mirabelli (*Polyanthea*, 1503), Jean Tixier de Ravisi, a.k.a. Ravisius Textor (*Officina*, 1520), Giglio Gregorio Giraldi (*De Deis Gentium*, 1548), Natale Conti (*Mythologiae*, 1551), and Vincenzo Cartari (*Imagini*, 1556). The same period also saw the preparation and publication of editions of medieval treatises, such as those by Palaephatus, Fulgentius, and Albricus.[38] The two major vernacular Spanish contributions to this burgeoning tradition came at relatively late stages. The first was by the mathematician and mythographer Juan Pérez de Moya, whose *Philosofía secreta de la gentilidad* [Secret Philosophy of the Pagan Gods] was first published in Madrid in 1585 and then reprinted at least four times in the course of the next century (1599, Zaragoza; 1611, Alcalá; 1628 and 1673, Madrid).[39] Drawn from both the classical and the contemporary worlds, Pérez de Moya's sources are many and varied. He clearly knew many of the aforementioned works of Renaissance mythography; his greatest, though largely unacknowledged, debts are to Boccaccio and Conti, but he also draws freely from other writers, including the early fifteenth-century bishop Alfonso de Madrigal, famous across Europe as 'El Tostado' in the sixteenth and seventeenth centuries, and Pérez Sigler.[40] In the first of seven books, Pérez de Moya outlines the five principal ways in which mythological tales can be understood: literally ('literal'), allegorically ('alegórico'), anagogically ('anagógico'), tropologically ('tropológico'), and in accordance with physical or natural laws ('físico/natural').[41] In the next

[38] For more on the tradition of mythological handbooks, see Seznec, 'The Science of Mythology in the Sixteenth Century', in *Survival*, 219–56; and the essays collected in Rembrandt Duits and François Quiviger (eds.), *Images of the Pagan Gods: Papers of a Conference in Memory of Jean Seznec*, Warburg Institute Colloquia, 14 (London: Warburg Institute, 2009).

[39] Juan Pérez de Moya, *Philosofía secreta. Donde debaxo de historias fabulosas se contiene mucha doctrina provechosa a todos estudios. Con el origen de los Idolos o Dioses de la Gentilidad. Es materia muy necessaria para entender Poetas y Historiadores* (Madrid: Francisco Sánchez, 1585). All subsequent quotations are from *Philosofía secreta*, ed. Carlos Clavería, LH, 404 (Madrid: Cátedra, 1995).

[40] On Pérez de Moya's debts to these and other writers, see Carlos Clavería's introduction in *Philosofía secreta*, 13–39; Consolación Baranda Leturio, 'La mitología como pretexto: la *Filosofía secreta* de Pérez de Moya (1585)', *Príncipe de Viana. Anejo*, 18 (2000 = *Homenaje a Francisco Ynduráin*), 49–65; and Guillermo Serés, 'Antecedentes exegéticos de la *Filosofía secreta* de Juan Pérez de Moya (1585)', in Christophe Couderc and Benoit Pellistrandi (eds.), *«Por discreto y por amigo». Mélanges offerts à Jean Canavaggio*, Collection de la Casa de Velázquez, 88 (Madrid: Casa de Velázquez, 2005), 633–48. On El Tostado, see *Alfonso Fernández de Madrigal, El Tostado*, ed. Roxana Recio and Antonio Cortijo Ocaña, *La corónica*, 33 (2004), 5–162.

[41] *Philosofía secreta*, 69.

six books he goes on to discuss: gods; goddesses (Books ii and iii making up 80 per cent of the work); heroes, heroines, and demigods; those condemned to Hades (i.e. 'fábulas para exhortar a los hombres huir de los vicios y seguir la virtud' [stories designed to urge men to abandon vice and follow virtue]); further metamorphoses; and the dangers faced by man when dead ('fábulas para persuadir al hombre al temor de Dios' [stories designed to lead men to fear God]). In the case of each of the several hundreds of gods, goddesses, and other figures discussed, the relevant (group of) individual(s) is described, an account is given of the various tales they are involved in, and then, finally, the meaning(s) and significance of each tale are explained (under the headings *declaración* and/or *sentido*). Pérez de Moya shows far greater interest in the truths hidden in the tales than in the tales themselves, and as a result very brief accounts of tales are then followed by often lengthy *declaraciones/sentidos*. His attempts to decipher each tale, as if it were simple code conveying profound moral, natural, astrological, historical, or euhemeristic truths, often border on the absurd, as evinced by his discussion of the role of Neptune in the tale of Mars, Venus, and Vulcan:

> No quererlos soltar Vulcano de las cadenas, hasta que Neptuno mucho se lo rogó, significa que los torpes y necios amadores, en cadenas de sus viles deseos presos, nunca cesan de ser habidos por viciosos ni de sus malos hechos publicados, hasta que el tal ardor en ellos se amata, obedeciendo a la virtud, lo cual convenientemente se significa por Neptuno, el cual es dios del mar, y las aguas con su frialdad resfrían el calor libidinoso, y esto es soltarle de las prisiones, que son por ellas entendidos los deseos libidinosos en que los amantes están enredados.[42]

> [The fact that Vulcan did not want to free them from the chains until Neptune had pleaded with him to do so means that the clumsy and foolish lovers, imprisoned in the chains of their own base desires, never stop being seen as depraved or exposed by their evil deeds until their desires die down, paying obeisance to virtue, which is duly represented by Neptune, who is god of the sea, and the coldness of his waters cools lustful heat, and this is to free them from their fetters, which symbolize the lustful desires in which the lovers are entangled.]

The second influential Spanish manual was Baltasar de Vitoria's *Teatro de los dioses de la gentilidad* [Theatre of the Pagan Gods], published in Salamanca in two parts in 1620 and 1623. The first part examines the

---

[42] *Philosofía secreta*, 229. Discussions of the tale of Mars, Venus, and Vulcan are found in each of the three chapters dedicated to these gods: Vulcan, ii.15 (pp. 220–31); Mars, ii.26 (pp. 288–93); and Venus, iii.5 (pp. 378–86).

principal male gods: Saturn, Jupiter, Neptune, Pluto, Apollo, and Mars. The second then turns to Mercury, Hercules, Juno, Minerva, Diana, and Venus, with a seventh book dedicated to lesser divinities, such as Fortune, Nemesis, and Momus. In both parts Vitoria draws together a wide range of authorities, making the tales under examination acceptable through reference to and direct quotation from innumerable classical and contemporary poets, scholars, and mythographers: Ovid, Boccaccio, Petrarch, Ravisius Textor, Guillaume du Choul, Garcilaso, Lope, Cervantes, Góngora, and others. Vitoria's emphasis on literary points of reference and his apparent lack of concern for the allegorical significance of each tale are what most distinguish the *Teatro* from Pérez de Moya's 'decidedly anti-aesthetic compendium'.[43] Whilst the tale of Mars, Venus, and Vulcan is alluded to in passing on several occasions, Vitoria's most comprehensive examination of it comes in *Primera parte*, 'Libro sexto de Marte', chapter IV, entitled 'De los amores del Dios Marte, y Venus' [On the Loves of the God Mars and Venus]. Like many of the works discussed thus far, Vitoria's account draws together elements from a number of different classical tellings, as seen, for example, in his handling of the tale's denouement, which combines details from Homer (the intervention of Poseidon/Neptune and Venus's flight to Cyprus), Ovid (Venus's revenge against Apollo), and Lucian (the metamorphosis of Gallus/Alectryon):

> Solo el Dios Neptuno se compadeció de los delinquentes, y en favor dellos pidió absolucion del delito, y él les desenmarañó la red, como lo dize Homero, y con esto se fue Marte corrido a Tracia: y por el descuydo que tuvo su page, le convirtió en gallo, quedandose con el mismo nombre, y con mas cuydado del que tuvo, para que su amo no se viera en la afrenta que se vio: y assi quando entiende que viene el Sol, luego da vozes, y canta anunciando su venida a todos los de la casa donde vive. La Diosa Venus se fue a su isla de Cypro muy afrentada, y vergonçosa, y se vengó del Sol en muchas ocasiones que pudo, de su generacion, y de sus amigas.

> [Only the god Neptune felt pity for the wrongdoers, and on their behalf he asked for absolution for their crime, and he untangled the net for them, as Homer recounts it, and at that moment Mars went off in shame to Thrace: and, on account of his servant's negligence, he turned him into a cockerel, who kept the same name, and acted with greater care than before, so that his master did not find himself in the same embarrassing situation: and so when he senses that the Sun is rising, he cries out, and announces its arrival by singing to all those in the house where he lives. The goddess Venus went off to the island of Cyprus very embarrassed, and ashamed, and she took revenge against the Sun, his offspring, and his beloveds as often as she could.]

---

[43] Torres, 'Introduction: *Con pretensión de Fénix*', 8.

The chapter ends with quotation of the relevant passage from the *Metamorphoses*, first in Latin and then in Spanish, the latter taken directly from Sánchez de Viana's *Transformaciones*. Vitoria also seems to borrow from Sánchez de Viana a number of details that, as we shall see in later chapters, come to prominence in contemporary poetic accounts: the inappropriateness of Vulcan's wedding to Venus ('el casamiento tan desproporcionado'); her preference for brave warriors or braggart soldiers ('valentones y bravos'); and Apollo's friendship with Vulcan and his envy of Mars ('era envidioso de semejantes gustos, y . . . muy amigo de Vulcano').[44]

ILLUSTRATED OVIDS

As noted above, in Renaissance Europe the most widely known source of the tale of Mars, Venus, and Vulcan was the account found in *Metamorphoses* IV. Over the course of the sixteenth and seventeenth centuries Ovid's work appeared in many and varied forms. These ranged from the original Latin text with scholarly commentary to works anchored in the emblematic tradition, and from vernacular translations with lengthy allegorical exegeses to model books aimed at painters, sculptors, and other artists. From the late fifteenth century, through the whole of the sixteenth, and well into the seventeenth, book illustration enjoyed a great vogue in Europe. The *Metamorphoses* was one of the most frequently and heavily illustrated works in this period, perhaps second only to the Bible. The first printed edition of the *Metamorphoses* to feature woodcut illustrations was the *Ovide moralisé*, mistakenly attributed to Thomas Walleys, published in Bruges by Colard Mansion in 1484. The formula adopted therein, namely a series of small cuts of the principal gods and goddesses and then a large plate introducing each of the fifteen books, is found in many editions of works derived from the *Ovide moralisé*, including the *Bible des poètes*, which went through multiple editions in the first half of the

[44] Baltasar de Vitoria, *Primera parte del Teatro de los dioses de la gentilidad* (Madrid: Imprenta Real, 1657 [1620]), 654–8. For more on Vitoria and the *Teatro*, see Cossío, *Fábulas mitológicas*, 68–71; Belén Tejerina, 'El *De Genealogia Deorum gentilium* en una mitografía española del siglo XVII: el *Teatro de los dioses de la gentilidad*, de Baltasar de Vitoria', *Filología moderna*, 55 (1975), 591–601; Genoveva Calonge García, 'El *Teatro de los dioses de la gentilidad* y sus fuentes: Bartolomé Cassaneo', *Cuadernos de Filología Clásica: Estudios Latinos*, 3 (1992), 159–70; Virginia Salamanqués Pérez, 'El tratamiento de los dioses paganos en la obra de Baltasar de Vitoria', in José María Maestre Maestre, Joaquín Pascual Barea, and Luis Charlo Brea (eds.), *Humanismo y pervivencia del mundo clásico. Homenaje al profesor Antonio Fontán*, 5 vols. (Madrid: Laberinto, 2002), iv. 1863–8; and Guillermo Serés, 'El enciclopedismo mitográfico de Baltasar de Vitoria', *La Perinola*, 7 (2003), 398–421.

sixteenth century.[45] Early printed editions of the commentaries of Regius and Giovanni Bonsignori would later mark a departure from this format, with increasing numbers of images incorporated into the text proper.[46]

Despite its apparently minor role in Ovid's poem, serving principally as a prologue to another story, the tale of Mars, Venus, and Vulcan was one of the most frequently illustrated tales from the early 1490s on.[47] One of the earliest illustrations of the tale to appear in print was an anonymous wood-cut that formed part of a cycle of fifty-three illustrations used in both the 1497 and 1501 editions of Bonsignori's *Ovidio Metamorphoseos vulgare* (Fig. 1.1). The left half of the image sees Apollo visiting Vulcan to break the news of Venus's infidelity. The smith stands stock-still, frozen at the forge, the hammer that has just fallen from his raised right hand now lying at his feet (a detail also present in Bonsignori's text). The sun-god raises the index finger on his left hand, either to point in the direction of Vulcan's marital bed or, perhaps, to impress upon the smith the need to gain revenge for such an affront. At right we find a scene from the end of the same tale, the lovers now bound fast to the bed by Vulcan's net. Saturn, Apollo, and Mercury contemplate the lovers' plight from just behind the bed. In the centre of the image, Neptune —identified by his trident and adopting a pose that recalls that of Apollo at left—is seen reprimanding Vulcan and calling on him to free the lovers. The fact that this detail is drawn not from Ovid but from Homer is further proof of the fact that, even at this early stage in the Renaissance dissemination of classical mythology, the lines between different tellings of the same tale were often already blurred.

By the middle of the sixteenth century larger cycles of more sophisticated cuts were in circulation. The most influential sixteenth-century illustrations were those of the French illustrator Bernard Salomon, whose cycle of 178 cuts first appeared in *La Métamorphose d'Ovide figurée*, published in Lyons

---

[45] For more on French translations of the *Metamorphoses*, including the *Bible des poètes* and the *Grand Olympe*, see Ghislaine Amielle, *Recherches sur des traductions françaises des Métamorphoses d'Ovide* (Paris: Jean Touzot, 1989).

[46] Though Bonsignori's paraphrases and allegories, modelled on Giovanni del Virgilio's early fourteenth-century Latin commentaries, were written in the 1370s, they did not appear in print until the publication of the *Ovidio Metamorphoseos vulgare*, the earliest published Italian translation of the *Metamorphoses*, in Venice in 1497. For more on this work, see Bodo Guthmüller, *Ovidio metamorphoseos vulgare. Formen und Funktionen der volkssprachlichen Wiedergabe klassischer Dichtung in der italienischen Renaissance* (Boppard am Rhein: Boldt, 1981); Edith Wyss, *The Myth of Apollo and Marsyas in the Art of the Italian Renaissance: An Inquiry into the Meaning of Images* (London: Associated University Presses, 1996), 83–92; and Giovanni Bonsignori, *Ovidio Metamorphoseos vulgare*, ed. Erminia Ardissino, Collezione di opere inedite o rare, 157 (Bologna: Commissione per i testi di lingua, 2001).

[47] The subject is also found in illuminated manuscripts, as seen, for example, in BNF, Richelieu, MS. Fran. 137, a fifteenth-century *Ovide moralisé* (for Vulcan casting his net over the lovers, see fol. 46ᵛ).

.IIII.   xxVIII

S I come Alcitoe haue dita la sua fabula cioe de Pirão Leu conoe cõincio adire la sua E diffe cufi la mia forella Alcitoe ha dito de amore & io diro anchor de amore E incomincio in quefta forma. Vede/te uoi quefto fole elqual illumia el mõdo: Gia fo tempo che effo fe inamoro Ela cagiõe perche eli fo prefo de amore fo quefta. Voi ben fapete che Vul/chano figliolo de Iunone haue p moglie Venere; Ma Marte fe giacea con Venere. Impcio che Venere amaua molto Marte e Marte amaua liei: E facendo Marte fpeffe uolte quefto: El fole elquale entra per ogni picola apritura; Entro in la cafa doue giacea Marte e Venus uedédo q̃fto el fole fo molto turbato per amore de Vulchano. Onde el fole ando a Vulchano e tro/uolo che faetauano le faete di Ioue: A cui diffe cufi; uedi molto me increfce chio te lo dico. Io uoglio che tu fapi fi como Marte fe giace con Venus tua dõna: E fapi che Venus te pora le corne i capo. Odédo Vulchano q̃fte cofe fi li cade el martello diman e fubito ufi

diffe p lo dolore. Ma puoi che gli fo tornato in fua memoria Comincio afa bricare & alauorare una rete de filo de azaio e de diamãte tãto fotiliffima: chel uifo nõ la podea difcernere; fi che niũo fe faria de quella poduto guarda re; E portola a cafa e pofela fopra el lecto e quãdo Marte e Venus andaro e Saliro fu el lecto & abraciati che furono ifieme: Vulchão pfe la corda di la rete E copfe luno e laltro; p modo che niũo fe podea mutar. Et fato che Vulchão hebe q̃fto: ando e cõuoco tuti li dei ala fua cafa. Si como fuorõ détro: Vulchão apfe tute le feneftre fi che tuti li dei uidero aptaméte Marte e Venus fu lo lecto a cauallo abraciati p modo che nõ fe podeão foglier lũo dal altro; alhora li dei uedédo q̃fto comicio rõ forte aridere; p modo che tu hauerefti potuto cauarli tuti li déti che non hauerião fentito. Eftãdo cufi coftoro foprauene neptũo & fi prego Vulchano che li laffafe dapoi che li erano cufi fuergognati. Alhora coftoro p li p̃ghi de Neptuno fono folti e liberati.

A legoria.   Cap.   X.
                                      d iiii

Fig. 1.1. Giovanni Bonsignori, *Ovidio Metamorphoseos vulgare* (Venice: Zoane Rosso, 1497), fol. 28ʳ, featuring an anonymous woodcut illustration of the tale of Mars, Venus, and Vulcan.

in 1557.[48] Salomon's cuts form the backbone of a work inspired by the emblem tradition, each cut introduced by a short title in French and then followed by eight lines of French verse providing a brief outline of the narrative depicted. The relevant illustration appears under the title 'Mars & Venus surpris par Vulcan' (Fig. 1.2). At right the lovers lie naked in each other's arms, oblivious to the fate that awaits them. In the right foreground lies Mars's armour, discarded in his haste to experience the pleasures of love. Top right, an *amorino*—Cupid?—lifts the curtain draped around the bed to reveal the lovers *in flagrante*. Centre left, Vulcan moves towards the bed to cast his net over the lovers. This means of entrapment represents a departure from most of the tale's principal literary sources, for here, as in Reposianus, Vulcan imprisons the lovers directly. Behind the smith the sun's rays pour through an opening at top left, shedding light on the lovers' disgrace and recalling Apollo's role in proceedings. Framed in the same opening, the other gods—and, here, goddesses—take in the spectacle before them. Those at the front point, jeer, and gossip, whilst those at the back jostle for a better view. Significantly, the final two lines of the accompanying verse do not draw out any specific moral, underlining instead the laughter associated with the gods' response: 'Adonc Vulcan trestous les Dieux appelle, | Qui rient fort de ce plaisant soulas' [Then Vulcan calls out to all the gods, who laugh hard at this amusing shambles].

Salomon's series exerted considerable influence on many cycles in the next hundred years, including those of Virgil Solis, Pieter van der Borcht, Christoph Murer, Antonio Tempesta, and Crispin (van) de Passe. The Nuremburg engraver Solis's series went into circulation a few years after Salomon's, when his cuts appeared in two works published in Frankfurt in 1563.[49] Solis's debt to Salomon can be seen clearly in his illustration of the tale of Mars, Venus, and Vulcan (Fig. 1.3). He includes the same elements as his French forebear: the lovers naked in bed; Mars's arms abandoned beside the bed; Vulcan poised with the net raised above his head; the *amorino* lifting

[48] *La Métamorphose d'Ovide figurée* (Lyons: Jean de Tournes, 1557). A second French edition appeared in 1564, with a third following in 1583. Salomon's cycle would be used in several subsequent versions of the *Metamorphoses*, including Gabriele Simeoni's *La vita et Metamorfoseo d'Ovidio figurato i abbreviato in forma d'epigrammi da G. Symeoni* (Lyons: Jean de Tournes, 1559). On Salomon's cycle, and its influence on later artists and engravers, see Peter Sharratt, *Bernard Salomon: illustrateur lyonnais* (Geneva: Droz, 2005), 150–65, 181–207.

[49] Johannes Spreng, *Metamorphoses Ovidii* (Frankfurt: Georg Corvinus, Sigmund Feyerabend, heirs of Wygand Galle, 1563); and Johann Posthius, *Tetrasticha in Ovidii Metamor. lib. XV* (Frankfurt: Georg Corvinus, Sigmund Feyerabend, heirs of Wygand Galle, 1563). In the former, each cut is accompanied by a prose summary of the episode illustrated (drawn from Lactantius Placidus's *Narrationes Fabularum Ovidianarum*), and Spreng's own verse exposition (*enarratio*) and allegory (*allegoria*), all in Latin. In the latter, each cut is framed by four lines of Latin verse above and four lines of German verse below.

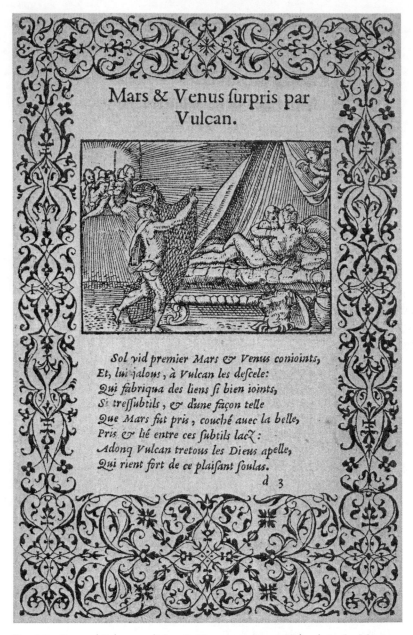

OVIDII METAM. LIB. IIII. 49

Veneris cum Marte adulterium. III.

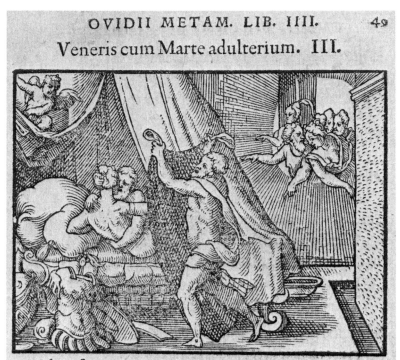

SOl poſtquam Martem olim cum Venere coë-
untem cerneret, ad Vulcanum eius maritū hoc
facinus detulit, qui ſupra modum indignatus, ca-
tenis tenuiſsimis, inſtar retiū, cubile circumdedit,
quibus Martem cum Venere rem habentem ſic
implicauit, ut alter ab altera diuelli nullo modo
poſſet. Patefactó deinde cubiculo, ambos omniū
Deorum oculis ſpectandos ſubiecit, & eorum ma-
litiam apertè hoc pacto retexuit.

COncubitum Titan Veneris cum Marte præhendens,
Vulcano retegit furta nefanda tori.

G

Fig. 1.3. Virgil Solis, 'Veneris cum Marte adulterium', in Johannes Spreng, *Metamorphoses Ovidii* (Frankfurt: Georg Corvinus, Sigmund Feyerabend, heirs of Wygand Galle, 1563), fol. 49ʳ.

Fig. 1.4. Pieter van der Borcht, 'Veneris cum Marte adulterium', in *Metamorphoses* (Antwerp: Ex off. Plantiniana, Widow and Jean Moretus, 1591), p. 103.

the drape; the gods leaning in through the opening; and so on. The biggest change in an otherwise straightforward transposition sees Solis move Vulcan to the centre, giving greater prominence to both the smith, now right on the brink of ensnaring the lovers, and the other gods of Olympus, who once more revel in the scene played out before them. Later versions of the same scene, though still heavily influenced by Salomon, bring further changes. In Fig. 1.4, for example, Van der Borcht makes a number of modifications (the type of bed, a more clearly defined indoor setting, etc.), the most significant of which sees the gods of Olympus (including Hercules, with his club, and Mercury, with his caduceus, at the front) no longer peering in through the window thrown open by Vulcan, but standing in the same room, and on the same level, as the husband and the lovers.[50] Significantly, each of Van der Borcht's illustrations occupies a whole recto page (with the relevant prose summary in Latin by Lactantius Placidus on the facing verso), marking an

[50] *Metamorphoses, argumentis brevioribus ex Luctatio Grammatico collectis expositæ: una cum vivis singularum Transformationum iconibus in æs incisis* (Antwerp: Ex off. Plantiniana, Widow and Jean Moretus, 1591), 102–3. On De Passe's series of 132 illustrations, published in Cologne in 1602 and 1607, see Ilja M. Veldman, *Profit and Pleasure: Print Books by Crispijn de Passe*, trans. Michael Hoyle and Clara Klein, Studies in Prints and Printmaking, 4 (Rotterdam: Sound and Vision, 2001), 73–84, 317–84.

important stage in the shifting of the balance between the literary and the visual—that is, in the transition from images as accompaniments to texts to images as principal subjects in their own right.

The Italian painter and engraver Antonio Tempesta produced another important series of illustrations, executed in the mid-1580s, and in circulation by the late 1590s, but not published until 1606.[51] Tempesta's cycle underlines the greater subtlety of nuance and expression available through engraving as opposed to the more primitive medium of the woodcut. Whereas earlier illustrators of the tale under examination had tried to capture a sense of continuous narrative by combining different episodes in one single image, Tempesta dedicates two separate engravings, from a cycle of 150, to the one story. Plate 33, 'Coniugis furtum Sol Vulcano detegit' (Fig. 1.5), captures the moment when Apollo delivers

33.   ⁵   *Coniugis furtum Sol Vulcano detegit.*

Fig. 1.5. Antonio Tempesta, 'Coniugis furtum Sol Vulcano detegit', in *Metamorphoseon sive transformationum Ovidianarum libri quindecim* (Amsterdam: Wilhelm Janson, 1606), Plate 33.

---

[51] *Metamorphoseon sive transformationum Ovidianarum libri quindecim, aeneis formis ab Antonio Tempesta florentino incisi, et in pictorum antiquitatisque studiosorum gratiam nunc primum exquisitissimis sumptibus a Petro de Iode antuerpiano in lucem editi* (Amsterdam: Wilhelm Janson, 1606).

news of Venus's infidelity to Vulcan. At right, Apollo addresses Vulcan whilst standing on a platform of cloud. The sun-god points into the distance with his left index finger, gesturing towards Vulcan's marital bed where he has just spied the lovers *in flagrante*. Once again, the bewildered smith stands frozen at the forge as he attempts to come to terms with Apollo's news. In the foreground lie arms forged by Vulcan and his assistant(s), the same arms that lie discarded by Mars at the foot of the smith's marital bed in Plate 34, 'Martem Venerem[que] adulterantes Vulcanus reti suo implicat' (Fig. 1.6). Here Tempesta turns to the scene examined above, the husband's surprise and shock having turned to rage and now a desire for revenge. The influence of Salomon and his followers is evident in terms of the scene's composition. However, by placing Vulcan on the other side of the bed (thus making him face the viewer), Tempesta captures a greater sense of movement as a surprisingly muscular Vulcan prepares to punish the lovers—here, seemingly all too aware

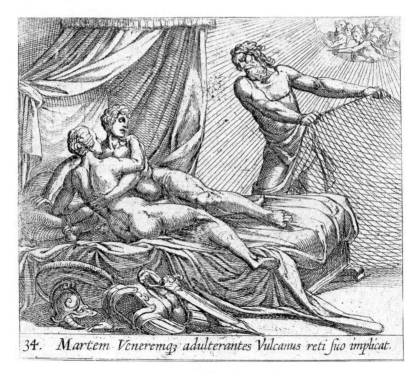

34. *Martem Veneremq3 adulterantes Vulcanus reti suo implicat.*

Fig. 1.6. Antonio Tempesta, 'Martem Venerem[que] adulterantes Vulcanus reti suo implicat', in *Metamorphoseon sive transformationum Ovidianarum libri quindecim* (Amsterdam: Wilhelm Janson, 1606), Plate 34.

of their fate—for their indiscretion. The focus is on the three central protagonists, as the other gods are relegated to a much smaller opening top right.

In 1589–90 the Dutch artist Hendrick Goltzius designed a series of forty engravings to accompany the first two books of the *Metamorphoses*, in the process 'rais[ing] the level of representations of Ovid's work available at the time'.[52] In an earlier engraving, entitled *Venus and Mars Surprised by Vulcan* (1585; Fig. 1.7), Goltzius presents a much more complex design for the scene in question. In the bottom half of the engraving, Vulcan is seen preparing to throw his net (here a large sheet) over the lovers lying naked in bed before him. In the top half, from the vantage-point of a platform of clouds, their fellow gods (from left to right, Neptune, Mercury, Jupiter, Apollo, and Hercules) look down upon them, both literally and figuratively. An opening at left reveals Vulcan's forge, the setting for the revelation that triggered the chain of events that led to this scene. In a humorous foreground detail, Cupid can be seen aiming his bow and arrow up at the gods, perhaps as punishment for laughing at his mother's predicament (his arrow counterbalancing the thunderbolt that Jupiter is about to send down to punish the lovers).[53] In a second engraving from three years later (Fig. 1.8), based on a design by Bartolomeus Spranger, Goltzius returns to the start of the tale.[54] In a strikingly erotic pose, Venus reclines in Mars's arms, her breast exposed to the viewer, her right arm drawing Mars's lips to hers in a passionate embrace. Mars's left hand rests tenderly on his lover's neck, whilst his right hand makes a beeline for her genitals. Cupid stands at the foot of the bed, whilst three other *amorini* draw back the canopy to reveal the lovers. Although the focus is on the lovers' foreplay, the tale's denouement is foreshadowed by the presence at top left of Apollo driving the chariot of the sun across the sky. The allusion to Apollo's role as informant—and, thus, by extension, to the lovers'

---

[52] Nadine M. Orenstein, 'Finally Spranger: Prints and Print Designs 1586–1590', in Huigen Leeflang and others, *Hendrick Goltzius (1558–1617): Drawings, Prints and Paintings* (New York: Metropolitan Museum of Art, 2003), 81–114 (p. 112).

[53] At the foot of the engraving four lines of Latin by Cornelius Schonaeus outline the moral: 'Ut Phoebus nitido lasciuum lumine Martem, | Et Paphiae prodit turpiae furta Deae: | Sic fucata Deus sceleratae crimina vitae | Cernit, et occultum non sinit esse nefas' [As Phoebus with his shining light betrays the debauchery of Mars and the secret infamies of Venus, so God sees the gross transgressions of people who live in crime and He does not allow the sin to remain hidden].

[54] On Spranger and Goltzius, see Ann H. Sievers, Linda D. Muehlig, and Nancy Rich, *Master Drawings from the Smith College Museum of Art* (New York: Hudson Hills, 2000), 57–60.

Fig. 1.7. Hendrick Goltzius, *Venus and Mars Surprised by Vulcan*, 1585. Engraving.

Fig. 1.8. Hendrick Goltzius (after Bartolomeus Spranger), *Mars and Venus*, 1588. Engraving.

punishment—and the presence of another moralizing Latin subscript add a veneer of respectability to an otherwise erotically charged scene.[55]

After Goltzius, the most significant departure from the Salomon model was introduced by the German engraver and miniaturist Johann Wilhelm Baur, who from 1639 to 1641 worked on a series of 150 engravings, published in Vienna in 1641.[56] Though similar in scope to the cycles of Tempesta and De Passe, Baur's cycle is more firmly anchored in the contemporary world: 'Il juxtapose monde réel et monde imaginaire—les palais, les jardins, les fontaines évoquent l'Italie, une Italie mythique—et cette vision se fond en une interprétation forte et originale du texte d'Ovide' [He juxtaposes real and imaginary worlds—the palaces, gardens, and fountains evoke Italy, a mythical Italy—and this vision is based on a strong and original interpretation of Ovid's text]. For Régine Bonnefoit, what ultimately distinguishes Baur's engravings from all previous versions is 'l'inégalée théâtralité, le feu de la gestuelle et les mimiques de ses personnages' [the unrivalled theatricality, the fiery body language, and the gestures and expressions of their figures]. This heightened sense of theatre is evident from his representation of the tale of Mars, Venus, and Vulcan (Fig. 1.9). Both Baur and his later imitator Jean Lepautre (Fig. 1.10) capture a strong sense of theatre, as the gods appear to burst onto the stage, at left, on a dais of clouds.[57] More detailed than their forebears, these scenes draw the viewer's eye as much to the divine onlookers as they do to the traditional protagonists, the customary

[55] The Latin text at the foot of the page reads: 'Mundi oculus Phoebus, mundi lux, omnia cernit, | Sub nitido arcanum est Sole, latensque nihil. | Martis adulterium blanda cum Cypride, nexu | Mulceribis, dictis praebet abunde fidem. | Nudus uterque iacet: nil sic celatur, et atra | Nox operit, prodat quin, reseretque dies' [Phoebus, the eye and the light of the world, sees all; under the shining Sun nothing remains secret or concealed. Mars's adultery with sweet Venus, in Vulcan's net, makes this saying very believable. Both lie there naked: thus nothing is concealed, and black night hides nothing but that the day betrays and reveals it]. For more on these two works, and for the source of the translations here and in n. 53, see Huigen Leeflang, 'Various Manners of the Best Masters: Prints and Drawings 1575–1585', in Leeflang and others, *Hendrick Goltzius*, 33–55 (pp. 50–3), and Orenstein, 'Finally Spranger', ibid. 96–7. For a further drawing of Mars and Venus (*c.*1609), see Emil K. J. Reznicek, *Hendrick Goltzius: Drawings Rediscovered 1962–1992* (New York: Master Drawings, 1993), 47.

[56] Johann Wilhelm Baur, *Dem hoch edlen unnd gestrengen Herren* (Vienna: [n. pub.], 1641). Baur's cycle was reissued several times in the following decades, including, for example, in the *Bellissimum Ovidii theatrum*, published in Nuremberg in 1687. For more on Baur, and on his influence on later artists and engravers, see Rodolphe Rapetti and others, *Johann Wilhelm Baur 1607–1642: maniérisme et baroque en Europe* (Strasbourg: Musées de Strasbourg, 1998).

[57] On Lepautre, see Roger-Armand Weigert and Maxime Préaud, *Inventaire du fonds français. Graveurs du XVIIᵉ siècle*, 17 vols. (Paris: Bibliothèque nationale de France, 1939–99), XI (1993), *Antoine Lepautre, Jacques Lepautre et Jean Lepautre (première partie)*, esp. p. 117 (no. 178), and XII (1999), *Jean Lepautre (deuxième partie)*.

Fig. 1.9. Johann Wilhelm Baur, untitled engraving of the tale of Mars, Venus, and Vulcan, in *Dem hoch edlen unnd gestrengen Herren* (Vienna: [n. pub.], 1641), Plate 38.

Fig. 1.10. Jean Lepautre, untitled engraving of the tale of Mars, Venus, and Vulcan, in *Oeuvre de Le Pautre* ([Paris]: Mariette, [*c.*1660(?)]).

shot of Vulcan ensnaring the lovers now relegated to the bottom-right corner of the stage. Whereas Salomon had set the benchmark for illustrations of the *Metamorphoses* for the previous eighty-four years, from 1641 on, it would be Baur who would set the standard for the following decades, his cycle being copied and adapted time and again over the course of the next century.

The sheer volume of illustrated editions of the *Metamorphoses* suggests that many poets and painters in early modern Europe would have known the tale of Mars, Venus, and Vulcan through both textual and visual sources. Whilst none of the aforementioned cycles was designed or printed in Spain, illustrated editions of the *Metamorphoses* published in France, Germany, Italy, and the Low Countries circulated freely across the continent. The most successful cycles of woodcuts and engravings were printed, reprinted, and imitated through tens of editions. Through one channel or another, the works of Salomon, Solis, Tempesta, and others found their way into the Iberian Peninsula. Originally published in Frankfurt in 1563, Solis's cycle, for example, was included in the 1595 edition of Bustamante's *Transformaciones*, published in Antwerp but aimed, for obvious reasons, at a predominantly Spanish market. The fact that this edition also includes Pérez Sigler's allegories underlines the fluid nature of works relating to the *Metamorphoses* at this time, Ovid's epic poem—either in Latin or vernacular translation—being just one of many possible components of publications bearing his name.[58] In Renaissance Europe the poem itself became indissolubly bound up with—and indeed was often substituted by—other texts and images, including scholarly commentaries, prose summaries, allegorical exegesis, moralizing verse (octaves, tetrastichs, etc.), woodcut emblems, and single-sheet engravings. These many and varied epitomes—some of Ovid's multiple identities in the Renaissance—'all reduced the [mythological] fables to a form in which they were readily digested and easily memorized'.[59] Moss's observation is particularly valid for the above images. The increasing popularity of, and thus demand for, ever-more detailed illustrations of the *Metamorphoses* points to the important role played by woodcuts, engravings, and prints in the dissemination of Ovid in the Renaissance, and to the mark left by such works on the European imagination and the way in which successive

[58] Another example of this fluidity is the 1570 Paris edition of Spreng's *Metamorphoses Ovidii*, which features Salomon's series of illustrations instead of the Solis cycle found in the 1563 *editio princeps*. Two of the most commonly seen components were Lactantius Placidus's Latin prose summaries and Posthius's Latin tetrastichs, both of which were recycled time and again in the period.
[59] *Latin Commentaries*, 136.

generations of writers, painters, and other artists viewed, understood, and remembered popular classical tales.[60]

Even a brief overview of the reception and transmission of the tale of Mars, Venus, and Vulcan gives an indication of the remarkable range of sources available to poets and painters in the sixteenth and seventeenth centuries. Depending on a particular individual's command of the ancient languages, and indeed of other European vernaculars, a given writer or artist could have known versions of the tale through any one or more of innumerable different outlets, ranging from Homer's *Odyssey* in the original Greek to the 'moralized Ovids' of Bersuire and others; from Reposianus's *De Concubitu* to the emblem-style works made popular by the *Métamorphose d'Ovide figurée*; from vernacular translations of Lucian to iconographical handbooks in the tradition of Boccaccio's *De Genealogia*; and from scholarly commentaries on Ovid to the engravings of Tempesta, Goltzius, and Baur. As will become apparent, many of the translations, handbooks, and illustrations discussed above—including, most notably, Pérez's *La Ulyxea*, Vitoria's *Teatro*, and Tempesta's illustrations—left an immediate and indelible mark on the reception of the tale in question.

As we have seen, though there are clear differences between the principal classical tellings, the boundaries between them are often blurred in the Renaissance. Elements specific to individual classical accounts—Poseidon's intervention (Homer), Venus's revenge against Apollo (Ovid), the figure of Alectryon (Lucian), etc.—were often incorporated into the same telling or illustration, as seen in Sánchez de Viana's *Anotaciones*, Vitoria's *Teatro*, and the anonymous woodcut in Bonsignori's *Ovidio Metamorphoseos vulgare*. This blurring of the boundaries between the different accounts is indicative of what might be seen as a progressive voyage away from the principal classical sources. The translations/allegories of Pérez Sigler and Sánchez de Viana and the handbooks of Pérez de Moya and Vitoria offer good examples of this general movement. In wide circulation in Golden Age Spain, all four works pool details present in different classical tellings and subject them to a number of different—sometimes even contradictory—readings. When searching for new subjects and sources of inspiration, Golden Age poets and painters could turn to such works for readily accessible storehouses of competing tellings and different 'interpretaciones, imágenes y metáforas'

[60] For more on illustrations of Ovid's *Metamorphoses*, see Max D. Henkel, 'Illustrierte Ausgaben von Ovids Metamorphosen im XV., XVI. und XVII. Jahrhundert', in *Vorträge der Bibliothek Warburg, herausgegeben von Fritz Saxl: Vorträge 1926–27* (Leipzig: Teubner, 1930), 58–144; and Fátima Díez Platas, 'Tres maneras de ilustrar a Ovidio: una aproximación al estudio iconográfico de las *Metamorfosis* figuradas del XVI', in María Carmen Folgar de la Calle, Ana Goy Diz, and José Manuel López Vázquez (eds.), *Memoria Artis. Studia in memoriam Mª Dolores Vila Jato* (Santiago de Compostela: Xunta de Galicia, 2003), 247–67.

[interpretations, images, and metaphors].[61] Whilst, on the one hand, these works gave poets and painters instant access to a wide range of material on the tale of Mars, Venus, and Vulcan (and significant freedom in terms of which aspects of the tale to highlight), on the other, their existence made it less likely that such individuals would have direct and detailed knowledge of the particulars of each individual classical text. Some poets and painters doubtless had a sound grasp of Homer, Ovid, Lucian, and perhaps even Reposianus, but others would have been entirely reliant upon intermediaries that, as we have seen, often conflate or gloss over the particulars of and the differences between the various classical tellings.

Also apparent from the above overview is the existence of a constant tension between Horace's twin ends of entertainment (*delectare*) and profit (*prodesse*). An important feature of Demodocus's song, this tension between the comic and the serious lies at the heart of many subsequent treatments of the tale of Mars, Venus, and Vulcan. As we have seen, the question of (im)morality is central to the reception of the tale, from the times of Xenophanes and Plato on. In the notes to his early eighteenth-century translation of the *Odyssey*, Alexander Pope declared that classical thinkers and their medieval and Renaissance disciples had 'by an unnecessary violence endeavoured to reduce [the story of Mars and Venus] to allegory'.[62] The medieval tendency to use mythological tales as vehicles for moralizing allegory casts a long shadow over readings of this and other stories in the Renaissance. The concern for allegory, embodied by the *Ovide moralisé*, lives on in the hands of Bonsignori and Regius, Horologgi and Sánchez de Viana, Pérez de Moya, and others. The more radical solution presented by various forms of censorship/excision would also continue to plague the tale, as evinced by, for instance: (i) a *c.*1400 manuscript of the *Roman de la Rose*, from which a miniature of the *exemplum* of Mars and Venus has been excised; (ii) a Parmigianino pen-and-ink drawing of Mars and Venus being revealed to the gods, from which the lovers have been deleted; (iii) a copy of the 1570 Paris edition of Spreng's *Metamorphoses Ovidii*, in which the lovers have been inked out of the relevant Salomon illustration; (iv) the version of the ode 'A son lict' found in the 1578 Paris edition of Ronsard's *Oeuvres*, from which lines 21–4 (describing the rocking of the bed and the banging of the headboard) have been removed; and (v) Jean Mathieu's illustration of the tale (in Nicholas Renouard's French prose translation of 1619), which takes Tempesta's 'Martem Venerem[que] adulterantes . . .' as its model but which sees the lovers' nether regions deliberately covered

61 Cossío, *Fábulas mitológicas*, 38.
62 *The Odyssey of Homer*, ii. 210. For Pope's vindication of Homer and a notable discussion of classical and Renaissance attitudes to the tale of Mars, Venus, and Vulcan, see the extensive annotations contained in the 'Observations on the Eighth Book' (pp. 193–222), esp. the introduction (pp. 193–4) and the notes on the relevant lines (pp. 209–14).

through the addition of a carefully draped sheet.[63] While it is impossible to say for certain when the various images were butchered, in each case the tale of Mars, Venus, and Vulcan was singled out for special treatment. Even in the sixteenth and seventeenth centuries, the indecorous and lascivious nature of the tale was, it seems, still too much for some.

However, whilst on the one hand the obsession with morality lived on well into the Renaissance, on the other, the same period brought about an evolution in the presentation and understanding of mythological tales. Whereas the *Ovide moralisé* enshrined the spirit of fourteenth- and fifteenth-century attitudes to Ovid, the *Métamorphose d'Ovide figurée* captured the essence of mid-sixteenth-century attitudes to the same poet, 'remplaçant l'approche moralisante et allégorisante du Moyen Age par une appréciation à la fois littérale et hédoniste' [replacing the moralizing and allegorizing approach of the Middle Ages with an appreciation that was both literal and hedonistic].[64] Other examples of this increasingly undogmatic approach to mythology—and of the growing appreciation of classical tales as sources of sensual and aesthetic pleasure—can be seen, for example, in Goltzius's engravings, which foreground the eroticism of each bedroom scene (relegating any didacticism to the accompanying verse), and Vitoria's *Teatro*, which shows little or no interest in developing the various kinds of readings put forward by Pérez de Moya. The presence of a number of light-hearted details in the various Ovid illustrations (the gossiping immortals in Solis, the Cupid taking aim at the gods in Goltzius, the elderly looking Mars attempting in vain to cover Venus's chest in Van der Borcht, etc.) also points to a newly rediscovered enjoyment of the humour inherent in the main classical tellings. In sum, then, in the Golden Age of Spain 'the storehouse of mythology received by writers and artists . . . was neither as uniform, as allegorically dominated, nor indeed as depleted of potential as we are sometimes led to believe'.[65] As we shall now see, the poets and painters of the Spanish Golden Age were quick to exploit the potential inherent in Demodocus's song of Ares and Aphrodite.

---

[63] On (i), see Heidrun Ost, 'Illuminating the *Roman de la Rose* in the Time of the Debate: The Manuscript of Valencia', in Godfried Croenen and Peter Ainsworth (eds.), *Patrons, Authors and Workshops: Books and Book Production in Paris Around 1400*, Synthema, 4 (Leuven: Peeters, 2006), 405–36 (p. 405, n. 2); on (ii), see David Ekserdjian, *Parmigianino* (New Haven: Yale University Press, 2006), 113–14 (which also shows that the same fate was suffered by an engraving by Enea Vico); on (iii), see the copy of Spreng's *Metamorphoses Ovidii* (Paris: Jérôme de Marnef and Guillaume Cavellat, 1570) held in the Bibliothèque nationale de France, FRBNF31046941; on (iv), see *Les Oeuvres de P. de Ronsard . . . Rédigées en sept tomes, Reveuës, et augmentées . . .* (Paris: Gabriel Buon, 1578), i. 259; and on (v), see 'Mars et Venus Surpris', in *Les Métamorphoses d'Ovide traduites en prose françoise, et de nouveau soigneusement reveuës, corrigées en infinis endroits, et enrichies de figures à chacune fable. Avec XV discours contenant l'explication morale et historique* (Paris: veuve Langelier, 1619), 104.

[64] Sharratt, *Bernard Salomon*, 151.

[65] Torres, 'Introduction: *Con pretensión de Fénix*', 11.

2

Mythological Subtexts: The Art of Allusion

Though some mythological motifs, references, and characters are present in the works of canonical fifteenth-century Spanish poets such as Íñigo López de Mendoza, Marquis of Santillana, and his friend and contemporary Juan de Mena, interest in classical mythology as a source of inspiration for secular poetry did not become widespread in Spain until the second quarter of the sixteenth century. As mapped out in the last chapter, Renaissance humanism provided the tools necessary for the rediscovery and dissemination of ancient Greek and Latin texts. It was not long before the explosion of interest in classical authorities such as Homer, Ovid, and Lucian was reflected in the literary culture of the period. The 1520s and 1530s were decades of considerable import in the history of Spanish literature, as the first generation of Golden Age poets—with Garcilaso, Juan Boscán, and Diego Hurtado de Mendoza to the fore— began to experiment with classical forms, genres, subjects, and styles. All the while, writers and thinkers of the Italian Renaissance played a vital role as intermediaries between the culture of Antiquity and the culture of sixteenth-century Spain.

A range of approaches to the gods and their affairs can be seen in the works of the aforementioned poets, who soon seized upon classical mythology as an encyclopedia of ready-made narratives, situations, images, metaphors, and themes. Mythological references fast established themselves as a common currency of Golden Age poetry, opening up new lines of communication between individuals with even a basic grasp of classical literary culture. Mentions of figures drawn from the world of classical mythology are common in the works of most sixteenth- and seventeenth-century Spanish poets. Such references are often employed as simple formulae, to allude to conventional associations or characteristics in an economical manner. According to this form of shorthand, which would remain in use throughout the Golden Age, Argus represents keen sight, Cacus theft, Flora fertility, the Giants rebellion against authority, Icarus and Phaethon the folly of youthful overambition, the river Lethe forgetfulness, the phoenix eternal rebirth, Tantalus the torture of unfulfilled desire, Zephyr the west wind, and so on. Following this scheme, Mars is a metonym for war and the embodiment of martial valour; Venus a metaphor for erotic love and the epitome of female beauty; and Vulcan the archetypal master-craftsman and cuckold. In the sixteenth century, which was dominated by the figure of the soldier-lover, it is not surprising that references to Mars and Venus abound. The figure of Mars, for example, is often adduced, in conjunction with one or more stock epithets—*airado, belicoso, duro, fiero, riguroso, sangriento*, etc.—to introduce the subject of war, to refer to the profession of the soldier, or to extol an individual's military qualities.[1]

Alongside this relatively simple reference system, the secular poetry of the period also offers examples of more complex and ambitious responses to its classical inheritance. Throughout the Golden Age, poets engaged in full-scale imitations of individual classical tales. The earliest example of this phenomenon is Boscán's *Leandro*, which, stretching to almost 2,800 lines of free verse, offers an extensive account of the tale of Hero and Leander based on the version of the story told by the late Greek lyric poet Musaeus. First published in 1543, a year after Boscán's death, this poem set a trend that would continue until well into the next century, as classical tales fired the imagination of the leading lights of successive generations of poets.[2] As we shall see in the next chapter, the tale of Mars, Venus, and Vulcan would inspire its own lengthy imitations in the first quarter of the seventeenth century. In the sixteenth century, however, the tale left its mark in a more subtle way, as a number of poets developed and exploited the art of erudite allusion, transforming ideas and details borrowed from the tale before weaving them together to form mythological subtexts in their poems.

GARCILASO DE LA VEGA

Little is known about the early life of Spain's first, and greatest, Renaissance poet. The second son of an aristocratic family from Toledo, at 20 Garcilaso enlisted in the household guard of the Holy Roman Emperor Charles V.

---

[1] Numerous examples of this form of shorthand can be seen, for instance, in the works of Garcilaso, Hernando de Acuña, Gutierre de Cetina, and Fernando de Herrera. The last of these, for example, has frequent recourse to this device, as evinced by the opening lines of his poems 'Del fiero Marte el canto numeroso' (Sonnet XXIII) and 'En tanto que, Malara, el fiero Marte' (Elegy VI); see Fernando de Herrera, *Poesía castellana original completa*, ed. Cristóbal Cuevas, LH, 219 (Madrid: Cátedra, 1997), 518, 562.

[2] The poem was first printed in *Las obras de Boscan y algunas de Garcilasso dela Vega repartidas en quatro libros* (Barcelona: Carles Amorós, 1543), fols. 73ᵛ–117ᵛ. For a modern edition of the poem, see Juan Boscán, *Obra completa*, ed. Carlos Clavería, LH, 453 (Madrid: Cátedra, 1999), 245–324.

He fought in the civil war against the *Comuneros* (1521), was made a member of the prestigious Order of Santiago, served against the French in Navarre (1523), and in 1525 married a lady at court, Elena de Zúñiga, with whom he had five children. In 1529 he was ordered to attend the emperor in Italy. In the following years he was sent on military and diplomatic missions to Italy, Germany, and France, but this promising career was interrupted in 1532 when he was arrested and exiled from Spain for his involvement in the elopement of his nephew with the young daughter of the Duke of Albuquerque. Garcilaso travelled to Bavaria to seek the emperor's pardon, but failure in this mission led to him being imprisoned on an island in the Danube (a chapter of his life famously commemorated in his Canción III). When, after three months, his sentence was commuted to permanent exile from Spain, he went to Naples where he joined the court of the recently appointed viceroy, Pedro Álvarez de Toledo. In 1535 Garcilaso took part in the emperor's campaign against the Ottoman Turks in Tunis (the backdrop for Sonnet XXXIII). In October of the following year he died as the result of a head wound suffered whilst leading troops in an attack on an insignificant tower in the hamlet of Le Muy near Fréjus in southern France.

Two years, 1526 and 1532, are of particular significance for Garcilaso's development as a poet. In March–September 1526 Garcilaso's friend and fellow poet Boscán travelled with the court to Seville and Granada for the wedding of the emperor Charles V and Princess Isabel of Portugal. Amongst those in attendance were two famous Renaissance men of letters, the papal nuncio Baldassare Castiglione, author of *Il libro del Cortegiano* [The Book of the Courtier] (1528), which Boscán would translate into Spanish in 1534, and the Venetian ambassador and humanist Andrea Navagero, who encouraged Boscán to experiment with Italianate metres.[3] Legend has it that Garcilaso was also in Granada, and that it was there that he fell in love with the empress's lady-in-waiting Isabel Freire.[4] Boscán's own account of this trip, however, implies that Garcilaso was not with him and that it was only on Boscán's return that the two friends discussed the project suggested by Navagero.[5] Though Garcilaso took up the challenge

---

[3] Boscán's translation of Castiglione appeared as *Los quatro libros del cortesano, compuestos en italiano por el conde Balthasar Castellon y agora nuevamente traduzidos en lengua castellana* (Barcelona: Pedro Monpezat, 1534). The preface by Garcilaso was written in 1533 when he visited Boscán in Barcelona having been granted leave to set foot in Spain on a diplomatic mission.

[4] For an introduction to the legend of Isabel Freire—long held to be the inspiration behind much of Garcilaso's finest poetry—and modern scepticism concerning it, see Daniel L. Heiple, 'Garcilaso's Critics and the Question of Sincerity', in *Garcilaso de la Vega and the Italian Renaissance* (Pennsylvania: Pennsylvania State University Press, 1994), 1–27.

[5] For Boscán's account, see the dedicatory epistle to the Duchess of Soma in *Obras*, fols. 19–21.

with great enthusiasm, it seems it was not until his arrival in Naples in 1532 that he began to study and write in earnest. Once there, he soon became a member of the Accademia Pontaniana, founded by the Latin poet Giovanni Pontano, where he met a brilliant circle of men and women of letters. Several of Garcilaso's extant poems celebrate the cultured life-style of a group that in his day included the literary theorist Antonio Minturno, the poets Bernardo Tasso and Luigi Tansillo, and the Spanish polymaths Juan Ginés de Sepúlveda and Juan de Valdés. Inspired, no doubt, by discussions about classical and Italian literature at the academy, in the last four years of his life Garcilaso composed a series of increasingly assured and ambitious poems in new forms and subjects imitated from the classical genres of ode, epistle, elegy, and eclogue.

As is the case with many subsequent Golden Age poets, Garcilaso's works were not published during his own lifetime.[6] His poetry first appeared in print in 1543, with the publication in Barcelona of *Las obras de Boscan y algunas de Garcilasso dela Vega repartidas en quatro libros* [The Works of Boscán and Some by Garcilaso de la Vega Divided into Four Books]. This joint edition was one of the most important works of the Golden Age. For the poet Pedro Salinas, a member of the Generation of 1927, it 'began a revolution that was to determine definitively the course of Spanish poetry in modern times'. Boscán had died in the autumn of 1542, so it was brought out by his widow, Ana Girón de Rebolledo, whom Salinas called 'the greatest benefactress of Spanish poetry—so many poems have been written for a woman, these have been saved by a woman'.[7] The fourth and final book of the work is dedicated to forty poems by Garcilaso.[8] This small corpus of poetry was reissued as part of the joint *Obras* a score of times up to 1597 in Spain, Flanders, and Italy. The first solo printing of Garcilaso came in 1569; this was followed in 1574 by a critical edition by the humanist Francisco Sánchez de las Brozas, who corrected innumerable errors found in the 1543 text, added ten new poems from an old manuscript, and illustrated classical sources and models for Garcilaso's poetry. El Brocense's edition canonized Garcilaso as the first classic of the Spanish Renaissance. It also provoked a massive counterblast from Fernando de Herrera, whose *Anotaciones* [Annotations] (1580) famously does not mention the earlier

---

[6] On the transmission of poetry in the Golden Age, see Antonio R. Rodríguez-Moñino, *Construcción crítica y realidad histórica en la poesía española de los siglos XVI y XVII* (Madrid: Castalia, 1965).

[7] Pedro Salinas, 'The Idealization of Reality: Garcilaso de la Vega', in *Reality and the Poet in Spanish Poetry* (Baltimore: Johns Hopkins University Press, 1940), 65–93 (pp. 67, 75–6).

[8] *Obras*, fols. 163ᵛ–237ᵛ. For a modern edition of his works, see Garcilaso de la Vega, *Obra poética y textos en prosa*, ed. Bienvenido Morros, Clásicos y Modernos, 10 (Barcelona: Crítica, 2003).

edition of his rival commentator. A third important commentary appeared with the Toledan Tomás Tamayo de Vargas's edition of 1622. His notes cite the opinions of a host of contemporary poets, including Góngora, thus confirming Garcilaso's status as a classic and showing that study of the Toledan poet had by then become obligatory.[9]

Garcilaso's surviving poetry in Castilian, much of which was written in Naples during the last four years of his life, now comprises fifty-nine poems: eight *coplas*, forty sonnets, five *canciones* (including the Horatian *Ode ad florem Gnidi*), two elegies, one epistle, and three eclogues. Whilst, unlike Boscán, Garcilaso did not indulge in long retellings of mythological tales, classical mythology plays a prominent role in many of his extant Italianate poems. He draws on several tales in his works, including most prominently those of: Apollo and Daphne (Sonnet XIII; Eclogue III, 145–68); Hero and Leander (Sonnet XXIX); Icarus (Sonnet XII); Iphis and Anaxerete (Canción V, 66–110); Narcissus and Echo (Eclogue II, 597–601); Orpheus and Eurydice (e.g. Eclogue III, 9–16 and 121–44); Phaethon (Sonnet XII); Philomela (Eclogue I, 231–4); Tantalus (Canción IV, 90–100); and Venus and Adonis (Eclogue III, 169–92). In all of these tales, motifs of loss, death, and absence predominate, as individuals are either punished for their own actions or left to grieve over another's passing.[10]

Another of the mythological tales on which Garcilaso draws, and one of very few not to end in death, is that of Mars, Venus, and Vulcan. While Cammarata simply includes the tale in a long line of mythological themes present in Garcilaso's works, Heiple underlines the importance of this particular myth for the poet, placing special emphasis on the interplay between Venus and Mars.[11] The conflict between love and war, the

[9] On the history of editions of Garcilaso's poetry and the rivalry between El Brocense and Herrera, see Oreste Macrí, 'Recensión textual de la obra de Garcilaso', in *Homenaje. Estudios de filología e historia literaria lusohispanas e iberoamericanas publicados para celebrar el tercer lustro del Instituto de Estudios Hispánicos, Portugueses e Iberoamericanos de la Universidad Estatal de Utrecht* (The Hague: Van Goor Zonen, 1966), 305–30; Elias L. Rivers, 'Garcilaso divorciado de Boscán', in J. Homer Herriott (ed.), *Homenaje a Antonio Rodríguez Moñino: estudios de erudición que le ofrecen sus amigos o discípulos hispanistas norteamericanos*, 2 vols. (Madrid: Castalia, 1966), i. 121–9; Eugenio Asensio, 'El Brocense contra Herrera y sus *Anotaciones* a Garcilaso', *El Crotalón. Anuario de Filología Española*, 1 (1984), 13–24; *Las 'Anotaciones' de Fernando de Herrera. Doce estudios*, ed. Begoña López Bueno (Seville: Universidad de Sevilla, 1997); and Bienvenido Morros Mestres, *Las polémicas literarias en la España del siglo XVI: a propósito de Fernando de Herrera y Garcilaso de la Vega*, Biblioteca General, 20 (Barcelona: Quaderns Crema, 1998).

[10] On Garcilaso's use of classical mythology, see Luis M. Schneider, 'Apuntes sobre la mitología greco-romana en Castillejo y Garcilaso', *Revista de Filología Hispánica*, 2 (1960), 295–322; Gustavo Correa, 'Garcilaso y la mitología', *HR* 45 (1977), 269–81; Joan Cammarata, *Mythological Themes in the Works of Garcilaso de la Vega* (Madrid: José Porrúa Turanzas, 1983); Anne J. Cruz, 'La mitología como retórica poética: el mito implícito como metáfora en Garcilaso', *Romanic Review*, 77 (1986), 404–14; Antonio Gargano, *Fonti, miti, topoi: cinque saggi su Garcilaso* (Naples: Liguori, 1988); and Heiple, *Garcilaso, passim*.

[11] Cammarata, *Mythological Themes*, 82–3; and Heiple, *Garcilaso*, 279–395.

competing demands of the lover and the soldier, and the metaphor of love as a form of warfare are all embodied in the relationship between them. In several poems Garcilaso appropriates the Mars/Venus contrast, which was a commonplace of Latin classical poetry, and deploys it as a form of mythological subtext. An example of this is seen in Elegy II, a self-mocking poem in *tercetos* addressed to Boscán and centred on the intertwined themes of war and sexual jealousy. Lines 49–69 compare the effects of absence from the beloved on the metaphorical fire of love to those of water on an actual fire: whilst 'la breve ausencia', like 'el agua moderada', makes the fire burn with greater brightness and intensity, 'el ausencia larga', like 'el agua en abundancia mucha', extinguishes the flame. The reason for the speaker's own lengthy absence is his career as a soldier, as made clear in lines 94–9:

> ¡Oh crudo, oh riguroso, oh fiero Marte,
> de túnica cubierta de diamante
> y endurecido siempre en toda parte!
> ¿Qué tiene que hacer el tierno amante
> con tu dureza y áspero ejercicio,
> llevado siempre del furor delante?

[O harsh, O severe, O fierce Mars, covered in an adamantine tunic and forever hardened in every part! What can the tender lover do with your hardness and rough profession, always led on by martial fury?]

The speaker's complaint about the soldier's lot is introduced through an apostrophe to Mars. Garcilaso's brief sketch of the god of war draws on traditional epithets, underscored through anaphora and tricolon, together with a detail reminiscent of Horace, *Odes*, 1.6.13–14: 'quis Martem tunica tectum adamantina | digne scripserit . . . ?' [Who could fittingly tell of Mars clad in his adamantine tunic?].[12] The exclamation is followed immediately by a rhetorical question: how can the speaker reconcile his duties as a soldier with his desires as a lover—that is, his desires as, or indeed for, the 'tierno amante'? Plying Mars's trade means having to contemplate his 'amado y dulce fruto en mano ajena' [beloved and sweet fruit in another's hand]. Denied the comfort of a literal and rapid death in battle, the speaker is destined, in a fate ironically akin to that of Vulcan, to die a protracted metaphorical death whilst imagining another man enjoying his lady's company. The speaker's commitment to the sphere of Mars thus appears to preclude engagement in that of Venus.

Garcilaso's Canción V, the *Ode ad florem Gnidi* [Ode to the Flower of Gnidus], offers a contrasting perspective on the relationship between the two

---

[12] Horace, *Odes and Epodes*, trans. Charles E. Bennett, LCL (Cambridge, Mass.: Harvard University Press, 1995), 20–1.

gods.[13] Lines 1–30 of this poem develop the conditional clause introduced in the opening line, 'Si de mi baja lira . . .' (the last word of which is now used to refer to the metre that Garcilaso introduces into Spanish in this poem): if the poet had the power of Orpheus, he would sing not of war but of the Neapolitan belle Violante Sanseverino and of her effect on 'el miserable amante' [the wretched lover], later identified as the poet's close friend Mario Galeota. The third *lira* introduces the figure of Mars:

> no pienses que cantado
> sería de mí, hermosa flor de Gnido,
> el fiero Marte airado,
> a muerte convertido,
> de polvo y sangre y de sudor teñido. (11–15)

[do not think, fair flower of Gnidus, that I would sing of fierce and wrathful Mars, who is forever set on death, stained with dust, blood, and sweat.]

Serving once more as a synecdoche for war, Mars is portrayed as an agent of death standing on the battlefield caked in dust, blood, and sweat. The pun *Marte/muerte*, reminiscent of Latin *Mavors/mors*, confirms that death is his trade. The address to the 'hermosa flor de Gnido', the allusion to the figure of the *Venus armata* [armed Venus] in line 25 ('el aspereza de que estás armada'), and the wordplay on *viola* in line 28 ('convertido en viola') cement the link, suggested by the poem's title, between Violante and Venus.[14] Mario is then introduced through a playful periphrasis:

> Hablo d'aquel cativo,
> de quien tener se debe más cuidado,
> que 'stá muriendo vivo,
> al remo condenado,
> en la concha de Venus amarrado. (31–5)

[I speak of that captive, of whom greater care should be taken, who is going through a living death, condemned to row, chained in Venus's conch shell.]

---

[13] The poem's title plays on the double meaning of 'Gnidus': an upmarket district of old Naples (Nido); and a Doric city in Caria celebrated for its nude statue of Venus, attributed to Praxiteles and held to be the most perfect image of beauty in the classical world (Cnidus).
[14] The subject of an epigram in the *Greek Anthology*, the figure of the *Venus armata* was commonplace in Spanish Golden Age poetry, as evinced by Diego Hurtado de Mendoza's humorous short poem 'A Venus' [To Venus]: 'Venus se vistió una vez | en hábito de soldado; | Paris, ya parte y jüez, | dijo de vella espantado: | «Hermosura confirmada | con ningún traje se muda. | ¿Veisla cómo vence armada? | Mejor vencerá desnuda»' [Venus once dressed up as a soldier; as both litigant and judge, Paris said in fear when he saw her: 'Proven beauty is not changed by any attire. See how she conquers when armed? She'll conquer even better when naked']; see Diego Hurtado de Mendoza, *Poesía*, ed. Luis F. Díaz Larios and Olga Gete Carpio, LH, 328 (Madrid: Cátedra, 1990), 386. For an analysis of the epigram 'On the Armed Aphrodite in Sparta', see Irving P. Rothberg, 'Lope de Vega and the Greek Anthology', *Romanische Forschungen*, 87 (1975), 239–56.

His predicament is portrayed in a striking visual metaphor that combines the topos of love as a form of captivity, the paradox of love as a living death, a contemporary reference to galley slaves (i.e. *galeotes*, with a pun on Galeota's surname), and an image of Venus's conch shell (*venera*) reminiscent of Sandro Botticelli's *Birth of Venus* (*c.*1485). A slave to love, Mario is condemned to row in the service of Venus.[15] In imitation of Horace, *Odes*, 1.8 ('Lydia, dic, per omnes'), the next four stanzas, each introduced with the anaphora of 'Por ti . . . ' [Because of you . . .], outline a series of pursuits integral to the life of the ideal Renaissance man that have been neglected by Mario as a result of his service to Venus/Violante.[16] Mario's imprisonment leads him to lose his natural vigour, neglect his passion for horses, arms, and letters, and spurn his male friends. The emphasis on Venus's *concha*, both 'conch shell' and 'pudenda', underlines an ironic disparity between text and subtext: whereas Horace's Sybaris has been weakened by too much sex, Garcilaso's friend Mario has been affected by not getting any at all. The power exercised by Violante is presented in negative light: the cruelty of the hard-hearted and pitiless Petrarchan lady disrupts the social order and triggers a veiled warning in the second half of the poem through the vehicle of the cautionary tale of Iphis and Anaxarete.

Whilst, as these two examples show, Garcilaso has frequent recourse to the Mars/Venus contrast, for an allusion to the tale of Mars, Venus, and Vulcan one must turn to Canción iv. Betraying the strong influence of both Petrarch and the early fifteenth-century Catalan poet Ausiàs March, this poem focuses on the struggle between reason and passion, which culminates here in the subjugation of the former to the latter.[17]

[15] The image of the lover as a galley slave would become another commonplace of Golden Age literature, as seen in Góngora's *romance de cautivo* 'Amarrado al duro banco' (1583) and, echoing Garcilaso, lines 593–5 of his play *Las firmezas de Isabela* (1610): 'y al fin . . . | de la concha fue de Venus | tan forzado galeote'; see Luis de Góngora, *Teatro completo*, ed. Laura Dolfi, LH, 355 (Madrid: Cátedra, 1993), 92.

[16] Horace, *Odes and Epodes*, 26–7.

[17] For a critical edition of the poem, see Garcilaso de la Vega, *Obras completas con comentario*, ed. Elias L. Rivers (Madrid: Castalia, 1974), 189–202. On the influence of Petrarch and March, the problematic question of dating, and Garcilaso's use of the Mars, Venus, and Vulcan tale, see Joseph-Sebastien Pons, 'Note sur la Canción iv de Garcilaso de la Vega', *Bulletin Hispanique*, 35 (1933), 168–71; Rafael Lapesa, *La trayectoria poética de Garcilaso* (Madrid: Revista de Occidente, 1948), 67–72; William J. Entwistle, 'Garcilaso's Fourth Canzon and Other Matters', *MLR* 45 (1950), 225–8; Pedro Bohigas, 'Más sobre la Canción iv de Garcilaso', *Ibérida*, 5 (1961), 79–90; Sharon Ghertman, 'Intra-Strophic Syntactic Patterning in the Extended Canzone: Garcilaso's Fourth *Canción*', in *Petrarch and Garcilaso: A Linguistic Approach to Style*, CTSA: Monografías, 44 (London: Tamesis, 1975), 76–92; Heiple, 'Mars and Venus Shamed: The Paradox of Love and Civilization', in *Garcilaso*, 281–315; Bienvenido Morros Mestres, 'La canción iv de Garcilaso como un infierno de amor: de Garci Sánchez de Badajoz y el Cariteo a Bernardo Tasso', *Criticón*, 80 (2000), 19–47; and Margot Arce de Vázquez, 'El caso de la "Canción iv"', in her *Obras completas: literatura española y literatura hispanoamericana*, ed. Matilde Albert Robatto and Edith Faría Cancel (San Juan: Universidad de Puerto Rico, 2001), 209–14.

In the opening lines the poet expresses the desire to confess his woes, before going on to explain the reasons behind his imminent metaphorical death. After telling the reader of how he has been dragged by his hair along a rough path by 'un tan desatinado pensamiento' [such a foolish thought] (lines 7–20), of the failure of his reason and judgement to protect him from danger (21–60), and of how he is now captivated by the distant and disdainful lady (61–100), the poet expands on the conflict between reason and passion in a meditation on his recent humiliation:

> De los cabellos de oro fue tejida
> la red que fabricó mi sentimiento,
> do mi razón, revuelta y enredada,
> con gran vergüenza suya y corrimiento,
> sujeta al apetito y sometida,
> en público adulterio fue tomada,
> del cielo y de la tierra contemplada.
>   Mas ya no es tiempo de mirar yo en esto,
> pues no tengo con qué consideralloo;
>   y en tal punto me hallo,
> que estoy sin armas en el campo puesto,
> y el paso ya cerrado y la hüida. (101–12)

[From her golden hair was woven the net created by my feelings, where my reason, upset and entangled, to its great shame and embarrassment, subdued and subjugated by desire, was caught in public adultery, witnessed by both heaven and earth. But now is not the time for me to think about this, since I have no faculties with which to do so; I find myself in such a weak position, defenceless on the battlefield, unable either to press on or to flee.]

In a reworking of the Petrarchan topos of the 'net of love', *razón* and *apetito* have been caught in a net forged from the lady's golden hair. In the *Anotaciones*, Herrera suggests that Garcilaso's source here is the opening lines of *Canzoniere*, CLXXXI: 'Amor fra l'erbe una leggiadra rete | d'oro e di perle tese sott'un ramo' [Love weaves amid the grass a gay net of gold and pearls, under a branch]. Lines 4–5 of the *canzone* 'Perché quel che mi trasse ad amar prima' also describe a trap formed from the beloved's hair: 'Tra le chiome de l'òr nascose il laccio, | al qual mi strinse Amore' [within the locks of gold was hid the noose with which Love bound me tight] (*Canzoniere*, LIX). The above lines from Canción IV thus form part of a well-established Petrarchan tradition—centred on the effect on the lover of seeing the lady's blonde locks—that would be imitated by many subsequent writers of the Spanish Golden Age, including Herrera, Cervantes, Lope de Vega, and Quevedo.[18] Garcilaso refreshes the three topoi of the 'red de amor', love as a form of captivity, and the paradoxical emotional struggle between reason and passion by combining them with a metaphor based on the tale of Mars, Venus, and Vulcan. El Brocense and Herrera both draw attention to the presence of this mythological subtext. Herrera's commentary on line 106, which begins with the statement 'Moraliza la fábula de Venus i Marte', develops El Brocense's comment on line 101: 'Moraliza la fábula de Venus, que fingen los poetas que la prendió Vulcano con una sutilísima red, tomándola en adulterio con el Dios Marte' [This section moralizes the story of Venus, who was, poets say, trapped by Vulcan in a very fine net, catching her *in flagrante* with Mars].[19] Although no subtext is explicitly mentioned by Garcilaso, the conjunction of the net, adulterers caught 'en público adulterio', and an audience of onlookers brings the Homeric and Ovidian episode to mind. The points of comparison between the capture of the poet's *razón* and *apetito* and the imprisonment of Mars and Venus are multiple. The net forged from fine steel threads by Vulcan is succeeded by a metaphorical net forged from the beloved's fine golden hair by the poet's own *sentimiento* (and not by Love, as in the above examples from Petrarch). Both sets of adulterers are snared in a strong yet invisible net, caught *in flagrante delicto*, and exposed to the contemplation of both the heavens and the earth. Like the lovers, the poet's reason, 'revuelta y enredada', struggles frantically but in vain to free itself from the net whilst experiencing acute shame and embarrassment ('gran vergüenza . . . y corrimiento'). In the final two lines of the section quoted above the

---

[18] Examples of the topos of the 'red de amor' formed from the lady's golden hair are found in Herrera's sonnet which begins 'Destas doradas hebras fue texida | la red en que fui preso y enlazado'; lines 32–4 of Lenio's song on love in Book IV of Cervantes's *La Galatea* (1585): 'red engañosa de sotil cabello | que cubre y prende en torpes actos feos | los que del mundo son en más tenidos'; the opening lines of Lope de Vega's sonnet 'Con nuevos lazos, como el mismo Apolo, | hallé en cabello a mi Lucinda un día' (*Rimas*, no. 68); and Quevedo's madrigal on a lady's hairnet 'Alma en prisión de oro' (Q409), which begins 'Si alguna vez en lazos de oro bellos | la red, Flori, encarcela tus cabellos'. For more on this topos, see Paul Julian Smith, *Quevedo on Parnassus: Allusive Context and Literary Theory in the Love-Lyric*, MHRA Texts and Dissertations, 25 (London: MHRA, 1987), 65–8; and, on the oft-glossed sonnet 'Dígame quien lo sabe: ¿de qué es hecha | la red de amor?', Trevor J. Dadson, 'Cómo se hacía un soneto en el Siglo de Oro: el caso de «Amor, la red de amor digo que es hecha»', in María Cruz García de Enterría and Alicia Cordón Mesa (eds.), *Actas del IV Congreso Internacional de la Asociación Internacional Siglo de Oro (AISO)*, 2 vols. (Alcalá de Henares: Universidad de Alcalá, 1998), i. 509–24.

[19] For El Brocense's and Herrera's comments on the lines under discussion, see *Garcilaso de la Vega y sus comentaristas: obras completas del poeta acompañadas de los textos íntegros de los comentarios de El Brocense, Fernando de Herrera, Tamayo de Vargas y Azara*, ed. Antonio Gallego Morell, 2nd rev. and exp. edn. (Madrid: Gredos, 1972), 273, 406–7.

hopeless situation faced by the poet is confirmed in the image of his being 'sin armas en el campo puesto'. The word *campo*, a metonym for the sphere of Mars, introduces another Petrarchan topos, that of the bed as the battle-field of love: like Mars, the poet is stripped of his arms, defenceless, and unable either to proceed or to flee ('el paso ya cerrado y la hüida').[20] Unlike the god of war, however, he will not be freed, rearmed, and restored to his divine status as soon as the episode draws to a close. A second dispar-ity between text and subtext recalls that seen in the *Ode ad florem Gnidi*: whereas Mars and Sybaris both pay a price for having too much sex, the protagonist of Canción IV and Mario Galeota both suffer from not having any at all. A third, related to the first two, has to do with tone: in Ovid, for example, the gods look on and laugh; here, however, the absence of any levity is determined by the serious emotional dilemma of the speaker, whose paradoxical situation, one closely associated with Petrarch, is effect-ively conveyed by means of the Mars/Venus borrowing.[21]

In his *Anotaciones*, after a brief summary of allegorical interpretations of the tale, Herrera outlines the sources behind Garcilaso's mythological sub-text, citing the *Odyssey*, *Metamorphoses* VIII (rather than IV), and Ariosto, *Orlando furioso*, XV.56:

> Havea la rete già fatta Vulcano,
> di sottil fil d'acciar, ma con tal arte,
> che saria stata ogni fatica in vano
> per ismagliarli la più debil parte;
> et era quella, che gia piedi e mano
> havea legati a Venere et a Marte,
> la fe il geloso, et non ad altro effetto
> che per pigliargli insieme ambi nel letto.[22]

[Vulcan had made the net out of finest steel meshes but with such craft that to try snapping the weakest link would have been a wasted effort. This was the

---

[20] The metaphor of the bed as the battlefield of love, inspired by Petrarch, *Canzoniere*, CCXXVI ('et duro campo di battaglia il letto') is imitated by innumerable Golden Age poets, including Garcilaso (Sonnet XVII, line 8: 'y duro campo de batalla el lecho'), Góngora (*Soledad primera*, line 1091: 'a batallas de amor campo de pluma'; also see below, p. 88), and Quevedo (Q359, line 8: 'y duro campo de batalla el lecho'). For more on imitations and re-workings of this topos, see Antonio Vilanova, *Las fuentes y los temas del 'Polifemo' de Góngora*, Anejos de la *Revista de Filología Española*, 66, 2 vols. (Madrid: CSIC, 1957), ii. 200–6.

[21] For an example of Petrarch's characterization of the reason/passion struggle as a perpetual war, see the second tercet of the sonnet 'Lasso, ben so che dolorose prede' (*Canzoniere*, CI): 'La voglia et la ragion combattuto ànno | sette et sette anni; et vincerà il migliore, | s'anime son qua giù del ben presaghe' [Passion and reason have fought for seven and seven years; and the better one will win, if souls down here can see the good to come].

[22] Fernando de Herrera, *Anotaciones a la poesía de Garcilaso*, ed. Inoria Pepe and José María Reyes, LH, 516 (Madrid: Cátedra, 2001), 522–3.

net with which he had bound Venus and Mars hand and foot—the jealous god had made it for no other purpose than to catch the pair of them in bed.][23]

In the surrounding *ottave* Ariosto gives a brief history of what happened to Vulcan's net after this episode. It was seized by Mercury and used to catch the nymph Chloris, then preserved for centuries in the temple of Anubis at Canopus, before, after three thousand years, being stolen by the giant Caligorant, who placed it in the sand to ensnare passers-by. Finally it was taken by Astolfo, who defeated Caligorant by blowing his horn, scaring the giant into his own trap, and then cuffing him with one of the net's links. Whilst Canción IV, 101–7, may recall the above stanza from the *Orlando furioso*, Garcilaso's use of the mythological tale is much more sophisticated than that of Ariosto. In an example of what Heiple terms 'dissimulative imitation', Garcilaso calls to mind the tale of Mars, Venus, and Vulcan without the names of any of the gods being revealed.[24] Instead of foregrounding his imitation of the classical tale, Garcilaso relies on the cultured reader to spot the allusions to it, weave them together into a coherent subtext, and reflect on their significance for the poem as a whole. Whereas Ariosto sketches out the central section of the tale in order to give a sense of remote mythological heritage to Caligorant's net, Garcilaso embeds in the *canción* an ekphrasis-like visual snapshot of a single scene from the tale—reminiscent of some of the early woodcuts discussed in the previous chapter—to give an original twist to his treatment of the commonplace clash between reason and passion.[25]

Whilst Ariosto cites the tale of Vulcan's net to lend variety and erudition to the narrative, Garcilaso alludes to the tale to develop ideas and motifs present in the first one hundred lines of the poem. First and foremost, the shameful entrapment of the poet's reason and passion represents the climactic episode in the struggle between them that is mapped out in lines 21–60. Having set out in fear on the 'áspero camino' [harsh path], reason strives to protect the poet, only to be left tired, wounded, and defeated by a then as yet unidentified opponent. This adversary is finally named in line 105, when *razón* is conquered and subjugated by *apetito*. Lines 101–12 also draw together a number of the poem's other strands: mention of the

[23] Ludovico Ariosto, *Orlando furioso*, trans. Guido Waldman, Oxford World's Classics (Oxford: Oxford University Press, 1998), 159–60.

[24] *Garcilaso*, 58.

[25] For Leo Spitzer's definition of *ekphrasis* as 'the poetic description of a pictorial or sculptural work of art', see 'The "Ode on a Grecian Urn", or Content vs. Metagrammar', *Comparative Literature*, 7 (1955), 203–25 (p. 207). On the tradition of ekphrasis in Spain, see Emilie L. Bergmann, *Art Inscribed: Essays on Ekphrasis in Spanish Golden Age Poetry*, Harvard Studies in Romance Languages, 35 (Cambridge, Mass.: Harvard University Press, 1979).

lady's hair offers a bitter reminder of how the poet had been dragged along by his own hair, leaving behind a trail of blood, in lines 7–20; after the sun-like eyes, whose power over the poet is described in lines 61–72, the golden hair represents a second element in the traditional Petrarchan catalogue of the lady's fragmented features; the metaphor of love as a form of captivity picks up on the image of the galley slave's clanking chains in lines 85–6 ('. . . está sonando | de mis atados pies el grave hierro'); the emphasis on *vergüenza* and *corrimiento* develops out of the image of reason setting out 'de pura vergüenza constreñida' (line 32) and the poet's admission of shame and embarrassment in lines 53–5 ('Entonces yo sentíme salteado | d'una *vergüenza* libre y generosa; | *corríme* gravemente . . .'; my emphasis); the identification of the poet as a naked and defenceless soldier continues the military metaphor of love as war introduced in the images of battle ending in defeat in lines 41–6 ('peleando | en mi defensa', 'en mil partes ya herida', 'mi razón vencida'); and, finally, the use of erudite classical allusion follows on from the end of the previous stanza in which Garcilaso draws on the figure of Tantalus to establish a subtext relating to the suffering of continual unsatisfied desire (lines 93–100).

In sum, far from being mere ornament, the veiled allusions to the tale of Mars, Venus, and Vulcan in Canción IV cohere to form a complex metaphor that is indissolubly bound up with the development of the poem's central concerns. As in many of his extant works, Garcilaso's use of classical mythology in this poem is characterized by allusion through periphrasis, subtle modifications to individual narrative elements, and unexpected parallels between situations faced by the poem's protagonists and those involving the gods of Antiquity. As we have seen, the presence of the subtext relating to the shaming of Mars and Venus enables Garcilaso to refresh a number of conventional poetic topoi, including those relating to the Petrarchan lady's golden hair, the 'red de amor', and the metaphors of love as captivity and love as war. In lines of considerable conceptual density and economy, these topoi are combined and played off against each other not to 'moraliza[r] la fábula de Venus i Marte', as both El Brocense and Herrera would have it, but to offer a striking depiction of the climactic moment in the struggle between reason and passion. Given the above, Garcilaso's use of mythological allusion in Canción IV should not be analysed in relation to the concept of sincerity, at best patchy knowledge of the poet's biography, and the legend of his frustrated love for Isabel Freire. As Heiple reminds us, sincerity is always a construct: '[whilst] the tone of the lyric is often personal and intimate . . . its metaphors and rhetoric, along with the narrative stance of the speaker, must be fictional.'[26]

---

[26] *Garcilaso*, 11.

Detailed examination of the presence and function of classical allusion in the above lines sheds light not on Garcilaso's emotional and psychological states in response to the marriage of Isabel Freire but on his attitude to the intellectual currents of the Renaissance, his innovative reworking of poetic commonplace, and the complex relationship between imitation and invention that lies at the heart of the work of Spain's first Renaissance poet.

DIEGO HURTADO DE MENDOZA

Born into one of the most famous aristocratic families in Castile in or around the same year as Garcilaso, Diego Hurtado de Mendoza was a direct descendant of the Marquis of Santillana. Like his more famous contemporary, whom he outlived by almost forty years, Hurtado de Mendoza was a soldier-poet who spent long periods of his life outside Spain. After studying canon and civil law in Salamanca, he moved to Italy, where he combined service in the Spanish armies with attendance at lectures at universities including Rome and Padua. In 1536, in his first diplomatic mission, he was sent to London as Charles V's ambassador-extraordinary to propose a marriage between Henry VIII's daughter, Princess Mary, and Charles's brother-in-law, the Infante of Portugal. Although this mission ultimately proved unsuccessful, Hurtado de Mendoza was later made ambassador, first to Venice (1539–46) and then to Rome (1547–52). Whilst in Venice he sat for Titian, kept company with Italian Renaissance poets and humanists—including such luminaries as Pietro Aretino and Benedetto Varchi—and cultivated his interests in poetry, languages (Italian, Latin, Greek, Arabic, etc.), and collecting (books, manuscripts, coins, antiquities, etc.). He returned to Spain in the mid-1550s and moved with the Court to Madrid in 1561. In 1568, as the result it seems of a quarrel over a woman, he was imprisoned and then exiled in Granada. He died in 1575, leaving an impressive library to Philip II.[27]

Although individual poems by Hurtado de Mendoza were included in earlier works by other writers, such as the 1543 Boscán/Garcilaso *Obras*, much of his poetry was not published until an edition by Juan Díaz

---

[27] For more on his life, works, and library, see Ángel González Palencia and Eugenio Mele, *Vida y obras de don Diego Hurtado de Mendoza*, 3 vols. (Madrid: Instituto de Valencia de Don Juan, 1941–3); the editors' introduction in Hurtado de Mendoza, *Poesía*, 9–47; and Anthony Hobson, *Renaissance Book Collecting: Jean Grolier and Diego Hurtado de Mendoza, their Books and Bindings* (Cambridge: Cambridge University Press, 1999), esp. 70–92.

Hidalgo containing ninety-six poems was printed in Madrid in 1610.[28] Hurtado de Mendoza experimented widely with both traditional Spanish (e.g. *endechas, quintillas, redondillas*) and Italianate (e.g. sonnet, *tercetos, octavas reales*) forms. His poems range from sonnets in the Petrarchan tradition to verse epistles dedicated to contemporaries such as Boscán, and from satires of court life to humorous pieces on mundane subjects such as fleas, carrots, and grey hair. He also wrote several poems on mythological subjects.[29] The longest of these, at 824 lines, is the 'Fábula de Adonis, Hipómenes y Atalanta', an imitation in *octavas* of the tale of Atalanta and Hippomenes and its frame narrative of Venus and Adonis as found in Ovid, *Metamorphoses*, x.519–739. The majority, however, are not serious poems in the mould of Boscán's *Leandro*, but burlesque sonnets that poke fun at gods such as Venus, Cupid, and Diana.[30] The following sonnet, one of several burlesque poems to be censored in the 1610 *Obras*, serves as an example:

> ¡Oh Venus, alcahueta y hechicera,
> que nos traes embaucados tierra y cielo,
> cuántas veces, por falta de una estera,
> has hecho monipodios en el suelo!
>
> ¡Cuántas veces te han visto andar en celo
> tras los planetas machos, cachondera,
> pegada y abrazada pelo a pelo
> y pellejo a pellejo dentro y fuera!
>
> No me andes rodeando, puta vieja,
> que no tengo tan dura la costilla;
> guarda, que esta mi mano te apareja,

---

[28] *Obras del insigne cavallero Don Diego de Mendoza, embaxador del Emperador Carlos Quinto en Roma. Recopilados por Frey Ivan Diaz Hidalgo* (Madrid: Juan de la Cuesta, 1610). Two examples of poems published in earlier works are his epistle to Boscán, 'El no maravillarse hombre de nada', and the 'Fábula de Adonis, Hipómenes y Atalanta', included in the joint Boscán/Garcilaso *Obras* of 1543 (Barcelona) and 1553 (Venice), respectively.

[29] On Hurtado de Mendoza's mythological poems, see José Ignacio Díez Fernández, 'Algunos poemas atribuidos a don Diego Hurtado de Mendoza', *Revista de Filología Románica*, 4 (1986), 181–95; Cossío, *Fábulas mitológicas*, 89–97; Antonio Alatorre, 'Andanzas de Venus y Cupido en tiempos del romancero nuevo', in Beatriz Garza Cuarón and Yvette Jiménez de Báez (eds.), *Estudios de folklore y literatura dedicados a Mercedes Díaz Roig* (Mexico: El Colegio de México, 1992), 337–90 (esp. pp. 378–83); and Joaquín Roses Lozano, 'La "Fábula de Adonis, Hipómenes y Atalanta" de Diego Hurtado de Mendoza: grados de la imitación renacentista', in Juan Matas Caballero and others (eds.), *Congreso Internacional sobre Humanismo y Renacimiento*, 2 vols. (León: Universidad de León, 1998), ii. 123–50.

[30] On these sonnets, and the question of their attribution, see Hurtado de Mendoza, *Poesía*, 393–40; and Adrienne Laskier Martín, 'The Pre-Cervantine Burlesque Sonnet in Spain', in *Cervantes and the Burlesque Sonnet* (Berkeley: University of California Press, 1991), 41–65.

con un cuarto abrochado y candelilla,
un *memini* raudal de rabo a oreja
cual nunca dio a mujer hombre en Castilla.

[Oh Venus, you witch and procuress, how you bring us earth and heaven,
caught up [as we are] in your deceptions! How many times, for want of a
mat, you've done dirty deeds on the bare floor! How many times you've been
seen chasing after the male planets, sex-crazed and on heat, with your hair
and hide clinging to and rubbing up against theirs, both inside and out! Stop
following me around, old whore, 'cos I'm not that well off; look at what I'm
holding in my hand: a bag of change and this little rod, with which I'll make
sure you never forget being shafted from arse to ear, no man in Castile's ever
given a woman such a good seeing to.]

Reminiscent of Fernando de Rojas's bawd Celestina, this Venus is an old
prostitute, sorceress, and procuress. When not preparing for or engaging
in intercourse on earth, the sex-obsessed goddess chases male planets
across the night sky. In a parody of classical and Petrarchan tradition,
the poet instructs Venus, whom he addresses directly as 'puta vieja', to
stop following him around, not because he cannot endure the suffering
associated with love but because he is hard up. In the final tercet Hurtado
de Mendoza takes the poem's crudity to extreme lengths. A string of
euphemisms, vulgar plays on words, and obscene expressions drawn from
contemporary slang rounds off this apostrophe in memorable fashion: if
Venus accepts the poet's payment, albeit only a meagre 'cuarto abrochado',
then he will show her a truly unforgettable time.[31]

A different, yet related, attitude to the gods is seen in Hurtado de
Mendoza's '¿Qué hace el gran Señor de los romanos . . . ?', an epistle in
tercetos to the historian and ambassador Luis de Ávila y Zúñiga. The poem's
emphasis on describing aspects of an ambassador's life and the mention
on several occasions of Venice suggests that it was composed shortly after
Hurtado de Mendoza's arrival in Venice, or at least at some point during
his embassy there. In lines 10–12 the poet begins a long meditation on the
ambassador's lot: '¡Oh embajadores, puros majaderos, | que, si los reyes
quieren engañar, | comienzan por nosotros los primeros!' [Oh ambassa-
dors, complete fools, for, if kings want to deceive people, they start with
us first!] After describing a series of challenges faced by the ambassador,
including the consternation experienced when opening dispatches from
his king, the poet changes tack in line 100, commenting on the brevity of

---

[31] On the slang connotations of this phrase, see María Inés Chamorro, *Tesoro de villanos.
Diccionario de germanía. Lengua de jacarandina: rufos, mandiles, galloferos, viltrotonas, zurrapas, carcaveras, murcios, floraineros y otras gentes de la carda* (Barcelona: Herder, 2002), 52
(s.v. *abrochados*).

human life and the need to enjoy each and every day to its full. This leads into a surprising digression from the principal subject of embassy:

> Tú, Vulcano, dios de los plateros,
> poderoso en el fuego y el metal,
> a quien también adoran los herreros,
>   hazme un vaso de plata hondo y tal,
> que mida san Martín ocho cuartillos
> y otro santo si hay con su caudal. (106–11)

[You, Vulcan, god of silversmiths, with your mastery of fire and metals, you who are also worshipped by blacksmiths, make me a silver cup so deep that it takes four litres of San Martín de Valdeiglesias and another saint to keep him company if there's enough capacity.]

The poet calls on the smith-god to forge him a drinking vessel large enough to contain 'ocho cuartillos' (≈ four litres) of the famous 'vino de San Martín de Valdeiglesias', and, in a light-hearted wordplay, more wine named after another saint if the size of the cup permits. This address to Vulcan is an imitation of a specific Anacreontic song in which Hephaestus is also instructed to make a deep silver cup. The song survives in three different versions, in *Anacreontea*, IV, *Greek Anthology*, XI, 47–8, and Aulus Gellius, *Attic Nights*, XIX. The first of these runs thus:

> Work your silver, Hephaestus, and make me not a suit of armour—what have I to do with battles?—but rather a hollow cup, as deep as you can. Put no stars on it for me, no Wain, no gloomy Orion: what do I care about the Pleiads or the fair Ploughman? Put vines on for me with bunches of grapes on them and Bacchants picking them: put a wine-press and men treading it, the satyrs laughing, Loves all in gold, Cythere laughing together with handsome Lyaeus, Love and Aphrodite.[32]

In lines 112–35 of his epistle Hurtado de Mendoza adheres closely to the structure of his model, listing a number of subjects not to be engraved on the cup before proceeding to explain what should appear instead. The first half of this section is introduced with the words 'No entalles . . . ' [Do not engrave . . .] and punctuated by the anaphoric repetition of 'no' at the start of each of the following three *tercetos*. Whereas, in *Anacreontea* IV, Hephaestus is ordered not to decorate the cup with a series of constellations (the Bear, Orion, the Pleiades, and the Plough), here Vulcan is

---

[32] *Anacreontea*, IV, in *Greek Lyric*, trans. by David A. Campbell, LCL, 5 vols. (Cambridge, Mass.: Harvard University Press, 1982–93), ii. 165–7. On the question of which of the three versions served as Hurtado de Mendoza's principal model, see Irving P. Rothberg, 'Hurtado de Mendoza and the Greek Epigrams', *HR* 26 (1958), 171–87.

instructed not to engrave thunder and lightning, hell, the extremes of winter and summer, the sun and the seven planets of the Ptolemaic system, and Mars, 'el sangriento señor de las batallas' [the bloody master of battles]. Instead of these images that reflect metaphorically some of the hardships associated with embassy, as detailed in lines 10–99, Vulcan is commissioned—now as in the model—to depict a Bacchanalian scene associated with the enjoyment of life prescribed in lines 100–5:

> Entalla muchas uvas coloradas
> con sus vides, que en torno las rodeen,
> con las revueltas yedras entricadas.
>   Los amores estén que se meneen
> espirando aquel fuego glorïoso
> cuyas llamas ardiendo no se veen;
>   el dios Baco, borracho y dormijoso,
> las horas todas doce al derredor,
> el tiempo sano y mozo y con reposo.
>   Tal será la razón de la labor,
> padre Vulcano, que me has de hacer,
> y a ti te cabrá parte del sabor. (127–38)

[Engrave lots of red grapes with vines and intricate, interwoven ivy all around them. Let there be Amores going round breathing out that glorious fire whose flames burn invisibly; the god Bacchus, drunk and sleepy, all twelve Hours around, and Time healthy, young, and at rest. Such, father Vulcan, will be the nature of the work you are to do for me, and some of the taste will be left for you.]

The image of the grapes and the vines trailing up the vessel is closely based on the Anacreontic model. The motif of the interwoven vines and ivy represents a classically inspired metaphor for the harmony associated with reciprocated love, a metaphor that stands in contrast to earlier images of disorder and strife associated with suffering in love. At the centre of the relief lies the god of wine, Bacchus; drunk and drowsy, he is surrounded by the Hours, the companions of Venus in times of joy and festivity. Whereas the model places emphasis on the treading of grapes and the pressing of wine in preparation for Bacchanalian festivities, here the proposed relief work depicts the after-effects of the wine's consumption. The grapes have been made into the wine of Bacchus, whilst the extreme conditions evoked in lines 112–17 have been replaced by an idyllic, harmonious backdrop. When Vulcan completes the commission, he too will be able to enjoy the pleasure and effects of the wine.

The endings of the three versions of the Anacreontic song differ with regard to the number and identity of figures to appear on the silver cup.

The most extensive is that of *Anacreontea* IV (the only one, for example, to include Aphrodite/Venus), but none of the three prepares the reader for Hurtado de Mendoza's expansion of his source:

> Harás sentar a tabla tu mujer,
> que no pesará ello a don Luis;
> tú entrarás a lo hondo en el beber.
>   Nunca estimáis en dos maravedís
> que el ojo y pie se acuerdan, los cornudos,
> ni miráis lo que pasa ni sentís.
>   Todos seremos ciegos, sordos, mudos,
> y tú haz la labor que sea divina,
> que te la pagaremos en escudos. (139–47)

[You'll make your wife sit at the table, for that won't displease Don Luis; you'll get stuck into drinking. You cuckolds don't place much value on the eye and the foot being in tune with one another, nor do you watch or sense what's going on. All of us will be blind, deaf, and mute; you just make sure that the work is something divine, for we'll pay you for it in coins of gold.]

The festive spirit of the ekphrasis is carried over into the final section of the address to Vulcan, as the smith is instructed to bring his wife to join the poet and the poem's dedicatee at their table. In a humorous aside, it is suggested that Luis de Ávila will not mind keeping Venus, the most beautiful of all the goddesses, company whilst Vulcan dedicates himself to drinking freely. Though neither Venus nor Mars is explicitly named, the last two *tercetos* of the inset address to Vulcan contain allusions to the tale of Mars, Venus, and Vulcan that force the reader to reconsider the relationship between the classical song and its new context. The penultimate *terceto* reminds the reader that the world of reciprocated love, Bacchanalian festivity, and wine-induced slumber is not one to which Vulcan is accustomed. Wordplay on the verb *cabrá* in line 138 paves the way for an explicit reference to cuckoldry in lines 142–4.[33] Addressing 'los cornudos' directly, the poet states that cuckolds continually fail to see or sense what goes on around them, thus recalling Vulcan's obliviousness to his wife's affair with Mars, 'el sangriento señor de las batallas'. In the final *terceto* the poet assures Vulcan that everyone will turn a blind eye to his wife's affair and decline to gossip about it if he successfully completes his latest commission: 'todos seremos ciegos, sordos, mudos.' The shift to the first-person plural in *seremos* and *pagaremos* creates the impression of a

---

[33] 'Llamar a uno cabrón, en todo tiempo y entre todas naciones es afrentarle. Vale lo mesmo que cornudo, a quien su mujer no le guarda lealtad, como no la guarda la cabra, que de todos los cabrones se deja tomar' (Cov. s.v. *cabra*).

knowing audience made up not of the male gods of Antiquity but of the poet, Don Luis, and their unidentified companions (perhaps including the reader). Vulcan will be paid handsomely for his labour; not with the miserly sum of two *maravedís* but, ironically, in *escudos*, both valuable gold coins and, as shields, the trappings of his rival Mars's military splendour. At this point the digression formed by the appeal to Vulcan draws to a close and the poet returns to his discussion of his current situation for the final three *tercetos* and the closing four-line envoi. In sum, the poet's meditation on the life of an ambassador frames a section made up of fourteen *tercetos* in imitation of a specific Anacreontic song. As noted earlier, Hephaestus/Vulcan is renowned for his sublime talent as the divine master-craftsman. Objects created by him—such as the shield of Achilles (Homer, *Iliad*, xviii.483–608) or the relief-work on the doors of the palace of the sun (Ovid, *Metamorphoses*, ii.1–18)—represent the pinnacle of artistic achievement. Taking inspiration from his classical model, Hurtado de Mendoza presents a form of ekphrasis to rival previous descriptions of works forged by Vulcan. However, he modifies the end of the song by introducing references to Venus's affairs. The serious address to Vulcan, the divine artificer and god of silversmiths and blacksmiths, thus becomes, in a new ending, a playful address to Vulcan, the arch-cuckold. Whilst the gods of Antiquity are not seen through the same distorting lens as that offered by the burlesque sonnets, they are, nevertheless, still seen in a playfully comic light.

FRANCISCO DE ALDANA

One of the leading lights of the next generation of Spanish poets was Francisco de Aldana. Born in 1537 in Naples, where his father served as captain in the forces of Pedro de Toledo, Aldana was brought up in the cultured world of Renaissance Italy. Like Garcilaso, Hurtado de Mendoza, and other early sixteenth-century Spanish writers, such as Hernando de Acuña and Gutierre de Cetina, Aldana was a soldier-poet: after formative years in Naples and then at the Medici court in Florence, he spent the majority of his adult life in military campaigns in Flanders, France, and North Africa. His last years were spent in the service of Philip II's nephew, King Sebastian of Portugal. In 1578, whilst leading the infantry in Sebastian's expedition in North Africa, Aldana was killed, together with Sebastian and large numbers of Portuguese nobles, at the Battle of Alcazarquivir in Morocco.[34]

[34] For a detailed account of Aldana's life, see Elias L. Rivers, *Francisco de Aldana, el divino capitán* (Badajoz: Institución de Servicios Culturales, 1955), 9–123.

Like both Garcilaso and Hurtado de Mendoza, Aldana did not see his poetry published during his own lifetime. His poems were collected by his brother, Cosme, and published more than a decade after his death in two parts dedicated to Philip II, the *Primera parte* in Milan in 1589 and the *Segunda parte* in Madrid in 1591.³⁵ Though Aldana has long been neglected as a poet, a fact bemoaned by successive generations of twentieth-century critics, 'el divino capitán' was held in the highest regard by later Golden Age writers of the stature of Cervantes, Lope, and Quevedo. Shaped, no doubt, by his years in Renaissance Italy, Aldana's poetry betrays the influence of not only Petrarchism but also Neoplatonic philosophy. This is evident from his most famous poem, the 'Carta para Arias Montano sobre la contemplación de dios y los requisitos della' [Letter to Arias Montano on the Contemplation of God and its Requirements], 'a profound and moving meditation on friendship as a pathway to Divine contemplation'.³⁶ Written predominantly in *tercetos, octavas reales*, and sonnet form, Aldana's other poems range from pastoral sonnets (e.g. 'Mil veces digo, entre los brazos puesto') and reflections on the theme of the *vida retirada* ('Gózate, rey, subido allá en tu alteza') to imitations of Italian works such as Sannazaro's *De Partu Virginis* ('Del Parto Virginal, que vino al suelo') and religious pieces on the Creation ('Señor universal de cuanto alcanza') and the Last Judgement ('Un cerco de oro, al cielo muy vecino').³⁷

Several of his poems feature the gods of Antiquity, and a small number of them focus explicitly on specific mythological tales. These include 'Entre el Asia y Europa es repartido', a line-by-line gloss on Garcilaso's sonnet on Hero and Leander, and the 'Fábula de Faetonte', an imitation, stretching to over 1,200 lines of free verse, of the tale of Phaethon told by

³⁵ *Primera parte de las obras que hasta agora se han podido hallar del Capitan Francisco de Aldana* (Milan: Paolo Gottardo da Ponte, 1589); and *Segunda parte de las obras que se han podido hallar del Capitan Francisco de Aldana* (Madrid: Pedro Madrigal, 1591). For a modern edition, see Francisco de Aldana, *Poesías castellanas completas*, ed. José Lara Garrido, LH, 223 (Madrid: Cátedra, 1985).

³⁶ Julian Weiss, 'Renaissance Poetry', in David T. Gies (ed.), *The Cambridge History of Spanish Literature* (Cambridge: Cambridge University Press, 2004), 159–77 (p. 172).

³⁷ For critical studies of Aldana's poetry, see Rivers, *Francisco de Aldana*; Otis H. Green, 'On Francisco de Aldana: Observations on Dr. Rivers' Study of "El Divino Capitán"', *HR* 26 (1958), 117–35; Carlos Ruiz Silva, *Estudios sobre Francisco de Aldana* (Valladolid: Universidad de Valladolid, 1981); D. Gareth Walters, *The Poetry of Francisco de Aldana*, CTSA: Monografías, 128 (London: Tamesis, 1988); Alfredo Mateos Paramio, 'Francisco de Aldana: ¿un neoplatónico del amor humano?', in Manuel García Martín (ed.), *Estado actual de los estudios sobre el Siglo de Oro: actas del II Congreso Internacional de Hispanistas del Siglo de Oro*, Acta Salmanticensia, Estudios Filológicos, 252, 2 vols. (Salamanca: Universidad de Salamanca, 1993), ii. 657–62; Dolores González Martínez, *La poesía de Francisco de Aldana (1537–1578): introducción al estudio de la imagen*, Scriptura, 4 (Lleida: Edicions de la Universitat de Lleida, 1995), esp. 99–113 (on Aldana y mythology); and Álvaro Alonso, *La poesía italianista* (Madrid: Laberinto, 2002), 206–17.

Ovid in *Metamorphoses*, I.750–II.400. Two further poems on mythological subjects develop aspects of the relationship between Mars and Venus. The first of these is a 552-line fragment dating from 1565–70, published in the *Segunda parte* under the title 'Octavas del mismo capitán Francisco de Aldana, en diversas materias descontinuadas y desasidas' [Octaves by the Same Captain Francisco de Aldana, on Diverse Unrelated and Unfinished Subjects].[38] The sixty-nine *octavas* of this episodic poem without beginning or end contain versions of the tales of Mars, Venus, and Vulcan, Jupiter and Europa, and Hercules and Omphale. The first *octava* sketches out the opening sections of the first of these three tales:

> Marte, dios del furor, de quien la fama,
> por público pregón, había salido
> estar ardiendo de amorosa llama
> por la hermosa madre de Cupido;
> que esto así se entendió porque en la cama
> los vino a hallar el cojo su marido,
> y los cogió a los dos, ambos desnudos,
> en una red de indisolubles ñudos. (1–8)

[Mars, god of martial fury, whom fame had revealed, through public proclamation, to be burning with passion for the beautiful mother of Cupid; this was held to be true because her lame husband found them together in bed, and he caught the pair both naked in a net of indissoluble knots.]

This stanza picks out several important details from the tale: the episode's fame and notoriety, Mars's burning passion for Venus, the lovers' capture *in flagrante* at the hands of Vulcan, and the unbreakable net. The three protagonists are either associated with or identified by a particular quality: Mars with his *furor* [martial fury], Venus by her *hermosura* [beauty], and Vulcan by his *cojera* [limp]. Picking up on line 8, the second stanza focuses on the spectacle of the lovers' imprisonment in the 'red de indisolubles ñudos':

> Hizo a los dioses, de una y otra parte,
> estar mirando en círculo vecino,
> y ver en esta lucha al fiero Marte
> preso y vencido (¡oh dulce desatino!).

---

[38] *Segunda parte*, fols. 44ʳ–54ᵛ; and *Poesías castellanas completas*, 251–74. On the dating, unity, purpose, and artistic merit of these *octavas*, see Juan Ferraté, 'Una muestra de poesía extravagante', in *Dinámica de la poesía. Ensayos de explicación, 1952–1966* (Barcelona: Seix Barral, 1968), 215–23; Ruiz Silva, *Estudios*, 170–3; Walters, *Poetry*, 9–17; and Guillermo Alonso Moreno, 'Otra fuente de los versos sobre Júpiter y Europa de Francisco de Aldana', in José María Maestre Maestre, Joaquín Pascual Barea, and Luis Charlo Brea (eds.), *Humanismo y pervivencia del mundo clásico. Homenaje al profesor Antonio Prieto*, 5 vols. (Madrid: CSIC, 2008–10), i. 79–89.

Cosa de admiración, ver con cual arte
el cuerpo de la diosa alabastrino
se aovilla, encoge, encubre y se retira,
por no ser vista y ver a quien la mira; (9–16)

[He [i.e. Vulcan] made the gods, from all corners, look on in a circle next to them, and see in this struggle fierce Mars imprisoned and defeated (oh sweet folly!). It is a thing of wonder to see the artful movements of the goddess's alabaster body curling up, shrinking, covering up, and hiding, so as not to be seen and see all those watching her.]

As Mars struggles in vain to escape, in a scene reminiscent of early illustrations of this episode (e.g. Fig. 1.1), his peers form a 'círculo vecino' around the bed. The second half of the stanza turns to Venus's 'cuerpo . . . alabastrino'. This description of her body represents an amusing play on the Petrarchan metaphor of the lady's skin as smooth, white alabaster. Here, what the onlookers get is not a fleeting, tantalizing glimpse of the skin on Venus's neck, breast, or limbs but a totally unrestricted view of her naked, sculpted body in all its glory. After a series of pluperfects and preterites in the opening twelve lines, line 15 shifts to the immediacy of the present tense. Four different verbs are strung together in a form of chiasmus to capture the sense of Venus's desperate, and ultimately futile, struggle to maintain her dignity: 'se aovilla, encoge, encubre y se retira.'[39] In another humorous detail, the final line suggests that she is just as concerned with uncovering the identities of the spectators as she is with the task of covering her own body. The last of the three stanzas dedicated to the tale expands upon the responses of the three main protagonists:

ceñido de una hembra al dios furioso
después considerar, por otro lado,
estar cual jabalí fiero y cerdoso
que tiene el perro en monte acorralado;
tras esto el cojo andar muy querelloso,
Venus corrida, Marte encarnizado,
con furia de relámpagos rodando
los ojos, que a Vulcano están hablando. (17–24)

[and then, on the other hand, to see the ferocious god held in the embrace of a female, acting like a fierce wild boar cornered by a dog in the hills; and then the lame god going around most quarrelsome, Venus humiliated, Mars enraged, with rolling eyes flashing menacingly at Vulcan.]

---

[39] The accumulation of verbs is characteristic of Aldana's poetry; see e.g. 'Fábula de Faetonte', lines 123–30: 'afloja, aprieta, deja, toma, vuelve, | prueba, finge, rodea, mueve y sacude, | ciñe, gime, reposa, tienta, impide, | se cierra, se dilata . . . ' (*Poesías castellanas completas*, 152).

Imprisoned in the net, Mars is compared to a fierce wild boar cornered by a dog during the hunt. Whilst Vulcan is left feeling aggrieved, Venus is ashamed and Mars enraged by their predicament. Particular emphasis is placed on the reaction of the god of war, who is described shooting at his captor not daggers but bolts of lightning.

At the start of the fourth stanza the poet acknowledges that the opening three form a digression from his 'principal y nuevo intento' [principal and new aim]. Building on the above 'cimiento | de Marte y Venus' [foundation of Mars and Venus], the next fifteen stanzas offer an innovative continuation of the tale by charting Mars's attempts to win Venus back, having been abandoned by her after their very public shaming. The narrative that unfolds mirrors the classical tale mapped out in the opening digression, only now it is Mars, not Vulcan, who discovers Venus's infidelity. This original continuation comprises an exchange between Mars and Cupid, who tells Mars that Venus has forgotten all about him and taken up with an ugly satyr (lines 33–88); Mars's furious response to this news, which triggers a frantic search for his former lover in a pastoral *locus amoenus* populated by satyrs (89–128); and, finally, as implied by the scale of his pained response to a 'dura vista cruel' [harsh, cruel sight], Mars's discovery of Venus and the satyr *in flagrante* (129–52). As Ruiz Silva notes, these stanzas are punctuated by several humorous details: the description of Cupid as an *alcahuete*, 'procurer' (42); the narrator's warning to Mars not to laugh at Venus's go-between (43–4); the ominous 'sospiro crudo y lamentable' [heavy and lamentable sigh] that prefaces Cupid's words to Mars (56); the contrast between Mars fighting on the battlefield and Venus 'dando y tomando | frutos de amor' [giving and receiving the fruits of love] (65–8); the repeated emphasis on the speed with which Venus descends from the heavens in her eagerness to consort with the 'sátiro bestial, bajo y grosero' [crude, lowly, and bestial satyr] (69–72, 77–80); and Mars's response to Cupid's news with the cry of '¡Arma, arma!' [To arms!], accompanied by the sound of him gnashing his teeth (89–96).[40] The suggestion that Mars has taken the place of Vulcan as Venus's cuckolded husband is reinforced by his *querella* (94), a word that echoes the earlier description of Vulcan, confronted by the spectacle of the lovers' imprisonment, as 'muy querelloso' (21). An ironic contrast is set up between stanzas 2–3, which describe in detail the original lovers' response to being caught in Vulcan's net, and stanzas 18–19, which state little but imply much about what Mars sees, inviting the reader to imagine Venus in the arms of her new lover. It is at this point, at the end of stanza 19, that the poet signals his desire to move on again, this time to the subject of 'los afetos de Amor' [Love's affects]. The rest of the fragment turns to the trials and tribulations of other gods.

[40] *Estudios*, 172.

The second poem relevant to this discussion is Aldana's sonnet entitled 'Marte en aspecto de Cáncer' [Mars in the Aspect of Cancer] (*c*.1565). This poem also focuses on the power of love, but it offers an entirely different perspective on the relationship between Mars and Venus:

> Junto a su Venus, tierna y bella, estaba,
> todo orgulloso, Marte, horrible y fiero,
> cubierto de un templado y fino acero
> que un claro espejo al sol de sí formaba,
> y mientras ella, atenta, en él notaba
> sangre y furor, con rostro lastimero
> un beso encarecido al gran guerrero
> fijó en la frente y dél todo colgaba.
> Del precioso coral tan blando efeto
> salió que al fiero dios del duro asunto
> hizo olvidar con nuevo, ardiente celo.
> Oh fuerza extraña, oh gran poder secreto,
> que pueda un solo beso, en sólo un punto,
> ¡los dioses aplacar, dar ley al cielo!⁴¹

[Next to his tender and lovely Venus was Mars, full of pride, horrendous and fierce, covered in a fine, tempered steel that formed a clear mirror to the sun; and while she, attentive, saw in him blood and martial fury, she planted a delightful kiss on the great warrior's forehead and draped herself all over him. Such a tender effect came from her lovely coral lips that it made the fierce god forget about his hard task with a new, burning passion. Oh strange force, oh great secret power, that a single kiss, in a single spot, can appease the gods and bring order to the heavens!]

As Rivers notes, each stanza in the sonnet relates to a different aspect of the moment described: situation (lines 1–4), action (5–8), result (9–11), and commentary (12–14).⁴² The opening quatrain sets the scene, introducing the gods and establishing a balanced, yet seemingly irresolvable, contrast between the 'tierna y bella' Venus on the one hand, and the 'horrible y fiero' Mars on the other. Through skilful manipulation of word-order, Aldana briefly mentions the former in the first line before moving on to a more detailed description of the latter in the rest of the stanza. In lines that recall the portrait of Mars in Garcilaso's curse on war—'Oh crudo, oh

---

⁴¹ *Primera parte*, 38ᵛ; and *Poesías castellanas completas*, 233–4. On this sonnet, see Rivers, *Francisco de Aldana*, 153–5; Green, 'On Francisco de Aldana', 130–1; Ruiz Silva, *Estudios*, 87–8; Alexander A. Parker, *The Philosophy of Love in Spanish Literature, 1480–1680*, ed. Terence O'Reilly (Edinburgh: Edinburgh University Press, 1985), 63; and Walters, *Poetry*, 32–3.

⁴² *Francisco de Aldana*, 155.

riguroso, oh fiero Marte, | de túnica cubierta de diamante | y endurecido siempre en toda parte'—Mars is presented as not only 'todo orgulloso' and 'horrible y fiero' but also 'cubierto de un templado y fino acero'.[43] His impressive armour glints in the sun, serving, at the same time, as a mirror to the greater, metaphorical sun that is Venus. In the rest of the poem Mars is described in similar terms, characterized first by 'sangre y furor' and then presented as the 'gran guerrero' and the 'dios del duro asunto'. At this point the focus is firmly on Mars: the more formidable he is made to seem, the greater the perceived power of Venus in the second half of the sonnet.

The second quatrain builds up to the moment when Venus plants a kiss on Mars's forehead whilst draping her arms around his neck. In contrast to the four imperfects that serve as rhyme words in lines 1, 4, 5, and 8, the preterite *fijó* at the beginning of line 8 underlines the importance of this simple action. As Walters observes, the 'brief instant of tension and uncertainty suggested by the last word of the second quatrain . . . yields to a feeling of serenity reflected in the smooth and sonorous line that immediately follows'.[44] The kiss is issued from Venus's 'precioso coral', a commonplace Petrarchan metaphor for the coral-red mouth of a woman. The first tercet explores the result of Venus's kiss on Mars, contrasting, in another of the sonnet's semantic and structural oppositions, its 'blando efeto' with his status as the 'dios del duro asunto'. This single 'beso encarecido' has the power to placate Mars and make him forget his natural inclination to violence. As a result of Venus's action, he turns his mind from war to love, a 'nuevo, ardiente celo'.

According to classical and Renaissance tradition, the power to subdue Mars is unique to Venus. In the invocation to her at the start of his *De Rerum Natura* [On the Nature of Things], the first-century BC Roman poet and philosopher Lucretius paints a portrait of Mars reclining in her lap, vanquished by love:

> nam tu sola potes tranquilla pace iuvare
> mortalis, quoniam belli fera moenera Mavors
> armipotens regit, in gremium qui saepe tuum se
> reicit aeterno devictus vulnere amoris,
> atque ita suspiciens tereti cervice reposta
> pascit amore avidos inhians in te, dea, visus,
> eque tuo pendet resupini spiritus ore. (31–7)

[43] This image of Mars's adamantine armour is reworked in lines 34–9 of Herrera's *canción* 'Con dulce lira, el amoroso canto': '¿Quién a Mavorte crudo, | d'adamantina túnica cubierto, | cuando en l'áspera Tracia'l campo abierto | mueve, teñido en sangre, el duro escudo, | podrá escrevir, si al fin le falta el buelo, | i se despeña dend'el alto cielo?' (*Poesía castellana*, 784).

[44] *Poetry*, 32.

[For thou alone canst delight mortals with quiet peace, since Mars mighty in battle rules the savage works of war, who often casts himself upon thy lap wholly vanquished by the ever-living wound of love, and thus looking upward with shapely neck thrown back feeds his eager eyes with love, gaping upon thee, goddess, and as he lies back his breath hangs upon thy lips.][45]

The idea that Venus is the only individual capable of placating Mars is developed by several Renaissance thinkers, including the fifteenth-century Florentine Neoplatonist Marsilio Ficino:

Conciosia, che quando Marte posto nelli Angoli, o nella seconda, o vero nella ottava casa delle Geniture, minaccia i Nati di casi infelici: Venere spesse volte venendoli congiunta od opposta, o ricevendolo o guardandolo di aspetto Sestile, o Trino, Ammorza (per dir or così) la malignità di quello.[46]

[When Mars is in the angles or in the second or perhaps eighth house of the geniture, he threatens those born with unfortunate circumstances. Often moving towards Mars, or in opposition to Mars, or receiving or looking at Mars from the sextile or trine aspects, Venus abates (so to speak) his malignancy.]

In his *Diálogos de amor* [Dialogues of Love], León Hebreo, a Portuguese Jew forced into exile from Spain in 1492, confirms that Venus acts as a counterpoint to Mars:

Así que la concupiscente Venus suele enamorarse del ardientísimo Marte; por lo cual los astrólogos ponen grandísima amistad entre estos dos planetas, y dicen que Venus corrige con su benigno aspecto toda la malicia de Marte.

[And so lustful Venus usually falls in love with Mars, full of burning ardour; for this reason astrologers see a very close relationship between these two planets, and say that with her benign aspect Venus counters all of Mars's malevolence.]

Building on Ficino, Hebreo describes in great detail the positions of the stars and the movements of the planets, offering astrological and allegorical explanations for specific classical tales. Whereas Jupiter and Venus are 'buenos y portadores de óptima fortuna . . . de los que siempre procede todo bien' [good and bringers of excellent fortune . . . from whom always comes great good], Saturn and Mars are 'malos e infortunados . . . de los

---

[45] Lucretius, *De Rerum Natura*, trans. William H. D. Rouse, LCL (Cambridge, Mass.: Harvard University Press, 1966), 4–5.

[46] Marsilio Ficino, *Sopra lo amore o ver' Convito di Platone* (Florence: Neri Dortelata, 1544), 112.

que se deriva todo mal' [bad and unfortunate . . . from whom derives all evil].[47] Throughout this, his most famous work, Hebreo dedicates sections to Mars and Venus, both the gods and the planets. Their conjunction symbolizes peace and harmony, as Mars's negative characteristics are held in equilibrium with Venus's positive qualities. The contrast between them seen in the opening stanzas of Aldana's sonnet is thus resolved in the first tercet through the Neoplatonic concepts of *discordia concors* and *coincidentia oppositorum*. In line with Hebreo's theories, the poem relates not only to the relationship between the gods but also to the conjunction of the planets and to the proximity of Mars and Venus in the night sky. The sonnet's title refers to the moment when Mars and Venus are closest to one another, the moment when Mars abandons its own sign, Scorpio, and moves into the house of Cancer.

The final tercet expresses wonder at the power of love, confirming the fact that a fundamental shift in the dynamic between Mars and Venus has taken place. The 'fuerza extraña' and 'gran poder secreto', which would have been associated with Mars in the first quatrain, are now associated with Venus, whose love has the power to subdue the gods and give order and structure to the heavens. These lines round off what, on one level, constitutes, 'una alegoría al amor cósmico como pacificador del universo' [an allegory of cosmic love bringing peace to the universe].[48] After four imperfects and three preterites in the first three stanzas, the sudden switch to the present subjunctive in the penultimate line suggests that this force is constant and universal. If the poem's opening recalls the contrast present in Lucas van Leyden's engraving of Mars and Venus (Fig. 2.1), memorable for the prominent vertical formed by Mars's sword, its end has more in common with Titian's sensuous painting of the lovers sharing a kiss (Fig. 2.2), which captures some sense of Venus's irresistible hold over Mars. Any discord between Mars and Venus is resolved, as an overriding sense of harmony, underlined through repetition (*solo/sólo*) in line 13 and chiasmus in line 14, comes into effect as the result of a single, tender kiss.

[47] León Hebreo, *Diálogos de amor*, trans. Carlos Mazo del Castillo, ed. José-María Reyes Cano (Barcelona: Promociones Publicaciones Universitarias, 1986), 127, 230–1. Published in Italian in 1535 (though completed much earlier, in 1502), Hebreo's *Dialoghi d'amore* was translated into Spanish twice in the sixteenth century, first by Guedella Yahia (Venice, 1568) and then by Carlos Montesa (Zaragoza, 1582). Both translations were re-edited and reprinted before the end of the sixteenth century.

[48] Alicia de Colombi-Monguio, '"Al simple, al compuesto, al puro, al misto": la amada como microcosmos', in Keith McDuffie and Rose Minc (eds.), *Homenaje a Alfredo A. Roggiano: en este aire de América* (Pittsburgh: Instituto Internacional de Literatura Iberoamericana, 1990), 91–110 (p. 103).

Fig. 2.1. Lucas van Leyden, *Mars, Venus, and Cupid*, 1530. Ink on paper/engraving.

Fig. 2.2. Titian, *Mars, Venus, and Cupid*, *c.*1550. Oil on canvas.

LUIS DE GÓNGORA

Amongst the next generation of Spanish men of letters were Luis de Góngora and Lope de Vega, two of the most celebrated writers of the Golden Age. Born in Córdoba in 1561, Góngora studied at the University of Salamanca in 1576–80 before returning to Andalusia to take up a post as prebendary of Córdoba cathedral in 1586. After several years undertaking trips to various parts of Spain on cathedral business, he moved to Madrid in 1617 where he was made chaplain to Philip III at the behest of the king's first minister and Góngora's then patron, the Duke of Lerma. After Lerma's fall from power in 1618, and the execution of his other principal patron, Rodrigo Calderón, in 1621, Góngora struggled in vain to secure the patronage and preferment of leading lights at the court of Philip IV and his *valido* [first minister], the Count-Duke of Olivares. Suffering from the after-effects of a stroke, Góngora returned to Córdoba in penury less than a year before his death in 1627.[49]

Though Góngora did not reach the height of his fame until the mid-1610s, with the circulation at Court of the *Fábula de Polifemo y Galatea* [Fable of Polyphemus and Galatea] and the unfinished *Soledades* [Solitudes], his works of the 1580s and 1590s soon established him as one of the leading poets of his day. In 1605 an influential anthology of contemporary poetry compiled by Pedro de Espinosa featured more poems by Góngora than by anyone else.[50] In the late sixteenth and early seventeenth centuries Góngora mastered both Spanish and Italianate forms, with poems ranging from humorous *letrillas* to beautifully crafted examples of the Renaissance sonnet, from heroic *canciones* on historical events to stinging satires of the evils of the Court, and from burlesque treatments of classical tales to open attacks on rival poets and their works. In the 1580s both Góngora and Lope were leading exponents of the *romance artístico*, a new genre based on the imitation and updating of the traditional ballad.[51] Góngora's «Ensíllenme el asno rucio» ["Saddle me the grey ass "] (1585), a *contrafactum* of Lope's famous *romance morisco* «Ensíllenme el potro rucio» ["Saddle me the grey colt "] (1583), marks the beginning of a rivalry between the two poets that would stretch into the mid-1630s, almost a decade after the Cordovan poet's death.[52] Composed in the mid-1580s, both poems were published anonymously in the ballad

[49] For a brief introduction to Góngora's life and works, see Terry, 'Luis de Góngora: The Poetry of Transformation', in *Seventeenth-Century Spanish Poetry*, 65–93.

[50] *Primera parte de las Flores de poetas ilustres de España, dividida en dos libros. Ordenada por Pedro Espinosa* (Valladolid: Luis Sánchez, 1605).

[51] For an introduction to the rise and development of this genre, see Nigel Griffin and others (eds.), *The Spanish Ballad in the Golden Age*, CTSA: Monografías, 264 (Woodbridge: Tamesis, 2008).

[52] Emilio Orozco Díaz, *Lope y Góngora frente a frente* (Madrid: Gredos, 1973), 26–39.

anthology *Flor de varios romances nuevos* (1591), with Góngora's, introduced as 'otro romance contrahecho', following on immediately from Lope's.[53]

Whereas Lope's poem tells of the Moor Azarque's preparations for battle overseas and his enforced separation from his beloved Adalifa, Góngora's parody focuses on the preparations of the peasant dolt Galayo for sex down on the banks of the river Tagus. Each poem begins in direct speech, with the master ordering his servants to equip him for the task(s) ahead. In Lope's ballad the cumulative effect of the long list of items ordered, framed by the imperative *denme* [give me] in lines 3 and 12, is ennobling: the qualities of the various items reflect those of the speaker Azarque, who is, one intuits, every inch the archetypal noble Moor. In the opening twelve lines of his *contrafactum* Góngora parodies his model by substituting the Moor's impressive trappings with a ragbag of peasant paraphernalia: Azarque's colt is transformed into an ass, his leather shield into a cork lid, his strong suit of armour into a green overcoat, his plumed helmet into a feathered hood, and so on. The descriptions of the final items requested by first Azarque (*left*) and then Galayo (*right*) draw on two well-known mythological tales:

y aquella medalla en cuadro	y aquella patena en cuadro
que dos ramos la guarnecen	donde de latón se ofrecen
con las hojas de esmeraldas,	la madre del virotero
por ser los ramos laureles,	y aquel Dios que calza arneses
y un Adonis que va a caza	tan en pelota y tan juntos
de los jabalíes monteses,	que en nudos ciegos los tienen,
dejando su diosa amada,	al uno redes y brazos,
y dice la letra: «Muere». (13–24)	y al otro brazos y redes,
	cuyas figuras en torno
	acompañan y guarnecen
	ramos de nogal y espigas,
	y por letra: «Pan y nueces». (13–28)

[53] *Flor de varios romances nuevos. Primera y Segunda parte* (Barcelona: Iayme Cendrat, 1591), fols. 5ᵛ–8ᵛ. On Góngora's *contrafactum*, see Robert Jammes, *Études sur l'oeuvre poétique de Don Luis de Góngora y Argote*, Bibliothèque de l'École des hautes études hispaniques, 40 (Bordeaux: Féret et Fils, 1967), 145–8; Robert F. Ball, 'Góngora's Parodies of Literary Convention', unpublished doctoral thesis, Yale University (1976), 267–317; José Rico Verdú, 'Dos personalidades literarias enfrentadas: comentario a dos romances de Lope y Góngora', *Hispanística*, 1 (1993), 38–53; the editor's notes in Luis de Góngora, *Romances*, ed. Antonio Carreira, 4 vols. (Barcelona: Quaderns Crema, 1998), i. 345–55; Antonio Carreño, 'De potros y asnos rucios: ludismo y parodia en Luis de Góngora', in Joaquín Roses (ed.), *Góngora Hoy*, VI: *Actas del Foro de Debate Góngora Hoy celebrado en la Diputación de Córdoba: Góngora y sus contemporáneos: de Cervantes a Quevedo del 14 al 16 de noviembre de 2002*, Colección de Estudios Gongorinos, 4 (Córdoba: Diputación de Córdoba, 2004), 59–87; and my '"Ensíllenme el asno rucio" (1585): Parody and Burlesque in a *Contrafactum*', in Oliver Noble Wood and Nigel Griffin (eds.), *A Poet for All Seasons: Eight Commentaries on Góngora*, Spanish Series, 156 (New York: Hispanic Seminary of Medieval Studies, 2013), 1–23.

[*Lope*: . . . and that square brooch decorated with two branches with emeralds for leaves, because the branches are laurels, and an Adonis portrayed heading off to hunt wild boar, leaving behind his beloved goddess, with a motto reading: *He dies.*]

[*Góngora*: . . . and that square dish where in latten you can see the mother of the chap who fires darts and that god who straps on armour, so naked and so close to one another, that they are held in invisible knots, one by nets and arms, the other by arms and nets, their figures accompanied and decorated all round with branches of walnut and ears of wheat, and the motto reads: *Bread and nuts.*]

In Lope's poem the picture of Adonis leaving his beloved Venus to hunt wild boar introduces a tragic subtext based on the tale of Venus and Adonis (a tale much treated by Renaissance artists); in particular, the death of Adonis, as recounted in Ovid, *Metamorphoses*, x.519–59 and 708–39. The inscription 'Muere' makes explicit what is implicit in the reference to *jabalíes monteses*, 'wild boar', namely that Adonis will be killed by a boar whilst out hunting—a death orchestrated, according to some versions of the tale, by Venus's jealous ex-lover Mars (see, for example, Nonnus, *Dionysiaca*, xli.208–11). One infers from this that, just as Adonis died moments after leaving Venus, so too will Azarque die soon after leaving his beloved Adalifa—only this time on the battlefield.

Góngora's ekphrasis draws not on Venus's love for Adonis, but on her affair with Mars. The lovers are introduced through the belittling periphrases of 'la madre del virotero' and 'aquel Dios que calza arneses'. Venus is not the 'diosa amada', Adonis's 'divine beloved', but the mother of the pesky little chap who fires off phallic darts (*virotes*), i.e. Cupid. As seen in the previous chapter, a motif present in many illustrations of this scene, from Salomon and Solis on, is that of Mars's arms (*arneses*) lying abandoned at the foot of Vulcan's marital bed. The circumlocution 'aquel Dios que calza arneses' not only represents a bathetic subversion of commonplace references to the warrior-god ('el fiero Marte airado', 'belicoso Marte', 'el sangriento señor de las batallas', etc.), but also reminds us that this Mars is just as likely to be caught out of his armour as in it. The touching scene of Adonis's departure for the hunt is replaced by the comic spectacle of the lovers' imprisonment in Vulcan's net. The *nudos ciegos* provide an economical means of reference to both a metaphor for an amorous embrace (that of the *nudo* or *ñudo*) and the fact that the net's links are so fine as to be 'blind' or invisible (*Odyssey*, viii.279–81; *Metamorphoses*, iv.176–9). The polysyndeton of *y* in lines 21–8 and the chiasmus in 23–4 underline the absurdity of the lovers' predicament, the syntax of these lines mirroring the tangled web of nets and limbs created as the lovers struggle in vain to maintain their dignity.

The final quatrain of Galayo's first address subverts the tragic implications of Lope's inscription; the figures of Mars and Venus are accompanied not by garlands of laurels with emerald-green leaves but by 'ramos de nogal y espigas'. The inscription that follows underlines the comic tone of the 1585 retelling; rather than point to the impending death of the handsome youth Adonis, the inscription 'Pan y nueces' underlines the absurdity of the scene depicted on Galayo's mock breastplate. Here, 'Pan y nueces' works on at least three levels. First, as reinforced by the chiasmus in 27–8, there is a link between the *nogal* and *nueces*, on the one hand, and between *espigas* and *pan*, on the other. Second, Góngora's *letra* calls to mind contemporary proverbs such as 'No todas veces pan y nueces' [You can't always have bread and nuts] and 'Pan i nozes [nueces], saben a amores' [Bread and nuts taste of love]—for their part, the lovers certainly seem to have had too much of a good thing, their latest period of indulgence leading to their imprisonment and public shaming.[54] Last, but by no means least, the inscription alludes to the lovers' sexual organs—Venus's *pan*, '*cunnus*' and Mars's *nueces*, 'testicles'—driving home the point that they are powerless to cover their modesty.[55] In a remarkably economical quatrain, Góngora subverts the serious subtext of Lope's original through play on sex and rustic fare, a formula to which he will return in the second half of the poem.

The scenes depicted on their respective arms shape the words of both Azarque and Galayo when, in preparation for departure, they address their respective beloveds:

Trajéronle la medalla,	Trajéronle la patena,
y, suspirando mil veces,	y, suspirando mil veces,
del bello Adonis miraba	del Dios garañón miraba
la gentileza y la suerte:	la dulce Francia y la suerte;
«Adalifa de mi alma,	piensa que será Teresa
no te aflijas ni lo pienses;	la que descubren y prenden
viviré para gozarte,	agudos rayos de envidia,
gozosa vendrás a verte;	y de celos nudos fuertes:
breve será mi jornada,	«Teresa de mis entrañas,
tu firmeza no sea breve.	no te gazmies ni ajaqueques,
Procura, aunque eres mujer,	que no faltarán zarazas
ser de todas diferente;	para los perros que muerden.

[54] Gonzalo Correas, *Vocabulario de refranes y frases proverbiales*, ed. Louis Combet (Bordeaux: Institut d'études ibériques et ibéro-américaines de l'Université de Bordeaux, 1967 [1627]), 260, 458.

[55] Louis Combet, 'Lexicographie et sémantique: quelques remarques à propos de la réédition du *Vocabulario de refranes* de Gonzalo Correas', *Bulletin Hispanique*, 71 (1969), 248–50; and Pierre Alzieu, Robert Jammes, and Yvan Lissorgues, *Poesía erótica del Siglo de Oro* (Barcelona: Crítica, 1984), 153, n. 13.

no te parezcas a Venus,
aunque en beldad le pareces,
en olvidar a su amante
y no respetalle ausente.» (33–48)

Aunque es largo mi negocio,
mi vuelta será muy breve,
el día de san Ciruelo
o la semana sin viernes.

    No te parezcas a Venus,
ya que en beldad le pareces,
en hacer de tantos huevos
tantas frutas de sartenes.» (37–56)[56]

[*Lope*: He was brought the brooch, and sighing a thousand times, he contemplated handsome Adonis's elegant bearing and fate: 'Adalifa of my soul, do not worry or even think about worrying. I will live to enjoy your company, and you will come to enjoy yourself. I shall not be long away, may your constancy remain unshaken. Try, even though you are a woman, to be different from all the others; do not be like Venus, even though you match her in beauty, by forgetting about her lover and failing to respect him when he is away.']

[*Góngora*: He was brought the dish, and, sighing a thousand times, he contemplated the stud god's abundance of good fortune. He thinks Teresa will be the one to be discovered and trapped by penetrating shafts of envy and strong links of jealousy: 'Teresa of my inward parts, don't get all worked up or give yourself a migraine, for there'll be plenty of poison for any dogs that sink their teeth into you. Although my task is great I'll be back very shortly, either on 30 February or in the week without a Friday. Don't be like Venus, since you're like her in terms of beauty, by making so many fritters out of so many eggs/testicles.']

Developing the play on terms relating to four-legged animals introduced in the opening line of the *contrafactum*, Góngora presents Mars as the 'Dios garañón', a god of great sexual prowess, likened to a stallion put out to stud.[57] Whereas Azarque contemplates 'la gentileza y la suerte' of Adonis, Galayo focuses on 'la dulce Francia y la suerte' of Mars. In Góngora's poem *suerte* has a meaning strongly contrasting with that

---

[56] Both 'el día de san Ciruelo' and 'la semana sin viernes' are proverbial expressions associated with broken promises. The former, like 30 February, is a day that will never come: '*san ziruelo*] Por santo no determinado ni zierto. *para el día de san ziruelo*] es dezir: para nunka xamás' (Correas, *Vocabulario*, 666). According to Cov. (s.v. *viernes*), the latter refers to a week when Christmas Day falls on a Friday, so that it does not count, as other Fridays do, as a day of penitence and abstinence; Correas makes it clear that this is also a day that will never arrive, or at least one for which one will have to wait an eternity: '*la semana ke no tenga viernes*] o no tuviere Viernes. Dan a entender kon esto ke no se hará lo ke se pide o promete' (*Vocabulario*, 185).

[57] Cov. s.v. *garañón*: 'Al hombre desenfrenado en el acto venéreo, especialmente si trata con muchas mujeres, suelen llamar garañón, aludiendo al uso que hay destas bestias.'

in Lope's poem: it alludes not to Adonis's imminent 'fate' (i.e. death at the tusks of a wild boar) but to Mars's 'good fortune' (i.e. lying in carnal embrace with Venus). This meaning is reinforced by 'la dulce Francia', 'Reino opulentísimo y abundante de todo' (Cov. s.v. *Francia*), the phrase echoing the French 'la douce France'.[58] For a second time, Góngora adds a quatrain to develop some of the comic potential inherent in the tale of Mars, Venus, and Vulcan. In lines 41–4 Galayo draws a parallel between the scene depicted on the *patena* and his own circumstances. Fearful of the consequences of his departure, he imagines Teresa as another Venus, lying in the arms of another man, her unfaithfulness revealed to others by the 'agudos rayos de envidia' of those who learnt of it (like the rays of the envious all-seeing sun-god Apollo), their envy/jealousy figuratively weaving a mesh around her which held her prisoner (like the strong links of the jealous husband's net).[59] Galayo's absurd plea to Teresa is thus delivered by a man who sees himself not in the position of the lover Mars but in that of the cuckolded husband Vulcan.

In Lope's ballad Azarque's appeal to Adalifa contains a commonplace reference to the fickle nature of women: 'varium et mutabile semper | femina' [woman is ever a fickle and changeable thing] (Virgil, *Aeneid*, iv.569–70). Whilst praising her by comparing her beauty to that of Venus, Azarque calls on her to reject the example set by the goddess of love in her treatment of men, fearing that Adalifa will take advantage of his absence to deceive him just as Venus deceived first Vulcan and then Mars. The noble sentiments expressed by the lover, often taken to reflect Lope's own fears concerning his then love Elena Osorio, are undermined through Góngora's bathetic treatment of the same situation.[60] Galayo's appeal opens not with the serious 'Adalifa de mi alma' but with the base 'Teresa de mis entrañas'. Azarque's comforting words are replaced with Galayo's 'no te gazmies ni ajaqueques'. On one level he orders her not to get worked up in his absence

---

[58] The phrase also denotes a 'sexual climax': 'Con el término *Francia* también se aludía al disfrute venéreo, y más concretamente al orgasmo final, y por ello pasó a aplicarse a cualquier cosa hecha bien o que era muy buena, y se decía: *dulce Francia*' (Chamorro, *Tesoro de villanos*, 412, s.v. *Francia*).

[59] Vulcan's net is described in similar terms in lines 75–6 of Alberto Díez y Foncalda's 'Fábula de Venus y Marte' (1653), in which the chains are 'tan sutiles, y tan fuertes, | como si hechas de celos' [as fine and as strong as if they were made of jealousy] (for more on this poem, see Chapter 4).

[60] On Lope's Moorish and pastoral masks, see Alan S. Trueblood, *Experience and Artistic Expression in Lope de Vega: The Making of 'La Dorotea'* (Cambridge, Mass.: Harvard University Press, 1974), 48–85; Antonio Carreño, *El romancero lírico de Lope de Vega* (Madrid: Gredos, 1979), 13–184; Felipe B. Pedraza Jiménez, *El universo poético de Lope de Vega*, Colección Arcadia de las Letras, 16 (Madrid: Laberinto, 2003), 13–50; and Antonio Sánchez Jiménez, *Lope pintado por sí mismo: mito e imagen del autor en la poesía de Lope de Vega Carpio*, CTSA: Monografías, 229 (Woodbridge: Tamesis, 2006), 20–41.

and to avoid the migraines associated with *jaquecas*. Here, however, the verbs *gazmiarse* and *ajaquecarse* also play on the nouns *gazmio* and *jaque*, two slang terms for a 'pimp'. On a second level, therefore, Galayo instructs Teresa not to team up with a pander who will (enable her to) tout her sexual wares. If she fails to heed this warning, Galayo will deal with any men who try to take advantage of her; like dogs, they will be killed off with feed containing crushed glass and needles (Cov. s.v. *zarazas*). Galayo also calls on his lady to reject the example of Venus. However, whereas Azarque cites Venus's affairs to express his fear that Adalifa will turn her attentions elsewhere whilst he is away, Galayo alludes in more obscene terms to the sexual proclivities of the libidinal Venus. The idea of the goddess making innumerable *frutas de sartenes*, 'fritters' made from an egg-based paste, out of innumerable *huevos*, both 'eggs' and 'testicles', brings together once more the worlds of rustic comestibles and humour based on sex.[61] Galayo is worried that Teresa will take advantage of his absence to consort with a very large number of men.

In sum, whereas Lope employs the tale of Venus and Adonis, 'a story of love and loss set in a timeless landscape', to create a tragic subtext by alluding to Azarque's imminent death, Góngora exploits the comedy inherent in the tale of Mars, Venus, and Vulcan, 'a comic tale of illicit lust played out in a domestic setting', to parody his rival's well-known Moorish ballad.[62] Góngora punctuates his absurd rewriting of Lope's ballad with allusions to the tale, subverting the original *romance morisco* through play on the motifs of sexual indiscretion, shameful entrapment, and cuckoldry. Tautology, derogatory circumlocution, obscene wordplay, and underworld slang (*germanía*) are all employed to draw out the tale's comic potential. Mars is portrayed as a 'dios garañón' who spends more time stark naked, preparing for or engaging in carnal embrace, than he does dressed, preparing for or engaging in battle; Venus as a capricious nymphomaniac, whose example is to be avoided at all cost; and Vulcan as a pathetic cuckold racked by jealousy. As we shall see in due course, all three of these caricatures will come to the fore in later, full-length mythological burlesques.

Another example of Góngora's incorporation of humorous allusions to the tale of Mars, Venus, and Vulcan is seen in the *romance* 'Arrojóse el mancebito' [The little lad threw himself . . .] (1589), a burlesque retelling of the tale of Hero and Leander aimed, at least in part, at Boscán's

---

[61] Cov. s.v. *freír*: 'De freír se dijo fruta, *quasi* friuta, como fruta de sartén.' The same entry explains the cautionary meaning of the popular phrase 'Al freír de los huevos lo veréis': 'you will find out what you don't know about now', as Venus, so embarrassingly for her, did when she was caught in Vulcan's net.

[62] Malcolm Bull, *The Mirror of the Gods: Classical Mythology in Renaissance Art* (London: Allen Lane, 2005), 217.

monumental *Leandro*. When the light guiding the impetuous youth
Leander across the Hellespont is extinguished by the wind, Hero prays to
Venus and Cupid in an attempt to ensure her lover's safe passage:

> Ella entonces derramando
> dos mil perlas de ambas luces,
> a Venus y a Amor promete
> sacrificios y perfumes.
> Pero Amor, como llovía
> y estaba en cueros, no acude,
> ni Venus, que con Marte
> está cenando unas ubres. (41–8)

[Then, shedding two thousand pearls from each of her beacons, she promises
sacrifices and incense to Venus and Cupid. But Cupid, as it's raining and he's
naked, doesn't come running, and nor does Venus, because she's eating to her
heart's content with Mars.]

In line 42 a mixture of hyperbole and precision makes a mockery of the
commonplace Petrarchan metaphors of *perlas* (tears) and *luces* (eyes). Tear-
ful Hero's promise of offerings to Cupid, Venus, and Mars is immediately
undermined when it is revealed in the next stanza that the gods are otherwise engaged. The first joke at their expense is based on the traditional
depiction of Cupid as a naked boy. Given the earlier description in lines
15–16 of the night undoing its trousers and the clouds urinating on
Leander ('se desató la noche, | y se orinaron las nubes'), it is hardly sur-
prising that Cupid should want to stay indoors. For her part, Venus is too
busy 'cenando ubres' with her lover Mars to be bothered with the perils and
prayers of Hero and Leander. Here, Góngora plays established metaphor
(*cenar ubres*, 'to feed with abundance') off against literal sense (*cenar ubres*,
'to sup udders'): the lovers are shown in comic light, gorging themselves
not on the ambrosia associated with their classical forebears but on coarse
rustic fare. As Eric Southworth notes, wordplay on *ubres* contains 'an
additional hint that the udders in question are those of the bare-breasted
goddess'. Again, an allusion to the affair of Mars and Venus introduces an
ironic disparity: whereas the gods enjoy one another's company in a dis-
torted classical idyll, Hero and Leander will never be reunited, as both are
destined to die before the night is out.[63]

Góngora makes different use of the relationship between Mars and
Venus in the poem '¡Qué de invidiosos montes levantados | . . . !' [What

---

[63] For a detailed analysis of this ballad, see Eric Southworth, 'Luis de Góngora y Argote
(1561–1627), "Arrojóse el mancebito" (1589)', in *The Spanish Ballad*, 41–57 (on the lines
discussed here, pp. 50–1).

envious lofty mountains . . . !], dated 1600 by Chacón and published, along with thirty-six other poems by Góngora, in Espinosa's *Flores de poetas ilustres*.[64] In this *canción*, inspired by Petrarch and Torquato Tasso, the jealous poet imagines being a voyeur at his lover's nuptials with another man. His 'noble pensamiento' [noble thought] is personified and sent to spy on the couple's lovemaking. In the first two of six nine-line stanzas, the poet's *pensamiento* negotiates each and every obstacle between him and his lover, flying like a bird over snow-capped mountains, across frozen or flooding rivers, and past the locks and keys on the lady's body. In the final lines of the second stanza Góngora introduces the metaphor of sex as a form of military engagement. Moving from the present tense to the future, the poet suggests that every move made by the husband will be catalogued by his winged thought: 'ni emprenderá hazaña | tu esposo, cuando lidie, | que no la registre él, y yo no envidie' [when he fights, your husband will not undertake any feat that is not registered by it or envied by me]. The third stanza brings a change in addressee, as thought, now apostrophized, swoops down on the lovers' bed in eager anticipation of the sight that will greet it. However, at the start of the fourth stanza, in a turning point marked by the poem's only preterite (*batiste*), thought arrives too late to witness the lovemaking:

> Tarde batiste la invidiosa pluma,
> que en sabrosa fatiga
> vieras (muerta la voz, suelto el cabello)
> la blanca hija de la blanca espuma,
> no sé si en brazos diga
> de un fiero Marte, o de un Adonis bello;
> ya anudada a su cuello
> podrás verla dormida,
> y a él casi trasladado a nueva vida. (29–36)

---

[64] *Primera parte de las Flores*, 42ʳ–3ʳ. For a modern critical edition of the poem, see Luis de Góngora, *Canciones y otros poemas en arte mayor*, ed. José María Micó, Clásicos Castellanos, NS 20 (Madrid: Espasa Calpe, 1990), 84–91. Notable contributions to the study of this *canción* include: Dámaso Alonso, *Góngora y el «Polifemo»*, 6th edn., 3 vols. (Madrid: Gredos, 1974), ii. 199–204; Juan Ferraté, 'Ficción y realidad en la poesía de Góngora', in *Dinámica de la poesía*, 297–334; Giulia Poggi, '*Exclusus amator* e *poeta ausente*: alcune note ad una canzone gongorina', *Linguistica e letteratura*, 8 (1983), 189–222 (repr. in her *Gli occhi del pavone. Quindici studi su Góngora* (Florence: Alinea, 2009), 15–34); Raymond P. Calcraft, 'The Lover as Icarus: Góngora's "Qué de envidiosos montes levantados"', in Salvador Bacarisse and others (eds.), *What's Past is Prologue: A Collection of Essays in Honour of L. J. Woodward* (Edinburgh: Scottish Academy Press, 1984), 10–16; José María Micó, 'La superación del petrarquismo', in *La fragua de las «Soledades». Ensayos sobre Góngora* (Barcelona: Sirmio, 1990), 59–102; and Jesús Ponce Cárdenas, *«Evaporar contempla un fuego helado»: género, enunciación lírica y erotismo en una canción gongorina* (Málaga: Universidad de Málaga, 2006).

[You beat your envious feathers too late, for you would have seen the white daughter of the white foam, unable to speak and with her hair untied, enjoying delightful fatigue, either in the arms—shall I say?—of a fearsome Mars or a handsome Adonis; you will be able to see her sleeping with her arms around his neck, with him almost transported to a new life.]

The images of thought's swift flight in the first half of the poem give way in the fourth and fifth stanzas to a still of the lovers' post-coital slumber. The erudite circumlocution of 'la blanca hija de la blanca espuma' identifies the lady as Venus/Aphrodite, whose birth from the sea's foamy waves is recounted in Hesiod, *Theogony*, 185–200 (and later immortalized in Botticelli's painting). By extension, the man must be either Venus's divine lover Mars ('un fiero Marte') or the goddess's mortal lover Adonis ('un Adonis bello'). Parallelism (line 32), chiasmus (34), and sibilance (41–2: 'que el silencio le bebe | del sueño con sudor solicitado') all contribute to an overwhelming impression of post-coital bliss: as he recovers from his exertions, she sleeps in his arms, her hair loose, her arm bare, her chest exposed. In lines 43–54 the identity of the addressee changes again, as the poet implores the new couple to sleep, safe in the knowledge that the winged god Cupid is standing guard over them with his finger on his lips. Contrasting his own lonely exile in a rocky desert with the lovers' joyous union in bed, the poet extends the earlier military metaphor by introducing the Petrarchan topos of the battlefield of love: 'sea el lecho de batalla campo blando' (line 54). In a surprising shift, intense sexual jealousy thus gives way to an unexpected ray of nobility as the poet instructs the lovers to make the most of the marriage bed. In the three-line envoi, the poet addresses the song directly and asks it to tell his *pensamiento* to draw the curtain across the bed and return to him.

Adopting a psychoanalytic, or more specifically Freudian, approach to the *canción*, Steven Wagschal argues that the wanderer is Vulcan and that Góngora's poem fuses 'two divergent and irreconcilable versions of the myth', one in which Venus's husband is Mars and another in which she is married to Vulcan.[65] However, whereas in Garcilaso's *canción* the allusions to the tale of the lovers' capture cohere to form a clear mythological subtext, here they do not. The identification of the wanderer as Vulcan is based not on evidence drawn from the text but on a simple leap of the imagination. Whilst the jealous speaker spurned by Venus in favour of Mars (or Adonis) shares much in common with Vulcan, the emphasis on marriage,

---

[65] Steven Wagschal, 'Writing on the Fractured "I": Góngora's Iconographic Evocations of Vulcan, Venus, and Mars', in Frederick A. de Armas (ed.), *Writing for the Eyes in the Spanish Golden Age* (Lewisburg, Pa.: Bucknell University Press, 2004), 130–50; and 'Myth and the Fractured "I" in Góngora', in *The Literature of Jealousy in the Age of Cervantes* (Columbia, Mo.: University of Missouri Press, 2006), 136–56.

the speaker's show of goodwill towards the newly-weds, and the absence of any desire for revenge all make it difficult to support Wagschal's identification. The central section of Góngora's poem does, however, form part of a long literary and pictorial tradition of descriptions of couples identified as or with Mars and Venus (before, during, or after sex). Góngora's still of the lovers' post-coital bliss recalls not only Renaissance paintings, including those by Botticelli and Piero di Cosimo (as shown by Wagschal), but also literary renditions of the scene such as those of Lucretius and Reposianus. Whereas in 'Arrojóse el mancebito' Góngora draws on the lovers' tryst for comic effect, here his emphasis is firmly on the sensuous eroticism of the scene.

Thus far I have discussed some notable examples of reworkings of the tale of Mars, Venus, and Vulcan in the works of four canonical sixteenth-century Spanish poets: Garcilaso, Hurtado de Mendoza, Aldana, and Góngora. Significantly, none of them indulges in extensive retelling of the tale made famous by Homer, Ovid, and others; the tale itself is never the principal subject of the poem. With the exception of Aldana, who flags up his source in the first three stanzas of the 'Octavas en diversas materias', these poets do not explicitly refer to the tale in question. They choose instead to employ erudite allusion to particular aspects of the story—the lovers' imprisonment, Vulcan's cuckoldry, Venus's fickleness, etc.—in order to create subtexts which add new layers of meaning to their respective works. Particularly fine examples of this art of allusion are seen in Garcilaso's *canción*, Hurtado de Mendoza's epistle, and Góngora's *contrafactum*: all three contain veiled references to the tale that must be spotted, pieced together, and deciphered by the alert reader. The basic strategy is simple, yet remarkably effective: in each case, single words or succinct phrases ('en público adulterio', 'cabrá', 'en nudos ciegos') call the classical tale to mind, forcing the reader to consider its relevance for, or compare and contrast it with, the specific situation in hand. On each occasion the precise nature of the relationship between allusion and new context is not made explicit, so the onus is on the reader to work to resolve any potential ambiguity. Though drawn from the same common storehouse, such allusions both refresh and are refreshed by their new contexts. The same elements of the tale are called to mind time and again, but on each occasion they are seen and interpreted in new light. In these examples mythological allusion is no mere ornament, but a highly economical and flexible device that enabled poets to challenge and inspire *admiratio* in audiences who could be relied upon to have a firm grasp of classical tradition.

The poems discussed in this chapter also introduce a number of radically divergent attitudes to the gods of Antiquity. The two ends of the spectrum are seen in Hurtado de Mendoza's scurrilous attack on Venus in '¡Oh Venus, alcahueta y hechicera!' and Aldana's memorable snapshot of the power of the same goddess in 'Marte en aspecto de Cáncer'. The latter paints the gods in traditional light, focusing on the respective qualities of bellicose Mars and beautiful Venus. The former, on the other hand, turns this conception upside down, portraying Venus not as a youthful belle but as an old madam. Whilst one sonnet builds up towards the harmonious resolution of seemingly irreconcilable oppositions, the other reaches its climax in a string of obscene euphemisms and plays on words. Hurtado de Mendoza's sonnet is the most extreme example of a playful irreverence that seems already firmly established by the second half of the sixteenth century. The humour evident in several of the above poems not only picks up on and develops that seen in the various classical sources but also anticipates the dominant tone of many seventeenth-century tellings. Later poets would continue to draw out the tale's inherent comic potential, fleshing out the caricatures of Mars the braggart soldier, Venus the shrewd prostitute, and Vulcan the arch-cuckold. Not only are these figures present—at least, in embryonic form—in some of the poems discussed in this chapter, but the same is also true of some of the techniques that would be sharpened by seventeenth-century poets, most notably, the development of wordplay and the use of contemporary slang and/or *germanía*. The first generations of Golden Age poets also synthesized a number of Petrarchan and Neoplatonic topoi, which, as we shall see, would in due course be subtly parodied, mercilessly mocked, turned on their heads, or taken to their logical extremes. As if there were not already enough supplies in the mythological storehouse stocked by their classical forebears, Garcilaso, Hurtado de Mendoza, Aldana, and Góngora all gave later writers interested in the tale of Mars, Venus, and Vulcan further food for imitation.

3
Mythological (Mock) Epics: The Stage of Honour

Nulla quidem esset apibus gloria, nisi in aliud et in melius inventa converterent.[1]

[There would be no value in what the bees do if they did not turn what they gathered into something different and better.]

The second half of the sixteenth century saw an explosion of interest in narrative poetry, sparked by the reception and dissemination of the works of both classical authors such as Homer, Virgil, and Lucan and Italian Renaissance writers such as Boiardo, Ariosto, and Tasso. Though Petrarchan lyric would remain in vogue throughout the Golden Age, the third quarter of the sixteenth century saw the emergence and growing popularity in Spain of this new style of poetry. In a famous study Frank Pierce charts the rise of epic poetry in Spain from the 1550s on, highlighting works such as Alonso de Ercilla's *La Araucana* (1569–89), on the Spanish conquest of Chile, Juan Rufo's *La Austriada* (1584), on the achievements of the military commander Juan de Austria, and Lope's *La Dragontea* (1598), on the final years of Sir Francis Drake, as seminal contributions to a then burgeoning genre.[2] For inspiration, poets turned not only to contemporary history, as in these three cases, but also to religious subjects, Italian epics, and the world of classical mythology.

Following in the footsteps of Boscán, innumerable Golden Age poets indulged in long retellings of tales drawn principally from the *Metamorphoses*. Inspired by the *Leandro*, and catalysed by the appearance

---

[1] Francesco Petrarca, *Rerum familiarium*, 1.8.23, in *Le familiari*, trans. Ugo Dotti, 3 vols. (Rome: Archivio Guido Izzi, 1991–4), i. 62.

[2] *La poesía épica del Siglo de Oro*, trans. J. C. Cayol de Bethencourt, 2nd rev. and exp. edn. (Madrid: Gredos, 1968). On the rise of epic, see also Arthur Terry, 'The Literary Epic', in *Seventeenth-Century Spanish Poetry*, 180–207; and Elizabeth B. Davis, *Myth and Identity in the Epic of Imperial Spain* (Columbia, Mo.: University of Missouri Press, 2000).

of translations of Ovid and iconographical handbooks, mythological narrative poetry remained in vogue until well into the seventeenth century. Notable examples of this practice include Hurtado de Mendoza's *Fábula de Adonis, Hipómenes y Atalanta* (1553), Acuña's *Fábula de Narciso* (1568–9), Aldana's *Fábula de Faetonte* (*c.*1570), Luis Carrillo y Sotomayor's *Fábula de Acis y Galatea* (1611), Juan Espínola y Torres's *Transformaciones y robos de Júpiter* (1619), and Juan de Jáuregui's *Orfeo* (1624). Founded on the principles of imitation and emulation, and ranging in length from a few hundred lines to several cantos, such poems recorded, modified, expanded upon, and sought to excel previous tellings of well-known classical tales. The jewel in the crown of this subgenre was Góngora's *Polifemo* (1613), a retelling of the story of Acis and Galatea as found in Ovid, *Metamorphoses*, XIII.738–897. Together with the *Soledades* (1613–14), the *Polifemo* served as the manifesto of a new poetic style (*cultismo*), characterized by highly wrought Latinate vocabulary and syntax, elaborate conceits, daring flights of metaphor, and cryptic allusions to classical mythology. The appearance of the *Polifemo* gave mythological narrative poetry fresh impetus. It also meant that, from the mid-1610s on, poets who chose to imitate classical tales did so firm in the knowledge that they were inviting comparison with their famous Cordovan forebear.

By far the most common metre for narrative poetry in the Spanish Golden Age was the Italianate *octava real*. First employed by Boccaccio, *ottava rima* was the verse form of the great Italian Renaissance epics, including Boiardo's *Orlando innamorato* (1495), Ariosto's *Orlando furioso* (1532), Tasso's *Gerusalemme liberata* (1581), and Marino's *Adone* (1623). Introduced into Spanish by Boscán and Garcilaso, the metre was then appropriated by scores of writers in the period 1550–1650, proving especially popular for translations and imitations of classical and Italian epic poetry. Though in practice the *octava* proved suitable for a wide range of subjects and tones, many contemporary theorists were prescriptive about its use. At the start of his analysis of Garcilaso's Third Eclogue, Herrera concludes his brief discussion of the form with the statement that *octavas* 'Quieren alteza, i con ella ganó Ariosto el primer lugar' [They require loftiness, and in this regard Ariosto won first place].[3] Later critics, such as El Pinciano and Francisco Cascales, restricted the use of the form to epic poetry: 'la octava solamente queda perfecta, consumada y buena para la épica' [the octave is perfect, consummate, and appropriate only for epic poetry].[4] As we shall now see, the first two long narrative retellings of the

[3] *Anotaciones*, 937–9 (p. 939).
[4] Alonso López Pinciano, *Philosophía antigua poética*, in *Obras completas*, ed. José Rico Verdú, 2 vols. (Madrid: Biblioteca Castro, 1998), i. 319; see also Francisco Cascales, *Tablas poéticas* (Madrid: Antonio de Sancha, 1779 [1617]), 95–8, 148.

story of Mars, Venus, and Vulcan, by Juan de la Cueva and then Lope de Vega, both played on a disparity between the traditional epic weight of the *octava* and the humour of the Homeric and Ovidian tale.

JUAN DE LA CUEVA, 'LOS AMORES DE MARTE Y VENUS' (1604)

Born in Seville in 1543, the poet and playwright Juan de la Cueva was a member of the generation of Seville writers associated with the humanist circle of Juan de Mal Lara and 'el Divino' Fernando de Herrera. As with many writers of the period, little is known about large parts of his life. His adolescence was, it seems, marked by an infatuation with a certain Felipa de la Paz, the dedicatee, under the Petrarchan pseudonym Felicia, of much of his early amatory verse. In 1574, for reasons that are still unclear, he travelled to Mexico with his brother Claudio. Upon his return to Spain in 1577 he became immersed once again in the literary academies of Seville, most notably as an active participant in the famous academy hosted by Fernando Enríquez Afán de Ribera, the third Duke of Alcalá, at the Casa de Pilatos.[5] In this hotbed of intellectual activity, Cueva dedicated himself to the mutually complementary disciplines of poetry, drama, and translation of the classics (including Martial, Horace, Propertius, and Juvenal). The last few years of his life took him to Cuenca and then to Granada, where he died in 1612.[6]

Though in recent decades attention has increasingly been paid to his poetry, Cueva is still best known for the part he played in the rise and development of the *comedia nueva*, a new type of theatre that came to prominence in Spain in the late sixteenth and early seventeenth centuries. His fourteen extant plays, which were performed in Seville's public theatres between 1579 and 1581 and then published in 1583, mark him out as an important and immediate precursor to Lope, whose name became synonymous with the new style in the 1590s and early 1600s.[7] Cueva's *Ejemplar poético* [Poets' Guide], a treatise on poetry and drama from *c.*1606–9, was composed only shortly before Lope's own, more famous

[5] José María Reyes Cano, *La poesía lírica de Juan de la Cueva* (Seville: Artes Gráficas Padura, 1980), 18.

[6] For a brief biography of Cueva and an overview of his extant plays (and critical responses to them), see David G. Burton, 'Juan de la Cueva (1543–1612)', in Mary Parker (ed.), *Spanish Dramatists of the Golden Age* (Westport, Conn.: Greenwood Press, 1998), 87–95.

[7] The plays were published in *Primera parte de las comedias y tragedias de Juan de la Cueva dirigidas a Momo* (Seville: Andrea Pescioni, 1583); though reprinted in 1588, no second part ever came out.

treatise on the dramatic art, the *Arte nuevo de hacer comedias* [The New Art of Writing Plays] of 1609. Whilst Cueva claims, in the third epistle of the *Ejemplar poético*, to have pioneered a number of important theatrical practices—amongst them, the mixing of tragedy and comedy, the introduction of kings and gods as characters, the reduction of the number of acts from five to four, and the use of polymetric verse forms—his most significant contribution to the development of the *comedia* is, as Jonathan Thacker notes, his use of subjects drawn from Spanish history, medieval balladry, and classical Antiquity.[8]

As a poet, Cueva experimented with a wide range of forms and styles; his poetry includes elegies, *canciones*, sonnets, madrigals, eclogues, a *sextina*, a mock epic in the style of the pseudo-Homeric *Batrachomyomachia*, and the *Conquista de la Bética*, a long historical epic on the reconquest of large parts of Andalusia under Ferdinand III in the second quarter of the thirteenth century. Of greater significance for this study, however, are his two long mythological narrative poems. The first of these, the 'Llanto de Venus en la muerte de Adonis' [Venus's Tears on the Death of Adonis], is a retelling of the story of Venus and Adonis, published, in a collection dominated by amatory verse inspired by Petrarchan tradition, in Seville in 1582. In the second, 'Los amores de Marte i Venus a Don Enrrique de la Cueva' [The Loves of Mars and Venus Dedicated to Don Enrique de la Cueva], Cueva turns to the story of Mars, Venus, and Vulcan. Though likely penned in the 1580s or 1590s, the earliest-known version of this poem is found in a manuscript, currently held in the Biblioteca Capitular y Colombina in Seville, dated 1604.[9]

---

[8] Thacker, *A Companion to Golden Age Theatre*, 16–17. On Cueva as dramatist, see Camillo Guerrieri Crocetti, *Juan de la Cueva e le origini del teatro nazionale spagnuolo* (Turin: Giuseppe Cambino, 1936); Norman D. Shergold, 'Juan de la Cueva and the Early Theatres of Seville', *BHS* 32 (1955), 1–7; and Melveena McKendrick, *Theatre in Spain, 1490–1700* (Cambridge: Cambridge University Press, 1989), 53–7. On the *Ejemplar poético*, see Richard F. Glenn, 'The *Poets' Guide*', in *Juan de la Cueva*, TWAS, 273 (New York: Twayne, 1973), 130–7; and Juan de la Cueva, *Exemplar poético*, ed. José María Reyes Cano (Seville: Alfar, 1986).

[9] Juan de la Cueva, 'Llanto de Venus en la muerte de Adonis', in *Obras de Juan de la Cueva, dedicadas al ilustrísimo señor don Juan Téllez Girón* (Seville: Andrea Pescioni, 1582), fols. 121^r–35^v; and 'Los amores de Marte i Venus a Don Enrrique de la Cueva. 1604', in *Segunda parte de las Obras de Iuan de la Cueva. Anno 1604*, BCC, Ms. 82-2-5, fols. 59^r–84^v. For more on later manuscript versions of 'Los amores', see Cebrián García, *La fábula*, 46–7. On Cueva's poetry, see Glenn, *Juan de la Cueva*; Reyes Cano, *Poesía lírica*; José Cebrián García, *Estudios sobre Juan de la Cueva* (Seville: Secretariado de Publicaciones, 1991); and José Valentín Núñez Rivera, '«Y vivo solo y casi en un destierro»: Juan de la Cueva en sus epístolas poéticas', in *La epístola*, ed. Begoña López Bueno, Literatura, 42 (Seville: Universidad de Sevilla, 2000), 257–94; and 'Cueva, Barahona y tal vez Cervantes. Más paradojas en la segunda mitad del XVI', in his edition of Cristóbal Mosquera de Figueroa, *Paradojas*, Textos Recuperados, 27 (Salamanca: Universidad de Salamanca, 2010), 91–109.

Dedicated to a little-known relative, and written in 137 *octavas reales*, Cueva's 'Los amores' is the first long narrative poem in the Golden Age to take as its main subject the tale of Mars, Venus, and Vulcan. The poem's metre and length, equivalent to one canto, suggest that it is a form of epic; following in the footsteps of El Pinciano, Cueva himself notes, in *Ejemplar poético*, III, 94–6, that, though appropriate for a variety of discourses, the *octava* is particularly suited to epic poetry: 'Esta es la rima otava, en quien florece | la heroyca alteza i épica ecelencia, | i en dulzura a la lírica engrandece' [This is the octave, in which flourish heroic greatness and epic excellence, and which ennobles lyric poetry with its sweetness]. The sense that, on one level, 'Los amores' is a form of epic is reinforced by the poem's structure. The 137 *octavas* can be split into the following sections: a summary of the subject to be treated (1–2); a dedication to Enrique de la Cueva (3–4); the introduction of the protagonists (5–10); Mars's courtship of Venus (11–26); Apollo's discovery of the lovers' affair (27–57); the forging of the net (58–75); the setting (76–91) and springing (92–103) of the trap; Vulcan's return home (104–11); the smith's appeal to Jupiter and the unveiling of the lovers (112–32); the lovers' release (133–5); and, finally, a promise of further poems on Enrique's 'hechos celebrados' [famous deeds] (136–7).[10] The main narrative, comprising stanzas 5–135, is thus embedded in the epic frame of stanzas 1–4 and 136–7.

This epic frame features several commonplaces inherited from classical and Italian Renaissance tradition, including the poet's 'furor natural poético' (2*a–d*); the inspiration of Apollo and the Muses (2*e–f*); the humility topoi of 'mediocritas mea' and 'excusatio propter infirmitatem' (3*a–d*); and the promise of further poems in praise of Enrique's glorious deeds (136).[11] Designed to seize the audience's attention, the opening stanza summarizes the subject to be treated:

> La red que con ingenio y sutil arte
> a la madre de Amor y la belleza
> prendió, y en nudo estrecho ligó a Marte,
> en sujeción poniendo su fiereza,
> el ruego de los dioses que desparte

---

[10] Cebrián García, *La fábula*, 66–8. All references to 'Los amores' are to the edition found in Juan de la Cueva, *Fábulas mitológicas y épica burlesca*, ed. José Cebrián García (Madrid: Editora Nacional, 1984), 117–56. Numbers will be used to denote stanzas and italicized letters to denote lines within stanzas (e.g. 1, 37*e–h*).

[11] For a discussion of 'el furor natural poético', see López Pinciano, *Obras completas*, i. 109–31. On the topos of 'excusatio propter infirmitatem', see Ernst Robert Curtius, *European Literature and the Latin Middle Ages*, trans. Willard R. Trask (London: Routledge & Kegan Paul, 1953), 83.

del ígneo dios la saña y aspereza,
la red suelta, el insulto perdonado,
será de mi terrestre voz cantado. (1)

[The net which with subtle and ingenious skill trapped the mother of Love
and beauty, and bound Mars in a tight knot, subjugating his ferocity, the
gods' plea that placates the god of fire's severity and fury, how the net was
loosed and the offence pardoned, all this will be sung by my earthly voice.]

Emphasis is placed on elements central to the principal classical tellings:
the ingenious net, the lovers' imprisonment, the gods' response to Vulcan's
appeal, and the lovers' eventual release. The use of asyndeton, the delaying
of the main verb ('será . . . cantado') until the final line of the *octava*, and the
choice of the verb *cantar*—with its echo of the openings of Virgil's *Aeneid*
('Arma virumque cano . . . ') and innumerable Renaissance imitations of
the archetype of secondary epic—all give the impression that what follows will be a serious treatment of a lofty subject grounded in Renaissance
theories of imitation.[12] In stanzas 2–4 the poet adopts a position of
affected humility, protesting his own inadequacy for the task ahead and
underlining the unrefined nature of his 'terrestre voz'. He contrasts his
own 'débil fuerza' [weak force] (2*c*), 'plectro humilde' [humble style] (2*g*),
and 'musa temerosa' [timid muse] (3*b*) with the heroic task ahead, 'una
empresa tan grave' [so serious an undertaking] (2*d*), and the magnificence
of the poem's dedicatee. At its end the poem will come full circle: what is
introduced as a 'don indigno' [unworthy gift] (3*a*) is later presented as a
'don humilde' [humble gift] (137*e*), the first of many poems in praise of
Enrique's achievements to be offered up, if fortune permits, by the poet's
Orphic lyre. Paradoxically, it is by adopting the posture of 'mediocritas
mea' that Cueva invites comparison with canonical classical and Renaissance forebears. While the narrator does not directly invoke the protection
of Apollo and the Muses, he claims, in one of innumerable examples of
erudite circumlocution, that his poem is already 'inspirado del coro de las
nueve | y del retor a quien está sujeto' [inspired by the choir of the nine
Muses and the leader to whom they are subject] (2*e–f*). His dedicatee's
'aliento soberano' [sovereign inspiration] will enable him to surpass his
classical forebears in the spirit of eristic imitation. Specifically, he will be

---

[12] 'Primary epic is folk epic or oral epic, secondary epic a self-conscious literary
imitation of the oral variety'; Joseph Farrell, 'Towards a Rhetoric of (Roman?) Epic', in
William J. Dominik (ed.), *Roman Eloquence: Rhetoric in Society and Literature* (New York:
Routledge, 1997), 131–46 (p. 132). For the use of the verb *cantar(e)*, compare, for example,
the openings of Ariosto's *Orlando furioso* ('Le donne, i cavalier, l'arme, gli amori, | le cortesie,
l'audaci imprese, io canto') and Tasso's *Gerusalemme liberata* ('Canto l'arme pietose e 'l capi-
tano | che 'l gran sepolcro liberò di Cristo').

able to 'exced[er] al que cantó en dulce armonía | la vitoria greciana y fin troyano' [excel the one who sang with sweet harmony of the Greek victory and the Trojan defeat] (4*c–d*). Cueva thus sets out to surpass both the Homer of the *Iliad*, who sang of the siege of Troy that led to the 'vitoria greciana', and, more pertinently, the Homer of the *Odyssey*, who sang the story of Odysseus's arduous return home after the 'fin troyano' (related to this, one might also add the Virgil of the *Aeneid*).

The narrative proper takes as its principal model Demodocus's song of Ares and Aphrodite in *Odyssey*, VIII.266–369. Cueva's poem contains several features that are found in Homer's telling but not in the accounts of Ovid, Lucian, and Reposianus. The clearest example is the important role accorded to Neptune in the tale's denouement. In stanzas 125–32 Neptune expresses his disapproval of his peers' laughter, rebukes Mercury and Apollo for their witty asides, calls for the lovers to be freed, and, finally, guarantees payment of the compensation due to Vulcan. Details of the gods' response to the sight that greets them when they come down from Olympus are also imitated from Homer. In 123*f–h* (*below left*), the moral asides that bad deeds never end well and that the lame can catch the healthy and fleet of foot may be borrowed in part from the corresponding lines of Pérez's *La Ulyxea* (*right*):

«nunca tiene buen fin ni en bien acaba	Nunca tienen buen fin las malas obras
la mala obra, y bien se ha visto en esto,	ni parte con virtud: que al fin se vee,
pues así alcanza el cojo al sano y presto.»	que el más pesado alcanza al más ligero.[13]

In the exchange between Apollo and Mercury that follows in 124*e–h* (*left*), Cueva goes on to paraphrase Pérez's translation (*right*):

«Pluguiera a Jove, hacedor del mundo,	«Plugiesse a Dios que fuesse,
que en cien mil lazos más viera	o Rey Apolo,
conmigo	y que a mí me tuviessen otros lazos
a Venus, y que estando de aquel modo	tres tantos muy mayores y más graves,
me viera el celestial colegio todo.»	y que vosotros Dioses, y las Diosas,
	siquiera me estuviéssedes mirando,
	con tal que yo durmiesse así en los
	brazos
	de Cytherea Venus la amorosa.»[14]

Other details drawn from Homer include the description of the fine threads of the net as 'tan sutiles . . . | que ecedían a Aragne en sutileza' [so fine . . . that they surpassed Arachne's webs in fineness] (73*f–g*) and

---

[13] *La Ulyxea*, 258.   [14] *La Ulyxea*, 259.

the mention in stanzas 133–4 of Mars hastily putting on his arms before leaving for Thrace and of Venus being clothed and then whisked off to Cyprus by the Three Graces.

Significantly, however, whilst Cueva takes Homer as his main model, he also draws inspiration from a wide range of other sources. References to other classical tales abound: Atreus and Thyestes (28*g–h*), Bacchus and Ariadne (65*e–f*), Jupiter and Alcmene (108*e–h*), and so on. Whereas the majority are brief, passing references of little structural import, Cueva's allusion to the Judgement of Paris forms part of a notable departure from Homer. We saw earlier how in *Odyssey* VIII the goddesses do not come down from heaven: 'Meanwhile the gods the dome of Vulcan throng . . . But modesty withheld the goddess train.' In 'Los amores', the narrator states that the goddesses returned home out of shame (115*e–h*); yet Juno and Pallas Athene are the first witnesses to comment on the lovers' capture: a glimpse of Venus's 'deshonra cierta' [certain dishonour] (102*d*) and a chance to pass comment on her predicament constitute revenge for the shame the two goddesses experienced when Paris adjudged Venus to be the fairest of the three and, as a result, awarded her the golden Apple of Discord (116–18). Only once the goddesses' calls for Vulcan to free the lovers have been rejected does Cueva return to his main source as outlined above. In other parts of the poem Cueva turns to Ovid for inspiration. When Apollo delivers his message to Vulcan, the smith is so shocked that he drops his hammer. Not present in Homer, this detail is suggested by *Metamorphoses*, IV.175–6 ('quod opus fabrilis dextra tenebat | excidit . . . '), before being spelt out in vernacular translations (e.g. Bustamante's 'se le cayeron de las manos las tenazas y el martillo' [he dropped his tongs and his hammer]).[15] The final lines of the narrative are also inspired by Ovid: Venus's imprisonment instils in her 'implacable saña y mortal furia | contra el Sol . . . ' [ruthless fury and mortal rage against the Sun] (135*e–f*), mention of her desire for revenge hinting at the suffering in love endured by Apollo that forms the core of Leuconoe's narrative in *Metamorphoses*, IV.166–284.

Whilst he draws direct inspiration for many sections of the poem from classical sources—or sixteenth-century vernacular translations of them— Cueva also adds long sections of new material. In a poem that is 1,096 lines long it is not surprising that there should be some significant additions to the basic Homeric narrative. As we have seen, the final *octavas* follow their model(s) fairly closely. In contrast, the first two-thirds of the poem present a dramatic *amplificatio* of the source text. A simple comparison with Pérez's *La Ulyxea* makes the scale of this expansion clear.

---

[15] *Las Transformaciones*, fol. 56^r.

At the end of stanza 91 Vulcan leaves home, having set his trap: after almost 700 lines we come to the point in the story reached by Pérez after just thirty-eight.[16] Cueva adds to the tale by developing old sections of the narrative and introducing new ones. Notable modifications include a detailed description of Mars's courtship of Venus, the lovers' first kiss, and the consummation of their passion (10–26); a lengthy examination of Apollo's initial uncertainty as to what to do about his discovery (27–41); a drawn-out exchange between Apollo and Vulcan when the former goes to deliver his message (42–58); a long account of Vulcan's deliberation as to how to gain revenge, his orders to the Cyclopes, and the forging of the net (59–75); and an innovative section on Vulcan's setting of the trap, his interruption of the lovers' tryst, and their response to his sudden and unexpected appearance (80–95). By delaying the dramatic highpoint of the lovers' unveiling, Cueva fundamentally alters the tale's basic structure. The more deliberate build-up to the tale's denouement makes the structure of the poem akin to that of a play. Whereas Homer focuses on resolution (i.e. what happens after the lovers are trapped), Cueva gives equal weight to both introduction and complication (i.e. what happens before the lovers are trapped) and thus balances the Aristotelian beginning, middle, and end.[17]

Focusing on the movement from order destroyed to order restored, the tale would naturally lend itself to theatrical development. Like many contemporary plays, it is shaped by the interplay between three main characters: a male protagonist (Vulcan), a male antagonist (Mars), and a female who brings about the antagonism (Venus).[18] With its emphasis on adultery, deception, deceit, *engaño/desengaño*, revenge, confrontation, revelation, and honour, the plot of 'Los amores' would not be out of place on the seventeenth-century stage. The tale is rich in inherently dramatic scenes, such as Apollo's discovery of the affair, the capture and unveiling of the lovers, and the wronged husband's appeal for justice to the king of the gods. In the tale's final scene, which brings the entire cast together on stage, an apparent impasse is resolved through a *deus ex machina*: through the sudden intervention of Neptune order is restored to the celestial sphere.

---

[16] *La Ulyxea*, 255.

[17] The poem's structure is thus more in line with Lope's three-act division of the *comedia* than with Cueva's own four-act scheme: 'En el acto primero ponga el caso, | en el segundo enlace los sucesos | de suerte que, hasta el medio del tercero, | apenas juzgue nadie en lo que para' [In the first act introduce the subject, and in the second connect events together so that, until halfway through the third, no one can quite predict the end]; Lope de Vega, *Arte nuevo de hacer comedias*, ed. Enrique García Santo-Tomás, LH, 585 (Madrid: Cátedra, 2006), 147 (lines 298–301).

[18] Donald R. Larson, *The Honor Plays of Lope de Vega* (Cambridge, Mass.: Harvard University Press, 1977), 1.

To this foundation Cueva adds a number of other features which, even at this relatively early stage in its history, are readily associated with the *comedia*. Often uncertain as to how to act, Cueva's gods engage in long periods of self-reflection. For example, attention is paid to Vulcan's thought processes both before (58–61) and after (77*e*–9*h*) the forging of the net. On each occasion the process of self-questioning that he goes through would be appropriate for a soliloquy voiced by a dishonoured husband on the stage. When Vulcan heads home to set his trap, we see a scene played out in numerous *comedias*: the husband's unexpected return at night interrupts a tryst between the lovers, throwing them into panic and forcing the woman to hide her lover from her husband (a detail that recalls the painting by Tintoretto discussed in the Introduction).[19] Another theatrical device exploited by Cueva is that of dramatic irony. Notable examples of humour springing from a character's ignorance of the reality of a particular situation are Vulcan's misreading of the reasons behind Apollo's visit to the forge (43–5*d*), Venus's belief that she has successfully deceived her husband and thus safely negotiated his untimely return (87–92), and Mars's display of overweening pride moments before the lovers' fall (94–5).

Closer examination of Mars's courtship of Venus sheds further light on Cueva's handling of the story. Stanzas 5–9 introduce the protagonists, contrasting the lovers' carefree sexual indulgence with the husband's unremitting labour at the forge. Several of the motifs examined in the previous chapter are reworked in these stanzas. The narrative begins with very deliberate polyptoton designed to show that Mars can be conquered only by Venus: 'Venció . . . | . . . | al invencible Marte' [she conquered … the unconquerable Mars] (5*a*–*c*). As he begins his courtship of her, Mars is rendered subservient to Venus, whose charms enslave both mortals and immortals alike:

> del tracio dios la saña horrible allana,
> el brazo liga siempre vitorioso,
> y así cativo della, ante ella puesto
> dice, rendido al soberano opuesto . . . (10*e*–*h*)

[she tempers the Thracian god's terrible fury, she binds his ever victorious arm, and so, captive to her, prostrate at the feet of his sovereign opponent, he says . . .]

---

[19] At this point, Vulcan is driven by 'celosos accidentes' (79*e*), a feverish condition that, in the guise of 'el accidente de [sus] celos' (line 1876), will later afflict Gutierre in Pedro Calderón de la Barca's wife-murder play *El médico de su honra*. In two parallel scenes framing the central act of this play, Calderón reworks the motifs of the husband's unexpected return and the lover's need to hide, as first her ex-lover Enrique and then her husband Gutierre visit Mencía under the cloak of night.

Metaphors of love as a form of captivity or servitude recall Garcilaso's galley slave condemned to row 'en la concha de Venus amarrado'. The poem suddenly shifts from the general to the specific, as Mars, kneeling at Venus's feet, launches into a long declaration of his love (11–16). He addresses her with a string of periphrases ('luz del tercer cielo' [light of the third sphere of heaven], 'hija de Jove' [daughter of Jove], 'madre de Cupido' [mother of Cupid]; 11*a–b*), promising to be forever enslaved to her if she accedes to his wishes, heaping praise on her whilst at the same time extolling his own qualities, and expressing his horror that her divine beauty should be enjoyed by 'un cojo, un feo, de tizne y humo lleno, | que en nada es nada, y para nada bueno' [a lame and ugly fellow, covered in soot and smoke, who is useless at everything and good for nothing] (15*e–h*).[20] Mars is horrified that 'tal monstro' [such a monster] should have the pleasure of Venus's company, for he alone is worthy of 'tal tesoro' [such a treasure]. Despite Mars's claim that he would do anything to please her—including even dethrone Jupiter—Venus is unimpressed by his overtures:

> Venus las oye, sin que en ella pueda
> el afición, ni los desgarros nada;
> que los desgarros del amante fiero,
> son de menos efeto que el dinero. (17*e–h*)

[Venus listens to them, without either his affection or his boasting having any effect on her; for the fierce lover's boasting holds less sway than money.]

It is stated that *desgarros* have no influence on Venus, for soldiers' self-aggrandizing talk is less persuasive than money.[21] Venus's reply confirms this assertion. Claiming already to have known of Mars's passion and of the extent to which he would go to win her affection, Venus rebuffs Mars's outpouring by stating that actions speak louder than words: ' . . . los que hablan menos | para amantes y amados son los buenos' [those who talk less are best as far as lovers and beloveds are concerned] (19*g–h*). Women are more susceptible to gifts ('el regalo tierno', 20*a*) than to obnoxious bluster ('el desgarrar horrible', 20*b*), an assertion that recalls Celestina's remarks to Calisto in the first *auto* of the *Celestina*: 'dile que cierre la boca y comence abrir la bolsa; que de las obras dubdo, quanto más de las palabras' [tell him to shut his mouth and start opening his purse, because I don't trust

---

[20] The planet Venus was the third sphere in the Ptolemaic system; thus the goddess's epithet of 'luz del tercer cielo'; compare, for example, Garcilaso, Eclogue 1, 400–3: 'y en *la tercera rueda*, | contigo mano a mano, | busquemos otro llano, | busquemos . . . ' (my emphasis).

[21] Cov. s.v. *desgarrar*: 'Desgarro, la bravata de un soldado fanfarrón y glorioso.'

his deeds, let alone his words].[22] Even the wildest woman, 'que es animal terrible, | indómita por tal' [who is a wild animal, and as such indomitable] (20*f–g*), can be tamed through such means. Accordingly, Venus instructs Mars to abandon his sword and to exchange the attributes of the fierce soldier for those of the tender lover, including gifts, sweet nothings, and infinite patience (21*e–h*). The idea of exchanging the weapons of the soldier for those of the lover would later be developed by Quevedo in one of his burlesque sonnets on Apollo and Daphne, when the sun-god is instructed to follow the example of Mars in his pursuit of the nymph: ' . . . trata de compralla: | en confites gastó Marte la malla, | y la espada en pasteles y en azumbres' [. . . try to buy her: Mars pawned his armour for sweets, and his sword for cakes and litres of wine] (Q536: 6–8). Whilst the advice given by Venus is not as explicit about the requirement for Mars to pawn his weapons, what is made clear is the need for plenty of *crédito* (21*d*), both 'buena opinión y reputación' [good standing and reputation] and, more importantly, 'entre mercaderes, abono de caudal y correspondencia con los demás' [amongst traders, a wealth of credit and good dealings with others] (Cov.).

Acting on Venus's advice to 'hacer más' [do more] (19*g*), Mars recovers this unpromising situation by planting a kiss on her lips: 'recoge el brazo, el rostro allega della | al suyo y los purpúreos labios sella' [he raises his arm, pulls her head in towards his, and seals her crimson lips] (23*g–h*). In an inversion of the 'beso encarecido' of Aldana's sonnet, it is Mars who placates Venus through the medium of a kiss: 'Así el enojo reconcilia y mueve | la voluntad airada en mansedumbre' [Thus he defuses her irritation and tames her angry will] (24*a–b*). Although the end is the same, the means by which the lovers are reconciled undermines the usual process by which *discordia concors* is achieved. Cueva juxtaposes a euphemistic description of the climax of the lovers' tryst (25–6) with Apollo's discovery of them 'en infame nudo asidos' [trapped in a disgraceful knot] (27–32). Horrified by the spectacle, Apollo's first thought is to turn his chariot around in order to shroud the lovers' union in darkness. Concerned by the affront to Vulcan, but, tellingly, also motivated by envy (27*f* and 31*c*), he craves immediate vengeance but is uncertain how to proceed. Whereas Homer's and Ovid's gods are spontaneous in their actions and responses, Cueva's gods are hesitant and full of doubt. Stanzas 30–9 are dedicated to the deliberations that lead to Apollo's decision to tell Vulcan of his wife's affair. After a brief moral digression which starts with the chiastic '¡Oh miserables amadores vanos, | oh vanos

---

[22] Fernando de Rojas, *La Celestina*, ed. Dorothy S. Severin, LH, 4 (Madrid: Cátedra, 2000), 116.

amadores miserables!' [Oh vain and wretched lovers, oh wretched and vain lovers!] (40–1), the scene switches to Vulcan's forge. When Apollo arrives, Vulcan leaves the forge, wiping soot from his face. Unaware of the reason for Apollo's visit, the smith launches into a hyperbolic address, expressing his good fortune to have in his house the 'sacro dios de Delo' [sacred god of Delphi] (43*f*) and offering to forge anything that his new guest should wish to commission.

Throughout the poem emphasis is placed on the immorality of the lovers' actions, their affront to Vulcan's honour, and the smith's desire for revenge. The statement, in stanza 5, that Mars acts 'en ofensa | de Vulcano' [causing offense to Vulcan] (5*c*–*d*) prepares the reader for a tale focused on honour. Cueva has constant recourse to nouns (*alevosía, fama, insulto, ofensa, oprobrio, osadía*, etc.), verbs (*adulterar, afrentar, infamar, ofender, profanar, vengar*, etc.), and adjectives (*afrentoso, aleve, infame, injuriado, injusto, vergonzoso*, etc.) relating to this central theme. The same is true of the gods' direct speech (a form that takes up over fifty stanzas, or a good third, of the whole poem). When Apollo finally informs Vulcan of his wife's infidelity, the sun-god outlines the smith's predicament in the language of societal and familial honour codes:

> «Esta pues que tú *honras* y amas tanto
> te ofende, menosprecia y te *deshonra*,
> sin cuidar de tu afán ni tu quebranto,
> compra el contento suyo con tu *honra*;
> Marte el desgarrador, que pone espanto
> oír su numbre, adulterando tu *honra*
> con Venus, sin mirar *honor* ni puntos,
> los dejo a entrambos en tu casa juntos.» (51; my emphasis)

[This woman that you so love and honour insults, scorns, and dishonours you, and, without any concern for your ardour or your suffering, she buys her own happiness with your honour; boastful Mars, whose very name inspires fear, compromising your honour with Venus, with no thought for honour or propriety, I have just left both of them in your house together.]

The quick-fire repetition of words relating to honour—the verbs *honrar* and *deshonrar* and the nouns *honra* and *honor*—and the placing of three of them in the rhyme positions in 51*b*, *d*, and *f*, highlight the disparity between Vulcan's love for Venus and her flagrant disrespect for him. Vulcan's own language confirms that this is a matter of personal honour. When, after much deliberation, he finally decides that a net is the best way to 'restaurar la fama' [restore his reputation] (59*f*), Vulcan addresses the Cyclopes and impresses on them the unique nature of their next work. As in Hurtado de Mendoza's poem, a series of potential commissions—Jupiter's thunderbolts, Neptune's trident, Ariadne's golden diadem, Aeneas's arms, etc. (64–5)—is rejected in favour of an 'obra más perfeta' [more perfect work] (66*d*) on which Vulcan's honour now depends (63*h*). From this point on, Vulcan's primary concern is the restoration of his honour. When he discusses the question of the lovers' release with Neptune, his words recall those of Apollo:

> «Mas una cosa en lo que pides quiero
> (por lo que toca a mi sosiego y *honra*
> ante el potente Jove) hacer primero
> que es la que en esto me restaura y *honra*:
> que a Venus que traspasa el santo fuero
> de Himeneo, y cual ves, mi *honor deshonra*,
> repudialla, y ella ha de volverme
> el dote que le di para así verme.» (129; my emphasis)

[But one of the things you ask for I want to do first (because of its bearing on my peace and honour before powerful Jove) and that is the one that saves my face and honour: that Venus, who breaks Hymen's sacred laws, and as you can see, dishonours my honour, be condemned, and that she must return the dowry that I gave her only to see myself in this position.]

The emphasis placed by Vulcan on infamy, dishonour, and treachery— 'una horrible alevosía' (68*d*), 'este infame daño' (69*a*), 'esta injuria tan grande y afrentosa' (69*b*), 'mi oprobrio horrible' (70*d*), etc.—invites the reader to draw links between the smith's situation and similar predicaments faced by characters in the *comedia*. The concern for honour, echoed throughout the poem, reflects not only contemporary social norms but also the currents of Cueva's own plays, the majority of which deal with questions relating to honour and vengeance.[23]

However, whilst the poem's focus on the themes of honour, jealousy, and revenge hints at common ground with late sixteenth- and early seventeenth-century honour plays, it is clear from the outset that Cueva's telling is far from serious and that the effect he strives for is not so much epic as mock-heroic. Cebrián García asserts that 'Los amores' is punctuated by 'detalles humorísticos y jocosos que aportan una nota de ironía y desenfado' [humorous and jocular details that lend a note of irony and entertainment]. Several of the passages analysed thus far—including Venus's initial rejection of Mars's courtship, his subsequent transformation into a fawning lover, and the presence of the goddesses at the

---

23 Cossío, *Fábulas mitológicas*, 174.

lovers' shaming—are playful in terms of their undermining of the reader's expectations. However, not all of the poem's humour is the product of what Cebrián García terms 'la fina ironía del poeta' [the poet's subtle irony].[24] Many of the rhetorical devices found in 'Los amores'—most notably, circumlocution, classical allusion, and simile—underpin its mock high style. Take, for example, Cueva's insistent recourse to periphrasis when referring to Venus: introduced in the first stanza as 'la madre de Amor y la belleza' [the mother of Cupid and beauty] (1*b*), she then becomes 'la diosa en Idalio venerada' [the goddess revered in Idalion] (5*b*), 'luz del tercer cielo, y diosa eterna, | hija de Jove, y madre de Cupido' [light of the third sphere of heaven, daughter of Jove, and mother of Cupid] (11*a–b*), 'la diosa que premió el pastor en Ida' [the goddess awarded the prize by the shepherd from Ida] (18*b*), 'la bella diosa a quien adora Gnido' [the beautiful goddess worshipped by Gnidus] (86*e*), 'la bella diosa Citerea' [the beautiful goddess Cytherea] (92*a*), 'bella diosa, a quien adora | la deleitosa Chipre' [beautiful goddess, worshipped by pleasure-giving Cyprus] (93*a–b*), 'bella hija del potente | retor de la celeste monarquía' [beautiful daughter of the powerful ruler of the heavenly monarchy] (95*a–b*), and so on.[25] Whilst the phrases in themselves are not comic, the accumulation of such elaborate periphrases soon helps to create an air of the ridiculous.

In several *octavas* the effect created is one not of subtle irony but of deliberate incongruity or absurdity. For example, the descriptions of the reactions of both Apollo and Vulcan on first learning of the lovers' affair tip over into comic exaggeration. When Apollo catches sight of the lovers, his immediate response is to turn his chariot around in order to shroud the affair in darkness, 'cual hizo huyendo | por no mirar de Atreo el hecho horrendo' [as he did when fleeing in order not to see Atreus's terrible deed] (28*g–h*). The lovers' affair is apparently so objectionable that it bears comparison with the gruesome revenge carried out by Atreus on Thyestes as punishment for his brother's adultery with his wife Aerope: killing, dicing, and stewing his brother's sons, serving them up to him at a feast, and then having their heads, hands, and feet brought in when Thyestes asked to see them.[26] If the allusion to Atreus's 'hecho horrendo' seems inappropriate, a second simile, comparing Apollo in his state of great consternation to a

[24] *La fábula*, 89.

[25] For more on this and other rhetorical devices employed by Cueva, see Esteban Calderón Dorda, 'La mitología clásica en la obra poética de Juan de la Cueva', in Ricardo Escavy Zamora and others (eds.), *Amica verba: in honorem Prof. Antonio Roldán Pérez*, 2 vols. (Murcia: Servicio de Publicaciones de la Universidad de Murcia, 2005), i. 133–54.

[26] Apollodorus, *The Library of Greek Mythology*, trans. Robin Hard, Oxford World's Classics (Oxford: Oxford University Press, 1997), 145–6.

rock battered by the elements, gives Cueva's emphasis on Apollo's reaction the air of absurd hyperbole:

> cual roca al mar en quien su furia brava
> hiere, a sus duros golpes puesta en medio,
> que por un cabo y otro con frecuencia
> le aqueja el mar y el viento con violencia. (30*e–h*)

[like a rock in the sea lashed by its furious ferocity, placed amidst its hard blows, that from one end to the other is frequently battered by wave and wind.]

Apollo's comical overreaction prepares the reader for that of Vulcan, who drops his hammer, loses the power of speech, and bursts into floods of tears: 'de agua abundante por el rostro vierte | un Tanais' [a Tanais of abundant water flows down his face] (54*e–f*). Cueva's description of the husband's tears in terms of a river flowing from the smith's face is patently absurd, even more so when we consider that the Tanais, the offspring of Oceanus and Tethys, was famed not only for its great volume but also for rushing down a mountainside: 'Tánais flu. Scythiæ ex Riphæis montibus defluens' [Tanais: a Scythian river flowing down from the Rhiphaean mountains].[27] An extended simile that takes up the whole of the next stanza leaves the reader in no doubt as to the poem's mock-heroic tone: like a sudden deluge that gives birth to a rapid torrent that sweeps away everything in its downward path, Vulcan's tears form a river that flows down his face sweeping away the encrusted 'hollín, humo, y tizne' [smut, smoke, and soot] (55*h*).

When the lovers are caught, Mars's reaction takes up five stanzas (97–101), that of Venus just two (102–3). Mars furiously struggles to free himself, drawing breath only to rattle off a series of rhetorical questions expressing his dismay at being subjected to such ignominy by a lesser divinity. Once more, Cueva uses a simile—this time comparing Mars to a proud lion trying to escape from captivity—to convey the full force of a character's state:

> que cuanto más trabaja y más se aíra,
> más se revuelve y ve más oprimido
> de la ingeniosa trampa que lo aprieta,
> y nudo y lazo y red más lo sujeta. (100*e–h*)

[the more he struggles and the more he gets angry, the more he tosses and turns, the tighter he is squeezed by the ingenious trap that snares him, and the more knot, chain, and net subdue him.]

---

[27] Ravisius Textor includes this entry under the heading 'Fluvii praecipui nominis' [Names of major rivers] in *Officinae Ioannis Ravisii Textoris epitome*, 2 vols. (Lyons: Sébastien Gryphius, 1551), i. 413.

Mars's efforts are futile: the more he struggles, the tighter the net closes around him, the tangled verse resulting from the polysyndeton of *y* reflecting, as in Góngora's *romance*, the tangled web he is in. In contrast to Mars, Venus does not put up a fight: her delicate flesh is no match for Vulcan's great steel net. Bursting into tears, she at last spares a thought for her husband, foolishly thinking that 'si él así la viera | de lástima y de amor se enterneciera' [if he saw her like this he would be moved by pity and love] (103*g–h*). The lovers' dismay is soon contrasted with Vulcan's ecstatic response to Apollo's news that his trap has been successful. Perhaps the most inappropriate of all the comic details comes when the smith's celebrated limp is forgotten as he acquires remarkable fleetness of foot in his rush to get home:

> No le impedía el suelto movimiento
> de la quebrada pierna la torpeza,
> que el deseo le da y la ira aliento,
> y lo llevan con suelta ligereza;
> no usaba de temor, y andar a tiento,
> sintiendo en desmandándose flaqueza,
> que a ver esto, aunque cojo y de pies malo,
> ecediera a Filón, Canisio, y Talo. (110)

[His clumsy, mangled foot did not impede his nimble movement, because anger and desire spur him on and drive him on with fleetness of foot; he felt no fear and did not go carefully, feeling weakness as he lost control of himself; for if you saw this, although lame and with bad feet, he would surpass Philonides, Canistius, and Thalus.]

Vulcan becomes so nimble that he outstrips three classical figures renowned for their speed as runners: Alexander the Great's courier Philonides, who ran 1,305 stadia in a single day; the Spartan courier Anystis/Canistius, who accomplished the same feat; and Thalus, a bronze giant who paced around the shoreline of Crete three times a day to guard the island from invaders.[28]

The presence of these and other incongruous details confirms the tone of Cueva's telling as mock-heroic. It also brings us back, by way of a brief conclusion to this section, to the question of sources. We saw above how an entry in Ravisius Textor's *Officina* helps to explain Cueva's choice of the river Tanais. The same is also true of his choice of famous classical runners, for Philonides, Anystis/Canistius, and Thalus are all included, in the space of just a few lines, in the section of the *Officina* headed 'Cursores

---

[28] On Philonides and Anystis/Canistius, see Pliny, *Natural History*, VII.20.84; on Thalus, Apollonius Rhodius, *Argonautica*, IV.1638–44.

velocissimi' [Very quick runners].[29] Such references may, at first sight, pass for erudite classical allusion, but they are soon revealed to be nothing more than empty borrowing from one of the most widely known commonplace books of the sixteenth century—another in a long line of storehouses freely plundered by Cueva in his imitation of Demodocus's song.

LOPE DE VEGA, 'LA ROSA BLANCA' (1624)

The most renowned poet-playwright of his day, Lope de Vega (1562–1635) was, and to a certain extent still is, as famous for his colourful life as for his remarkable literary output. Many of the facts of his life remain shrouded in legend, drawn as they are not from reliable and objective evidence but from the pages of Lope's own works. He is known, however, to have served in the Azores in 1583, been exiled from Madrid in 1588–95 for libellous attacks on the family of an ex-lover (Elena Osorio), married twice thereafter and engaged in a string of other affairs (fathering several legitimate and illegitimate children), taken holy orders as a priest in 1614, and, all the while, forged a long career as a poet, playwright, and secretary to members of the nobility (most notably, the Duke of Sessa).[30]

As noted earlier, Lope's name is synonymous with the development of the *comedia nueva* and the emergence of the figure of the professional dramatist. However, like Cueva, he also experimented with a wide range of poetic forms, styles, and subjects. His poetry for the page, as opposed to the stage, ranges from religious lyric to popular Moorish and pastoral ballads, from historical epic on figures such as Sir Francis Drake (the aforementioned *La Dragontea*) to mock epic in the style of the *Batrachomyomachia*, and from beautifully crafted examples of the Renaissance sonnet to stinging attacks on rival poets and humorous burlesques of contemporary literary styles (most notably, Góngora and *cultismo*). In contrast to many of his forebears and contemporaries, including, most famously, Góngora and Quevedo, Lope saw collections of his poems published on a regular basis throughout his own lifetime, the most notable being his *Rimas* [Poems] (1602), *Rimas sacras* [Sacred Poems] (1614), and *Rimas humanas y divinas del licenciado Tomé de Burguillos* [Sacred and Secular Poems by the Licentiate Tomé de Burguillos] (1634). Perhaps as a conscious attempt to rival Góngora, whose *Polifemo* is still regarded as the finest and most polemical mythological poem of the Golden Age,

---

[29] *Officinae*, i. 454.
[30] For an overview of Lope's life and works, see the essays published in Alexander Samson and Jonathan Thacker (eds.), *A Companion to Lope de Vega*, CTSA: Monografías, 260 (Woodbridge: Tamesis, 2008).

Lope also wrote four long narrative poems on mythological subjects.[31] The first two, 'La Filomena' [Philomena] and 'La Andrómeda' [Andromeda], were published in *La Filomena con otras diversas rimas, prosas y versos* [Philomena with Various Other Poems, Prose Pieces, and Verses] (1621). The last two, 'La Circe' [Circe] and 'La rosa blanca' [The White Rose] were included in a second miscellany entitled *La Circe con otras rimas y prosas* [Circe with Other Poems and Prose Pieces] (1624). Whilst recent years have witnessed an increasing number of studies of Lope's plays on mythological subjects, his four long mythological poems have continued to receive little critical attention.[32]

Whilst *La Circe* as a whole is dedicated to the Count of Olivares, who had been Philip IV's first minister since 1621, 'La rosa blanca' bears the dedication 'A la ilustrissima señora doña Maria de Guzman, hija unica del Excelentissimo Señor Conde de Olivares' [To the most illustrious lady doña María de Guzmán, the only child of the most excellent Lord Count of Olivares]. Born in 1609, María de Guzmán was one of three children born to Olivares and his wife, Inés de Zúñiga y Velasco.[33] She was, however, the only one to survive infancy. Whilst in 1624 Olivares may still have hoped for a son of his own, no child had been born to his wife for several years; by the date of publication of *La Circe* it looked increasingly likely, therefore, that it would fall to María to provide a male heir to continue the family line. Just as the end of Cueva's 'Los amores' promises

---

[31] Terry, *Seventeenth-Century Spanish Poetry*, 113.

[32] On Lope and classical mythology, see Michael D. McGaha, 'Las comedias mitológicas de Lope de Vega', in Ángel González, Tamara Holzapfel, and Alfred Rodríguez (eds.), *Estudios sobre el Siglo de Oro en homenaje a Raymond R. MacCurdy* (Madrid: Cátedra, 1983), 67–82; Rosa Romojaro, *Lope de Vega y el mito clásico* (Málaga: Universidad de Málaga, 1998); Enrique Ramos Jurado, 'Comedia mitológica y comedia histórica: la tradición clásica en Lope de Vega', in *Cuatro estudios sobre tradición clásica en la literatura española. Lope, Blasco, Alberti y Mª Teresa León y la novela histórica* (Cadiz: Universidad de Cádiz, 2001), 11–43; Juan Antonio Martínez Berbel, *El mundo mitológico de Lope de Vega: siete comedias mitológicas de inspiración ovidiana* (Madrid: Fundación Universitaria Española, 2003); and Frederick A. de Armas, '*Adonis y Venus*: hacia la tragedia en Tiziano y Lope de Vega', in Frederick A. de Armas, Luciano García Lorenzo, and Enrique García Santo-Tomás (eds.), *Hacia la tragedia áurea. Lecturas para un nuevo milenio* (Madrid: Iberoamericana, 2008), 97–115. On *La Filomena* and *La Circe* in particular, see the editor's prefatory remarks in Lope de Vega, *Obras poéticas*, ed. José Manuel Blecua, Clásicos Planeta, 18 (Barcelona: Planeta, 1969), 555–65, 917–26; and Ali Rizavi, '*Novelas a Marcia Leonarda*', in *A Companion to Lope de Vega*, 244–55.

[33] Lope dedicated a number of works to the future Count-Duke and his immediate family in the first years of Olivares's rule, but was, it seems, ultimately unsuccessful in securing his patronage. On attempts by Lope and others to curry favour with the new *valido*, see José Simón Díaz, 'Libros de autores andaluces dedicados al Conde-Duque de Olivares', in Sonsoles Celestino Angulo (ed.), *De libros a bibliotecas. Homenaje a Rocío Caracuel* (Seville: Universidad de Sevilla, 1995), 389–402; and 'Sesenta y dos libros dedicados al Conde-Duque de Olivares en los años 1621–1642', *Trabajos de la Asociación Española de Bibliografía*, 2 (1998), 143–74.

further poems on Enrique de la Cueva's glorious exploits, the final stanza of Lope's 'La rosa blanca' promises an epithalamium in honour of María's future marriage. On 10 October 1624 a marriage contract was signed between the 14-year-old María and Ramiro Pérez de Guzmán, thus bringing an end to both intense speculation surrounding Olivares's choice of son-in-law and the hopes of several eligible bachelors including Olivares's own nephew Don Luis de Haro. Though the marriage was celebrated on 9 January 1625, a matter of months after the publication of *La Circe*, María died just over a year and a half later, on 30 July 1626, after giving birth to a stillborn child.[34]

The form and length of 'La rosa blanca', which comprises 109 *octavas reales*, give Lope's panegyric of Olivares's daughter an air of heroic weight and significance.[35] The poem's length is the result not of dramatic *amplificatio*, as in Cueva's poem, but of a form of *ars combinatoria*. Whereas 'Los amores' focuses on a single tale, 'La rosa blanca', like Espínola y Torres's *Transformaciones y robos de Júpiter*, is eclectic, collating a wide range of previously disparate tales to form a single, overarching narrative centred on an individual god(dess). Though, as we shall see, the poem's frame focuses on María de Guzmán and the white rose (a central motif on her coat of arms), the main body of the poem forms a biography of Venus, from her birth from the foam of the sea to a duel with her rival Pallas Athene over the dedication of the red rose. In order to construct this linear narrative, Lope makes modifications to well-known episodes, plays different accounts of tales off against one another, and introduces new material to make subtle transitions between separate narrative strands. Though one of several mythological stories reworked in the body of 'La rosa blanca', the tale of Mars, Venus, and Vulcan lies at the heart of Venus's biography, occupying more than twice as many *octavas* as any other; if, as Pedraza Jiménez suggests, 'cada episodio es una joya que se engarza sin violencia a los demás' [each episode is a jewel that sets off the others without compromising them], then the poem's centrepiece is Lope's account of the tale under examination.[36]

The first eleven stanzas of 'La rosa blanca' introduce its subject and dedicatee, reworking commonplace elements of the exordium. The poem's opening line, the start of an address to 'Hermosa Venus, alma Citerea',

[34] John H. Elliott, *The Count-Duke of Olivares: The Statesman in an Age of Decline* (New Haven: Yale University Press, 1986), 19, 163–7, 275–82.

[35] *La Circe, con otras rimas y prosas* (Madrid: viuda de Alonso Martín, 1624), fols. 90ʳ–108ʳ. For a more recent edition of 'La rosa blanca', see Lope de Vega, *Obras poéticas*, 1059–83.

[36] *El universo poético*, 173.

recalls Lucretius's celebrated invocation to 'alma Venus' at the start of *De Rerum Natura*:

> Aeneadum genetrix, hominum divomque voluptas,
> alma Venus, caeli subter labentia signa
> quae mare navigerum, quae terras frugiferentis
> concelebras . . . (1.1–4)

[Mother of Aeneas and his race, darling of men and gods, nurturing Venus, who beneath the smooth-moving heavenly signs fillest with thyself the sea full-laden with ships, the earth with her kindly fruits . . .][37]

In the final couplet of the opening stanza Lope draws on the bard topos: 'que se digne de dar tu luz hermosa | vida a mi voz para cantar tu rosa' [may your beautiful light deign to give life to my voice to sing of your rose]. Lope's poem is inscribed in a long literary tradition of representations of the rose, a tradition that stretches back from Lope and Góngora, through Torquato Tasso, Garcilaso, and Jean de Meun, to the biblical *Song of Songs* and classical writers such as the Latin poets Catullus and Virgil and the Greek poets Bion, Anacreon, and Homer.[38] However, in the second stanza Lope makes a claim to originality, acknowledging this tradition only to dissociate himself from it. Contrasting the white rose, 'que no fue cantada | de lira humana, griega ni latina' [which was not sung about by any human lyre, either Greek or Latin] (2*a–b*), with the red rose, about which 'varias y difusas | dóricas liras y romanas musas' [many and varied Doric lyres and Roman muses] have sung (2*g–h*), he promises what Ariosto termed 'cosa non detta mai in prosa nè in rima' [a subject never before treated in either prose or verse] (*Orlando furioso*, 1, 18). As he explains in stanza 8, Lope presents an inversion of classical tradition, suggesting that the white rose developed from, and not into, the red rose, a less virtuous flower formed from the blood of Venus.

Following on from this brief introduction, stanzas 3–6 begin the transition to the dedication. First the poet rebukes himself for invoking the inspiration of the 'Venus de la tierra' (earthly Venus) instead of that of 'la celestial' (heavenly María). After the initial appeal to 'hermosa Venus' [beautiful Venus], the poet launches into a second invocation to 'sacra Venus' [sacred Venus], not the classical goddess but María, who, due to her purity and chastity, is a superior force. Though similar to Venus, María offers 'más viva luz' [more intense light], for the circumstances of her

---

[37] Lucretius, *De Rerum Natura*, pp. 2–3.

[38] For a brief overview of this tradition and a more detailed history of poetic representations of the rose in Spain and Latin America, see Juan Pérez de Guzmán (ed.), *La Rosa. Manojo de la poesía castellana*, 2 vols. (Madrid: Imprenta y Fundación de M. Tello, 1891).

birth excel those found in the celebrated Hesiodic account of the birth of Venus. Whereas Venus was born from 'las ondas espumosas' [the foamy waves], María was born 'entre armiños' [amongst ermine], brilliant furs known for their pure white colour.[39] As the offspring of 'el claro sol' [the noble/radiant sun] (i.e. Olivares) and 'la madre de perlas' [the mother of pearls] (Inés de Zúñiga), she is the 'único parto de tan rica aurora' [the only offspring of such a beautiful dawn] (5*g*).[40] The hyperbolic praise continues in stanzas 6–11. It is only when Lope addresses his dedicatee directly as 'ilustrísima María' [most illustrious María] in the first line of stanza 7 that the nature of the relationship between María and Venus (or the celestial Venus and the terrestrial Venus) becomes clear.[41] Stanzas 9–10 draw on the tale of Cleopatra and the two pearls. In Pliny, *Natural History*, IX.59, Cleopatra dissolves one of a pair of valuable pearls in vinegar before drinking the solution. Saved from the same fate, the second pearl is then dedicated to Venus by Augustus. In Lope's poem it is this now unique pearl that is captured by the divine features of Olivares's daughter. In a second address to 'ilustrísima María' she is cast as the phoenix, the mythical Arabian bird of eternal rebirth. Exploiting the idea of a family line without end, the long introductory section thus closes with an expression of hope for María's future well-being and, by extension, the continuation of the illustrious house of Guzmán.

Whereas Lope's panegyric suggests that the poem will focus on the original subject of the white rose, its origins, and its dedication to María, the main body of the poem (stanzas 12–89) reverts to tales about Venus and the red rose: her birth and arrival on Olympus (12–14); the gods' courtship of Venus and her eventual marriage to Vulcan (15–25); the birth of Cupid (26–30) and then, some years later, Anteros (31–6); the tale of Mars, Venus, and Vulcan (37–52); the marriage of Thetis and Peleus (53–5); the Judgement of Paris and the start of the Trojan War (56–64); the tale of Venus and Adonis (65–71); the birth of the red rose (72–4); a second struggle between Juno, Pallas Athene, and Venus over the dedication of this new flower (75–82); the resulting duel between Athene and an Armed Venus (83–7); and Jupiter's placing of the Rose of Discord in a

---

[39] Cov. s.v. *armiño*: 'para encarecer la blancura de alguna cosa decimos ser blanca como un armiño.'

[40] The dedication in stanzas 4–11 of 'La Circe' presents Olivares as the moon to Philip IV's sun, in line with the conceit of the Planet King: 'que mientras duerme el sol, velando puede | sustituir su luz vuestro cuidado' (lines 41–2). For more on this conceit, see Elliott, *The Count-Duke of Olivares*, 177–8.

[41] Repeated in lines 10*d* and 109*b*, these words recall the addresses to 'ilustre y hermosísima María' at the start of Garcilaso's Third Eclogue and in the opening line of a 1583 sonnet in imitation of Garcilaso by Góngora.

temple in a wood sacred to Flora (88–9).[42] Only at this point does the poet signal the end of this lengthy digression and begin his song about the white rose: 'llega la ocasión, hermosa Venus | en que se ha de cantar tu blanca rosa' [here comes the point, beautiful Venus, at which one has to sing about your white rose] (89*g–h*). Jupiter falls for Amaryllis, a beautiful nymph whose complexion mirrors that of the red rose.[43] When, out of spite, his wife Juno turns the red rose white, ruining Amaryllis's complexion, Jupiter returns all but six petals to their original colour, thus not only restoring but in fact enhancing Amaryllis's beauty. Enraged, Juno scatters the flower's petals only for separate red and white roses to spring from the ground as it takes up the petals. The poem comes to a swift conclusion in the final stanza with a return to the poem's frame, a final comparison between María and the white rose, and the promise of an epithalamium in her honour.

The source for the majority of the tales contained in Lope's potted biography of Venus is almost certainly Vitoria's *Teatro*, which was published just shortly before *La Circe*, in 1620–3. The fact that Lope wrote an *aprobación*, dated 2 September 1619, for the *Primera parte*, in which he praises Vitoria's 'suma lección, y erudición' [supreme learning and erudition], suggests that he was well acquainted with the work.[44] Vitoria's compendium had, of course, already carried out the task of compiling stories relating to Venus; in the 'Libro sexto de la diosa Venus' of the *Segunda parte*, Vitoria dedicates over a hundred pages to the one goddess. In these pages, which draw on a whole host of classical and Renaissance authorities, he discusses both well-known stories associated with Venus, including the birth of Cupid, the tale of Venus and Adonis, and the origins of the red rose, and more recondite ones, such as the birth of Anteros, the tale of Cleopatra and the pearls, and the duel between Pallas Athene and the Armed Venus—all tales present in 'La rosa blanca'.[45] Other tales central to Lope's poem mentioned only in passing in this book receive more detailed coverage elsewhere; the marriage of Thetis and Peleus and

---

[42] For a summary of each inset episode, see María de la Almudena Zapata Ferrer, 'La mitología en *La rosa blanca* de Lope de Vega', in Francisca Moya del Baño (ed.), *Los humanistas españoles y el humanismo europeo (IV simposio de filología clásica)* (Murcia: Secretariado de Publicaciones, Universidad de Murcia, 1990), 261–6.

[43] Amaryllis is often seen as a mask for Lope's then love Marta de Nevares; see e.g. Pedraza Jiménez, *El universo poético*, 173.

[44] For his part, Vitoria certainly knew Lope's work well; the *Teatro* contains numerous citations of poems by Lope, including, for example, the following sonnets from the *Rimas*: 'Cleopatra a Antonio, en oloroso vino' (no. 3), 'Sentado Endimión al pie de Atlante' (no. 16), 'La antigua edad juzgó por imposibles' (no. 74), 'Pasando el mar el engañoso toro' (no. 87), 'Atada al mar Andrómeda, lloraba' (no. 89), 'Perderá de los cielos la belleza' (no. 99), and 'Al rey Niño, Semíramis famosa' (no. 187).

[45] Baltasar de Vitoria, 'Libro sexto de la diosa Venus', in *Segunda parte del Teatro de los dioses de la gentilidad* (Madrid: Imprenta Real, 1657 [1623]), 347–466.

the Judgement of Paris, for example, are discussed at length in the chapter on Paris in the book on Jupiter in the *Primera parte*.

Vitoria's handbook provides the inspiration not only for Lope's choice of tales, but also for many of the specific details found in individual sections of the poem. In the build-up to the tale of Mars, Venus, and Vulcan, Lope tells the stories of the births of Cupid and Anteros, both of which are included in chapter 7 of Vitoria's book on Venus, entitled 'De Cupido hijo de la Diosa Venus' [On Cupid, the Son of the Goddess Venus]. According to Lope, Cupid is either the result of an affair between Venus and Mercury (26), the child of Chaos (28*a–d*), or the offspring of Poros, god of abundance, and Penia, goddess of poverty (28*e–h*). All three possibilities are given by Vitoria. Lope also seems to follow Vitoria on the subject of the birth of Anteros. When, after seven years, Cupid stops growing, a distraught Venus consults the oracle Themis in the hope of a solution. The oracle declares that Cupid needs a sibling to return his affection in order to continue to grow. It is only at this point that Venus turns her attention to Mars, having earlier rejected his courtship. When Venus first arrived in the heavens soon after her birth, Mars and Apollo were the first two gods to compete for her attention, 'entrambos encendidos | en rayos, en amor, en ira, en celos' [both consumed by pain, love, anger, and jealousy] (15*g–h*). In stanza 16, in an extended version of the battlefield-of-love metaphor, Mars charges at Venus as if she were an opposing army, brandishing his phallic 'fogosa espada' [ardent sword]. The failure of this comical attempt at courtship leads to a dramatic change in attitude. Learning the art of a more benign form of warfare, Mars the soldier soon turns into Mars the lover, as he abandons the 'fosos y trincheras' [moats and trenches] (32*h*) associated with real military conflict for the 'dulcísimas batallas' [most sweet battles] (32*f*) of love. Stanzas 33–4 underline this marked change of disposition, detailing the arms discarded by Mars in order to engage with Venus on the battlefield of love. Lope's Mars has, it seems, anticipated the advice given by Cueva's Venus: a long list of weapons, defensive fortifications, and siege engines has already been exchanged for diamonds, civilian clothing, and longing sighs. When the trappings of Mars's past military splendour are placed as an offering at her feet, this time Venus is more receptive to Mars's overtures:

> Venus, que vio sus armas arrogantes,
> sus banderas, sus tropas y gobiernos
> rendidos a sus pies, quiso piadosa
> ser Palas a su lado belicosa. (34*e–h*)

[When she saw his proud arms, flags, troops, and estates lying in tribute at her feet, she was moved to want to be a warlike Pallas Athene at his side.]

Having seen Mars adopt characteristics associated with the lover, Venus dreams of being a soldier and taking the place of Pallas Athene at Mars's side on the battlefield. The notion of the exchanging of roles takes the Neoplatonic theory of *discordia concors* to its logical extreme, marking another important stage in the shift towards burlesque accounts of Mars's courtship of Venus. Following this courtship, the gods immediately consummate their relationship. Anteros is born in the first line of the very next stanza, and, as soon as he reaches Cupid's age, Cupid begins to grow again in the face of reciprocated love.[46]

The tale of the birth of Anteros provides the background for Venus's affair with Mars, thus serving as an introduction to the story of Mars, Venus, and Vulcan. However, whilst Lope's account of the story of Anteros follows Vitoria's closely, his version of the tale under examination does not follow the one included in the book on Mars at the end of the first part of the *Teatro*, which, as we saw in Chapter 1, combines elements from several different classical sources. Lope's telling begins in stanza 37 when the sun finds its way into the house of 'bárbaro Vulcano' [barbaric Vulcan] without anyone noticing. Whereas in previous tellings Apollo's horror on discovering the affair was at least in part the result of moral indignation and/or a concern for Vulcan's honour, here it is simply the product of burning envy. Indeed, Apollo is so envious of Mars that he fails to heat the earth and light the heavens for an entire month. It is envy that drives his decision to visit Vulcan, a decision condemned as unworthy of such a figure: 'El sol, en fin, para tan noble lumbre | ejecutó la más indigna hazaña | . . . ' [In short, for such a noble light, the sun carried out the most disgraceful deed . . .] (38*a–b*).

A considerable proportion of Lope's account is dedicated to the exchange that ensues between Apollo and Vulcan. Lope's rendering of this exchange draws out some of its dramatic potential, placing emphasis on matters relating to honour, social reputation, and the world of 'el qué dirán' [what will people say?]. In a departure from his traditional role as messenger, Apollo begins not by informing Vulcan of what he has just seen but by rebuking the smith for knowingly putting up with Venus's affairs:

> «¿Cómo sufres, Vulcano, tanta afrenta?
> ¿Cómo permites que te ofenda Marte?
> Bastardos hijos en tu casa intenta;
> en Anteros y Amor no tienes parte.» (39*a–d*)

['How, Vulcan, do you put up with such an affront? How do you let Mars offend you? He's making bastard children in your house; you didn't father Anteros and Cupid.']

---

[46] For an earlier version of the story of Anteros/Contramor, see lines 97–138 of Herrera's elegy '¿Qu'onor vos pudo dar, bella enemiga, . . . ?', in *Poesía castellana*, 768–73.

The fact that Vulcan is seemingly already aware of his wife's infidelity, and thus to some extent content to accept it, marks another important stage in the development of representations of the tale. Apollo acts as the voice of social conscience, asking Vulcan how he can bear such an affront to his honour and chastising him for housing bastard sons in Cupid (fathered by Mercury) and Anteros. Because Vulcan's sons look nothing like him, they serve as a constant sign of his dishonour; their hair alone makes it clear that Vulcan is not their biological father. Apollo continues in stanza 40 by contrasting Mars's 'celada bélica' [military helmet], the helmet that Mars has long since abandoned, with his own 'corona de rayos' [crown of rays], the solar nimbus that sheds light on the lovers' affair. After boasting that there is nothing that his rays cannot illuminate, Apollo calls on Vulcan to take revenge, if not out of love for Venus then at least out of a concern for his own honour: 'Yo los he visto; la venganza intenta; | si no te mueve amor, basta la afrenta' [I have seen them; take revenge; if love doesn't spur you on then the affront should be enough to do so] (40g–h).

The first half of stanza 41 describes Vulcan's reaction to Apollo's 'funesta relación' [terrible story]. The fact that Vulcan's pale face is 'teñido | en humo, en ira y en dolor tan nuevo' [marked with smoke, anger, and such fresh pain] (41c–d) prepares the reader for a response similar to that of Cueva's Vulcan. However, the reader's expectations are turned upside down by the smith's reply: Vulcan rejects Apollo's claim and implies that the sun-god is lying. Playing with a series of basic oppositions—light/dark, insight/blindness, reality/illusion, truth/deceit, and honour/dishonour—he accuses him of imprudence, criticizes him for allowing his actions to be motivated by envy, and states that Apollo's words represent the only real threat to his honour:

> «¡Oh cuantas veces miras malicioso
> cosas en que te engañas! Ni tú puedes
> entrar en todas partes, y celoso
> atientas con tus rayos las paredes;
> soñaste, Sol, o amante o envidioso;
> dormiste, Sol, de la verdad excedes;
> y ¿qué puede decir un sol dormido
> de un planeta de luz de honor vestido?
>
> Venus es mi mujer, Marte mi amigo,
> y tú enemigo, Sol, que solo basta;
> pues ¿quién ha de creer a un enemigo
> en deshonor de una mujer tan casta?
> Contenta vive de vivir conmigo;

montañas de oro y de valor contrasta;
lo que has dicho en mi afrenta fue bajeza;
mas eres sol, y dasme en la cabeza.» (42–3)

['Oh, how many times, out of malice, you see things you're wrong about!
Not even you can get in everywhere, and, racked by jealousy, you feel for the
walls with your rays. You were dreaming, Sun, as either a lover or someone
consumed by envy. You were sleeping, Sun; you've gone beyond the truth.
And what can a sleeping sun say about a planet dressed in the light of honour? Venus is my wife, Mars my friend, and you, Sun, an enemy, and that's
that; because who's going to believe an enemy who speaks ill of such a chaste
woman? She lives contentedly living with me, offsetting even mountains of
gold and the power it has. The affront you've caused me was a despicable act;
but you're the sun, and you come striking me on the head.']

Vulcan questions Apollo's claim to be all-seeing, stating that he has confused
dream with reality, that envy has led him to stumble around in the dark,
and that there are some places that even he cannot reach. Undermined by
the implicit allusion to the horns of cuckoldry in the phrase 'da[r] en la
cabeza', Vulcan's impassioned rebuttal is rendered absurd by the dramatic
irony that results from the reader's knowledge of the build-up to this exchange. The smith was first introduced in stanza 21 as the last of Venus's
suitors. Though ugly, deformed, and self-deluded, he was chosen as her
husband, the competition for her hand humorously likened to a fight between bulls over a cow which ends with the spoils being taken by '[el] más
cobarde y flaco' [the weakest and most cowardly] (23*g*). Venus despises her
new husband because of his limp, thick beard, and satyr-like features, and
immediately turns her attentions elsewhere. The amusing description of
Vulcan in stanza 25 as both a 'retrógrado cancro' [crab that scuttles back-
wards] and a 'camello asirio' [Assyrian camel] marks the crippled hunchback out as a slow and dim-witted cuckold. The backstory formed by the
sections on Venus's marriage to Vulcan and the births of Cupid and Anteros thus makes a mockery of Vulcan's pretence of marital bliss, his claim
to count Mars amongst his friends, and his praise of Venus as a virtuous
goddess clothed in 'luz de honor'.

When a chastened Apollo leaves, it becomes immediately apparent
that Vulcan's response was simply an exercise in maintaining the façade of
social appearance. He knows Apollo to have been right, but the honour
code to which he adheres demands that he reject the sun-god's claims.
Like many figures on the contemporary stage, Vulcan says one thing
and does another. While his words are shaped by the need to save face in
front of one of his peers, his subsequent actions are designed to restore his
honour. In marrying Venus, a woman to whom he was totally unsuited,

Vulcan had demonstrated the archetypal Golden Age sin of *necedad* [folly]. Now, however, he is 'más cuerdo en responder que fue en casarse' [wiser in reacting than he was in getting married] (44*d*). Vulcan considers throwing himself into the forge, before tempering the fire of his rage with the water from his tears. Unlike Cueva's Vulcan, Lope's smith says nothing to his assistants, as making news of his wife's infidelity public at this stage would merely compound his dishonour. When the sun rises and reminds him of his predicament, Vulcan wanders metaphorically 'de dolor en dolor' [from grief to grief] and literally 'de monte en monte' [from hill to hill] pondering the right course of action. The statements used to explain Vulcan's silent deliberation—'quien mucho quiere hacer no dice nada' [someone with plenty to do says nothing] (45*b*) and 'un prudente | no resuelve lo grave fácilmente' [wise men don't take difficult decisions lightly] (45*g–h*)—are two of a number of sententiae found in the poem.[47]

The decision to forge the net is taken only when other solutions have been rejected:

> Y viendo que morir era imposible
> Venus, siendo inmortal, que muerte y diosa
> era imaginación incompatible,
> por implicar contradicción forzosa;
> hizo una red sutil, tan invisible
> que la alta rueda del pastor famosa
> por sus cien ojos verla no pudiera,
> si cada verde pluma un lince fuera. (46)

[And seeing as, being immortal, Venus could not die—for death and divinity were never compatible and to imagine them as such would be a violent contradiction—he made a fine net, so invisible that even the hundred eyes—once those of the shepherd Argus—set in the peacock's famed arching tail-plumage could not see it, even if each green feather possessed the vision of a lynx.]

In an allusion to the dramatic convention of uxoricide, Vulcan's first thought is to wash clean the stain of dishonour with Venus's blood. However, the simple fact that she is a goddess, and thus immortal, makes killing Venus, or sacrificing her to the false god of his honour, impossible. Vulcan thus forges the net in order to catch her *in flagrante*. Through a combination of periphrasis, erudite allusion, and hyperbole, Lope gives an original twist to the description of the net's traditional invisibility. To unlock the conceit in the second half of the above stanza, the reader must know the

---

[47] For an analysis of the presence and function of such remarks in *La Circe*, see Ernest Martineche, '*La Circe* y los poemas mitológicos de Lope', *Humanidades*, 4 (1922), 59–66.

tale of Io, as told in Ovid, *Metamorphoses*, I.568–749. The hundred-eyed *pastor* is the all-seeing giant Argus (Panoptes), who was charged by Juno with guarding Io—a beautiful girl who had been transformed into a white heifer—from her husband Jupiter's amorous advances. When Argus was killed by Mercury, at Jupiter's behest, Juno set the shepherd's eyes into the long train feathers of her royal bird, the peacock. Even if each of the one hundred eyes set in the peacock's green tail feathers had the sight of a lynx, an 'animal de aguda vista' [animal with keen sight] (Cov.), they would still not be able to make out the net. In lines of notable conceptual density, Lope thus obliges his reader to work through a chain of associations, from the hundred eyes of the shepherd Argus to the green tail feathers of the peacock and finally to the sharp-sightedness of the lynx.

At this point in Lope's telling, the scene switches not to Vulcan's marital bed but to a pastoral *locus amoenus*. The lovers are enjoying a post-coital midday siesta in a green meadow through which runs a gentle stream that reflects Venus's snowy-white foot.[48] Whilst the lovers sleep off their exertions, Cupid plays with Mars's helmet, sword, and shield. He covets the figures depicted in relief on Mars's golden shield, a potential rival to the shield of Achilles forged by Hephaestus described in the aforementioned ekphrasis in Homer, *Iliad*, XVIII.478–617. In stanza 48 Cupid and Anteros fight over the plumes in Mars's helmet, tearing out white and purple feathers described using commonplace *culto* metaphors as 'cándidas espumas' [white foam] and 'la morada flor del amaranto' [the purple flower of the amaranth] (48c–d). The description of their games underlines the point that the naked, sleeping Mars has been conquered by love: 'post proelia victor | victus amore' (Reposianus, *De Concubitu*, lines 77–8). The final couplet of the stanza underlines through hyperbole the power that Venus holds over Mars: 'para igualar de Venus los amores | no tiene arena el mar ni el campo flores' [the sea does not have as much sand nor the country-side as many flowers as Venus has Amores]. The setting of this scene in a *locus amoenus*, the focus on the lovers' post-coital repose, the image of the children playing with Mars's arms, and the overriding sense of 'omnia vincit amor' [love conquers all] (Virgil, *Eclogues*, x.69) all recall Sandro Botticelli's depiction of a similar scene in his *Venus and Mars* (c.1485; Fig. 3.1). While it is unlikely that Lope had ever seen Botticelli's painting,

---

[48] The scene recalls the opening stanza of the sonnet 'La clara luz, en las estrellas puesta' (no. 139) in Lope's *Rimas*; the rest of the sonnet sees Venus don Mars's arms and travel through Greece to Thebes, where she rebuffs a challenge from Pallas Athene with the words 'Cuando te atrevas, | verás cuánto mejor te vence armada | la que desnuda te venció primero' [When you dare, you'll see just how much more easily the one who conquered you when naked will conquer you again when armed], a boast that is echoed in 'La rosa blanca' in the section on the Armed Venus (87c–d).

Fig. 3.1. Sandro Botticelli, *Venus and Mars*, *c*.1485. Tempera and oil on poplar.

the similarity between the two scenes, one poetic, the other pictorial, is striking. The two works may share a common source in Reposianus's *De Concubitu*, which, as we saw in Chapter 1, paints a detailed portrait of Cupid playing with Mars's arms—testing the weight of his lance, hiding in his helmet upon the arrival of Vulcan, and marvelling at the power of his own arrows—as the god of war recovers next to Venus.[49]

Vulcan destroys the harmony and tranquillity of this idyllic scene by imprisoning the lovers—and, in a novel detail, Cupid and Anteros as well—at the start of the very next stanza. As in Reposianus's poem, Vulcan throws the net over the lovers as they sleep outdoors rather than setting it as a trap for them to fall into indoors.[50] In the second half of stanza 49 an incongruous simile sees the smith's action of trapping the lovers and exposing their crime to the heavens likened to that of an osprey (*aleto indiano*) sinking its curved beak into hapless wood pigeons (*tímidas torcaces*). A simple tricolon sums up the gods' response to the spectacle in the first half of stanza 50: Mars's plight is met with *envidia* [envy], Venus's with *celos* [jealousy], and Vulcan's with *dolor* [grief]. Instead of commenting on the traditional laughter of the gods, Lope draws on another simile to describe the lovers' struggle in the invisible and unbreakable net:

> Como suelen los peces ignorantes
> estar entre la red, el fuerte acero
> romper querían, mas no fue posible;
> que era muy fuerte, aunque era imperceptible. (50*e*–*h*)

[49] In 12–14 Lope's description of Venus's birth recalls Botticelli's painting of the same subject: born from the foam of the sea, Venus is propelled in her scallop shell by a 'blando céfiro' [gentle zephyr] to the shore of Cyprus, where she is taken up to the heavens by the Hours.

[50] As seen in Chapter 1, the image of Vulcan preparing to throw the net directly over the lovers is also common in cycles of illustrations of Ovid's *Metamorphoses* from Salomon and Solis onwards.

[As is usually the case with foolish fish when caught, they tried to break the strong steel of the net, but it was not possible, because it was very strong, even though it was invisible.]

In a development of the absurd idea of Vulcan as a fish-eating bird of prey, the lovers are compared to foolish fish struggling in vain to break free from the clutches of their captor. The long Homeric denouement, followed faithfully by Cueva, is rejected in favour of a much briefer conclusion:

> Pero a ruego de Júpiter salieron
> dando palabra Marte mal cumplida,
> que la que amando los peligros dieron,
> no fue jurada cuando fue rompida. (51*a–d*)

[But at Jupiter's plea they were set free, with Mars making a promise he would not keep, for the oath made in the midst of danger was no sooner sworn than broken.]

The telling included in Vitoria's *Teatro* follows Homer's account with regard to Neptune's role as negotiator. In 'La rosa blanca', however, it is Jupiter who secures the lovers' freedom—a change perhaps made with one eye on Jupiter's involvement in the innovative Amaryllis episode that takes up the final third of the poem. Lope alludes to the question of compensation but reworks this Homeric motif to begin the transition to the next part of Venus's biography. Mars promises to pay his debt to Vulcan but breaks his word as soon as he has given it. Such is Mars's response to the episode that Venus forgets all about him. Rather than being continued in the open, as is the case in the *Ars Amatoria*, the affair comes to a sudden and bitter end, as in the fragment of Aldana's poem in *octavas*. Despite her rejection of Mars, Venus does not return to Vulcan: such is her hatred of the ugly smith, now continually 'teñido en humo infame' [stained with disgusting smoke] (52*b*), that she seeks to distract herself with yet more *necedad* (52*e*).

The next chapter of Venus's biography begins with the marriage of Thetis and Peleus, which in turn leads into the Judgement of Paris. Whereas in Cueva's poem this episode predates the shaming of Mars and Venus, the reverse holds true here. When, in the next section, Venus falls for Adonis, a jealous Mars enlists the help of the Fury Alecto to have the handsome youth killed by a wild boar whilst his rival is out hunting. Seeing an opportunity to rekindle their affair, Mars chases Venus across both land and the night sky. One day, whilst fleeing from her ex-lover, Venus cuts her foot on a hidden bramble and the red rose forms from the blood spilt on the grass. As outlined above, the remaining stanzas tell the story of the origins of the white rose. First formed when Juno turns the red rose white, the white rose is formed again when Juno scatters the six white petals of the bicolour rose in the penultimate stanza. The potentially negative connotations of the red rose dedicated to Venus—lust, unbridled passion, and the transience of beauty and human life—are replaced by the unequivocally positive connotations of the white rose dedicated to María de Guzmán, which is much rarer than the red rose and, like the 'clara y ilustrísima María', 'cándida, pura, casta, honesta, hermosa' [white, pure, chaste, honest, beautiful] (109*b–c*). The poem thus comes full circle, returning to the original subject outlined in the opening stanzas.

In line with El Brocense's famous dictum, 'no tengo por buen poeta al que no imita los excelentes antiguos' [I do not consider anyone who does not imitate the excellent ancients to be a good poet], both Cueva and Lope borrow heavily from classical and Renaissance accounts of the story of Mars, Venus, and Vulcan.[51] However, whilst adhering to its basic outline, they develop the tale inherited from their forebears in new directions. They do so chiefly by drawing out the tale, collating it with other stories, and adding to it details suggested by a wide range of intermediaries, including translations of classical texts such as Pérez's *La Ulyxea*, mythological handbooks such as Vitoria's *Teatro*, and popular miscellanies such as Ravisius Textor's *Officina*. Like Seneca's bees, both Cueva and Lope draw inspiration from a number of sources, fusing such influences into distinct narratives that simultaneously both conceal and betray their hybrid origins.[52] Rather than compressing the tale into economical allusions which prick the intellect and imagination of the reader, they expand and rework it to create rival tellings that not only delight the reader with their variety but also surprise him/her with their unexpected departures from tradition.

Whilst, unlike their contemporary, the English Renaissance playwright Thomas Heywood, neither of them wrote a play on the subject, both Cueva and Lope appear to have been acutely aware of the potential for dramatic development inherent in the tale of Mars, Venus, and Vulcan.[53] To cite one of Lope's famous pronouncements from the *Arte nuevo*, 'Los

---

[51] *Garcilaso de la Vega y sus comentaristas*, 23.

[52] The commonplace metaphor for the practice of *imitatio* of bees gathering pollen from flowers and converting it into honey is seen in Seneca, *Epistulae Morales*, 84.3–5; for a brief discussion of the classical roots of this Renaissance topos, see *Antiquity and its Interpreters*, ed. Alina Payne, Ann Kuttner, and Rebekah Smick (Cambridge: Cambridge University Press, 2000), 10.

[53] The tale is reworked in Act IV of Heywood's play *The Brazen Age* (1613), in which Mars, Venus, and Vulcan appear on stage, alongside Apollo, Jupiter, Neptune, Mercury, Gallus, and Homer.

casos de la honra son mejores | porque mueven con fuerza a toda gente'
[Affairs of honour are best because they move everyone most forcefully].[54]
Perhaps both poet-playwrights were attracted to the tale because they saw
in it a ready-made 'caso de la honra', a plot steeped in jealousy, betrayal,
and revenge, and a colourful cast of clearly defined characters. As demonstrated above, both Cueva and Lope make important changes to the tale,
the majority of which serve first and foremost to tease out its dramatic
qualities. To a story already rich in drama, both poets add a number of
scenes, exchanges, and devices drawn straight from the world of contemporary Golden Age theatre. This fact can be seen, for example, in Vulcan's
untimely and unexpected returns home at night, his fierce rebuttals of
others' claims, his secret machinations and thoughts of wife-murder, his
overriding fear of dishonour, and his all-consuming need for revenge. In
both poems Vulcan plays to perfection the part of the husband wronged
by an unfaithful wife, a stock character on the contemporary stage. In
order to appreciate the innovative aspects of 'Los amores' and 'La rosa
blanca', the reader must, therefore, have both a firm grasp of previous tellings of the story of Mars, Venus, and Vulcan and an appreciation of the
wider context of the literary culture of the late sixteenth and early seventeenth centuries.

Whilst on one level Cueva and Lope saw in the tale a serious 'caso de la
honra', on another they saw a tale ripe for comic, even burlesque, treatment.
Another of Lope's dramatic precepts calls for 'lo trágico y lo cómico mez-
clado' [tragedy and comedy mixed together]; this mixing of the serious and
the comic, a hallmark of many works of Golden Age literature, is evident
in both 'Los amores' and 'La rosa blanca'. Though neither is an example of
the burlesque epic—a genre which has its roots in the *Batrachomyomachia*
and which finds expression in the Golden Age in works including Cueva's
La Muracinda (c.1608), Villaviciosa's *La Mosquea* (1615), and Lope's *La
Gatomaquia* (1634)—both poems display a number of features readily associated with mock-heroic. Much of the humour in them springs from
the addition of elements of farce, bathos, cliché, and dramatic irony. As
we have seen, a number of patently absurd or incongruous details also
punctuates the two tellings, with the gods fighting like bulls for the right to
mate with a prize cow, voluminous rivers of tears cascading down Vulcan's
face, the arch-cripple suddenly acquiring incredible fleetness of foot, the
smith swooping down on Mars and Venus like a bird of prey on a helpless
quarry, and the lovers wriggling like foolish fish caught in a net. In both
poems simile, metaphor, and erudite allusion are frequently employed to
pull the tone down, tipping the balance between the serious and the comic

---

[54] *Arte nuevo*, 149 (lines 327–8).

firmly in favour of the latter. Such details also help lend the two tellings, in the words of Gracián, 'la variedad, gran madre de la belleza' [variety, the great mother of beauty], and, as Lope explains in the *Arte nuevo*, 'aquesta variedad deleita mucho; | buen ejemplo nos da naturaleza, | que por tal variedad tiene belleza' [this variety pleases greatly; we find a good example of this in nature, whose beauty lies in its variety].[55]

Both 'Los amores' and 'La rosa blanca' hint, in their treatments of the gods and their affairs, at some of the directions in which the tale will be taken in the full-blown burlesques of Castillo Solórzano, Polo de Medina, Barrios, and others. As was the case with some of the poems discussed in the previous chapter, Cueva's and Lope's portraits of the gods present in embryonic form caricatures of Mars as a braggadocio, Venus as a prostitute, and Vulcan as a cuckold. The fleshing out of the backstory of the lovers' affair, which represents a significant addition to the basic narrative, gives both poets scope to sketch out these portraits and at the same time playfully to rework aspects of Petrarchan and Neoplatonic tradition. In both poems it is Mars who has to placate Venus, not the other way around; to do so he must pawn the trappings of his past military splendour, for words are powerless in comparison with money. Both poets play on a contrast between the boastful soldier's failure and the fawning lover's success in winning Venus over. In his description of Mars's courtship of her, Cueva depicts Venus as mercenary, open to bribery, and conversant in the language of buying and selling. Though Cueva does not make the link with prostitution explicit, the fact that Venus wears make-up, 'remedio que enseñó Naturaleza | para suplir las faltas de belleza' [a solution introduced by Nature to make up for beauty flaws] (8*g–h*; and 9*e–f*), suggests that she may carry certain physical and, by extension, moral blemishes associated with that oldest of professions.[56] Last but not least, Lope's succinct allusions to the smith's famed deformity (*retrógrado cancro, camello asirio,* etc.) and the hint that the wronged husband had known all along about his wife's infidelity point to the fate that awaits Vulcan in later tellings.

In sum, then, the two poems analysed in this chapter represent another important stage in the development of Golden Age treatments of the tale of Mars, Venus, and Vulcan. Cueva's dramatic amplification of the tale in 'Los amores' and Lope's imaginative reframing of it in 'La rosa blanca'

---

[55] Baltasar Gracián, *Agudeza y arte de ingenio*, ed. Evaristo Correa Calderón, CC, 14–15, 2 vols. (Madrid: Castalia, 2001), i. 48; Lope de Vega, *Arte nuevo*, 141 (lines 178–80).

[56] In *Los inventores de las cosas* (1607), iv.361–2, Cueva credits Venus with inventing this trade: 'Venus, fue la qu'el arte meretricia | inventó en Chipre . . . ' [Venus was the one who invented the art of prostitution in Cyprus]; Juan de la Cueva, *Los inventores de las cosas*, ed. Beno Weiss and Louis C. Pérez (Pennsylvania: Pennsylvania State University Press, 1980), 130.

offer two contrasting yet complementary responses to the tale under consideration. Together, they represent something of a halfway house: between serious imitation and burlesque parody; between unquestioning reworking of topoi inherited from the Petrarchan and Neoplatonic traditions and unrelenting subversion of the very same topoi; and between flattering portraits of the pagan gods as embodiments of divine virtues and irreverent caricatures of them as personifications of human vices. As such, they not only explore the implications of some of the details present in the erudite allusions discussed in the previous chapter but also pave the way for the sustained burlesques that are the subject of the next.

4

Mythological Burlesques: Pimps, Prostitutes, and *Pacientes*

Yo espero ver vuestro endiosamiento muerto de hambre, por falta de víctimas, y de frío, sin que alcancéis una morcilla por sacrificios, ocupados en sólo abultar poemas y poblar coplones, gastados en consonantes y en apodos amorosos, sirviendo de munición a los chistes y a las pullas.[1]

[I hope to see your deification die of hunger, thanks to a lack of victims, and of cold, without you getting even a blood sausage as a sacrifical offering, and you all doing nothing more than bulking out poems and inhabiting the pages of doggerel, used up as rhyme words and pet names, serving as ammunition for jokes and gibes.]

At the end of the sixteenth century and the beginning of the seventeenth, as the mythological tradition reached its peak in Spain, a vogue for humorous reworkings of mythological tales developed. Though, from the 1580s onwards, serious treatments of classical tales were still very much in evidence, more and more writers turned to parody, burlesque, and the grotesque when depicting the pagan gods and their affairs. Though, as we have seen, the adoption of humorous approaches to the gods of Olympus was not an invention of the late sixteenth century, nor indeed peculiar to Spain, mythological burlesque became one of the most popular sub-genres in Spain in the seventeenth century, as writers began to exploit mythological subjects as platforms for spectacular fireworks of humour, wordplay, and metaphysical wit.[2] By 1635, the date of publication of

---

[1] Francisco de Quevedo, *La Hora de todos y la Fortuna con seso*, ed. Jean Bourg, Pierre Dupont, and Pierre Geneste, LH, 276 (Madrid: Cátedra, 1987), 160.
[2] For examples of humorous treatments of the gods in Italy, France, and England, see e.g. Francesco Bracciolini, *Lo scherno degli dei* (Venice: Paolo Guerrigli, 1618); Charles Coypeau d'Assoucy, *L'Ovide en belle humeur* (Lyons: Nicolas Gay, 1650); and Alexander Radcliffe, *Ovidius exulans, or, Ovid travestie: A mock-poem on five epistles of Ovid* (London: Peter Lillicrap, 1673).

Quevedo's *La Hora de todos y la Fortuna con seso* [The Hour of All Men and Fortune with Wisdom], the curse hurled by Fortune on the 'fallen pantheon' of the pagan gods had already become reality.[3]

Whilst mythological burlesque was often incorporated into works of prose, as in the prologue and epilogue to *La Hora de todos* and the closing lines of the 'Premática del desengaño contra los poetas güeros, chirles y hebenes' [Proclamation against crap, shit, and pointless poets] in Quevedo's picaresque novel *El Buscón* [The Swindler] (1626), it was particularly prevalent in works of poetry. Examples of mythological burlesque can be found in many of the poetic forms current at the time, including the sonnet (e.g. Hurtado de Mendoza's '¡Oh Venus, alcahueta y hechicera!' or Quevedo's pieces on the tale of Apollo and Daphne, 'Bermejazo platero de las cumbres' (Q536) and 'Tras vos, un alquimista va corriendo' (Q537)), the *silva* (e.g. Gabriel del Corral's 'Fábula de las tres diosas'), the *octava real* (e.g. Castillo Solórzano's 'Fábula de Polifemo', a *contrafactum* of Góngora's *Polifemo*), and the *romance*.[4] Whereas, as we have seen, the *octava* was the most popular vehicle for extensive serious, or indeed mock-heroic, treatments of classical tales, the traditional *romance* became the most common form for extensive burlesque tellings of the same narratives.

Góngora's tellings of the stories of Hero and Leander ('Arrojóse el mancebito' (1589) and 'Aunque entiendo poco griego' (1610)), and Pyramus and Thisbe ('De Tisbe y Píramo quiero' (1604) and 'La ciudad de Babilonia' (1618)), mark important stages in the development of the mythological burlesque in Spain. The first pair of ballads depicts Hero and Leander not as tragic star-crossed lovers but as foolish and self-deceiving slaves to the Deadly Sin of Lust. In the very first line of the 1589 ballad, in which Leander is introduced with the derogatory diminutive *mancebito*, Góngora signposts the fact that his will not be a respectful, sentimental account of the story. In the rest of the poem he goes on to develop vulgar sexual and scatological wordplay to make the point that the lovers are not to be pitied, but rather condemned for their stupidity, their immodesty (in every sense of the word), and their 'upside-down values'.[5] The second pair, which recounts the 'lamentable comedy and most cruel death of Pyramus and Thisby' (Shakespeare, *A Midsummer Night's Dream*, I.ii.), is based on the same mismatch between subject and tone. Góngora's *Fábula de Píramo y Tisbe* of 1618 ('La ciudad de Babilonia'), a 508-line tour de

---

[3] The term 'fallen pantheon' is borrowed from James Iffland, *Quevedo and the Grotesque*, CTSA: Monografías, 69 and 72, 2 vols. (London: Tamesis, 1978–82), ii. 56.

[4] On these and other related poems, see *«Aunque entiendo poco griego … ». Fábulas mitológicas burlescas del Siglo de Oro*, ed. Elena Cano Turrión (Córdoba: Berenice, 2007).

[5] The term is taken from Southworth's detailed commentary on the 1589 poem (see Chapter 2, n. 63).

force of mock romance, vulgar slang, and mindless erudition, is his most sustained attack on both *necedad* and the high *culto* style associated with his own *Polifemo* and *Soledades*. In this ballad Góngora shows himself to be a master of both inappropriate detail and needless pedantry, as evinced by the first quatrain in which he questions whether or not the walls of Babylon were 'cooked or uncooked' (lines 3–4: 'fuesen de tierra cocidos | o sean de tierra crudos'), and by the portrait of Thisbe in which he draws an absurd odontological distinction between her twelve incisors and her twenty canines/molars (lines 63–4: 'entre veinte perlas netas | doce aljófares menudos').[6]

The earliest extant example of an unequivocally burlesque telling of the story of Mars, Venus, and Vulcan is by Alonso de Castillo Solórzano. Born in Tordesillas in or before 1584, Castillo Solórzano moved to Madrid in the late 1610s where he frequented the celebrated 'Academia de Madrid' of Francisco de Medrano and, later, Francisco de Mendoza.[7] Though now best known for a series of picaresque novels and short stories stretching over a period from the mid-1620s to the early 1640s—including *Tardes entretenidas* [Entertaining Evenings] (1625), *Las Harpías en Madrid* [The Harpies of Madrid] (1631), *La niña de los embustes, Teresa de Manzanares* [The Trickster Girl, Teresa de Manzanares] (1632), *Aventuras del bachiller Trapaza* [Adventures of Bachelor Trapaza] (1637), and *La garduña de Sevilla* [The Seville Thief] (1642)—his earliest extant work is a collection of light verse published in two parts in 1624 and 1625 under the title *Donaires del Parnaso* [Parnassus Pleasantries].[8] The fruits of Castillo

---

[6] Góngora had already revealed a playful attitude to these two tales in the early *letrilla* 'Ándeme yo caliente | y ríase la gente' (1581). This burlesque defence of the simple life (characterized by, amongst other things, birdsong, rustic food, and shaggy-dog stories) culminates in a rejection of commonplace sentimental tales. In the penultimate stanza swimming across the Hellespont to see one's beloved (in the style of Leander) is cast aside in favour of 'swimming' in home-made wine. The final stanza sees the poetic voice dreaming of Thisbe not as a tragic heroine impaled on a sword but as a delicious pastry impaled on his own tooth (lines 42–3: 'sea mi Tisbe un pastel, | y la espada sea mi diente').

[7] On Madrid academies, see Jeremy Robbins, *Love Poetry of the Literary Academies in the Reigns of Philip IV and Charles II*, CTSA: Monografías, 166 (London: Tamesis, 1997), esp. 7–46 (chapter 1: '"El seminario de los entendidos, el taller de los bien hablados, el colegio de los discretos": The Academy and Seventeenth-Century Spain').

[8] On Castillo Solórzano as poet and prose writer, see Peter N. Dunn, *Castillo Solórzano and the Decline of the Spanish Novel* (Oxford: B. Blackwell, 1952); Alan Soons, *Alonso de Castillo Solórzano*, TWAS, 457 (Boston: Twayne, 1978); Pablo Jauralde Pou, 'Alonso de Castillo Solórzano, *Donaires del Parnaso* y la *Fábula de Polifemo*', *Revista de Archivos, Bibliotecas y Museos*, 82 (1979), 727–66; Magdalena Velasco Kindelán, *La novela cortesana y picaresca de Castillo Solórzano* (Valladolid: Institución Cultural Simancas, 1983); Begoña Ripoll, 'Alonso de Castillo Solórzano', in *La novela barroca* (Salamanca: Universidad de Salamanca, 1991), 51–72; and Luciano López Gutiérrez, '"Donaires del Parnaso" de Alonso de Castillo Solórzano: edición, estudio y notas', doctoral thesis, Universidad Complutense de Madrid (2004) Available online at <http://eprints.ucm.es/4649/>.

Solórzano's labours during his time at the Madrid academy, the *Donaires* contain a number of mythological burlesques: in the first part, on Actaeon, the Rape of Europa, Pan and Syrinx, Apollo and Daphne, Polyphemus (i.e. the aforementioned *contrafactum*), and Adonis; and, in the second, on the birth of Vulcan.

The *Primera parte* also includes his 'Fábula de Marte y Venus' [Tale of Mars and Venus], a 454-line *romance* with a closing epigram in the form of a *décima*.[9] For reasons outlined below, this poem would have a profound influence on subsequent burlesque tellings of the myth. The second and third quarters of the seventeenth century saw several Castilian writers follow in Castillo Solórzano's footsteps by writing humorous accounts of the story in the traditional ballad form.[10] The first was the Murcian writer Salvador Jacinto Polo de Medina (1603–76). Having benefited in Murcia from the tutelage of the eminent humanist Francisco Cascales, in 1630 Polo de Medina travelled to Madrid where he became associated with the circle of Lope de Vega and Pérez de Montalbán. Later that year, under Lope's supervision, he published his earliest known works, the *Academias del jardín* [Academies of the Garden], a miscellany inspired by academy sessions, and *El buen humor de las musas* [The Good Humour of the Muses], a collection of humorous poetry which includes burlesques on the figures of Apollo and Diogenes and a 356-line *romance* entitled 'A Vulcano, Venus y Marte' [To Vulcan, Venus, and Mars].[11] Though not as well known as his burlesques on the tales of Apollo and Daphne ('Fábula de Apolo y Dafne', 1634) and Pan and Syrinx ('Fábula de Pan y Siringa', 1636), Polo de Medina's account of the tale of Mars, Venus, and Vulcan is

---

[9] Alonso de Castillo Solórzano, 'La fábula de Marte y Venus', in *Donayres del Parnaso. Primera parte* (Madrid: Diego Flamenco, 1624), fols. 53ᵛ–63ʳ.

[10] The Catalan poet Francesc Vicenç Garcia also wrote a burlesque version of the tale in his 'Faula de Vulcano, Venus y Marte', which was written before 1623 (the year of Garcia's death) but not published until it was included in his *La armonia del Parnás* (Barcelona: Rafel Figueró, 1700), 108–11. For discussion of this poem and its attribution, see Albert Rossich, 'Les faules mitològiques burlesques als segles XVII–XVIII', in Roger Friedlin and Sebastian Neumeister (eds.), *Vestigia fabularum. La mitologia antiga a les literatures catalana i castellana entre l'edat mitjana i la moderna*, Textos i Estudis de Cultura Catalana, 98 (Barcelona: Publicacions de l'Abadia de Montserrat, 2004), 113–41; and Pep Valsalobre, 'Mitologia burlesca, invenció barroca i catarsi: l'ànima frondosa de Fontanella o notes disperses a *Lo Desengany*', in Pep Valsalobre and Gabriel Sansano (eds.), *Francesc Fontanella. Una obra, una vida, un temps* (Bellcaire d'Empordà: Edicions Vitel·la, 2006), 281–318.

[11] Salvador Jacinto Polo de Medina, *El buen humor de las musas* (Madrid: Alonso Pérez, 1630). On Polo de Medina, see Antonio de los Reyes and others, *Polo de Medina: tercer centenario* (Murcia: Academia Alfonso X el Sabio, 1976); Juan Barceló Jiménez, *Polo de Medina: la sociedad y los tipos humanos en su obra* (Murcia: Academia Alfonso X el Sabio, 1978); Francisco Javier Díez de Revenga, *Polo de Medina, poeta del barroco* (Murcia: Real Academia Alfonso X el Sabio, 2000); and my 'Salvador Jacinto Polo de Medina (1603–76), "A Vulcano, Venus y Marte" (c.1630)', in *The Spanish Ballad*, 175–221.

more challenging, linguistically and conceptually, than either of its more illustrious companions.[12]

The third quarter of the seventeenth century saw the publication of at least three further burlesque accounts of the tale. The first of these is by the little-known Zaragozan writer Alberto Díez y Foncalda. His 152-line *romance* 'Fábula de Venus y Marte' [Tale of Venus and Mars] was included in the *Primera parte* (1653) of his *Poesías varias* [Various Poems], alongside tellings of the myths of Asteria and Jupiter, Caenis and Neptune, and Jupiter, Danaë, and Perseus.[13] The second is by the Marrano poet Miguel de Barrios, best known now as a victim of religious persecution who would convert, or rather revert, to the Jewish faith under the name Daniel Levi de Barrios. Barrios's 348-line *romance* 'A la fábula de Vulcano y Venus' [To the Tale of Vulcan and Venus] was first published in Brussels in 1665 in a collection entitled *Flor de Apolo* [Flower of Apollo].[14] This, his first published work, contains a number of poems in different verse forms on mythological and biblical subjects, including the tales of Venus and Adonis, Polyphemus and Galatea, Jupiter and Callisto, Echo and Narcissus, Judith and Holofernes, and, of course, Mars, Venus, and Vulcan. The last of the three is a ninety-six-line *romance* written for an academy in Salamanca in January 1672 by another little-known writer, Jerónimo Durán de Salcedo.[15]

The five poems by Castillo Solórzano, Polo de Medina, Díez y Foncalda, Barrios, and Durán de Salcedo share much in common; as a result, in the rest of this chapter they will be examined not one after the other, as in previous chapters, but side by side, in order better to pick out and examine

---

[12] For a modern edition of his more famous burlesques, see Jacinto Polo de Medina, *Poesía. Hospital de incurables*, ed. Francisco J. Díez de Revenga, LH, 268 (Madrid: Cátedra, 1987), 209–44.

[13] Alberto Díez y Foncalda, 'Fábula de Venus y Marte', in *Poesías varias. Primera Parte* (Zaragoza: Juan de Ibar, 1653), 149–55.

[14] Miguel de Barrios, *Flor de Apolo* (Brussels: Baltazar Vivien, 1665), 105–10; and, recently, ed. Francisco J. Sedeño Rodríguez (Kassel: Reichenberger, 2005), 253–64. On Barrios and his poetry, see Kenneth R. Scholberg, 'Miguel de Barrios and the Amsterdam Sephardic Community', *Jewish Quarterly Review*, 53 (1962), 120–59; José Luis Sánchez Fernández, *Poemas mitológicos de Miguel de Barrios* (Córdoba: Instituto de Historia de Andalucía, 1981); Julia R. Lieberman, '"Jonen Dalim", auto alegórico de Miguel (Daniel Leví) de Barrios', in Yedida K. Stillman and Norman A. Stillman (eds.), *From Iberia to Diaspora: Studies in Sephardic History and Culture* (Leiden: Brill, 1999), 300–15; Norman Simms, 'Confusion and Madness: Miguel de Barrios, alias Daniel Levi', in *Masks in the Mirror: Marranism in Jewish Experience* (New York: Peter Lang, 2006), 113–31; and Inmaculada García Gavilán, 'Notas sobre lo satírico y lo burlesco en el *Coro de las Musas* de Miguel de Barrios', in Alain Bègue and Jesús Ponce Cárdenas (eds.), *La poesía burlesca del Siglo de Oro* (= *Criticón*, 100) (Toulouse: Presses Universitaires du Mirail, 2007), 27–40.

[15] Jerónimo Durán de Salcedo, 'Venus y Marte', in *Academia que se celebró en la Universidad de Salamanca, en tres de enero de 1672, en casa del Señor Don Luis de Losada y Rivadeneyra su Rector* (Salamanca: Melchor Estévez, [n.d.]), 30–2.

some salient features of burlesque treatments of the tale in question.[16] I begin with a discussion of the representation of the three main protagonists, focusing on the fleshing out of the caricatures of Mars, Venus, and Vulcan hinted at in several of the poems examined in Chapters 2 and 3. Throughout my analysis greater attention will be paid to the more ambitious, complex, and innovative tellings of Castillo Solórzano, Barrios, and, in particular, Polo de Medina, who, as we shall see, takes to extreme lengths both caricatural distortion and the demands placed on the intellect and the imagination of the reader.

THE PIMP (MARS)

The respective lengths of their ballads suggests that, like both Cueva and Lope, Castillo Solórzano, Polo de Medina, and Barrios all add significantly to the narrative inherited from their classical and Renaissance forebears. Whilst the skeleton of the tale told by Demodocus and Leuconoe remains largely intact—the lovers' affair, Apollo's role as witness, the forging of the net, the lovers' entrapment, Vulcan's appeal for redress, etc.—each poet makes a number of additions, modifications, and changes of emphasis to the basic narrative. The most significant alterations made by Castillo Solórzano, for example, include a new setting in and around the world of contemporary Madrid; the inclusion of a parodic opening appeal to Apollo and the Muses; the introduction of detailed portraits of the main protagonists; the addition of an original backstory recounting Mars's courtship of Venus at a feast of the gods; the description of a *locus amoenus* prepared by the fertility goddess Flora for the lover's assignation; the presence of cuckoos, ill omens, and prophetic dreams; focus on the reactions of other gods to the lovers' shaming; and the addition of a closing epigram penned by Momus, the god of mockery. Whilst Polo de Medina and Barrios once more alter the setting—to the banks of the Danube and a *locus amoenus* reminiscent of the Garden of Eden, respectively—and whilst they dispense with the mock-epic opening, both of them pick up on many of these changes: the detailed portraits; the affair's backstory; the cuckoos, omens, and dreams; and, perhaps most significantly, the role accorded to Momus.

With the exception of Díez y Foncalda, each of the five poets begins the tale proper with what becomes a set-piece portrait of one or more of the protagonists: Castillo Solórzano and Barrios with Vulcan and Venus;

---

[16] For an overview of all five poems (and García's 'Faula de Vulcano, Venus y Marte'), see Diego Angulo Íñiguez, 'La fábula de Vulcano, Venus y Marte y *La Fragua* de Velázquez', *AEA* 33 (1960), 149–81 (repr. in his *Estudios completos sobre Velázquez* (Madrid: CEEH, 2007), 159–92); and Cebrián García, *La fábula*, 130–48.

Polo de Medina with Mars and Venus; and Durán de Salcedo with Vulcan. What picture of Mars emerges from his portrayal in these ballads? As we have seen, in sixteenth-century poetry Mars is often presented as the proto-typical soldier, the archetype of military might, and/or a metonym for war. He is often presented in a positive light, as the embodiment of certain virtues expected of the ideal Renaissance courtier. In the world of mytho-logical burlesque Mars is shown in a far less positive light. Both Castillo Solórzano (*below left*) and Polo de Medina (*right*)—the second of whom paints by far the most detailed portrait of the god of war—characterize him as an underworld rogue:

Entre los dioses festivos	El jaque de las deidades,
el bélico Marte hallóse,	todo bravatas y rumbo,
avalentado de vista,	que vive pared en medio
arriscado de bigotes;	del planeta boquirrubio;
hijo nacido sin padre,	el de los ojos al sesgo,
por la virtud de unas flores,	caribajo y cejijunto,
siendo la mayor patraña	de la frente encapotada
que Ovidio esparció en el orbe.	y mostachos a lo ruso;
Al fin, el hijo de Juno,	de Venus se enamoró,
airoso y galante joven,	que en la orilla del Danubio
atento miraba en Venus	muy arremangada estaba
la cifra de los primores. (149–60)	enjabonando un menudo. (1–12)

[*Castillo Solórzano*: Amongst the festive gods was warlike Mars, with a look of bravado in his eyes and menacing moustachios; a son born without a father, by virtue of some flowers, according to the greatest tall story that Ovid ever spread around the world. In the end, the son of Juno, an elegant and urbane youth, was carefully eyeing up Venus, the embodiment of perfection.]

[*Polo de Medina*: The pimp of the gods, who lives next door to the pretty-boy planet, is all bravado and show, with shifty eyes, head down and mono-brow, lowering forehead, and Russian-style moustachios. He fell in love with Venus, who was on the banks of the Danube, with her sleeves all rolled up, washing her smalls/dressing some giblets/scrubbing a penny.][17]

---

[17]   Much of the humour here is caused by the unexpected conjunction of the verb 'enja-bonar' and its object, 'un menudo'. Given that Venus has her sleeves rolled up on the banks of a river, the verb *enjabonar*, 'limpiar la ropa con jabón' (Cov. s.v. *jabón*), should mean that she is washing an item of clothing—her 'smalls'?—, but 'un menudo' could also denote either the entrails of a dead or butchered animal, or a small copper coin: '*Menudo*, se dice el vientre del carnero con manos y cabeza. *Menudos*, las monedas de cobre, a diferencia de las de plata y oro' (Cov.). The fact that the same verse is cited twice in *Aut.*, under both *enxabonar* and *menudo*, suggests that this is the only occurrence of these two words being put together in this way.

Whereas Castillo Solórzano acknowledges the tradition of 'el bélico Marte' as a young, powerfully muscular, and awe-inspiring embodiment of war, Polo de Medina's opening lines paint a portrait that stands in stark contrast to any image of Mars as an 'airoso y galante joven'. By introducing Mars as 'El jaque de las deidades', Polo de Medina makes explicit what is implicit in Castillo Solórzano's description of the warrior-god as 'avalentado de vista, | arriscado de bigotes'. The noun *jaque*, 'pimp', sets the tone for the rest of the poem, introducing not the elevated world of classical mythology but an underworld associated with thieves' cant (*germanía*), prostitution, and the picaresque. Better versed in the world of sexual commerce than in that of military engagement, Polo de Medina's warrior-god would not be out of place in the *Celestinesca*, the *cofradía* of Cervantes's 'Rinconete y Cortadillo' (notable parallels, both physical and moral, can be drawn with the crime syndicate's leader, Monipodio), Quevedo's *jácaras* (in particular, the figure of Escarramán), or his picaresque novel *El Buscón* (which ends with Pablos, Seville's 'rabí de los rufianes' [rabbi of ruffians], heading off to the New World in a desperate, and one suspects ultimately futile, attempt to improve his lot).

Like Monipodio, Polo de Medina's Mars is a physiognomist's delight: his shifty eyes, lowering monobrow, and Russian-style moustachios invite not admiration but rather a snigger from the reader. The idea of Mars 'cubierto de un templado y fino acero', as he was in Aldana's sonnet, is a distant memory, for Mars's chief attribute is no longer his impressive arms but his comical *bigotes* or *mostachos*. Whereas previously Mars's adamantine armour had symbolized many of the warrior-god's positive qualities, now Mars's facial hair serves to underline the fact that he is 'all mouth and no trousers', for according to Covarrubias, 'los que traen bigotes muy largos … pretenden parecer valientes y espantabobos' [those who have very long moustaches … try to seem brave and to come across as such to fools]. The image of Mars as a *valentón* [bravo], implicit in Castillo Solórzano's description, is also developed by Barrios. His Mars is labelled 'el dios pendenciero' [the quarrelsome god] (line 246); when Vulcan catches his wife's lover and pulls his hair, Mars responds by baring his teeth and scratching at the smith's face (lines 293–6)—all in all, a scrap most unbecoming for two of the twelve most important Roman deities. In Polo de Medina's poem, Mars is introduced as being 'todo bravatas y rumbo'. Characterized by his honeyed sweet nothings, empty boasts, and idle threats, he shares much in common with Quevedo's warrior-god, whose entrance in *La Hora de todos* is described thus: 'Marte, don Quijote de las deidades, entró con sus armas y capacete, y la insignia de viñadero enristrada, echando chuzos' [Mars, the Don Quixote of the gods, entered in his arms and helmet, with his wine-farmer's standard at the ready, tossing off idle boasts].[18] The rest of Polo de Medina's poem exposes him as a pompous, posturing, and strutting *jaque*, a soldier-turned-pander created in the mould of Plautus's *Miles Gloriosus* or the figure of Il Capitano from the Commedia dell'Arte.

While Mars is ridiculed through the description of his appearance and actions, his authority is further undermined, in Polo de Medina's poem, through the presentation of his verbal exchanges with Venus: first, we are told that he addresses her with the hyperbolic 'dos mil conceptos' [two thousand conceits]; next, in order to express his *ansias*, a word associated in contemporary slang with the relationship between a pimp and his prostitute, he employs 'dulces conceptos cultos' [sweet, learned conceits], 'razones verdes' [dirty words], and 'requiebros maduros' [tried and tested sweet nothings], only for Venus to dismiss them as 'bombardas y chuzos' (i.e. both 'weapons' and 'empty boasting'); and when Mars, metaphorically transformed into an *avechucho* [wretched little bird], flies down the chimney to see Venus on the occasion of their capture, he conducts himself in accordance with 'las jerigonzas del gusto' [amorous mumbo jumbo]. Whereas *jerigonza*, 'jargon', was 'la melopea rogativa de los ciegos' (i.e. the blind beggars' patter that Lázaro learns from his cruel and duplicitous first master in the anonymous *c*.1554 picaresque novel *Lazarillo de Tormes*) and 'jerga de germanía usada por rufianes y valentones' [underworld slang used by thieves and thugs] (*Lex.*), it was also associated with a derogatory approach to *cultismo*, as evinced by the opening lines of Quevedo's 'Receta para hacer soledades en un día' [Prescription for Writing *Solitudes* in One Day]: 'Quien quisiere ser culto en sólo un día, | la jeri (aprenderá) gonza siguiente … ' [Anyone who wants to be learned in just one day will pick up the following jargon …] (Q825: 1–2).[19] For Polo de Medina's gods, such *culto* mumbo jumbo is the common mode of parlance: despite their differences, Mars and Venus are 'unánimes en lo culto' [united in their use of learned language]; and Vulcan calls to the gods to come down from heaven 'en culta voz de becerro' [with all the learnedness of a bleating calf].

Though it is well known that Mars is one of Venus's lovers, exactly how he came to find himself in such an enviable position is uncertain. As in both

---

[18] *La Hora de todos*, 149–50.

[19] Quevedo associates *jerigonza* specifically with Góngora, a fact underlined in his infamous epitaph on his rival's death, 'Este que en negra tumba rodeado', which sends Góngora to Hell as a 'sacerdote de Venus y de Baco, | caca en los versos y en garito Caco' [a priest of Venus and Bacchus, who shits on the page and thieves like Cacus in the gambling den] (Q840: 9–10). According to Quevedo, Góngora befouled Spanish with his *jerigóngora*, confusing his mouth and his anus when he started writing about the one-eyed Cyclops Polyphemus: 'Éste a la jerigonza quitó el nombre, | pues después que escribió cíclopemente, | la llama jerigóngora la gente' [This chap made the word 'jargon' redundant, because after he wrote out of his one eye, everyone calls it 'jargongora'] (Q840: 17–19).

'Los amores' and 'La rosa blanca', conjecture as to Mars's wooing of Venus or as to the lovers' mating rituals provides a rich source of comedy. Like Cueva and Lope, both Castillo Solórzano and Polo de Medina introduce imaginative accounts of events leading up to the lovers' affair. In Castillo Solórzano's ballad, Mars falls for Venus when he is struck by one of Cupid's arrows at a feast of the gods. The affair is then consummated in a *locus amoenus* prepared for them by Flora, the lovers' *tercera* [go-between]. The first 160 lines of Polo de Medina's poem offer a far seedier background to the tale. The description of Mars's courtship of Venus, which parodies a number of stages associated with Courtly Love, tells the reader exactly how Mars intends to proceed, from voyeurism (disguised as a *pulpo*/octopus in lines 49–53), through the foreplay of kissing and petting (disguised as a *besugo*/ red bream in 61–4), to the desired goal of sexual intercourse ('el disfraz carnal', as opposed to 'el de cuaresma', in 81–4).[20] The various disguises adopted by Mars expose him as a perverted *necio* [fool] unable to control his basic instincts. Polo de Medina's Mars is also struck by one of Cupid's arrows. However, whereas Castillo Solórzano's poem plots the divine affair that ensues as a meeting of equals, Polo de Medina's poem sees Mars reduced to paying for sex to satisfy his desires; after a period of haggling, he drives Venus's asking price down from a *doblón* to an *escudo*. This Mars has already exchanged the accoutrements of war for cash, potential gifts/bribes, and postures associated with the male lover, thus following the example of his counterpart in Quevedo's sonnet, who, as we saw earlier, 'En confites gastó ... la malla, | y la espada en pasteles y en azumbres' (Q536: 7–8).

The comical swagger of Polo de Medina's Mars soon gives way to meek subservience. In his mock serenade to Venus he presents himself as a sacrificial lamb at the goddess's feet. The content of his address renders absurd the tradition of the lover's prostration before the beloved. Mars thinly veils his desires with a series of euphemisms relating to navigation, diving, and the dropping of anchors, before stating precisely what it is that he wants from her:

> Serás, oh Venus, mi manfla;
> yo seré, Venus, tu cuyo;
> serás de este Marte marta,
> que lo abrigues aun por julio;
> que si vengo a verme cuervo
> de esas bellas carnes, juro
> de darte seis tabaqueras
> para tabaco con humo. (129–36)

[20] The last stage recalls the battle between Don Carnal and Doña Quaresma in stanzas 1067–1209 of the fourteenth-century *Libro de buen amor*; see Arcipreste de Hita, *Libro de buen amor*, ed. Gerald B. Gybbon-Monypenny, CC, 161 (Madrid: Castalia, 1988), 335–60.

[Oh Venus, you'll be my courtesan and I'll be your lover. You'll be this Mars's prostitute; may you keep him under wraps even in the height of summer, because if I get to peck at that lovely flesh like a raven I swear I'll give you six pouches for smoking tobacco.]

In an absurd play on his own name, Mars invites Venus to be his *marta*, on one level a 'pine marten' but also a proper name associated with prostitution and hypocritical displays of piety.[21] In a second play on his name, this time based on the months of the Gregorian calendar, Mars asks Venus to keep him warm even in July—i.e. the height of summer. Mars intimates that he wants to have sex with her all year round. Ironically, in *germanía*, *abrigo* denotes the protection given by pimps to their prostitutes (*Lex.*). We are brought back to the relationship between the *cuyo/jaque* and the *manfla/madama*; yet here, in an incongruous inversion of the standard relationship between pimp and prostitute, it is Venus who will provide *abrigo* for Mars. This complements the reversal suggested earlier when Mars is presented as the prototypical Portuguese lover and Venus as a swaggering Turkish soldier: 'él tierno a lo portugués, | ella arrogante a lo turco' [he as affectionate as a Portuguese lover, she as boastful as a Turk] (lines 91–2). Whereas Mars may appear to be a fitting companion for Cervantes's Monipodio, 'el más rústico y disforme bárbaro del mundo' [the most coarse and deformed thug in the whole world], he is, in fact—in this 'mundo al revés' [world upside down]—an effeminate man, for whom true manhood runs not even skin-deep.[22] For his part, Díez y Foncalda takes this role reversal to its logical extreme: it is not Mars but Venus who initiates their affair, when she orders him to strip off and jump into bed: 'esto | ha de ser, pues ropa fuera | y vámonos a mi lecho' [this has to happen, so off with your kit and let's get into my bed] (lines 14–16). At the end of the section of Polo de Medina's poem cited above, Mars promises Venus six *tabaqueras*, here not an exotic present from the New World but a restorative cure for syphilis—something of which, as we shall now see, this Venus is in no little need.

---

[21] The figure of Marta is the subject of many popular sayings in the Golden Age, such as 'Kókale, Marta' and 'Habla Marta, rresponde Xusta; una puta a otra buska' (Correas, *Vocabulario*, 176 and 585), the second of these revealing a clear link with prostitution. On the proverbial character of Marta as 'a hypocritical woman who puts on the front of piety for show', as in Tirso de Molina's play *Marta la piadosa* (1615), see Francis C. Hayes, 'The Use of Proverbs as Titles and Motives in the *Siglo de Oro* Drama: Tirso de Molina', *HR* 7 (1939), 310–23 (p. 316).

[22] Miguel de Cervantes, *Novelas ejemplares*, ed. Harry Sieber, LH, 105–6, 2 vols. (Madrid: Cátedra, 1997), i. 211.

THE PROSTITUTE (VENUS)

Castillo Solórzano (lines 53–92), Polo de Medina (17–48), and Barrios (61–116) all dedicate several quatrains to the description of Venus. In doing so, each poet has the scope to play with conventional representations of female beauty—most notably, commonplace Petrarchan metaphors (hair as gold, eyes as suns, cheeks as roses, lips as rubies, teeth as pearls, necks as alabaster, and so on). In line with classical tradition, Castillo Solórzano's Venus excels the other goddesses in terms of beauty. As a result, she has no need for the make-up that was so prized by women in contemporary Madrid, not least because such lotions and potions (here labelled *artificios, solimanes, resplandores, alcanfores, albayaldes*, etc.) helped to conceal the facial disfigurement wrought by syphilis and other sexually transmitted diseases. In Polo de Medina's poem, however, the classical and Renaissance image of Venus as the paragon of female beauty is subverted, as we are shown a manly woman with black hair, a massive nose, a pot-belly, hairy legs, and gigantic feet. Her legs and thighs are 'gordas | como las letras de algunos' [ungainly like some people's ramblings] (lines 39–40), a passing reference to the *jerigonza* of both blabbering beggars and *culto* poets.[23] Polo de Medina's absurd portrait of Venus is encapsulated in the description of her as 'su divino bello bulto' [her divine and beautiful bulk] (line 78), the clumsy alliteration in *b–* driving home the point that this Venus is anything but divine. Barrios's fifty-six-line portrait of Venus also follows the traditional Petrarchan order, starting with her hair and moving down through the various parts of her body. The customary process of fragmentation is taken to an extreme, however, with individual quatrains devoted to her hair, brow, eyebrows, eyes, nose, cheeks, mouth, teeth, chin, neck, waist, hands, and feet.[24] His Venus *is* 'hermosa por excelencia' [beautiful par excellence] (line 121); rather than subvert Venus's traditional physical perfection, Barrios chooses instead to use his portrait of her as a platform for playful subversion of Petrarchan metaphor and erudite allusion. A memorable example of this is seen in the description of Venus's prominent aquiline nose as 'el águila de yelo' [the ice eagle], which

[23] For more on the play on *letras*, see my 'A Vulcano, Venus y Marte', 185–6.

[24] Polo de Medina presents a memorable parody of the traditional order of such descriptions in his 'Fábula de Apolo y Dafne', threatening to begin with Daphne's heels: 'y pienso comenzar por los talones, | aunque parezca mal al que leyere; | que yo puedo empezar por do quisiere' [and I think I'll start with her heels, even if that seems wrong to the reader; because I can start wherever I like] (lines 27–9). In the description that follows he mocks *culto* poets and their abuse of Petrarchan metaphor, crying out '¡oh, qué linda ocasión de decir *nieve* | si yo fuera poeta principiante' [oh, what a great chance to say *snow* if I were a novice poet!] (43–4) when he reaches the nymph's feet, '¡Qué tentación de rosas!' [How tempting to say roses!] (77) when he comes to her cheeks, and so on.

cleverly reworks the traditional Petrarchan paradox of the icy fire. As an eagle, the only bird reputed to be capable of looking straight into the sun, Venus's nose can look straight into her two sun-like eyes. As a frosty Petrarchan lady, it is fitting for it to be made of ice; despite its proximity to the goddess's fiery eyes, somehow it manages not to melt (lines 77–9).[25]

In all three poems Venus appears as a prostitute. Depending on her status (in other words, how much money she earns), she is a *buscona*, a *ramera*, a *cortesana*, or a *tusona*. The shell in which traditionally she arrives on the shore of Cyprus (as in Hesiod, Botticelli, Lope, etc.) allows Polo de Medina to associate her with prostitution through the double meaning of the word *concha*, both 'shell' and a symbol of the female sex organs. A conceit based on two meanings of *corte*—both 'cut' and 'court'—allows Castillo Solórzano to suggest that by becoming a *cortesana*/courtesan Venus is merely living up to the circumstances of her own birth, which stemmed from the conjunction of Uranus's castrated member (lopped off by his own son) and the waters of the ocean (Hesiod, *Theogony*, 185–200). The description of Venus that follows, structured upon the derogatory anaphora of 'de aquestas que' [one of those who], develops this image of her as one of many courtesans plying their trade in contemporary Madrid. However, Venus is not just representative of such women but actually the guiding star for all prostitutes sailing the ocean of Madrid: 'ella fue de todas norte' (line 92). As such, Castillo Solórzano's Venus conforms to the model not of the celestial Venus but of the terrestrial Venus responsible, according to Pérez de Moya and Cueva, for establishing the art of prostitution in Cyprus.[26] She is not at all fussy when it comes to choosing sexual partners, for she shamelessly consorts 'con galanes, a centurias | con billetes, a legiones' [with companies of handsome men and regiments of billets-doux], offering a 'mesa de trucos' [billiard table], at which men can engage in 'partidas de tocadillo' [games of slap and tickle] (lines 73–80). The hyperbole of 'a centurias' and 'a legiones' not only reveals that she does business with innumerable men but also prepares the reader for the fact that her next conquest/customer will be 'el bélico Marte', the god of war

---

[25] For more on Barrios's anti-portraits, see Francisco Sedeño Rodríguez, 'El antirretrato petrarquista: metamorfosis de la poética (paradigmas en Quevedo y Barrios)', in Gregorio Cabello Porras and Javier Campos Daroca (eds.), *Poéticas de la Metamorphosis. Tradición clásica, Siglo de Oro y modernidad* (Málaga: Universidad de Málaga-Universidad de Almería, 2002), 407–46.

[26] 'Ésta es la que comenzó hacer congregación de mujeres públicas en Chipre …; tuvo tan ardiente el deseo sensual que no sólo a algunos, mas a todos se dio; y por encubrir su deshonestidad, por común costumbre trujo a los de Chipre a esto mismo usar' [It was she who started to build up a group of prostitutes in Cyprus …; so strong was her sensual desire that she gave herself not just to a few people but to everyone; and to cover up her indecency, she made this a common practice amongst everyone in Cyprus] (*Philosofía secreta*, 379). For Cueva, see Chapter 3, n. 56.

and himself a guiding star for the men serving in such military units. The comparison drawn between Venus and a billiard table suggests that her services provide 'sport', 'entertainment', or even 'light relief' for any man willing to pay a presumably small and predetermined price. Whereas, in the prologue to Cervantes's *Novelas ejemplares* [Exemplary Tales] (1613), it is the 'mesa de trucos' of literature that provides 'horas ... de recreación donde el afligido espíritu descanse' [hours ... of recreation when the tormented spirit can rest], here it is sex that provides an altogether different kind of *entretenimiento* (and one that is not so *honesto*).[27] For his part, Barrios compares Venus not to a billiard table but to Pérez de Montalbán's well-known miscellany *Para todos* [For Everyone] (1632): 'no dando a ninguno el alma, | mandaba a todos el cuerpo' [refusing to give her soul to anyone, she gave her body to everyone] (lines 171–2). As one of her cult names suggests, Venus Pandemos is open to all comers.

Like Lope's Juana in the *Rimas humanas y divinas del Licenciado Tomé de Burguillos*, Polo de Medina's Venus is a common washerwoman. However, whereas Juana washes clothes in the Manzanares, Venus dresses giblets for her lover Adonis on the banks of the Danube. The epithet *madama* (also used by Castillo Solórzano) strengthens the association between Venus and prostitution. By describing Venus as an 'alhóndiga de belleza' [corn exchange of beauty] (line 101), a place where beauty or sex, like corn, is bought and sold, Polo de Medina's Mars introduces us to the commercial side of her trade. Having been a canny prostitute-in-the-making who sold her virginity on numerous occasions before dedicating herself openly to the art of prostitution (*Lex.* s.v. *apretada*), Venus is now, after years in the same business, an old hand (a 'moza redomada al uso'). She poses, however, not as a mere 'buscona de Chipre' [whore from Cyprus]—to cite Quevedo (Q682: 287)—but as a *tusona*, an escort of the highest class, as Tristán explains to the young Don García in Ruiz de Alarcón's *c*.1634 play *La verdad sospechosa* [The Suspicious Truth].[28] Accordingly, as in 'Los amores', she rebuffs Mars's initial approach and insists on payment, refusing to be swayed by his offer of six tobacco pouches:

«Las tusonas de mi porte
no temen fuerzas ni orgullos;
que en su golfo y mar sin norte
no se camina por rumbos.

---

[27] *Novelas ejemplares*, i. 52.
[28] Juan Ruiz de Alarcón, *La verdad sospechosa*, ed. José Montero Reguera, CC, 250 (Madrid: Castalia, 1999), 72–3: 'Hay una gran multitud | de señoras del Tusón, | que entre cortesanas son | de la mayor magnitud' (lines 329–32).

Todas son Troyas de bronce,
y sólo rompen su muro
un doblón con «Vida mía,
tómalo, que todo es tuyo.»» (141–8)

[Escorts of my standing are not afraid of force or boasting, for one doesn't get
by with lavish show in such waters without setting a course. All escorts are
like bronze Troys; their walls can be breached only with a doubloon and the
words, 'Love of my life, take it, for everything is yours'.]

Venus is adamant that her defences, ironically likened to the walls of
Troy, can be breached only through the vehicle of money, Mars's equivalent of Odysseus's Trojan Horse. After Venus's criticism of Mars's verbal
approach, the gods reach an impasse, before an extensive period of bar-
tering leads to resolution in the form of a financial transaction. Whilst
this transaction takes place on the conventional battlefield of love, the
trappings of Mars's past military splendour are transformed through simple punning into cash for sexual favours. The pair's exchange is based not
on love, friendship, and honour, but on the buying and selling of brothel
language. That Mars should end up paying an *escudo*, rather than the
original asking price of a doubloon, suggests that either he is proficient in
the art of haggling or business is slow for Venus. Either way, it is significant
that money now changes hands in advance, as payment to the woman for
sex, and not afterwards, as compensation to the husband for her adultery.

The terrestrial Venus, as filtered through the imaginations of Castillo
Solórzano, Polo de Medina, and Barrios, is the archetypal woman. She is
interested in men for purely financial reasons and—following the misogyn-
ist commonplace of the *bolsa*, both 'purse' and 'scrotum', milked dry—
squeezes every last drop of profit out of them before moving on to pastures
new. If Mars embodies the Deadly Sin of Lust, Venus embodies that of
Greed. Nothing escapes the clutches of her rapacious acquisitiveness.
Castillo Solórzano's Venus is representative of the sirens that endanger the
lives of men navigating the waters of Madrid. Stuffing their ears with wax
guaranteed Odysseus's crewmen safe passage through the waters of the
Sirens (*Odyssey*, xii.154–200), but there is no such respite or refuge for
men in contemporary Madrid: the sirens of the Court draw unsuspecting
men in with their superficial charms before stripping them of their every
last possession, right down to the wax in their ears: 'aun la cera de los oídos
| no le dejan al que cogen' (lines 55–6). Polo de Medina's Venus is first seen
'enjabonando un menudo'; as noted above, one possible meaning of this
phrase is that she is scrubbing a coin of insignificant monetary value.[29]
The idea of her as a devious, tight-fisted, penny-pinching prostitute is

[29] See above, p. 132, n. 17.

developed when she is then labelled *avarienta* [avaricious], compared to merchants and other popular targets of seventeenth-century satire, and associated with the rapacious, fast-flowing Danube, the 'Danuvius . . . rapax' of the pseudo-Ovidian *Consolatio ad Liviam*, 387. The suggestion that Venus is more interested in the state of her finances than the men she beds is taken to a logical extreme in Barrios's ballad, when it is stated that she sleeps not with her clients but with their money (lines 133–6). Like Quevedo in satirical mode (e.g. Q706, 'Quejas del abuso de dar a las mujeres'), both Polo de Medina and Barrios suggest that women are interested in men only because of their money and, in doing so, hint at the moral corruption of contemporary society by insinuating that all relationships between men and women are based upon sex and monetary exchange.

Unfortunately for her clients, Venus is riddled with disease. In the context of these ballads the popular saying can be read literally: 'A night in the arms of Venus leads to a lifetime on mercury.' In Castillo Solórzano's ballad Venus's line of work sees the health of Spaniards ('sanidades castellanas') threatened by syphilis, the 'French disease' ('humores franchotes'), the pejorative suffix *–ote* driving this unseemly point home. Had Vulcan known about his wife's indiscretions he would have been able to save himself from the *sudores* [sweats] associated with a common form of treatment for syphilis. Polo de Medina's description of the sight that greets the lovers' peers when they descend from heaven—as we saw in Chapter 1, the scene most frequently portrayed in illustrated editions of the *Metamorphoses*—also alludes to Venus's struggle against the disease:

> Halláronlos jadeando,
> por salir de aquel tabuco,
> y aunque de sudor aguados,
> estaban en cueros puros:
>   Venus, desgreñado el moño,
> desrizado su apatusco,
> y medrosa de otra espina,
> dos argentados pantuflos;
>   Marte con un tocador
> y escarpines que se puso,
> teniendo un francés catarro
> con dolores de Acapulco. (269–80)

[They found them panting, struggling to get out of that tiny space, and although they were covered in buckets of sweat, they were stark naked. Venus's hair was all dishevelled, her attire all undone, and fearful of another [porcupine] quill, she wore two silvered slippers. Mars was wearing a nightcap and some bedsocks that he'd put on, suffering from a French catarrh and aches and pains from Acapulco.]

The lovers are stark naked and covered in sweat, the first hint that Mars may have received, quite literally, rather more than he bargained for. Venus's fashionable hairstyle (*moño*) is all over the place, her curly hair totally dishevelled, and, to protect her from another *espina*, Venus now wears on her feet two 'silvered slippers'. The word *espinal/-o* incorporates a range of meanings: a porcupine spine; a penis; and, in *germanía*, a hospital for prostitutes suffering from sexually transmitted diseases (*Lex.*).[30] There are, therefore, at least two possible interpretations of the Gongorine *argentados*.[31] While *argentar* means 'to silver', more specifically it comes to refer to the process in Andalucía of applying a thin metallic layer or shine to the surface of leather shoes. This is the meaning that Góngora plays with in his 1584 ballad 'Noble desengaño', when the lady's dog pees liberally on the black patent-leather shoes of the unfortunate lover standing outside her house: 'me argentó de plata | los zapatos negros' (lines 63–4).[32] Like Góngora, Polo de Medina employs the verb *argentar* to suggest, in an inappropriately high register, that Venus's slippers have been decorated with a coating of urine (the conjunction of *argentar* and *pantuflo* itself may be inspired by line 160 of Góngora's 'La ciudad de Babilonia': 'argentaros el pantuflo'). If this is the case, then Venus must have wet herself at the thought of having to return to a correctional institution for prostitutes. It is also possible that Venus's footwear has been covered with *argento vivo*, 'mercury', to protect her from syphilis. In this case, the 'silvering' is deliberately carried out in preparation for extramarital sex and not an uncontrolled bodily response to being caught *in flagrante*. Either way, the subversion of the *culto* usage of this Latinate verb offers an example of the way in which erudite words could be incorporated into the grotesque lexicon of contemporary slang.

Unfortunately for Mars, he too contracts syphilis (here, a 'francés catarro') and suffers from 'dolores de Acapulco', a disease associated with the discovery and conquest of New Spain.[33] When Venus is later punished

---

[30] See also Chamorro, *Tesoro de villanos*, 384–5.

[31] Góngora frames the *Polifemo* with typically *culto* examples of the same verb: at the beginning it is used to describe the way in which the foamy Mediterranean 'silvers' the foot of Sicily's western promontory Lilybaeum ('Donde espumoso el mar sicil·iano | el pie argenta de plata al Lilibeo'; lines 25–6); and at the end, to paint a picture of Acis's now liquified bones 'silvering' the sands of the island's shore ('Corriente plata al fin sus blancos huesos, | lamiendo flores y argentando arenas'; lines 501–2).

[32] For more detailed discussion of this wordplay, see Eric Southworth, 'Luis de Góngora y Argote (1561–1627), "Noble desengaño" (1584)', in *The Spanish Ballad*, 24–40 (pp. 35–6).

[33] It is not clear to me whether the phrase refers to a specific disease that had been rife in that area—perhaps smallpox?—or whether the choice of Acapulco is determined simply by the assonantal rhyme scheme in *ú–o*.

for their affair, she is shipped off to Burgos 'sin coche y sin moño' [without her carriage and hairbun] (line 338), the former a stage for amorous encounters, the latter, as suggested above, both a fashion accessory and a means of concealing the hair loss caused by diseases contracted in the line of duty.[34] She is also sentenced to 'tres meses en ayuno' [three months on an empty stomach]; both a form of religious penitence and abstinence from eating meat or, in other words, practising as a prostitute/brothel madam. Polo de Medina's Venus is cut from the same cloth as the Venus of Quevedo's *La Hora de todos*, who arrives at the gods' assembly in a state of disrepair, her make-up only half done, her wig only half on.[35] Like Quevedo, Polo de Medina suggests that Venus is a slavish follower of the latest fads, fashions, and status symbols—or, rather, of anything and everything that can help mask her disease-ravaged body. Unfortunately, as Barrios stresses, Mars is not the only man to suffer as the result of a night in the arms of Venus:

> En la peste de su amor
> tantos por ella murieron,
> que para darles sepulcro
> hizo en Vulcano un carnero.

[In the plague of their love so many died for/because of her that in order to bury them Vulcan was made a ram/mass grave/charnel house.]

Here, the wordplay on *carnero* is a fine example of Barrios's wit. It cements the link between the pestilence spread by Venus and the horns of her husband's cuckoldry: Venus has killed so many of her lovers that her husband has become, at once, a cuckold, a ram sacrificed to Mars, and a 'common grave' (Cov.) or 'charnel house' (*Aut.*).[36] Unfortunately for men, consorting with women leads not just to the metaphorical death of their *bolsa* but also to their own literal death: on both levels, it will not be long before they hear the dreaded *Requiem aeternam*.[37]

---

[34] For more on the *mal francés*, see Jon Arrizabalaga, John Henderson, and Roger French, *The Great Pox: The French Disease in Renaissance Europe* (New Haven: Yale University Press, 1996).

[35] *La Hora de todos*, 151.

[36] Cov. s.v. *carnero*: 'dicho así porque se ofrecía al dios Marte en sacrificio.' Among the signs of the Zodiac, the ram—the sign for March—was an attribute of Mars in his planetary role.

[37] 'Mientras tuvieres que dar, | hallarás quien te entretenga, | y en expirando la bolsa, | oirás el *Requiem aeternam*' [So long as you've got something to give, you'll find someone to keep you company, and when your purse runs dry, you'll hear the *Requiem aeternam*] (Quevedo, Q726: 41–4); for a detailed discussion of these lines, see Colin Thompson, 'Francisco de Quevedo Villegas (1580–1645), "A la Corte vas, Perico" (date unknown)', in *The Spanish Ballad*, 115–33 (p. 123).

All three poets stress this link between Venus and death—or between sex and death (here, no longer simply a metaphor for a 'climax')—by describing her as, or comparing her to, death-dealing mythical or mythological creatures such as sirens, Gorgons, and basilisks. In Polo de Medina's poem Mars's complaint that he is powerless in the face of 'un estornudo | de [sus] basiliscos ojos' [a simple blink from her basilisk-like eyes] (lines 114–15) offers a burlesque reminder of Venus's unique ability to tame the warrior-god. The identification of Venus with the basilisk, whose evil eye was a symbol of destructive power and moral degeneration, allows for an economical reference to the Petrarchan commonplace that the look of a woman had the power to kill a man, as reworked in the opening to Quevedo's ballad 'Los médicos con que miras, | los dos ojos con que matas' [The doctors with which you look, the two eyes with which you kill] (Q706: 1–2). The basilisk is also the subject of Quevedo's poem 'Al basilisco': 'si está vivo quien te vio, | toda tu historia es mentira, | pues si no murió, te ignora | y si murió, no lo afirma' [if he who saw you is still alive, all your history is a lie, because if he didn't die, he isn't aware of you, and if he did die, he can't confirm it] (Q700: 53–6). Significantly, the basilisk could not stand its own appearance. It is ironic that a narcissistic Venus, so often seen in Renaissance and Baroque painting contemplating her reflection in a mirror (as, for example, in Velázquez's *Venus del espejo*; see Fig. 5.3), should be compared to an animal that has a fabled aversion to reflective surfaces. In medieval iconography warriors armed with a shield/mirror and a sword were often shown fighting the basilisk: perhaps Mars should be seen in such light when he breaks down Venus's defences with an *escudo*—both a gold coin and an impressive military shield.

THE *PACIENTE* (VULCAN)

In contrast to Polo de Medina, who delays the introduction of Vulcan until the second half of his ballad, both Castillo Solórzano and Barrios start their treatments of the tale with portraits of the smith. Whereas Castillo Solórzano briefly alludes to Vulcan's traditional physical defects—his ugliness, dirtiness, and deformity—Barrios goes into much more detail. The opening eleven stanzas of his ballad describe Vulcan from head to foot (*pelo* to *pie*), in anticipation of the portrait of his wife that follows. Through wordplay on a series of simple oppositions (*cielo/infierno*, *mojado/seco*, *canario/cuervo*, *cerrado/abierto*, *grande/pequeño*), Barrios presents Vulcan not only as ugly, lame, and slow-witted, but also as a Calvinist who suffers from baldness (he is 'Calvino de pelo'), facial disfigurement, horrendous breath, and unruly bodily functions. Touching on Vulcan's physical appearance only in passing, both Castillo Solórzano and Polo de Medina describe the lame smith's deformity using metaphors based on forms of doggerel. Whereas the former refers to Vulcan's corrective sandal as a 'fregenal estrambote', inelegant 'extra lines' at the end of a poem, the latter alludes to polt-foot Vulcan's physical abnormality by drawing a parallel between the smith's feet and lines of poetry that do not scan: '[sus] pies de copla | estaban de sílabas diminutos' (lines 211–12).[38] Just as a line of poetry that has either too many or too few syllables/feet is poetically deficient, Vulcan's feet are physically deficient (later on, 'micer Cornelio Castrucho' trips on the roots of a cork oak and falls down the stairs). Durán de Salcedo opts for a similar conceit.[39] For his part, Barrios rounds off his portrait of Vulcan by stating that the smith's feet are so big in comparison to the rest of his pygmyish body that they are the only part of him that can be seen. When others laugh at his *cojera*, he declares that it is a sign of his reverence for Venus, because it looks as if he is always bowing to her (i.e. performing *reverencias*).

In the world of seventeenth-century burlesque Vulcan appears not as the divine artist but as the archetypal cuckold. In *La Hora de todos* he is the 'dios de bigornia', *bigornia* deriving from the Latin *bicornis*, 'two-horned'.[40] In Quevedo's satirical poems Vulcan also appears as a sad cuckold: in a ballad written against the power of Cupid, Venus is a prostitute who allows her husband to rest while she evaluates Mars's erotic attributes (Q709: 17–28); in another, the poet claims that Venus made him Vulcan and that Mars made him a cuckold: 'Venus me dejó Vulcano, | cornudo me dejó Marte' (Q680: 103–4).[41] Whereas hints of cuckoldry shape the reader's perception of Vulcan in some of the poems analysed in previous chapters, in the mythological burlesque Vulcan's status as a cuckold is stressed every step of the way. Durán de Salcedo's poem, a tour de force on cuckoldry, focuses almost exclusively on the smith-god. Venus's husband is cowardly, clumsy, and dim-witted. However, as the arch-cuckold (or *marido resignado*, as in Lucian's *Dialogues*), his defining characteristic

---

[38] *Aut.* s.v. *diminuto*: 'defectuoso y falto de lo que debía tener para su cabal perfección.'

[39] 'Estaba, pues, Don Vulcano | en pie, que en dos no era fácil, | por haber prestado el uno, | para que se le glosasen' [So, Mr Vulcan was standing on one foot, because it wasn't easy for him to do so on two, having lent out one of them so that it could be glossed] (lines 17–20).

[40] *La Hora de todos*, 368.

[41] Gareth Walters argues that this is not true of Quevedo's love poems, suggesting that Vulcan, as the epitome of the mocked and the deceived, represents a vehicle through which the poetic voice can convey a sense of vulnerability, indignation, and injustice; see *Francisco de Quevedo, Love Poet* (Cardiff: University of Wales Press, 1985), 55–8, 163–8.

is his patience: 'Vulcano es insigne en la paciencia.'[42] The drudgery of the husband is frequently alluded to through references to slow, ponderous creatures such as snails, camels, asses, and oxen. Whilst Vulcan slaves away in the forge, Mars sleeps with Venus in the smith's marriage bed. As we have seen, forge and bed stand in opposition to one another in many sixteenth- and seventeenth-century paintings and illustrations of the tale, which serve as graphic reminders of Vulcan's folly and his fundamental incompatibility with his wife.

Vulcan's choice of wife marks him out as the archetypal *necio*. The smith's vanity, self-delusion, and lack of self-knowledge blind him to the fact that he is totally unsuited to Venus. In this regard, he is guilty of the same mistake as several husbands on the contemporary stage, such as the Duke of Ferrara in Lope's *El castigo sin venganza* [Punishment Without Revenge] (1631) or Gutierre Solís and Juan Roca, the protagonists of two of Calderón's wife-murder plays (*El médico de su honra* [The Surgeon of his Honour] (early 1630s) and *El pintor de su deshonra* [The Painter of his Dishonour] (late 1640s), respectively). That mistake is, of course, the failure to exercise good judgement (*discreción*), or the Cardinal Virtue of Prudence, when choosing a wife (though this is by no means the only mistake that they make). As suggested in the last chapter, such *comedias* focus on the husband's obsession with jealousy, his fear of the stain of dishonour, and the extreme lengths to which he will go to 'restore' his honour. In the mythological burlesque the emphasis is not on honour/dishonour but on cuckoldry, the humorous flip side of the same coin. It is no coincidence that the first half of the seventeenth century should see the parallel development of preoccupation with honour (one of the main concerns of the *comedia nueva*) on the one hand, and delight in cuckoldry (one of the principal subjects of contemporary satire) on the other.

All three poets stress the unfortunate symptoms and/or side-effects of cuckoldry. Vulcan is constantly plagued by headaches, ill omens, and prophetic dreams, from which there is no respite and for which there appears to be no antidote (despite the contemporary Anglo-Dutch poet William Fennor's suggestion to the contrary).[43] The emphasis on cuckoldry leads Castillo Solórzano to include in his telling the cuckoo, a notoriously bad omen for jealous husbands.[44] Once Vulcan has forged the net, he is then guided to the scene of the lovers' tryst by the cuckoo's call. In Polo de Medina's

---

[42] Cosme Gómez de Tejada de los Reyes, *León prodigioso: apología moral entretenida, y provechosa a las buenas costumbres, trato virtuoso y político* (Madrid: Francisco Martínez, 1636), fol. 235[r].

[43] William Fennor, *Cornucopiae, Pasquils nightcap: or, Antidot for the head-ache* (London: Thomas Thorp, 1612).

[44] Cov. s.v. *cuclillo*: 'Ave conocida y de mal agüero para los casados celosos.'

poem, before Apollo has even had the chance to deliver his message the very same call gives Vulcan advance warning of his fate. The bird's ominous call ushers in a nightmarish dream of his impending cuckoldry:

> Vulcano, que ya por cierto
> tiene del ave el abuso,
> que cantando hados presentes,
> predice agravios futuros,
>   y que se sueña animal
> jarameño y corajudo,
> convertido en puerco espín
> a garrochas y repullos;
>   y en un sueño vió dos cañas,
> que tenían sus cañutos,
> en su mujer las raíces,
> y en su cabeza los ñudos. (165–76)

[Vulcan has already got wind of the outrage from the bird that singing about present fates predicts future problems. He dreams of himself as a brave animal from Jarama, turned into a porcupine with spikes and little arrows. In a dream he saw two canes with their shoots, the roots of which were in his wife, and the knots of which were in his head.]

Having heard the dreaded call of the cuckoo, Vulcan has already been marked out as a disciple of the popular figure of Diego Moreno, the quintessential cuckold of Quevedo's *entremés* of the same name, and the last of the figures lampooned in his *Sueño de la muerte* [Dream of Death].[45] In the first half of his dream Vulcan imagines himself as a fighting bull which has been transformed into a porcupine, an animal capable of both defending itself at close quarters and attacking from distance.[46] However, as the second half of his dream makes clear, Vulcan is far from invincible. In fact he is utterly powerless to prevent other men from enjoying the benefit of his wife's company. He sees two *cañas*, 'canes', with two *cañutos*, 'shafts', which have their 'roots' in Venus and their 'knots' on his own head. On the one hand *cañutos* are the penises of Venus's clients; on the other, they are the horns of Vulcan's cuckoldry. It is entirely appropriate, therefore, that their *raíces*, 'los orígines y principios dellos', should be found in Vulcan's wife, while their *ñudos*, 'el nacimiento de los ramos' (Cov.), appear as shoots

---

[45] Francisco de Quevedo, 'Sueño de la muerte', in *Los sueños*, ed. Ignacio Arellano, LH, 335 (Madrid: Cátedra, 1999), 307–405 (pp. 399–405).

[46] The porcupine's mythical ability to throw its quills at attackers is reflected, for example, in Louis XII's choice of the animal as a symbol of invincibility—the French king's motto, 'Comminus et eminus', referring to the porcupine's capacity to fight both 'at close quarters' (*comminus*) and 'a spear's throw off' (*eminus*).

from Vulcan's temples. As Venus beds more and more men, the horns of her husband's cuckoldry grow and grow.

All five burlesque tellings contain a wide range of allusions to cuckoldry. The reader of these ballads encounters wordplay based on: animals with horns or animals that will soon grow horns (goats, rams, bulls, calves, etc.); words associated with such animals (e.g. *jarameño*, as above, or *hecatombe*, a sacrifice of 100 beasts to the gods); the noises or movements of animals with horns, most commonly the bull (snorting, charging, scraping hooves, etc.); astrological signs relating to animals with horns (i.e. Aries, Taurus, and Capricorn); the growth of shoots or branches (e.g. *cañutos*, *crecimiento*, *renuevos*), or figures associated with such growth (e.g. Pan, Vertumnus); horned shapes (e.g. crescent moons, particular types of leaf); words that contain *–corn–*, *–cuern–*, or other word-parts related to *cuernos*, 'horns' (e.g. *alcornoque, cornerinas, cornucopia*); items made out of horn or ivory (e.g. inkwells, hilt inlays); the cry of the cuckoo; or proper names related to any of the above (e.g. Cornelio, Panate, Ramiro). When used individually, near the beginning of a poem, such allusions serve as subtle pointers to the tale's denouement (compare, for example, the use of the verb *cabrá* in Hurtado de Mendoza's epistle). At times, however, they are rattled off in rapid-fire succession, creating impressive fireworks of linguistic wit. In Castillo Solórzano's account of Vulcan's appeal to the gods, for example, the smith's description of the temple dedicated to him and of the sacrifices made therein contains over twenty-five allusions to cuckoldry, with examples of all bar three of the categories outlined above:

> «Era el templo extraordinario,
> que villanos y escultores
> le formaron de cornijas,
> le enramaron de alcornoques.
>   La estatua de mi persona
> la guarnecen y componen
> de preciosas cornerinas
> con exquisitas labores.
>   La cornígera deidad
> de Pan, dios de los pastores,
> de pariente me ha tratado
> en nuestras corresponsiones.
>   El Aries, el Capricornio,
> y el Tauro, todos conformes,
> siempre me miran propicios
> sin que jamás se me enojen.
>   La luna, estando menguante,
> siempre que la vi bicorne

ha pretendido gustosa
que sus rayos me coronen.
Rebezos, corzos, y gamos,
con los ciervos corredores,
toros, cabritos, carneros,
para víctimas me escogen.
Hasta los tiernos chiquillos,
en sacrificios menores,
me van a ofrecer cornejas,
cuclillos, y caracoles.» (385–417)

[The temple was extraordinary, for villagers and sculptors constructed it out of crowns and adorned it with cork oaks. With exquisite skill, they decorated and embellished the statue of me with precious cornelian. The horned deity Pan, the god of shepherds, has treated me as a relative in our dealings. All alike, Aries, Capricorn, and Taurus always look favourably on me without them ever annoying me. Every time I have seen it two-horned, the moon, when waning, has taken pleasure in trying to crown me with its beams. Chamois, roes, fallow deer, along with fleet-footed stags, bulls, young goats, and rams, are all chosen as my victims. Even tender little kids, in smaller sacrifices, are going to be offered to me by crows, cuckoos, and snails.]

If the reader already knows that Vulcan is a cuckold, how can the poet surprise him? The emphasis here, as in many sections of these ballads, is on wit, verbal dexterity, and, in particular, accumulation. The poet provokes *admiratio* not through complex conceits, elaborate metaphors, and/or rhetorical embellishment, but through the deliberate and very self-conscious piling up or stringing together of different words associated with the horns of Vulcan's cuckoldry.

On other occasions we find more complex allusions to the same idea. In Polo de Medina's poem Vulcan's response to his peers' mockery offers a fine example of the linguistic and conceptual complexity of many quatrains:

Él, corriendo como un toro,
quisiera ser de un saúco,
si no pendiente espantajo,
cabrahígo de su fruto. (325–8)

[Running around like a bull, he would want to be, if not a scarecrow hanging in an elder, then the means by which the tree's fruit comes to maturity.]

The link drawn earlier between Vulcan and the finest fighting bulls in Spain, those from the lands bordering the river Jarama, is absurd, for the only point of comparison between Vulcan and a bull is their respective horns.[47] The rest of the quatrain develops a multifaceted conceit based on this simple point of comparison. Polo de Medina exploits the full range of semantic possibilities associated with the words *saúco, espantajo, cabrahígo*, and *fruto*. Vulcan is presented as a comical scarecrow hanging in the elder in order to frighten off his wife's possible suitors, who are busy trying to eat the fruit of the tree (that is, trying to have sex with Venus). Like some men, scarecrows command respect as unknown quantities; however, as Covarrubias explains (s.v. *espantajo*), their lack of substance soon leads them to be held in contempt, with the result that birds flock to eat from the trees they were designed to protect. Try as he may, Vulcan is powerless to prevent other men from sleeping with his wife. This seemingly light-hearted image of the scarecrow also carries more sinister resonances, for, according to popular pious legend, Judas Iscariot hanged himself from the branches of a *saúco*.[48] The rhetorical device 'si no *a, b*', closely associated with the poetry of Góngora, then throws light onto the *cabrahígo*, a wild fig that relies on another party in order to reach full maturity (Cov. s.v. *cabrahígo* and *higo*). Though Vulcan would like to be the one having sex with his own wife, he is forced to look on as other men impregnate her. In a remarkably dense quatrain, Polo de Medina points to Vulcan's impotence, the ease with which Venus offers up her fruit, and Mars's flagrant disregard for the presence of the knowing cuckold.

All three poems end on the theme of cuckoldry. Castillo Solórzano's ballad ends with Momus's burlesque epigram, a 'fregenal estrambote' in the form of a *décima* carved into marble and bronze so that word of Vulcan's cuckoldry can be passed down through the generations. At the end of Polo de Medina's poem Vulcan is rewarded for his patience by being made the 'abogado absoluto' [absolute arbiter] of 'maridos de cachas' [cuckolded husbands]. As such, he will hold the *cátedra* [chair] in cuckoldry studies of Quevedo's *El siglo del cuerno* [The Age of Horn] and have the final word on all cuckolds: 'no había de poder ser cornudo ninguno que no tuviese su carta de examen aprobada por los protocornudos' [there couldn't be any cuckolds not in possession of an exam certificate ratified by proto-cuckolds].[49] As if being a complaisant *marido resignado* were not already enough, cuckoldry is thus confirmed as the smith's new profession.

---

[47] 'cual suele acometer a jarameño, | toro feroz, de media luna armado' (Lope de Vega, *La Gatomaquia*, III, 240–1); see *La Gatomaquia*, ed. Celina Sabor de Cortázar, CC, 131 (Madrid: Castalia, 1982), 235.

[48] '*Fraile cuco, aceite de saúco. Fraile cuco, lámpara de saúco*: «que el tal fraile esté hecho lámpara de saúco, esto es, colgado de un saúco, como lámpara, a la manera de Judas»' (Correas, *Vocabulario*, 342).

[49] Francisco de Quevedo, 'El siglo del cuerno. Carta de un cornudo a otro', in *Prosa festiva completa*, ed. Celsa Carmen García-Valdés, LH, 363 (Madrid: Cátedra, 1993), 313.

The final quatrain sees him invent *guedejas* and *tufos*, two contemporary hairstyles banned in the 1630s, in a comical attempt to cover up the 'renuevos talludos' [mature shoots] that have started to grow from his temples—and which will serve as the insignia of his new-found trade. Last but not least, Barrios's poem draws to a close with a brief response from Jupiter to an exchange between Vulcan and Momus. The smith's complaint is given very short shrift, for Jupiter's mind is set firmly on his own affairs, in every sense of the word.[50]

THE SUPPORTING CAST

Whilst Mars, Venus, and Vulcan are the principal figures of fun in these ballads, a large supporting cast is also subjected to ridicule. This cast comprises both gods who traditionally play some part in the tale (e.g. Apollo) and a whole host of other figures previously unconnected with it (Cupid, Flora, Juno, Diana, Momus, etc.). According to Homeric and Ovidian tradition, it is Apollo who informs Vulcan of his wife's infidelity. The picture of the sun-god that emerges from these ballads is far from flattering. Whilst his actions are in part driven by a desire for revenge (angered by the insult to his friend Vulcan), they are also motivated by jealousy—or, more accurately, the Deadly Sin of Envy—for he, too, is consumed by desire for Venus (even when, in Díez y Foncalda's poem, he appears as Vulcan's father). Whereas Quevedo's Mars is accompanied by Bacchus, the divine alcoholic, Polo de Medina's Mars has Apollo for his planetary neighbour. The sun-god is introduced as the 'planeta boquirrubio' [pretty-boy planet], a naive *soplón* who is incapable of keeping a secret: 'Por lo de Marte y de Venus, | dicen que sois un soplón, | pues descubrís sus delitos | poniendo a riesgo su honor' [Because of the Mars and Venus affair, it's said you're a tell-tale, for you put their honour at risk by uncovering their crimes].[51] In Díez y Foncalda's poem Apollo's red hair leads to him being likened to Judas, the archetypal traitor—'como Judas bermejo' bringing to mind the opening line of Quevedo's sonnet 'A Apolo, siguiendo a Dafne' (Q536) in which Apollo is addressed as the 'Bermejazo platero de las cumbres'.

---

[50] For more on cuckoldry in seventeenth-century Spanish satire, see Ignacio Arellano Ayuso, *Poesía satírico burlesca de Quevedo. Estudio y anotación filológica de los sonetos* (Navarre: Universidad de Navarra, 1984), 66–72; and Félix Cantizano Pérez, 'El siglo del cuerno', in *El erotismo en la poesía de adúlteros y cornudos en el Siglo de Oro* (Madrid: Editorial Complutense, 2007), 37–74.

[51] For these lines, taken from another burlesque ballad in *El buen humor de las musas*, see 'Romance a Apolo', in Salvador Jacinto Polo de Medina, *Obras completas*, ed. José María de Cossío, Biblioteca de Autores Murcianos, 1 (Murcia: Tip. Sucesores de Nogués, 1948), 299–301 (p. 299).

For Castillo Solórzano and Polo de Medina, Apollo is the 'dios cochero' [coachman god]: on the one hand he whips his steeds into action as he drives the chariot of the sun across the sky; on the other, he mans *coches*, controversial 'carriages' associated in contemporary satire with illicit sexual encounters (see, for example, Quevedo's 'Sátira a los coches'; Q779). As if that were not enough, the final nail is driven into Apollo's coffin when the once-revered god of poetry—or 'Micer Apolo' or 'Apolillo', as he is now known—is dismissed as just another incomprehensible *culto* poet.

Several other gods come in for similar treatment in one or more of the poems: Cupid is a pesky little archer, 'inquietud y paz del orbe' [source of concern and peace in the world], responsible for setting the whole farce in motion by striking Mars with one of his gold-tipped arrows; Aurora is an executioner (of darkness); Flora is a go-between who prepares the stage on which the lovers consummate their affair; Adonis is a picaresque layabout, who engages in obscene foreplay with Venus, gorges himself on tripe, and faints after prolonged bouts of tenesmus; the Cyclopes are sweaty, one-eyed drudges (they are grotesque enough already not to require further deformation); Diana and her nymphs are unmasked as a brothel madam and her retinue of prostitutes; Pallas Athene is exposed as a moralizing prude; and Jupiter is too busy with his own marital problems to concern himself with Vulcan's complaint. When viewed as a whole, the gods are a 'caterva' [gang], a 'corro de poetas' [circle of poets], or a 'concejo en Galicia' [town council in Galicia], a shambolic rabble who gorge themselves, as in Góngora's 'Arrojóse el mancebito', not on the ambrosia associated with their classical forebears but on tripe, the coarsest of fare.

In one of the most important changes to the tale, already suggested in Cueva's 'Los amores', both gods and goddesses come down from on high to laugh at their peers' respective predicaments. Juno, Diana, and Pallas Athene are no longer in possession of the modesty that kept their Homeric counterparts at home. Polo de Medina gives the reactions of all three to the spectacle that greets them when the doors of heaven are flung open: Juno is displeased, being reminded of her own husband's affairs (and his transformations into a bull, a swan, a shower of gold, etc.); the virginal Pallas Athene screws up her face at the same time as trying to affect daintiness; and Diana, another virgin goddess, pretends to be appalled by what she sees, expressing horror at the lovers' shame and covering her eyes with her hands, but all the while peeks nonchalantly through the gaps between her fingers. At the end of Polo de Medina's poem the gods and goddesses return to the heavens, 'ellas en forma de urracas, | y ellos como abejorrucos' [the latter as a group of magpies, the former as bee-eaters]. The gods are *abejorrucos*, colourful 'bee-eaters', communal birds known for their song; the goddesses, meanwhile, are *urracas*, kleptomaniac 'magpies' but also idle 'chatterboxes' (the phrase 'hablar más que una hurraca' is still used today to refer to someone who suffers from verbal diarrhoea). On this evidence, the Roman gods are not a group of majestic divinities but a band of malicious, low-life gossips (compare, for example, the image of them at top right in Solis's illustration: Figure 1.3).[52]

In sum, the idealizing façade erected around the gods of Antiquity is exposed as a sham. However, that does not mean the mythological burlesque represents a wholesale rejection of classical authority. It marks, instead, a change in the model(s) being imitated. The most significant change of personnel in the tellings penned by Castillo Solórzano, Polo de Medina, and Barrios is the introduction of Momus—a change perhaps suggested by the role played by this figure at the end of Cueva's 'Llanto de Venus' or indeed by the prominent position given to him in the final book of Vitoria's *Teatro* (the latter published just months before Castillo Solórzano's *Donaires*). The presence of this figure previously unconnected with the tale marks a clear shift towards Lucianic satire (as does Díez y Foncalda's reintroduction of Mars's servant Gallus, a figure present in Lucian but not, as seen earlier, in Homer/ Ovid). As Covarrubias explains (s.v. *Momo*), Momus, god of mockery and fault-finding, does nothing but lampoon others, 'sin perdonar alguna falta, por pequeña que fuese' [without letting any error go, no matter how small]. This is his role in several of Lucian's works, including *Nigrinus*, 32, *Hermotimus*, 20, and *Vera Historia* [A True Story], 2.3 (all three of which touch on Momus's criticism of inventions by Athene, Poseidon, and Hephaestus); the *Deorum Concilium* [Council of the Gods] (which sees Momus launch a series of scathing attacks on his fellow gods and their crimes); and the *Zeus Tragoedus* [Zeus the Tragic Actor] (in which Momus tells his peers that, given the gods' upside-down world, it is only natural that men should begin to question the authority of those to whom their sacrifices are dedicated).[53] It is no surprise that Momus's eventual fate was to be cast down from Olympus on account of his inability to hold his tongue.

[52] The gods are presented in similar vein in Fortune's attack on Jupiter in Quevedo, *La Hora de todos*, 157.

[53] Momus appears frequently in early modern European literature, from Leon Battista Alberti's *Momus sive De principe* (*c*.1452) to John Dryden's *The Secular Masque* (1700). Alberti's allegorical satire was published in Spanish in Agustín de Almazán's translation *La moral y muy graciosa historia del Momo* (Alcalá de Henares: Juan Mey Flandro, 1553; repr. Madrid: Licenciado Castro, 1598). Momus plays a prominent part in many Spanish works contemporaneous with the poems under discussion in this chapter, including, for example, Alonso Gerónimo de Salas Barbadillo's *La estafeta del dios Momo* (Madrid: viuda de Luis Sánchez, 1627), a series of satirical epistles dedicated to the court preacher Hortensio Paravicino, and Sebastián Francisco de Medrano's *Las venganzas del amor* (1631), a mythological *comedia* featuring Mars and Venus, in which Momus plays the role of the *gracioso* (see his *Favores de las Musas* (Milan: Carlo Ferranti, 1631), 21–108). For more on Lucian and his reception in the Renaissance, see Chapter 1, n. 36.

Whereas in previous tellings (from Homer and Ovid to Cueva and Lope) gods such as Apollo and Mercury had voiced their envy of Mars, now it is Momus, 'el fisgón de los dioses' [the joker of the gods], who takes centre stage to pile misery on Vulcan. The emphasis on Neptune's mediation, Jupiter's judgement, and Mars's (empty) promise of compensation gives way to emphasis on Momus's cruel teasing, his malicious gossip, and his publication of Vulcan's infamy. Polo de Medina's Momus mocks Vulcan for being a 'bicorne búho' [two-horned owl]: the cuckold is labelled *búho*, in a play on the word *lechuzo*, not because of the bird's connection with wisdom but because of its association with ill omens and social recluses (Cov. s.v. *buho*). In Castillo Solórzano the god of mockery has the final word: Momus pens the burlesque *décima* with which the poem closes, ensuring that generations to come are familiar with the tale of Vulcan's cuckolding. As in John Dryden's poem *The Secular Masque*, in which the god of mockery exposes the vanity, self-delusion, and immorality of the gods (in this case Diana, Mars, and Venus), Momus is on hand to unmask the gods, to expose them as actors playing parts for which they are totally unfit, and to foil their attempts to pass themselves off as something they are not. Significantly, Polo de Medina's gods wear *coturnos*, the special platform shoes or 'buskins' worn by tragic actors. The gods' footwear marks them out as pretend gods, farcically striving to play in the 'tragic style'. When, in an attempt to make less noise during their descent from the heavens, they take off their *coturnos* and thus step down from their high platforms (physical and moral), their true nature is revealed.

As we have seen, Castillo Solórzano, Polo de Medina, and Barrios were all quick to seize on and develop the comic potential inherent in the tale of Mars, Venus, and Vulcan. Many of the changes they make to the basic narrative serve, first and foremost, to give them further scope to provoke laughter. A variety of stylistic devices is employed in the construction of what are unashamedly humorous tellings: accumulation, absurd hyperbole, derogatory suffixes, incongruous titles, neologisms and portmanteau words, argot and *germanía*, proverbs and popular sayings, sexual and scatological humour, wordplay on literal and metaphorical levels of meaning, and so on. In each *romance* the jokes come thick and fast, ranging from satire to empty wordplay, from slapstick to black humour, from parody to the grotesque, and from sexual innuendo to elaborate conceits. In Polo de Medina's poem alone we see jokes based on bullfighting, rustic fare, culinary preparations, carnival masquerades, fasting and religious abstinence, *culto* poetry, the Trojan War, sexually transmitted diseases and unsavoury medical conditions, storms at sea and menstrual cycles, classical references to Argus, Actaeon, and Aeneas's helmsman

Palinurus, astrology and signs of the Zodiac, the comic jargon of Basques, the remedial properties of plants from the New World, trees dedicated to Venus, far-flung corners of the Habsburg empire, the slang connotations of ornithological terms, contemporary fads and fashions, clothes associated with criminals on their way to the gallows, and so on and so forth.

One of the most common ways of introducing elements of bathos is through the conflation of the worlds of classical mythology and contemporary seventeenth-century society. Piquant anachronism sees the gods of Antiquity develop obsessions with early seventeenth-century fashions (make-up, farthingales, perfumed gloves, etc.), hairstyles (*moños, guedejas, tufos*, etc.), status symbols (carriages, theatre boxes, titles, etc.), and monetary denominations (*reales, escudos, doblones*, etc.).[54] Each poet also takes aim at a host of traditional targets: tradesmen and professionals (innkeepers, glovemakers, prison warders, merchants, lawyers, etc.); cuckolds, cowards, and nosy neighbours; narcissists, hypocrites, and homosexuals; the ugly, the syphilitic, and the physically deformed; and, perhaps most prominently, women, prostitution, and sexual commerce. Whilst Castillo Solórzano sets his telling in the Madrid of the *comedia* and the Prado, Polo de Medina sets his in the cynical modern world of the bordello, bringing together the previously antithetical worlds of the pagan gods and society's criminal underbelly. Mars is no longer the embodiment of martial valour, but an ugly, pompous, and self-deceiving *miles gloriosus* who has to pay a venal, rapacious, and disease-riddled professional for sex. The world of Aldana's sonnet could not be further away: the end product of the conjunction of Mars and Venus is no longer *discordia concors* but bathos and wit.

In terms of parody, it is not just serious treatments of classical mythology that find themselves in the firing line. Castillo Solórzano, Polo de Medina, and Barrios also take aim at a whole host of literary conventions associated with existing genres and styles. As we have seen, a number of topoi associated with conventions of Courtly Love and Petrarchan lyric are also parodied: the set-piece portrait of the divine beloved; the traditional order in which physical appearances are described; the male lover's worship of the female beloved; the lover's serenade to the beloved; the prostration of the lover before the beloved; the topos of the lover contemplating the beloved's reflection in a stream; the power of the beloved over the lover; the effects of the sight of the beloved on the lover; and the

[54] Many of these are the subjects of satirical poems by Quevedo. See e.g. the sonnets 'Si eres campana, ¿dónde está el badajo?' (Q516) and 'Si no duerme su cara con Filena' (Q522) on women and their accoutrements; the *letrilla* 'Poderoso caballero es don Dinero' (Q660) on the power of money; the *romance* 'Don Repollo y doña Berza' (Q683) on the obsession with titles; and the *romance* 'Tocóse a cuatro de enero' (Q779) on the vogue for *coches*.

metaphors of the bed as a battlefield of love and of love as a more benign form of war. Poetic tradition dictates that the lady be worshipped as a goddess. It is ironic, therefore, that Venus, the object of the male's affection, is already divine: rather than a mortal woman being elevated to the status of a goddess, we see a goddess exposed as the very embodiment of human moral weakness.

Conventions associated with epic and pastoral are also playfully reworked. The first thirty-two lines of Castillo Solórzano's poem, for example, parody the traditional appeal to Apollo and the Muses commonly found in the exordium to a long narrative poem: the Muses are addressed as a 'novenario virginal' [virginal nonet], likened to weathervanes atop Parnassus (as fickle and capricious women, they point in whatever direction the prevailing poetic winds blow); their legendary home is juxtaposed with the contemporary Court, a hotbed of vice and iniquity; wordplay on *vena* brings together the worlds of poetic inspiration and medicine (the administering of bloodletting or medicinal syrups); fourteen lines of Ovid are cited as the source for this mythological 'pastel de embote' [hotpot]; and finally the poet appeals to Armenian and Libyan muses for two hundred 'cultas bernardinas' [flashy learned words], so as to be able to 'show off' at appropriate moments in the rest of the poem. Later, when the lovers fall for one another at the gods' spring banquet, Mars and Venus withdraw to a shady clearing described in terms of flowers, birdsong, the mythological nightingale Philomela, babbling brooks, emerald-green grass, shade-giving trees (poplars, elms, and box trees), chattering cicadas, and so on. The description of this idyllic setting—a *locus amoenus* in the tradition of Theocritus (e.g. *Idylls*, VII.135–46), Virgil (e.g. *Eclogues*, I.51–8), and Garcilaso (e.g. Eclogue I, 43–56)—is punctuated by popular slang, absurd Latinisms, and inappropriate detail. This is, after all, the setting not for the unrequited loves of shepherds but for the unseemly affairs of Mars and Venus. The description of the lovers' union in terms of commonplace classical and Renaissance symbols of faithful, reciprocated love—such as the vine wedded to the trunk of the elm (e.g. Horace, *Epodes*, 2.9–10)—is inappropriate given the emphasis on instant sexual gratification. Barrios's setting is even more incongruous: what seems at first to be a *locus amoenus*, identified by birdsong, streams, flowers, and so on, is then revealed to be the Garden of Eden, with references to sin, temptation, and Venus eating fruit from the Tree of Knowledge of Good and Evil (lines 217–44).

As we have seen, the high *culto* style associated with Góngora and his followers is also frequently satirized. Unsurprisingly, it is Castillo Solórzano and Polo de Medina, the two poets writing in the wake of the great polemic surrounding *cultismo*, who most closely engage with aspects of this Latinate and highly erudite poetic style. Attacks on *cultismo* abound in their poems. In Castillo Solórzano's poem *culto* language is associated with a range of other targets, such as foreigners, heretics, and sodomites. As noted above, the poem's exordium reaches a climax in lines 21–32, with an appeal to the aforementioned foreign muses to teach him 'aquestas modernas voces' [those new words]; an obscure 'lenguaje biforme' [biform language] that is a source of bewilderment, unknown in Spain, devoid of substance, concerned only with ostentation, and opposed to the true language and religion of Castile. Apollo is a new-wave poet, but even he abandons his obfuscatory jargon and rhetorical flourishes to deliver his message to Vulcan: 'Pan por pan, vino por vino | son más claras locuciones, | no voces cultisonantes | que perturban el informe' [Calling a spade a spade and a bucket a bucket is clearer language, not those high-sounding learned words that obscure what one says] (lines 313–16). Throughout his ballad Polo de Medina undermines the authority of the pagan gods through burlesque and satirical descriptions of their words, actions, and appearances. Judging by the ironic gap between how the gods' words are presented and what they are designed to communicate, *cultismo* should be seen not as an ennobling form of the vernacular but as the incomprehensible mumbo jumbo of morally bankrupt *necios*. It is entirely appropriate that the pagan gods, who are false gods, should employ *culto* forms of discourse: *cultismo* is morally obfuscatory, for it prettifies and idealizes iniquity, most prominently here the Deadly Sins of Lust, Greed, Pride, and Envy.

When, in Polo de Medina's *Academias del jardín*, Álvaro attacks Jacinto for the *culto* nature of an epithalamium, the poet's alter ego defends himself thus:

no me infaméis con tan odioso nombre … que no lo merecen mis versos, que si hacen alguna resistencia al entendimiento nace de lo misterioso y retirado del concepto, no de lo forastero de las voces y marañada colocación de los términos.[55]

[do not slander me with such a loathsome name … because my poetry does not merit it, for if it is at all difficult to comprehend it arises from the mysterious and recondite conceits and not from any strange words or tangled ordering of terms.]

The ballads examined in this chapter are difficult, but any 'resistencia al entendimiento' stems not from the Latinate vocabulary and radical hyperbaton that are the hallmarks of *cultismo* (that is, 'lo forastero de las voces y marañada colocación de los términos') but from complex linguistic

---

[55] Polo de Medina, *Obras completas*, 154.

and conceptual play ('lo misterioso y retirado del concepto').[56] The links between several of these ballads, most notably those of Castillo Solórzano, Polo de Medina, and Barrios—the detailed portraits of the main protagonists, the presence of cuckoos and dreams, the role played by Momus, and so on—suggest that each poet was aware of an existing tradition of burlesque tellings. The drive to tell the same tale in different ways leads each poet to search for new and innovative conceits. A fine example of this can be seen in the various descriptions of the lovers' pre- or post-capture embrace. Whereas Aldana (the lovers are 'ambos desnudos, | en una red de indisolubles ñudos'), Góngora ('tan en pelota y tan juntos, | que en nudos ciegos los tienen'), and Cueva ('en infame nudo asidos') describe the scene simply in terms of naked flesh and indissoluble knots, the poets discussed in this chapter demand much more of the reader's intellect. Castillo Solórzano, Polo de Medina, Díez y Foncalda, and Durán de Salcedo all describe the scene through references to astrological signs (another common motif that suggests each poet was aware of previous tellings). Castillo Solórzano's account of Apollo's sighting of the lovers plays on the sign Gemini, its links to the month of May, and its zodiac symbol (♊): 'sin ser mayo, doraba | otro Géminis del bosque' [although it wasn't May, another pair of Twins was gilded in the woods] (lines 299–300). Durán de Salcedo and Díez y Foncalda also play on the same astrological sign. In contrast, when Polo de Medina's Apollo sees the lovers, they are:

> hechos al vivo un dibujo
> de aquel signo que a sus potros
> sirve de establo por junio. (246–8)

[acting out a sketch of the sign of the Zodiac that serves as a stable for his colts in June.]

As Covarrubias explains, *dibuxo* denotes a 'delineación de pintura escura sin colores' [simple line drawing without colours]. Mars and Venus, therefore, represent a real-life enactment of an outline drawing of a symbol associated with June, the month in which 'reyna el signo Cáncer' [the sign of Cancer reigns] (Cov. s.v. *junio*). This is not an invitation to picture the crab, for the fact that we are dealing with a *dibujo* points the reader in the direction of a more primitive symbol for the sign of Cancer. In order fully to understand this conceit, the reader must know that the *dibujo* in question is '♋'. In lines of notable conceptual density, Polo de Medina forces the reader to work through a chain of associations and to establish the correpondences between June and Cancer, between Cancer and a

---

[56] For more on Polo de Medina's relationship to Góngora and *cultismo*, see Giulia Bontempelli, 'Polo de Medina, poeta gongorino', in *Venezia nella letteratura spagnola e altri studi barocchi* (Padua: University of Pisa, 1973), 85–136.

particular *dibujo*, and between the glyph '℘' and a very specific sexual act. Similar conceits are employed throughout these ballads, as each poet shows a concern for conceptual complexity and mental gymnastics in the search for the most striking and original *conceptos*.

Throughout this chapter attention has been drawn to apposite parallels between the ballads under consideration and examples of the burlesque and satirical poetry of Quevedo, the period's most famous exponent of such verse. By way of conclusion to this chapter, one might note that much of the above analysis could be applied to the subjects, attitudes, and styles found in the poems grouped together under Thalia, the sixth muse of González de Salas's edition of Quevedo's *Parnasso español* [Spanish Parnassus] of 1648, which present 'descripciones graciosas, sucesos de donaire, y censuras satíricas de culpables costumbres cuyo estilo es todo templado de burlas y de veras' [humorous descriptions, charming events, and satirical attacks on blameworthy customs whose style is tempered throughout by jokes and truths]. The insistence, for example, on cuckoldry, physical deformity, and sexual and scatological wordplay—all hallmarks of Quevedo's burlesque and satirical works—is intended to make readers laugh, but it is also designed to disconcert them, challenging them to see through the *burlas* to the domain of *veras*. The ballads' emphasis on the moral degeneracy of the pagan gods—on their obsession with surface appearance (the world of *parecer* as opposed to *ser*), their failure to practise the Cardinal Virtues (especially Prudence and Temperance) and their subservience to the Deadly Sins (especially Greed, Lust, and Envy), and their (ab)use of language to prettify and/or justify their immoral thoughts, words, and actions—gives their readers serious food for thought:

> Burlas canto y grandes veras
> miento, que yo siempre he sido
> sermón estoico vestido
> de máscaras placenteras.
>   De el donaire en mi ficción
> cuide, pues, quien fuere sabio,
> que lo dulce sienta el labio
> y lo acedo el corazón.[57]

---

[57] These quotations are taken from the title page of the muse Thalia and the engraved frontispiece entitled 'Mimica lascivo gaudet sermone THALIA' in Francisco de Quevedo, *El Parnasso Español, monte en dos cumbres dividido, con las nueve musas castellanas* (Madrid: Pedro Coello, 1648), 399, 401. On Quevedo, González de Salas, and the muse Thalia, see Samuel Fasquel, 'La enunciación paradójica y las estrategias del discurso burlesco', in *La poesía burlesca*, 41–57; and my '«Vanitas vanitatum, et omnia vanitas»: bibliotecas y bibliofilia en la literatura del Siglo de Oro', in Oliver Noble Wood, Jeremy Roe, and Jeremy Lawrance (eds.), *Poder y saber. Bibliotecas y bibliofilia en la época del conde-duque de Olivares* (Madrid: CEEH, 2011), 277–96 (esp. pp. 279–81).

[I sing of jokes and disguise great truths, for I have always been a Stoic sermon dressed in delightful masks. As for the charms of my fictions, let anyone who aspires to wisdom take care that his lips taste the sweetness and his heart what is sharp or sour].

Paradoxically, it is, therefore, the burlesque and satirical romps of Castillo Solórzano, Polo de Medina, Barrios, and others that convey the most forceful moral lessons of all the poems analysed thus far, albeit only through the age-old principle of 'dorar la píldora' [sugaring the pill] and—adapting the words of Fray Juan Bautista in his *aprobación* to the *Novelas ejemplares*— the development of examples not of 'virtudes a seguir' [virtues to follow] but of 'vicios a huir' [vices to flee].[58]

---

[58] Cervantes, *Novelas ejemplares*, i. 45.

5

Mythological Paintings: Velázquez and the Cult of Ambiguity

Though, as we have seen, a wealth of material inspired by classical mythology can be found in Golden Age literature, in genres ranging from the traditional ballad to satirical prose and from the novel to works designed for the contemporary stage, mythological paintings by Spanish artists are by comparison few and far between. Whereas in Italy artists from Botticelli to Tiepolo frequently turned their attention to the fables of classical antiquity, and while innumerable paintings on mythological subjects by Italian and Dutch masters were either bought for or commissioned by the Spanish Habsburgs, few artists working in Spain turned to such subjects. The scarcity of mythological works is traditionally ascribed to restrictions imposed upon artists by notions of decorum and expectations as to the proper aims and ends of the art of painting. The post-Tridentine requirement for works of art to encourage devotion and prayer, or at least some form of morally beneficial response, appears at odds with the classical emphasis upon nudity and the apparently lascivious subject matter of many of the tales inherited from Homer, Ovid, and others.[1]

The relative status of mythological painting in Spain is reflected in Golden Age treatises on art, from Felipe de Guevara's *Comentarios de la pintura* [Commentaries on Painting] (*c*.1560) to Jusepe Martínez's *Discursos practicables del nobilísimo arte de la pintura* [Practicable Discourses of the Most Noble Art of Painting] (*c*.1675), which say little or nothing about the genre. When they do touch on it, it is normally in relation to the much-debated question of the painting of nudes. The emphasis on nudity in many classical tales posed painters (but not, as we have seen, poets) a serious problem. Whilst the nude enabled artists to demonstrate their mastery of the human form, 'la parte más difícil de la pintura' [the most difficult aspect of painting], it could also incite

---

[1] For an overview of mythological painting in the Golden Age, see Rosa López Torrijos, *La mitología en la pintura española del Siglo de Oro* (Madrid: Cátedra, 1985); and Diego Angulo Íñiguez, *La mitología en el arte español: del Renacimiento a Velázquez*, ed. and intro. José Manuel Pita Andrade (Madrid: RAH, 2010).

inappropriate responses from the viewer.[2] A long line of classical and Renaissance authorities voiced concern about such subjects, crediting Satan with their invention, suggesting that to paint or display them was a mortal sin, and banning them because they had the power to provoke 'deseos torpes, y aun acontecimientos abominables' [base desires and even abominable acts].[3] Even when part of representations of canonical biblical or classical tales, female nudes were more often than not viewed as 'pintura lasciva' [lascivious painting]. Venus was a source of particular controversy. Again, classical and Renaissance authorities give innumerable examples of young men falling for, and even trying to make love to, statues of her. In his chapter entitled 'De los templos, y estatuas de la Diosa Venus' [On the Temples and Statues of the Goddess Venus], Vitoria, for instance, gives several such examples before concluding that 'hermosura deshonesta, ni aun pintada se ha de ver, y los ejemplos pasados lo dan bien a entender cuan perjudiciales y nocivos son' [indecent beauty should not be seen even when painted, and past examples show well enough how damaging and harmful they are].[4]

The two most famous Golden Age treatises on art, Vicente Carducho's *Diálogos de la pintura* [Dialogues on Painting] (1633) and Francisco Pacheco's *Arte de la pintura* [Art of Painting] (1649), comment on mythological painting only in passing. The Madrid-based court painter Carducho touches on the treatment of mythological subjects in the course of a discussion of the decoration of 'galerías Reales' [royal galleries]:

> si acaso tal vez conviniere, o fuese gusto del dueño, pintar las obras de Virgilio, Homero, y las fábulas de Ovidio, procure demostrar con afecto y propiedad, la moralidad virtuosa que encierra en sí, oculta a la ignorancia, y no la corteza incasta, y descompuesta, atendiendo al provecho, no solicitando el daño.[5]

> [if ever deemed appropriate, or in line with the owner's tastes, to paint the works of Virgil, Homer, and Ovid's invented tales, try to show with care and

---

[2] Francisco Pacheco, *Arte de la pintura*, ed. Bonaventura Bassegoda i Hugas (Madrid: Cátedra, 1990 [1649]), 337.

[3] Juan de Butrón, *Discursos apologeticos, en que se defiende la ingenuidad del arte de la pintura* (Madrid: Luis Sánchez, 1626), fols. 83ᵛ–8ʳ (fol. 83ʳ).

[4] *Segunda parte*, 357–64 (p. 361). For a sample of approaches to the much-debated subject of the nude in Golden Age art, see Pierre Civil, 'Erotismo y pintura mitológica en la España del Siglo de Oro', *Edad de Oro*, 9 (1990), 39–49; López Torrijos, *La mitología en la pintura española*, 271–93; and Javier Portús Pérez, *La Sala Reservada del Museo del Prado y el coleccionismo de pintura de desnudo en la corte española 1554–1838* (Madrid: Museo Nacional del Prado, 1998); and 'Nudes and Knights: A Context for Venus', in Dawson W. Carr and others, *Velázquez* (London: National Gallery, 2006), 56–67.

[5] Vicente Carducho, *Diálogos de la pintura* (Madrid: Francisco Martínez, 1633), fol. 109ʳ.

correctness the virtuous morality contained within, hidden from ignorance, and not the immoral and ill-ordered outer shell, having regard for moral benefit, not soliciting harm.]

The Sevillian writer and painter Pacheco dissociates himself from 'los famosos pintores, que se han extremado con la licenciosa expresión de tanta diversidad de fábulas' [famous painters who have gone to great lengths with their licentious treatments of such a range of invented tales], and whose paintings 'ocupan los salones y camarines de los grandes señores y príncipes del mundo' [hang on the walls of the halls and chambers of the great nobles and princes of the world].[6] Together, these two asides underline the existence of continued belief in the surface immorality of classical tales and the subsequent need for moralization. In practice, mythological subjects were often incorporated into iconographical schemes in which they could be read allegorically, bringing to the fore the 'moralidad virtuosa que encierr[an] en sí'. As Marcia Welles observes, fine examples of this can be seen in the early seventeenth-century ceiling paintings in the library of the Sevillian poet Juan de Arguijo and the study of the Duke of Alcalá in the Casa de Pilatos.[7] Another oft-cited example is the cycle on the labours of Hercules completed by Francisco de Zurbarán for the Hall of Realms at the Buen Retiro, the controversial palace built by Philip IV and Olivares on the eastern outskirts of Madrid in the early 1630s. The meaning and function of the ten paintings—nine of major and minor labours and one of the hero's death and apotheosis—are clear: paralleling the military achievements of Hercules's glorious descendants, captured in the twelve battle paintings of recent Spanish victories hanging in the same hall, they embody the might, virtue, and immortality of the Habsburgs and underline their divine right to rule.[8]

Whilst the above asides suggest that mythological painting was held in low esteem in some quarters, they (and the above examples) also point to its popularity with royalty and the nobility. The passion of the Spanish Habsburgs for such works is well known. Titian was a particular favourite of both Charles V and Philip II. It was for the latter that the Italian painted six celebrated *poesie* on subjects drawn from the *Metamorphoses* between

[6] *Arte de la pintura*, 376.

[7] Marcia L. Welles, *Arachne's Tapestry: The Transformation of Myth in Seventeenth-Century Spain* (San Antonio, Tex.: Trinity University Press, 1986), 134–5. For more on these paintings, see Brown, 'Theory into Practice: The Arts and the Academy', in *Images and Ideas in Seventeenth-Century Spanish Painting* (Princeton: Princeton University Press, 1978), 63–83; and Mary E. Barnard, 'Inscribing Transgression, Siting Identity: Arguijo's Phaëthon and Ganymede in Painting and Text', in *Writing for the Eyes*, 109–29.

[8] On the construction and decoration of the Buen Retiro, see Jonathan Brown and John H. Elliott, *A Palace for a King: The Buen Retiro and the Court of Philip IV*, 2nd edn. (New Haven: Yale University Press, 2003).

1551 and 1562.[9] Other favourites of the Spanish Habsburgs included Tintoretto, Veronese, and, later, Rubens. Philip IV was a particularly avid collector of mythological paintings. When Rubens was in Madrid as foreign envoy between August 1628 and April 1629, the Flemish master copied 'todas las cosas de Ticiano que tiene el rey' [everything by Titian owned by the king], including 'los dos baños, la Europa, el Adonis y Venus, la Venus y Cupido . . . y otros muchos cuadros fuera de los que el rey tiene' [the two bathing scenes, the Europa, the Adonis and Venus, the Venus and Cupid . . . and many other works outside the royal collection].[10] The number of paintings in the royal collection on mythological subjects grew substantially in the middle decades of the seventeenth century, as Philip IV and Olivares bought up and commissioned myriad works for the various royal residences. Those in the Alcázar alone increased from fifty-eight in 1636 to 165 in 1686.[11] A famous addition to the royal collection in this period was a series of around sixty mythological paintings, mostly on subjects inspired by Ovid, completed by Rubens and his Flemish School disciples for the Torre de la Parada, the royal hunting lodge at El Pardo that was expanded and redecorated in 1636–8.[12]

The most significant additions, however, were mythological works by Philip IV's court painter, Diego Velázquez. Born in Seville in 1599, Velázquez became an apprentice to Pacheco in December 1610. At that time Pacheco, the artist's future father-in-law, was at the centre of a scholarly community that counted among its ranks leading poets, scholars, historians, theologians, and nobles of the day. Velázquez's apprenticeship thus gave him not only the tutelage of one of Seville's leading artists but also, and perhaps more importantly, total immersion in the city's famous academy of letters.[13] Velázquez's meteoric rise from young

---

9 On Titian's relationship with the Spanish Habsburgs and his paintings of Danaë, Venus and Adonis, Diana and Actaeon, Diana and Callisto, the Rape of Europa, and Perseus and Andromeda, see Jane C. Nash, *Veiled Images: Titian's Mythological Paintings for Philip II* (Philadelphia: Art Alliance Press, 1985); Fernando Checa Cremades, *Tiziano y la monarquía hispánica. Usos y funciones de la pintura veneciana en España (siglos XVI y XVII)* (Madrid: Nerea, 1994); and David Rosand, 'Inventing Mythologies: The Painter's Poetry', in Patricia Meilman (ed.), *The Cambridge Companion to Titian* (Cambridge: Cambridge University Press, 2004), 35–57.

10 Pacheco, *Arte de la pintura*, 197–201.

11 López Torrijos, *La mitología en la pintura española*, 73–4.

12 For more on Rubens and the Torre de la Parada, see Svetlana Alpers, *The Decoration of the Torre de la Parada* (London: Phaidon, 1971); Christopher Allen, 'Ovid and Art', in *The Cambridge Companion to Ovid*, 336–67; and Hélène Dubois and Natasja Peeters, 'The Mythological Decor of the Torre de la Parada', in Joost Vander Auwera and Sabine van Sprang (eds.), *Rubens: A Genius at Work* (Tielt: Lannoo, 2007), 250–63.

13 On the artistic environment in which Velázquez grew up, see Jonathan Brown, 'A Community of Scholars', in *Images and Ideas*, 21–43; Vicente Lleó Cañal, *Nueva Roma. Mitología y humanismo en el Renacimiento sevillano* (Seville: Diputación Provincial, 1979); and *Velázquez in Seville*, ed. Michael Clarke (Edinburgh: National Galleries of Scotland, 1996).

apprentice to Pacheco to painter to the king is well documented, as is his career at Court from 1623 to the year of his death in 1660.[14] His interest in mythological subjects, which would continue throughout the rest of his career, appears to have been piqued by contact with Rubens in late 1628 and early 1629.[15] Perhaps watching the Flemish master copy works by Titian was what encouraged him to turn to such subjects. A few months after Rubens's departure from Madrid, Velázquez's first extant mythological work, *Los borrachos* [The Topers] (1629), was sold to the Crown. This was, it seems, the last painting Velázquez completed before he set off on his first tour of Italy, between August 1629 and early 1631. Almost certainly encouraged and facilitated by Rubens, this trip, which took him to Genoa, Venice, Milan, Rome, and Naples, marked a defining point in Velázquez's career: exposure to classical sculpture, works by the great masters, and the latest developments in Italian art enabled him to develop his use of light and colour, his understanding of anatomy, and his mastery of gesture and expression.[16] It also brought his second foray into the world of mythological painting—and the only extant canvas from the Spanish Golden Age explicitly to take as its subject a scene from the tale of Mars, Venus, and Vulcan.[17]

LA FRAGUA DE VULCANO (1630)

During his first tour of Italy Velázquez 'synthesized [his] experiences in two history paintings in the Italian manner'.[18] Painted in Rome in 1630, and then sold to the Crown through Jerónimo de Villanueva in 1634 for the decoration of the Buen Retiro, *La túnica de José* [Joseph's Coat Brought to Jacob] and *La fragua de Vulcano* [The Forge of Vulcan] are two of a very

[14] See e.g. Jonathan Brown, *Velázquez: Painter and Courtier* (New Haven: Yale University Press, 1986).

[15] One of Velázquez's last works was his painting of *Mercury and Argus* (c.1659), the sole survivor of four mythological works completed for the redecoration of the Hall of Mirrors in the Alcázar (the others depicting Apollo and Marsyas, Venus and Adonis, and Cupid and Psyche); see Brown, *Velázquez: Painter and Courtier*, 246.

[16] On Velázquez's two trips to Italy, see Pacheco, *Arte de la pintura*, 206–9; Anna Coliva (ed.), *Velázquez a Roma. Velázquez e Roma* (Milan: Skiva, 1999); Salvador Salort Pons, *Velázquez en Italia* (Madrid: Fundación de Apoyo a la Historia del Arte Hispánico, 2002), 33–79; and Jonathan Brown, 'Velázquez and Italy', in Suzanne L. Stratton-Pruitt (ed.), *The Cambridge Companion to Velázquez* (Cambridge: Cambridge University Press, 2002), 30–47.

[17] A painting entitled *Marte y Venus sorprendidos por Vulcano*, attributed, possibly falsely, to Velázquez, was sold in Paris in 1867, but there is no more recent record of its existence (López Torrijos, *La mitología en la pintura española*, 282).

[18] Jonathan Brown, *The Golden Age of Painting in Spain* (New Haven: Yale University Press, 1991), 142.

small number of works undertaken by Velázquez without a commission after his arrival at Court. Together they represent his first attempts at history painting, thus marking an important stage in the development of his output and style. Golden Age art theorists underlined the need for painters to be acquainted with 'los buenos libros' [canonical texts]; that is, with history, scripture, and classical literature.[19] Both *La túnica* and *La fragua* are based on well-known stories, the former on the biblical tale of Joseph's Coat of Many Colours, as told in Genesis 37, the latter on the classical tale of Mars, Venus, and Vulcan.

La fragua (Fig. 5.1) depicts the moment in the Homeric and Ovidian tale when Apollo visits Vulcan to inform him of his wife's affair. The scene takes place in the smith's forge, complete with furnace, assorted tools, and pieces of armour. There is a clarity of action that is not present in many of Velázquez's other mythological works, including *Los borrachos* and the later *Las hilanderas* [The Fable of Arachne] (*c.*1657). At left the sun-god,

Fig. 5.1. Diego Velázquez, *La fragua de Vulcano*, 1630. Oil on canvas.

[19] See e.g. Felipe de Guevara, *Comentarios de la pintura*, ed. Rafael Benet (Barcelona: Selecciones Bibliófilas, 1948 [1588]), 104; and Pacheco, *Arte de la pintura*, 236. For more on Velázquez and history painting, see *Fábulas de Velázquez. Mitología e historia sagrada en el Siglo de Oro*, ed. Javier Portús Pérez (Madrid: Museo Nacional del Prado, 2007).

identified by his laurel crown and solar nimbus, is seen delivering his message. In response to this communication, Vulcan, sporting a beard and headscarf, stands frozen at the anvil, his hammer and tongs still in his hands. The messenger has, it seems, only just arrived, for Vulcan's tongs still hold a red-hot piece of metal on the block in front of him. The smith turns to face his visitor, his top half contorted in surprise, his lower half remaining hidden behind his station. Judging by the look on Vulcan's face, Apollo has already reached the crux of the matter. In the right foreground three assistants pause mid-work, turning or lifting their heads to face Apollo; they too are clearly taken aback by his message. In the background the face and body of a fourth foundry worker are less well defined, but news of Venus's infidelity seems to have reached even him.

Unlike poets, painters did not have the luxury of being able to retell classical tales *in toto*. Artists who turned their attention to such subjects had instead to select specific moments in them—to recreate imaginatively and capture scenes that were central to a given narrative, easy to identify, and which immediately called to mind the rest of the tale. At first Velázquez's choice of scene is surprising. In Renaissance and Baroque Europe the vast majority of artists who turned to the tale of Mars, Venus, and Vulcan drew inspiration from its end. The scene of the capture and/ or unveiling of the lovers was particularly popular with Dutch and Italian artists, a fact reflected, as noted in the Introduction, in works by painters including Martin van Heemskerck, Frans Floris, Joachim Wtewael, Hendrick de Clerck, and Luca Giordano.[20] As seen earlier, the lovers' imprisonment *in flagrante* was also the preferred choice in illustrated editions of the *Metamorphoses*, from Salomon and Solis on. Velázquez breaks this trend by taking us back to Apollo's visit to the forge—to the precise instant when Vulcan learns of his wife's infidelity. In doing so he avoids the potentially indecorous final scenes; and yet, by focusing on the exchange from which the rest of the tale unfolds, he invites the viewer to imagine the very scenes of the lovers' affair, their subsequent entrapment, and the tale's memorable denouement.

Two questions continue to cast a long shadow over critical debate about the work: why was Velázquez interested in the scene captured in *La fragua*, and what were his sources for it? Some consideration of suggested influences on the work will now lead onto a discussion of aspects of its meaning and significance. Velázquez may have known of the tale of Mars, Venus, and

---

[20] On the paintings by Van Heemskerck and Wtewael, for example, see Ilja M. Veldman, 'The "Vulcan Triptych"', in *Maarten van Heemskerck and Dutch Humanism in the Sixteenth Century*, trans. Michael Hoyle (Maarssen: Gary Schwartz, 1977), 19–42; and Anne W. Lowenthal, *Joachim Wtewael: Mars and Venus Surprised by Vulcan*, Getty Museum Studies on Art (Malibu, Calif.: J. Paul Getty Museum, 1995).

Vulcan through any number, or combination, of the many and varied works discussed thus far: classical tellings, Renaissance translations and illustrations, iconographical and mythographical handbooks, works of Golden Age poetry, and so on. Significantly, the principal classical tellings give very little detail about either the delivery of the message or the setting for Apollo's exchange with Vulcan. The opening lines of Pope's translation of Demodocus's song show how little attention is paid to this scene in the *Odyssey*:

> How the stern god, enamour'd with her charms
> Clasp'd the gay panting goddess in his arms,
> By bribes seduced; and how the sun, whose eye
> Views the broad heavens, disclosed the lawless joy.
> Stung to the soul, indignant through the skies
> To his black forge vindictive Vulcan flies:
> Arrived, his sinewy arms incessant place
> The eternal anvil on the massy base.
> A wondrous net he labours . . .

Pérez's *La Ulyxea* states quite simply that Apollo visited Hephaestus 'por mensajero' [as a messenger], and that, when he delivered his 'mensaje triste' [sad message], the smith headed to his forge bent on revenge.[21] What the song of Ares and Aphrodite gives us then is the basic outline of an exchange between the two gods but nothing by way of detail. Ovid's most famous account is also economical, but it does add two important details in noting that Apollo shows Vulcan where the adultery was committed and that Vulcan dropped his work on receiving the news (*Metamorphoses*, IV.173–6). Whilst the setting is not mentioned, this second detail suggests that, unlike in Homer, the encounter takes place in the forge, as in the scene at left in the anonymous woodcut in the 1497 edition of Bonsignori's *Ovidio Metamorphoseos vulgare* (Fig. 1.1).

The details added by Ovid are briefly fleshed out in some sixteenth-century translations of the *Metamorphoses*. The post-mortem inventory of his library shows that Velázquez owned at least two such translations: a 'Metamorfosis en romance', variously identified as that of Bustamante, Pérez Sigler, and Sánchez de Viana; and an Italian translation by Lodovico Dolce.[22] Whereas Pérez Sigler is very faithful to Ovid, Bustamante, Sánchez

---

21　*La Ulyxea*, 254.
22　On Velázquez's library, which also contained copies of Pliny's *Natural History*, Pérez de Moya's *Philosofía secreta*, and Cesare Ripa's *Iconologia*, see Francisco J. Sánchez Cantón, 'Los libros españoles que poseyó Velázquez', in Antonio Gallego y Burín (ed.), *Varia Velazqueña. Homenaje a Velázquez en el III centenario de su muerte 1660–1960*, 2 vols. (Madrid: Ministerio de Educación Nacional, 1960), i. 640–8; 'Inventario de las bienes que dejaron a su muerte D. Diego de Silva Velázquez y su mujer Doña Juana Pacheco', in *Varia Velazqueña*, ii. 391–400; and Pedro Ruiz Pérez, *La biblioteca de Velázquez* (Seville: Junta de Andalucía, 1999), 86, 168–70.

de Viana, and Dolce all add something to the original. Bustamante is more specific about the details introduced by Ovid, stating that Apollo 'mostrole la cama donde estaban' [showed him the bed where they were], that Vulcan 'quedó sin sentido' [was left without feeling], and that 'con la gran turbación y pesar se le cayeron de las manos las tenazas y el martillo' [with great dismay and sorrow he dropped his tongs and hammer].[23] Sánchez de Viana notes that, motivated by envy, Apollo showed '[e]l feo Vulcano, dios de la herrería | . . . el lugar do posa aquella fiesta' [ugly Vulcan, the smith-god . . . the place where the party takes place] and that 'El hijo de Junon lo supo apenas, | cuando hizo sutilísimas cadenas' [No sooner had Juno's son found out than he made some very fine chains].[24] No mention is made, however, of Vulcan dropping anything. Dolce's translation has Apollo draw a contrast between the smith sweating at the forge and the lovers lying in each other's arms, before going on to give a more detailed account of Vulcan's reaction:

> A questa nuova si senti Vulcano
> tutto ingombrar di freddo ghiaccio il core.
> Il lavor, che facea, gli uscì di mano;
> si dileguò dal volto ogni colore.[25]

[At this news, Vulcan felt his heart freeze over with cold ice. He dropped the work that he was doing, and all colour drained from his face.]

Whilst each translation has certain aspects in common with the scene depicted in *La fragua* (mention of the forge, Apollo's pointing finger, Vulcan's look of horror, etc.), none of them presents an obvious source. With the exception of Sánchez de Viana's *Transformaciones*, each translation picks out the detail of the dropped work or tools; in *La fragua*, however, Vulcan still has a firm grasp of his hammer and tongs. If he was well acquainted with Ovid, why did Velázquez choose to omit this motif? Does *La fragua* depict the moment just before Vulcan drops his tools, or is the smith shown holding them to signal that these will be the instruments of his revenge?

In Carducho's *Diálogos* the master splits history painting into 'la [parte] primera y principal', essential compositional motifs that must not be changed, and 'el modo o circunstancias', other elements that may be altered in order better to portray a particular subject.[26] As shown above,

[23] Bustamante, *Las Transformaciones*, fol. 56ʳ.
[24] Sánchez de Viana, *Las Transformaciones*, fol. 35ʳ.
[25] *Le Transformationi tratte da Ovidio* (Venice: Gabriel Giolito de' Ferrari, 1553), 85.
[26] *Diálogos*, fols. 113ᵛ–16ʳ.

whilst Homer and Ovid may have outlined the first of these, they left Velázquez considerable scope for innovation with regard to the second. The fact that the pictorial particulars of *La fragua* do not map neatly onto the principal classical sources has encouraged critics to look further afield in search of other influences. Two works, one pictorial and the other literary, are frequently cited as Velázquez's principal sources of inspiration. The first is Tempesta's 'Coniugis furtum Sol Vulcano detegit' (Fig. 1.5), which, as noted above, appeared in an illustrated edition of the *Metamorphoses* published in Antwerp in 1606.[27] Widely appreciated for their effective narratives, Tempesta's engravings were often used as starting points for artists' developments of mythological tales. In this case canvas and engraving have much in common, including: the setting of the forge, with armour in the foreground, an anvil at its heart, and a roaring fire behind; the attire, pointing finger, and prominent solar nimbus of Apollo; the central figure of Vulcan, bearded and naked from the waist up, standing at his station holding a hammer and tongs; the similarly shaped piece of metal being worked on the anvil; and the strong horizontals formed as Vulcan and his assistant(s) turn to face, and listen to, their visitor. Alongside the obvious transposition, there are also, however, some important differences between the two images. Most notably, *La fragua* includes four assistants, in contrast to the lone figure at left in the engraving.

The second suggested source is Cueva's 'Los amores de Marte y Venus'.[28] When Cueva first introduces Vulcan, the smith is shown working at his 'duro yunque' [hard anvil], beating armour into shape with his hammer, surrounded by his 'desnudos cíclopes' [naked Cyclopes] (7*a–d*). On Apollo's subsequent visit to the forge a similar scene is evoked, as Cueva offers a description of an 'oficina ardiente' [baking-hot workshop], full of 'el humo, el carbón, la tizne y el fuego' [smoke, coal, soot, and fire], where Vulcan works his assistants to the bone (42*a–d*). Seeing Apollo's imminent arrival, Vulcan leaves the forge to greet his visitor, who, he mistakenly assumes, has come to commission new work. When Apollo promptly disabuses him of this assumption with the news of his wife's infidelity, Vulcan reacts as follows:

> Oyendo a Febo estaba el dios Vulcano,
> y de aquejado, sin valor ni brío,
> se le cayó el martillo de la mano

---

[27] This source is first suggested by Pierre du Colombier, 'La Forge de Vulcain au Château d'Effiat', *Gazette des Beaux-Arts*, 81 (1939), 30–8.

[28] First made in Cossío, *Fábulas mitológicas*, 173–5, this suggestion was later developed in John F. Moffitt, 'Velázquez's "Forge of Vulcan": The Cuckold, the Poets and the Painter', *Pantheon*, 41 (1983), 322–6.

y todo se cubrió de un sudor frío;
quiso hablar, y aunque probó fue en vano,
que el dolor poseía el señorío
del corazón, y el corazón ligaba
la lengua, y casi muerto y mudo estaba. (53)

[The god Vulcan was listening to Phoebus, and, stripped of courage and spirit, in his suffering he dropped his hammer and his whole body broke out in a cold sweat. He wanted to speak, but his attempt to do so was in vain, because pain controlled his heart, and his heart tied his tongue, and he was almost dead and mute.]

It is easy to see the appeal of parallels between details given by Cueva and the scene depicted by Velázquez. The most seductive is Cueva's inclusion, a few stanzas later, of four assistants, who are addressed by Vulcan as Brontes, Pyracmon, Steropes, and Acmonides (66g–7a). However, as before there are also a number of basic differences between painting and suggested source. In *La fragua* the message is delivered in the forge, in front of Vulcan's assistants. As we have seen, Cueva's drawing out of the episode's dramatic potential in 'Los amores' dictates that the exchange take place elsewhere and in private: only after lengthy deliberation does Vulcan return to his forge, relay Apollo's message to his four assistants, and ask them for help in forging the net. Whereas Cueva adheres to the motif of the dropped work/tools, Velázquez, as noted above, does not. Whilst the reaction of Velázquez's Vulcan is theatrical, it is not a melodramatic over-reaction of the kind seen in 'Los amores', which has the smith holding his head in his hands, shedding abundant rivers of tears, and ripping out his own beard. It seems Cueva's influence, like that of Tempesta, goes only so far.

One can set the search parameters wider still, to include, for example, famous classical descriptions of Vulcan and his assistants labouring in the forge (e.g. Homer, *Iliad*, xviii.368 ff. and Virgil, *Aeneid*, viii.407–53), entries on the smith-god in iconographical handbooks (most notably Pérez de Moya's *Philosofía secreta*), or earlier Renaissance paintings of him at work in the forge (by artists such as Cornelis Cort, Jacopo Bassano, and Tintoretto), but links with the specific details of *La fragua* become yet more tenuous. As ever, the quest for sources runs the risk of being overly reductive, of glossing over differences in order to stress similarities, and of focusing on imitation to the detriment of invention. Given the subject, points of contact between *La fragua* and some, or indeed all, of the above works are inevitable; they should not be seen, therefore, as proof of an overriding debt to a specific visual or textual source. As we have seen in previous chapters, influences on individual handlings of mythological tales are many and varied—and, more often than not, such influences are combined, played off against one another, and refracted through the imagination of the particular poet/painter. To place too much emphasis, therefore, on links with Tempesta's engraving or Cueva's poem—to see *La fragua* as a copy of one or an illustration of the other, on the back of vague correspondences in terms of design, setting, the number of assistants, adherence to the motif of the dropped work and/or tools, etc.—is to turn a blind eye to the ways in which Velázquez develops the tale, to the aspects that he draws out, and to the significance of the scene he captures.

The fact that Velázquez was not catering, when painting *La fragua*, for the whims of an individual patron or responding to a carefully wrought iconographical scheme suggests once more that he had considerable room for experimentation and invention. However, the lack of any documentation relating to the reasons and circumstances behind its composition has helped give rise to profound uncertainty over the work's function and meaning, with the result that over the last hundred or more years *La fragua* has been interpreted in many and varied ways. It has been seen, for example, as a Christian allegory in which a Christ-like figure instructs men in the journey from ignorance and deceit to truth and virtue; an allegory of the arts, in which a representative of the Seven Liberal Arts illuminates the world of the manual arts; an expression of the power of words to influence feelings, emotions, and actions, and of the superiority of the world of ideas over the world of base labour; testament to the fact that evil and the abuse of power or position are always punished by higher authorities; a pendant to *La túnica*, with the two works capturing shots of detected and successful betrayal respectively; evidence of Velázquez's 'mastery of Italian classicizing art, including such techniques as dramatic gesture and expression, illusionistic space, [and] accurate anatomical draftsmanship'; and an example of mythological burlesque, in line with the dominant trends in contemporary poetry discussed in the previous chapter.[29]

[29] These and other readings are put forward in Carl Justi, *Diego Velázquez and his Times*, trans. Augustus H. Keane (London: H. Grevel & Co., 1889), 168–73; Angulo Íñiguez, 'La fábula'; Charles de Tolnay, 'Las pinturas mitológicas de Velázquez', *AEA* 34 (1961), 31–45; Moffitt, 'Velázquez's "Forge of Vulcan"'; Santiago Sebastián, 'Lectura iconográfico-iconológica de *La Fragua de Vulcano*', *Traza y Baza*, 8 (1983), 20–7; Stephen N. Orso, *Velázquez, Los Borrachos, and Painting at the Court of Philip IV* (Cambridge: Cambridge University Press, 1993), 132–40; Jonathan Brown and Carmen Garrido, *Velázquez: The Technique of Genius* (New Haven: Yale University Press, 1998), 46–56; Trinidad de Antonio, '"La fragua de Vulcano"', in Svetlana Alpers and others, *Velázquez* (Barcelona: Galaxia Gutenberg, 1999), 25–41; my 'Ovid and Velázquez: Re-examining Some of the Literary Sources for Velázquez's *La Fragua de Vulcano*', in *Latin and Vernacular in Renaissance Spain, III*, 147–61; and Escardiel González Estévez, 'En torno a la *Fragua de Vulcano* de Velázquez. Nuevas aportaciones a la interpretación de su significado', *Laboratorio de Arte. Revista del Departamento de Historia del Arte*, 21 (2008–9), 411–26. The last of these offers a useful summary of several such readings. The quotation is from Brown, *The Golden Age of Painting*, 142.

Several of these readings see allegory and moral purpose at the heart of the work, focusing, in the words of Carducho's master, not on the 'corteza incasta y descompuesta' but on the 'moralidad virtuosa' held within. Many such readings draw heavily on Pérez de Moya's *Philosofía secreta*, of which Velázquez is known to have owned a copy.[30] John Moffitt, for example, sees Pérez de Moya's handbook as '*the* indispensable source for a correct, "moral", reading of any of Velázquez's mythological paintings', claiming that knowledge of the relevant *declaración* enables 'apparently straight-forward pictorial composition[s] to be "*read*" in many, "*higher*", ways'.[31] Changing the lens through which *La fragua* is viewed, however, produces markedly different results. If one compares with to Cueva's treatment of the exchange between Apollo and Vulcan in 'Los amores', one sees a theat-rical still capturing the pivotal moment in a tale of honour, adultery, and revenge. If one examines it in the light of the burlesques of Castillo Solór-zano, Polo de Medina, and Barrios, one finds instead rambunctious play on the motifs of cuckoldry and public dishonour, an exaggerated sense of contrast between an effete sun-god and an all too down-to-earth smith, and a concerted effort to belittle the pagan gods and their affairs. These and other similar attempts to decipher the meaning of *La fragua* through reference to written accounts of the tale meet the same fate as the above attempts to pin down its sources. Whilst such accounts suggest several possible ways of reading the work, none seems entirely convincing, for, as Jonathan Brown reminds us, 'the juxtaposition of a literary reference to an image is no guarantee that the two are related'.[32]

The number and variety of readings of *La fragua* point to its status as a profoundly ambiguous work. But what precisely is it that gives rise to this ambiguity? The drama of the scene centres upon the exchange between Apollo and Vulcan, but it is not clear how either god is meant to be viewed. Is, for instance, Velázquez's Apollo to be seen as a Christ-like sun-god, a patron of the arts modelled on the Apollo Belvedere, a naive tell-tale akin to Polo de Medina's 'planeta boquirrubio', or a young model playing a part to which he is unaccustomed? The figure at left has all the trappings of a serious Renaissance sun-god—sandals, a laurel crown, a solar nimbus, and a billowing Italianate robe—and yet there is something disconcerting about his boyishness, the affected pose he adopts, and the slight cocking of his head. His stance is much more reminiscent of the sun-god at left in the 1497 woodcut than of the more dynamic Apollo who enters stage right

---

[30] See above, p. 168, n. 22.
[31] 'Velázquez's "Forge of Vulcan"', 324–5 (Moffitt's emphasis).
[32] Jonathan Brown, 'Velázquez, Rubens, and Van Dyck', in *Collected Writings on Velázquez* (Madrid: CEEH, 2008), 201–310 (p. 289, n. 153).

on a platform of cloud in Tempesta's engraving. His index finger illustrates the detail found in the *Metamorphoses*, but it seems to be raised almost as much in mock admonishment as for the purposes of showing Vulcan where the adultery was committed. As in previous handlings of the tale, envy cannot be ruled out as the prime motivation behind his visit to the forge (perhaps mirroring that shown by Joseph's brothers in *La túnica*). Indeed, ultimately, the joke may be at Apollo's own expense: those familiar with the context of Ovid's telling would know that the tell-tale would soon be punished by Venus for his actions.

The central figure of Vulcan is also ambiguous. As we have seen, two images of the smith emerge from classical tradition and are then reflected in the poetry of the Golden Age. The first sees Vulcan as the divine master-craftsman, the 'gran maestro' [great master] who produces remarkable works of art, the second as the archetypal cuckold, the manual labourer who drudges away at the forge whilst his wife sleeps with other men.[33] The context of the tale in question should allow us to identify Velázquez's smith with the second of these figures. However, Velázquez's portrait of Vulcan is much less one-dimensional than many of those discussed in previous chapters. Pérez de Moya states that Vulcan is depicted as 'un herrero lleno de tizne . . . muy feo, y cojo de una pierna' [a blacksmith covered in soot . . . very ugly and lame in one leg] and that portraits of him show signs of his having being cast down from heaven.[34] Cueva and Lope take this further, depicting Vulcan as an ugly good-for-nothing caked in soot and sweat. In 'La rosa blanca' Venus is so horrified by the prospect of marriage to a crippled hunchback—introduced, as we have seen, as a 'retrógrado cancro' and 'camello asirio'—that she immediately turns to other men for comfort. Later poets, including Castillo Solórzano, Polo de Medina, and, most prominently, Barrios, all develop exaggerated play on Vulcan's ugliness, dirtiness, deformity, and cuckoldry. In *La fragua*, however, there is no such explicit play on the smith's traditional defects.

The literary portraits of Vulcan found in burlesque treatments of the tale serve principally as springboards to complex linguistic and conceptual play. A more straightforward and detailed description of the smith is, however, found in Agustín de Rojas Villandrando's picaresque novel in dialogue form, *El viaje entretenido* [The Entertaining Journey] (1603). In Book III the author's alter ego, Rojas, entertains his friends on their travels

---

[33] The epithet is taken from a section in Garcilaso's Second Eclogue praising the quality of the relief-work on the urn revealed to Severo by the river Tormes: 'El artificio humano no hiciera | pintura que esprimiera vivamente | el armada, la gente, el curso, el agua; | y apenas en la fragua donde sudan | los cíclopes y mudan fatigados | los brazos, ya cansados del martillo, | pudiera así exprimillo el gran maestro' (Eclogue II, 1616–22).

[34] *Philosofía secreta*, 222.

with a *loa* that includes lengthy portraits of Mars, Vulcan, and Venus. Of the smith, he says:

> pinté en mi memoria un hombre
> de baja y humilde suerte.
> Digo que sería callado,
> sufrido, honrado, paciente,
> amigo de hacer su oficio
> y en lo demás no meterse;
> toda la cara tiznada,
> narices, orejas, frente,
> los brazos arremangados,
> dando martilladas siempre,
> con un devantal de cuero
> y en la cabeza un birrete;
> de buen cuerpo, corcovado,
> chica boca, grandes dientes,
> brazos, piernas, pecho, espaldas,
> tan blancos como la nieve,
> pero el vello sería tanto
> que pusiese espanto verle.[35]

[I pictured in my mind a short and lowly kind of man. He would be quiet, long-suffering, honest, patient, and dedicated to his work but not interested in anything else. His whole face (nose, ears, and forehead) would be covered in soot, his sleeves rolled up, and he would be forever hammering away, with a leather apron and a red cap on his head. He would be muscular, with a hunchback, a small mouth, big teeth, his arms, legs, chest, and back all as white as snow, but there would be so much hair on his chest that he would be a fright to see.]

What starts out as a seemingly straightforward description reaches a climax with the comic detail of Vulcan's unruly chest hair. Again, Velázquez does not have recourse to such patently grotesque details. In another painting of Vulcan housed in the Buen Retiro, Rubens's *Vulcan Forging Thunderbolts* (c.1634), the smith is shown with a corrective sandal on one foot. Here, however, Vulcan's legs are hidden from view. If what several critics, starting with Carl Justi, have seen as a deviation in Vulcan's spinal column *is* Velázquez's way of alluding to the smith's lameness, then it is an example not of glaring burlesque but of subtle and witty understatement.[36]

---

[35] Agustín de Rojas Villandrando, *El viaje entretenido*, ed. Jean Pierre Ressot, CC, 44 (Madrid: Castalia, 1972), 322.
[36] *Diego Velázquez and his Times*, 173.

Another source of ambiguity is Velázquez's translation of classical mythology into everyday terms. Vulcan and his assistants are presented as humans plying their trade in a realistic forge. Again, the absence of certain details is telling. Vulcan's assistants are not Cyclopes, the 'monóculos oficiales' [one-eyed workers] mentioned by Castillo Solórzano, but human foundry workers. The fact that they bear a striking resemblance to Jacob's sons in *La túnica* suggests that Velázquez used the same real-life models for both paintings. In his *Ovidio Metamorphoseos vulgare* Bonsignori notes that when Apollo visited the forge he found Vulcan producing thunderbolts for Jupiter, a detail picked up in several later tellings.[37] In *La fragua* Vulcan is not forging thunderbolts, or indeed any of the magnificent works attributed to him by classical tradition, but working a simple piece of metal that has just been heated in the furnace. Whereas Tempesta's sun-god stands on a dais of cloud, Velázquez's Apollo shares the same primitive smithy floor as Vulcan and his assistants. The sun-god's colourful robe, the carefully delineated foreground figures, the anatomically correct semi-naked bodies, and the dynamic network of individual poses, gestures, and expressions all suggest the influence of Velázquez's exposure to and assimilation of classical sculpture and contemporary Italian art. However, at the same time, the workers' loincloths, the setting's earthy tones, and the still-life elements scattered around the forge all anchor the work in the realist world of the artist's earlier Sevillian stage. The inclusion of the tools and pieces of armour in the foreground, of those hung on the pillar behind Vulcan, and of the items, including the enigmatic white jug, on the shelf above the fire creates a tension between the idealism associated with classical mythology and the realism of an ordinary scene, between the inclusion of the details required to identify the episode and a concern for verisimilitude, and between the grand manner of history painting and the lower genre of the *bodegón* [still life].

Velázquez thus complies with the advice given by Pacheco on the use of still-life elements, according to which 'grandes pintores' [great painters] may incorporate such details into history paintings, so long as 'procur[an] poner mayor cuidado en las cosas vivas, como figuras y animales, donde se conserva mayor opinión' [they make sure to take greater care with living things, such as figures and animals, which are held in higher esteem].[38] The still-life elements, which help to create an impression of depth, draw the different parts of the painting together, but do not detract from the

---

[37] *Ovidio Metamorphoseos vulgare*, ed. Ardissino, 220: 'el Sole andò a Vulcano e trovòlo che fabricava le saette de Giove' [the Sun went to see Vulcan and found him forging Jove's thunderbolts].
[38] *Arte de la pintura*, 511–12.

central drama of the exchange between Apollo and Vulcan. Throughout the *Diálogos* Carducho touches on the need for outward appearance to convey inner emotion.[39] The impact of Apollo's revelation is played out on Vulcan's face in a form of what Antonio Palomino termed a 'metáfora vultuosa' [facial metaphor]. Revealing 'las perturbaciones del ánimo' [the agitation of his soul], his expression betrays astonishment tinged with horror and anger.[40] His reaction is neatly underscored by those of his assistants, most notably that of the second figure from the right, who stares, mouth agape, in wide-eyed amazement at the visitor to the forge. Caught, it seems, completely unawares, Vulcan is struck dumb by the news of his wife's infidelity and thrust into an unenviable and precarious position.

Whilst it is not clear as to whether the viewer should respond to the smith's plight with sympathy or laughter, there can be no doubt about the piquancy of a scene that foregrounds the precise moment when a husband gets to know of his wife's infidelity. As several critics, including Trinidad de Antonio, have remarked, many similar scenes are found in the literature of the period.[41] The 'casos de la honra' [affairs of honour] that were popular on the contemporary stage throw up several; a husband's discovery of his wife's infidelity, real or imagined, or of a potential threat to his honour is a dramatic highpoint of many plays in the period. Playwrights found several novel ways of effecting this discovery. In Lope de Vega's *Peribáñez y el comendador de Ocaña* [Peribáñez and the Commander of Ocaña] (1605–8), for example, the husband Peribáñez chances upon a portrait of his wife Casilda, commissioned by her suitor Don Fadrique, in a painter's workshop. In Lope's *El castigo sin venganza* the Duke of Ferrera receives an anonymous letter informing him of his young wife Casandra's affair with his beloved bastard son Federico. Other plays depend for their dramatic effect on the gradual building up of evidence. In Calderón's *El médico de su honra*, for example, Gutierre finds 'proof' of his innocent wife Mencía's guilt in a series of untimely and unfortunate discoveries (a dagger dropped in Gutierre's house by Mencía's former lover Prince Enrique, an overheard exchange between Enrique and his half-brother King Pedro, a letter from Mencía to Enrique that cuts off at just the wrong moment, etc.). To an audience well versed in such scenes, the direct and very public nature of the husband's response in *La fragua* would have been striking.

---

[39] See e.g. *Diálogos*, fols 49ʳ–50ᵛ.

[40] Antonio Palomino de Castro y Velasco, *El museo pictórico y escala óptica. Teórica de la pintura*, 3 vols. (Madrid: Imprenta de Sancha, 1795–7), i. 60. See also Lía Schwartz, 'Linguistic and Pictorial Conceits in the Baroque: Velázquez between Quevedo and Gracián', in *Writing for the Eyes*, 279–300 (p. 295).

[41] '"La fragua de Vulcano"', 38.

Another memorable example of such a discovery is seen in Cervantes's exemplary tale 'El celoso extremeño' [The Jealous Extremaduran], which, like the tale under examination, features a jealous old husband (Carrizales), a beautiful young wife (Leonora), and a headstrong suitor (Loaysa). When Carrizales discovers Leonora lying in bed in Loaysa's arms, he concludes that the two are lovers and reacts accordingly:

> Sin pulsos quedó Carrizales con la amarga vista de lo que miraba; la voz se le pegó a la garganta, los brazos se le cayeron de desmayo, y quedó hecho una estatua de mármol frío; y aunque la cólera hizo su natural oficio, avivándole los casi muertos espíritus, pudo tanto el dolor, que no le dejó tomar aliento.

> [Carrizales was left senseless by the bitter sight that greeted him; his voice stuck in his throat, his arms fell limp at his sides, and he became a cold marble statue; and although anger did its usual thing, rousing his almost dead senses, the anguish was such that he could not draw breath.]

Cervantes's subsequent description of the arrival of dawn contains a veiled allusion to the tale of Mars, Venus, and Vulcan: 'Llegóse en esto el día, y cogió a los nuevos adúlteros enlazados en la red de sus brazos' [At that moment day broke and caught the new adulterers entangled in the net of their arms].[42] Without naming any gods, Cervantes sets up a parallel between Mars and Venus, the archetypal adulterers whose affair was uncovered at dawn by Apollo, and Loaysa and Leonora, the 'nuevos adúlteros', found lying in each other's arms first thing in the morning. The metaphor of the 'red de sus brazos', which describes the new couple's tangled web of limbs, points to the real net that Vulcan uses to trap Mars and Venus. The economical allusion establishes a link between Carrizales and Vulcan and hints at a possible course of action for the husband, who has only just rejected the idea of cleansing his honour with the lovers' blood. An ironic contrast is established, however, as, unbeknownst to Carrizales, and contrary to the evidence before him, Leonora has actually managed to fend off Loaysa's advances. Cervantes's reader knows that they are not 'nuevos adúlteros', but the link between Loaysa, Leonora, and Carrizales on the one hand, and Mars, Venus, and, Vulcan on the other, remains.[43]

Like Cervantes, Velázquez foregrounds and captures the precise moment of the husband's fateful discovery. In so doing, he strikes a balance between a potentially cold, academic study of human anatomy and the expression of a powerful psychological instant from a well-known mythological

---

[42] *Novelas ejemplares*, ii. 130.
[43] For more on the meaning and function of this allusion, see Stephen Boyd, 'A Tale of Two Serpents: Biblical and Mythological Allusions in Cervantes's *El celoso extremeño*', in *Rewriting Classical Mythology*, 71–89 (pp. 74–5).

tale. Recourse to the world of classical mythology enables Velázquez to undertake what the early twentieth-century Spanish philosopher and essayist José Ortega y Gasset labels an *experimentum crucis*, bringing a range of different ideas, techniques, and motifs into dialogue, reconciling the world of Italianate history painting with the world of still-life and genre scenes, and playing the spirit of classical idealism off against that of seventeenth-century Spanish realism.[44] Though *La fragua* is not marked by the scathing burlesque of many contemporary poetic treatments of the gods, it is anchored firmly in the world of the human and the everyday. The balance that Velázquez achieves between the human and the divine, the realist and the idealist, and the comic and the tragic underpins what is a profoundly ambiguous work—one whose meaning is difficult to establish with any certainty. As we shall now see, all of these qualities are integral to the air of ambiguity and ambivalence that lies at the heart of Velázquez's portrait of Mars a decade or so later.

MARTE (c.1640)

The title of Velázquez's *Marte* (Fig. 5.2) invites certain preconceptions: first, that the subject of the work will be the Roman god of war, Mars; second, that the image will be of a splendid armed figure personifying the essence of military power; and third, that the portrait will possess a clear function. Velázquez's depiction of Mars brutally undermines such expectations. In place of the traditional embodiment of war, a dishevelled, pensive, and apparently world-weary individual gazes blankly into the extra-pictorial space. Instead of a fearsome warrior adopting a posture of divine authority on a chariot or a campaign couch, we see an all too human figure adopting an introspective pose perched on the edge of a rumpled bed. It becomes immediately apparent that a new lexicon is required to describe the god of war, for the conventional Renaissance epithets—*airado*, *belicoso*, *duro*, *fiero*, *sangriento*, etc.—are no longer fitting. The incongruity of the god's appearance throws the initial identification into doubt; yet the arms at the figure's feet and the helmet on his head are clearly the possessions of Mars. The gap between iconographical tradition and the physical and mental reality of Velázquez's figure establishes profound ambiguity. If this is Mars, why is he depicted in this fashion? Is he to be seen in isolation from the world of mythological narrative, divorced from Venus and his traditional role as the god of war? Or is this scene also related to the tale of Mars, Venus, and Vulcan?

[44] José Ortega y Gasset, *Velázquez*, intro. Francisco Calvo Serraller (Madrid: Espasa Calpe, 1999), 63.

Fig. 5.2. Diego Velázquez, *Marte*, *c.*1640. Oil on canvas.

Like those of *La fragua*, the sources, origins, and meaning of *Marte* are uncertain. Again, a variety of possible influences has been put forward. Two of the most common suggestions concern sculptures of seated martial figures that Velázquez may have encountered during his first trip to Italy: the *Ares Ludovisi*, a second-century BC marble copy of a fourth-century BC seated bronze attributed to Scopas or Lysippus; and *Il Pensieroso* [The Thinker] (1521–34), a statue of Lorenzo de' Medici executed by Michelangelo for the Medici chapel at San Lorenzo in Florence. Other suggested sources range from images such as Hendrick Goltzius's *Mars* (*c.*1588), a half-length woodcut print of the warrior-god complete with moustache and helmet, and Hendrick ter Brugghen's *Sleeping Mars* (*c.*1625–6), which shows the same god at rest after battle, to works of literature such as Polo de Medina's 'A Vulcano, Venus y Marte', which begins, as we have seen, with a description of Mars as:

> El jaque de las deidades,
> todo bravatas y rumbo,
> que vive pared en medio
> del planeta boquirrubio;
> el de los ojos al sesgo,
> caribajo y cejijunto,
> de la frente encapotada
> y mostachos a lo ruso.[45]

It is tempting to seize on one or more shared details (the raised left knee, the introspective pose, the prominent moustache, the ornate helmet, etc.) to make a case for any or all of these suggested sources.[46] Once more, however, we are dealing with vague correspondences and not clear-cut sources. Velázquez may have known and been inspired by any, all, or none of these works, but whatever the case, comparing his portrait with them serves only to highlight its original features. What stand out are not the points of contact but the differences between them, and we find ourselves no closer to answering any of the above questions. In addition to this, the humanity and tangible physicality of the figure suggest that it too was painted from life, and not merely a straightforward copy or illustration of a previous literary or visual model.

[45] See above, p. 132.

[46] On Goltzius's *Mars* and Ter Brugghen's *Sleeping Mars*, the least well-known of these suggested sources, see Nancy Ann Bialler, *Chiaroscuro Woodcuts: Hendrick Goltzius and his Time (1558–1617)* (Amsterdam: Rijksmuseum, 1992), 95–101; and Leonard J. Slatkes and Wayne Franits, *The Paintings of Hendrick ter Brugghen 1588–1629: Catalogue Raisonné*, Oculi Studies in the Arts of the Low Countries, 10 (Philadelphia: John Benjamins, 2007), 144–7, 349.

The painting's existence is first recorded in an inventory of the Torre de la Parada, prepared after the death of Charles II, dated 1701. The relevant entry reads:

> [51] Yttem tres pitturas Yguales de mano de Velazquez la Una de Martte la Ottra de Ysopo y la ottra de menipus tassadas a Cinquenta doblones Cada Una.[47]

> [Item, three paintings of equal size by Velázquez, one of Mars, another of Aesop, and the third of Menippus, valued at fifty doubloons each.]

Though critical opinion has been divided over the question of dating, with attributions ranging from the late 1630s to the time of Velázquez's second trip to Italy (November 1648–June 1651) and beyond, it seems likely that the painting was commissioned for, or at least hung in, the hunting lodge at some point during or soon after its redecoration in 1636–8.[48] Velázquez played an important part in the redevelopment of the Torre de la Parada, made famous by Rubens's Ovid cycle, and several of his extant works, including, as the above entry attests, his portraits of Mars and the beggar-philosophers Aesop and Menippus, graced its walls. Significantly, the lodge was not an official, ceremonial palace, such as the Alcázar or the Buen Retiro, but a place to which Philip IV could retire in search of refuge and respite from the whirl of Court life. For Svetlana Alpers, *Marte* should be understood in the context of this setting: as a portrait of a disarmed god of war, it functions, first and foremost, as a symbol of peace. It constitutes Velázquez's response to the tradition of Mars at rest after battle, reflecting the weariness of the king and his entourage after a day of hunting, a pursuit which serves as the peaceful equivalent to, and training ground for, war.[49] Hanging in the same room as they, it may even be said to complement the portraits of Aesop and Menippus, two freed slaves suspicious of higher forms of thinking, who represent the wisdom of the simple life. Both pictorially and in terms of the physical distance that separates the hunting lodge from Madrid, together the three portraits symbolize life lived at a critical distance from the world of court artifice.

---

[47] 'Torre de la Parada', in *Inventarios reales. Testamentaria del Rey Carlos II 1701–1703*, ed. Gloria Fernández Bayton, 3 vols. (Madrid: Museo Nacional del Prado, 1975–85), II (1981), 169–82 (p. 174).

[48] For a brief summary of suggested datings, see Avigdor Arikha, 'Nota sobre el "Marte"', in Alpers and others, *Velázquez*, 43–55 (p. 45).

[49] *The Decoration of the Torre de la Parada*, 136. For more on Velázquez and his paintings for the hunting lodge, see Manuela B. Mena Marqués, 'Velázquez en la Torre de la Parada', in José Alcalá-Zamora and Alfonso E. Pérez Sánchez (eds.), *Velázquez y Calderón. Dos genios de Europa* (Madrid: RAH, 2000), 101–56.

Alpers's contextual reading—which, ultimately, can be validated only through the discovery of further documentary evidence relating to the work's origins—is just one of many attempts at definitive interpretation put forward in recent decades.[50] Three other popular readings see *Marte* as a didactic work with an overt moral exemplum, as a satirical portrait of the contemporary state of Spain, and as mythological burlesque. According to the first of these, the work is a simple allegory that can be decoded through reference to the appropriate *declaración* from Pérez de Moya's moralized and christianized reading of the tale of Mars, Venus, and Vulcan. The tale shows that 'los hombres viciosos que viven mal y obran peor, en ningunas fuerzas ni velocidad de pies confiados, podrán evitar el castigo de la ira de Dios' [debauched men who live badly and act even worse cannot rely on strength or speed of foot to escape punishment from God's anger].[51] According to this reading, Velázquez depicts the defeat of Mars, the embodiment of 'el calor libidinoso' [libidinous heat], and points to the triumph of Vulcan, the hard-working smith, who obliges Mars to conform to virtue, by publicizing his corruption and exposing him to ridicule. The unexpected portrayal of Mars thus serves as a warning against sin, offering:

[une] leço[n] où le spectateur averti peut discerner, en plus d'un sens litté-ral, un sens moral applicable à ses rapports avec les autres hommes, un sens psychologique pour le gouvernement de soi-même, [et] un sens anagogique concernant ses devoirs envers Dieu.[52]

[a lesson where the informed viewer can make out, in addition to a literal sense, a moral sense applicable to his relations with other human beings, a psychological sense relating to the government of himself, and an anagogic sense concerning his duties to God.]

Both *La fragua* and *Marte* thus mark the passage from ignorance to truth, and the victory of virtue over vice through the publication of infamy.[53]

---

[50] For a selection of readings of *Marte*, see López Torrijos, *La mitología en la pintura española*, 331–7; Welles, *Arachne's Tapestry*, 143–5; Antonio Domínguez Ortiz, Alfonso E. Pérez Sánchez, and Julián Gállego, *Velázquez* (New York: Metropolitan Museum of Art, 1989), 210–15; Brown and Garrido, *Technique of Genius*, 168–73; Lorenzo Hernández Guardiola, 'El Marte imprudente de Velázquez', *Ars longa: cuadernos de arte*, 1 (1990), 43–8; Arikha, 'Nota sobre el "Marte"'; Martin Warnke, *Velázquez: Form & Reform* (Cologne: DuMont, 2005), 112–21; Andreas Prater, 'Mars on the Bed of Venus', in *Venus at her Mirror: Velázquez and the Art of Nude Painting* (Munich: Prestel, 2002), 109–14; and my 'Mars Recontextualized in the Golden Age of Spain: Psychological and Aesthetic Readings of Velázquez's *Marte*', in *Rewriting Classical Mythology*, 139–55.

[51] *Philosofía secreta*, 291.

[52] Julián Gállego, *Vision et symboles dans la peinture espagnole du Siècle d'Or* (Paris: Klincksieck, 1968), 72.

[53] Moffitt, 'Velázquez's "Forge of Vulcan"', 326.

The second reading sees *Marte* as a veiled allusion to the historical decline of Spain, her armies, and her military prowess in the seventeenth century. Possibly in response to the Portuguese and Catalonian rebellions of 1640, or to the context of the Thirty Years War, Velázquez subverts the standard iconography of Mars to comment on the fortunes of the Spanish army at a time of widespread *desengaño* [disillusionment]. Mars is a shadow of his former self: an unarmed, unidealized human being, whose apparent exhaustion and resignation are more befitting of a moustachioed Breda *tercio* [infantryman] than a fearsome pagan divinity. *Marte* is thus a satirical portrait that ridicules the military and political pretensions, delusions, and failings of the government of Philip IV and Olivares, exposing the reality previously veiled behind the latter's carefully constructed propagandistic programmes. The portrait could even be read as a satirical reflection of the Count-Duke, in the guise of a *bufón* [fool], assuming a role for which he is clearly not fit. *Marte* serves as a veiled warning against the danger of Spain's continued weakness and failure. It provokes serious contemplation of the national situation, inviting reflection upon the characters of the monarch and his *valido*, and on the military reverses of the time.[54]

Like *Los borrachos* and *La fragua, Marte* can also be read as mythological burlesque, in which Velázquez subverts for comic effect the traditional picture of Mars as a young, powerfully muscular, and awe-inspiring representation of war. In contrast to both classical and Italian Mannerist representations of the warrior-god, Velázquez's Mars is a physically unfit, moustachioed figure, whose all too human qualities are accentuated at the expense of the divinity ascribed to him by Antiquity. Velázquez employs a series of pictorial details to mock his subject: Mars's baton of command serves only to support his weary frame; his right hand, previously a symbol of might as the hand that would wield his bloody sword, lies hidden, swathed in the red bedclothes; the juxtaposition of the cloth and the glittering accoutrements of war underscores the humanity and weariness of the figure; and the armour that lies mockingly at his feet and the incongruous gilded helmet, placed on the seat of reason, frame and accentuate both the inadequacy of the ageing body and the obscurity of the ill-defined face. This reading sees Velázquez's Mars as the companion of several figures examined in previous chapters, including Góngora's Mars, busy gorging himself with Venus; Quevedo's Mars, who pawns his accoutrements for fashionable delicacies in order to woo her (Q536: 7–8); and Polo de Medina's moustachioed braggart who is reduced to paying

---

[54] See Diego Angulo Íñiguez, 'Fábulas mitológicas de Velázquez', *Goya*, 37–8 (1960), 104–19 (p. 117) (repr. in his *Estudios completos*, 193–8); and Alfonso E. Pérez Sánchez, 'Velázquez and his Art', in Domínguez Ortiz, Pérez Sánchez, and Gállego, *Velázquez*, 21–56 (p. 40).

her for sex. Velázquez thus critically distances himself from classical mythology, offering an ironic critique of the subservience of Renaissance artists and writers to the culture of Antiquity. Simultaneously, he enters into competition with the linguistic wit of the period's poets, by displaying the virtuosity of his own *ingenio*, of his ability to caricature, ridicule, and present in any given light even the most revered pagan gods.[55] Each of these three popular readings is problematic. The objection voiced above to Moffitt's allegorical reading of *La fragua* also applies to *Marte*. Whilst Velázquez undoubtedly knew the *Philosofía secreta*, his mythological paintings are not mere illustrations of it. Reference to such works cannot wholly unlock the puzzle of a work of art, for within the Renaissance theory of *imitatio* there lies a certain component that relates to the creative, transformative process that the object of imitation undergoes as it passes through the individual mind of the artist. Any moral messages conveyed by *Marte* are not as clearly defined as those outlined by Pérez de Moya, for Velázquez's mythological paintings 'defy [the] unidimensional, allegorical exegesis' applicable to works such as the Arguijo/Alcalá ceiling paintings and Zurbarán's series for the Hall of Realms.[56] Knowledge of the historical reality of the 1630s and 1640s makes the second reading attractive. However, whilst it is not uncommon for court poets and painters to offer veiled (or even open) attacks on those in power, Velázquez's privileged position as painter and courtier was entirely dependent on the preservation of favourable relations with the ruling powers. Velázquez was not a political satirist in the mould of Quevedo, whose relations with Olivares soured to the extent that he was exiled and imprisoned, and it is improbable that he should criticize Philip IV's policies in a work designed for, or at least subsequently displayed in, a royal residence.[57] As for the third reading, it is tempting, given the fashion in contemporary poetry for unequivocal burlesque, to hold that Velázquez was doing something similar. However, this is not unambiguous caricature à la Castillo Solórzano, Quevedo, Polo de Medina, and others. Whilst the viewer's expectations are undoubtedly disturbed, and whilst the juxtaposition of incongruous elements does render the figure somewhat absurd, this is not Quevedo's 'don Quijote de las deidades' [Don Quixote of the

---

[55] For an early example of a reading of Velázquez's mythological paintings as Lucianic satire, see Narciso Sentenach y Cabañas, *La pintura en Madrid desde sus orígenes hasta el siglo XIX* (Madrid: Administración del «Boletín de la Sociedad Española de Excursiones», 1907), 89–128 (pp. 102, 118).

[56] Welles, *Arachne's Tapestry*, 135.

[57] On Quevedo's fall from favour, see John H. Elliott, 'Quevedo and the Count-Duke of Olivares', in James Iffland (ed.), *Quevedo in Perspective: Eleven Essays for the Quadricentennial* (Newark: Juan de la Cuesta, 1982), 227–50.

gods] or Polo de Medina's moustachioed Mars, caught *in flagrante* wearing nothing more than a nightcap and bedsocks.[58]

Much of the painting's ambiguity stems from the fact that this Mars, like Vulcan before him, does not resemble any of his literary forebears or counterparts, including, for example, that described in Rojas Villandrando's *El tarde entretenido*:

> . . . es dios que todo lo puede,
> quiero decir el dios Marte
> a quien el mundo obedece,
> a quien el cielo respeta
> y todos los hombres temen.
> Figuré en mi pensamiento
> un hombre de estraña suerte:
> alto, sufridor, nervioso,
> robusto, fiero, valiente,
> intrépido, denodado,
> animoso, bravo, fuerte,
> esforzado, guerreador,
> . . .
> un hombre de grande espalda,
> de facciones diferentes,
> cejijunto, patituerto,
> los ojos chicos y alegres.[59]

[. . . he is the god who can do everything, by that I mean Mars, whom the world obeys, heaven respects, and all men fear. I pictured in my mind a strange kind of man: tall, long-suffering, vigorous, robust, fierce, valiant, intrepid, daring, spirited, brave, strong, determined, warlike, . . . a man with a broad back and distinct features: a monobrow, bandy legs, small, bright eyes.]

A brief comparison of the two portraits underlines the strikingly innovative nature of Velázquez's canvas. In reality, his Mars is as different from the fearsome warrior of classical tradition (associated with the adjectives listed above) as he is from the blustering bravo of contemporary mythological burlesque (associated more with the physical features given above). To identify him with either figure, simply on the basis of the presence of the impressive arms at his feet or the bushy moustache on his face, is to fail to account for the subject's overriding air of melancholic self-absorption. In other contexts, Mars's moustache, like the 'mostachos a lo ruso' of Polo de Medina's *miles gloriosus*, would lend the portrait a humorous touch, but

---

[58] For more detailed discussion of these and other readings, see my 'Mars Recontextualized in the Golden Age of Spain'.
[59] *El viaje entretenido*, 321.

the pose adopted by Velázquez's subject pulls in a different direction. The motif of the elbow planted on the knee and the chin resting on the hand brings to mind traditional representations of melancholy, ranging from Durer's famous engraving *Melencolia I* (1514) to Cesare Ripa's description of *Melancholia* in his highly influential emblem book *Iconologia* (1593). The latter describes Melancholy as a sad, old woman, dressed in coarse clothing, sitting on a stone, 'con gomiti posati sopra i ginocchi, & ambe le mani sotto il mento' [with her elbows on her knees and both hands beneath her chin].[60] Velázquez must have known Ripa's text, a standard work of Renaissance iconography of which he owned a copy, but his portrait of Mars comes closer to the description of *Melancolía* given by Carducho's master just a few years before *Marte* was painted:

La melancolía, pensativos, y llenos de tristeza, los ojos hundidos, fijos en la tierra, la cabeza baja, el codo sobre la rodilla, la mano debajo de la quijada, echado debajo de cualquier árbol, o entrepiedras, o caverna, el color pálido y amarillo.[61]

[Melancholy: eyes thoughtful, sunken, full of sadness, fixed on the ground, head bowed, elbow on knee, hand under jaw, sitting beneath some tree, by rocks, or in a cave, pale and yellow-faced.]

Once again, Velázquez combines imitation and invention in his treatment of a specific code of representation. He draws on several aspects of the figure of the melancholic, but places him in an indeterminate bedroom interior and, in a common Baroque twist, shows him with his gaze fixed not on the ground but on the viewer.

The overwhelming impression of dejection and resignation has led one critic to link the work with the adage 'post coitum, tristis'.[62] Another possible explanation for this impression sees in the scene an illustration of the well-established poetic metaphor of love as war. Viewed from this angle, Mars's predicament recalls that of the poetic voice in Garcilaso's fourth *canción*, who, having seen his reason and passion caught in a net forged from the lady's golden hair, trapped 'en público adulterio', and shamefully exposed to both heaven and earth, sums up his position as follows:

. . . en tal punto me hallo,
que estoy sin armas en el campo puesto,
y el paso ya cerrado y la húida. (109–11)[63]

---

[60] Cesare Ripa, *Iconologia*, ed. Piero Buscaroli (Milan: TEA, 1992 [1593]), 261–2.

[61] *Diálogos*, fol. 142[r].   [62] Welles, *Arachne's Tapestry*, 145.

[63] See above, p. 58.

Whereas artists across Europe focused on the union of Mars and Venus to juxtapose flesh and arms, love and war, here Velázquez demonstrates that such a contrast can be played out in a single figure, not that of the armed Venus but that of the naked Mars. The rumpled bed becomes the battlefield of love, on which the god of war now finds himself totally defenceless. More usually a symbol of military strength and authority, Mars here experiences the lover's sense of weakness and loss of control. Traditionally, and as seen in the illustrations examined in Chapter 1, the god of war has to lay his arms to one side in order to engage with Venus. Here, however, the arms that lie at Mars's feet serve not only as an allusion to their creator, Vulcan, but also as an ironic reminder of their owner's former invincibility. The power of the beloved, the absent female *dueño*, causes him, like Garcilaso's friend Mario Galeota before him, to lose his natural vigour and his passion for arms. Previously a one-dimensional synecdoche for war, Mars is reborn in the guise of a three-dimensional individual, whose human frailty is every bit as tangible as his traditional divinity. Here, it seems, Griffin's statement about the gods' perennial ability to 'reassert their divinity, show their superiority to men, and retire from the realm of suffering and passion into their blessedness' does not apply.[64]

As a portrait of a lone figure, *Marte* stands in opposition to depictions of Mars and Venus by Renaissance artists such as Botticelli, Titian, and Veronese, which show the lovers, as we have seen, either sleeping off their exertions on the battlefield of love or engaged in a passionate embrace. Tradition dictates that the lovers should be painted together, so Venus's absence is striking. Velázquez isolates Mars in order to create discourse between visible text and implied extra-text; the absence of Venus becomes as important as the presence of Mars, pointing towards the absent beloved's emphatic presence in the *Venus del espejo* (*c.*1648; Fig. 5.3), the sole extant nude Venus painted during the Golden Age of Spain. Showing a life-size woman lying naked, lengthways across a bed, this portrait of the last of the tale's three protagonists reworks the twin Venetian traditions of the Toilet of Venus and the Reclining/Sleeping Venus. The viewer is afforded a playfully erotic view of the ideal female, who reclines in perfect serenity, blissfully unaware of the psychological disarray in the world of Mars. Venus lies with her back towards the implied onlooker, captivating the viewing eye through the sensuousness of her naked form. Velázquez alludes to the beauty and eroticism of the female form whilst playfully employing Cupid's mirror to place the goddess at an ironic remove from

---

[64] See Chapter 1, n. 5.

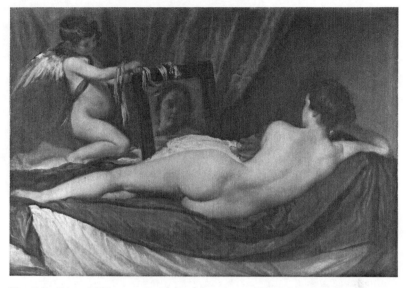

Fig. 5.3. Diego Velázquez, *La Venus del espejo*, *c*.1648. Oil on canvas.

the viewer, who experiences a sense of detachment and rejection similar to that suffered by Mars.[65]

One way of pulling many of these different aspects of the painting together is to see it not as moralizing allegory, political satire, or mythological burlesque but as an imaginative portrayal of the end of the tale of Mars, Venus, and Vulcan: 'The scene is the denouement of the amorous encounter between Mars and Venus, which has been interrupted by the cuckold Vulcan. Vulcan has set a trap for the lovers and invited the gods to witness the couple *in flagrante delicto*. Mocked, bemused, and abandoned to scorn, Mars seems befuddled, not bellicose.'[66] Having captured in *La fragua* a pivotal moment from the beginning of the tale, here Velázquez turns to its end, picturing the scene after both the lovers' release and the departure of Venus, Vulcan, and the other gods of Olympus. According to

[65] On the much-debated questions of the dating, sources, and meaning of the *Venus del espejo*, see e.g. Justi, *Diego Velázquez and his Times*, 462–6; Martin S. Soria, 'La Venus, Los Borrachos y La Coronación de Velázquez', *AEA* 26 (1953), 269–84; Francisco J. Sánchez Cantón, 'La Venus del espejo', *AEA* 33 (1960), 137–40; Charles de Tolnay, 'La "Venus au miroir", de Velázquez', in *Varia Velazqueña*, i. 339–43; Enriqueta Harris, *Velázquez* (Oxford: Phaidon, 1982), 136–40; Prater, *Venus at her Mirror*; and Peter Cherry, 'Velázquez y el desnudo', in *Fábulas de Velázquez*, 241–77 (pp. 255–64).

[66] Jonathan Brown, 'Velázquez in the 1630s and 1640s', in *Collected Writings on Velázquez*, 151–63 (p. 158). This reading is first put forward in Madlyn M. Kahr, *Velázquez: The Art of Painting* (New York: Harper & Row, 1976), 92.

this reading, Velázquez offers a second perspective on the story, depicting Mars's solitude as he sits on the bed that only minutes before had been the scene of another blissful encounter with Venus. Shocked, dejected, and bemused, Mars is left to rue his public humiliation and try to come to terms with the abrupt conclusion of his affair. Whilst it is undoubtedly satisfying to tie Velázquez's portrait of Mars into a specific mythological narrative, the 'solution' put forward by Kahr, Brown, and others raises as many questions as it answers. If this identification is correct, why does Velázquez not make it easier to reach? Why did Velázquez choose this scene over others that would have been more dynamic in terms of visual content and thus more in line with the vogue for grand-scale history painting?

Most paintings illustrating mythological tales depend for their effect on interplay between two or more readily identifiable figures and/or a strong sense of dynamism. How are we to respond to a lone figure sitting stock-still with his eyes fixed on the viewer? The conjunction of a semi-naked Mars, a rumpled bed, and arms on the floor may bring the tale of Mars, Venus, and Vulcan to mind, but the lack of other pictorial details linking this scene with the tale in question makes the identification difficult to confirm. Again, the principal classical sources say little about Mars's appearance after he is freed from the net. In Pope's translation the Homeric account notes only that '[the snares] burst; and Mars to Thrace indignant flies'.[67] Ovid says nothing about this moment, passing straight from the lovers' imprisonment and public shaming to the tale's subsequent notoriety. Whereas, as we have seen, Cueva, Lope, Castillo Solórzano, and Polo de Medina all flesh out the beginning of the tale, paying special attention to the background of the affair and the exchange between Apollo and Vulcan, none of them expands upon the moment in question. Once freed, Cueva's Mars, for example, immediately gets dressed in order to leave the scene of his shaming as quickly as possible:

> Luego que Marte en libertad se vio
> y que mover los fuertes brazos pudo,
> el fuerte arnés habiéndose vestido,
> se caló el yelmo y embrazó el escudo;
> empuñando la espada enfurecido,
> avergonzado y de coraje mudo,
> resuelto de vengar su desafuero,
> se fue desde allí a Tracia el tracio fiero. (133)

[When Mars was freed and he realized that he could move his strong arms, having put on his strong armour, he pulled on his helmet and took up his

---

67 *The Odyssey of Homer*, ii. 175.

shield; with his sword firmly grasped in his hand, enraged, ashamed, and stripped of courage, determined to avenge this outrage, the fierce Thracian went off from there to Thrace.]

The disparity between this description of Mars's release and Velázquez's portrait is striking, for the latter sees the god sitting completely motionless, with his armour, shield, and sword still piled on the ground. If, then, this is Velázquez's version of the end of the tale under examination, it is yet another in a long line of conscious reworkings of the tale whose origins are found in Demodocus's song of Ares and Aphrodite. As we have seen in previous chapters, Golden Age poets continually modified the tale, updating it through changes to the setting and order of events, the addition or suppression of individual scenes, and the creation of original backstories and continuations. There is no reason why Velázquez, a painter who set great store by *invención*, should not do the same.[68] Velázquez presents his viewer not with an explicit illustration of a scene from the tale of Mars, Venus, and Vulcan, but with a witty allusion to one possible continuation of it. As shown above, he presents his audience with a marked departure from both classical sources and earlier poetic treatments, for the thoughtful pose adopted by the semi-naked Mars is totally at odds with the emphasis elsewhere on frantic redressing followed by immediate flight. Equally, after his ignominious imprisonment Mars traditionally experiences a range of powerful emotions (anger, shame, the desire for revenge, etc.), but melancholy is not one of them. By focusing on a single figure, as opposed to a group narrative, Velázquez draws the viewer further into Mars's predicament, recording for posterity the aftermath of his capture *in flagrante* and parading his ability to subject even the most revered figures of the pagan world to his own prismatic vision.

If one takes the parallel with poetic treatments one step further, one might suggest that what Velázquez offers in *Marte* is the pictorial equivalent of a literary *concepto*. Rather than making the context of the scene explicit (as in *La fragua*), he paints an ambiguous and puzzling portrait and challenges the viewer to get to grips with it through intellectual effort. Viewers must use their knowledge of the tale in question to piece together the subtle allusions to it, supply the missing parts, and then use both their intellect and their creative imagination to understand and appreciate the significance of the changes that Velázquez makes. As demonstrated in the previous chapter, poetic conceits depend for their effect on striking juxta

---

[68] On Velázquez's emphasis on the importance of *invención* in a letter to the Bolognese historian and diplomat Virgilio Malvezzi dated 22 November 1649, see José Luis Colomer, '"Dar a Su Magestad algo bueno": Four Letters from Velázquez to Virgilio Malvezzi', *Burlington Magazine*, 135 (1993), 67–72 (p. 72).

positions of previously distinct, and often even antithetical, elements. Some of the most complex conceits see several ideas or motifs played off against one another in a very small number of words. A similar level of compression is seen in *Marte*. By bringing together a lone martial figure, items associated with the traditional iconography of the god of war, a posture linked with the figure of the melancholic, and a bedroom setting reminiscent of the scene of Mars's affair with Venus, Velázquez invites the viewer to consider the relationship between concepts previously held to be mutually exclusive, creating an economical network of implications that transforms once more the viewer's preconceptions of Mars. In the process he creates a portrait whose symbolic allusions and narrative associations produce an elegant synthesis of multiple parallel meanings—in sum, a portrait that is much more subtle, much more complex, and much less easy to categorize than any of those seen in the poetry of the period.[69]

On two separate occasions, then, Velázquez can be seen to draw inspiration from episodes associated with the tale of Mars, Venus, and Vulcan. Each time, he shuns the raucous and indecorous unveiling of the lovers to concentrate on a psychologically dramatic, or traumatic, moment associated with the 'perturbaciones del ánimo' of one of the tale's male protagonists. In both *La fragua* and *Marte* Velázquez displays considerable powers of invention, bringing to life scenes that are either largely undeveloped or completely unattested in the principal classical tellings. Though he would undoubtedly have known, and been influenced by, several earlier representations of the tale, through images such as Tempesta's engraving and through those written accounts found in vernacular translations of Homer and Ovid, iconographical handbooks such as the *Philosofía secreta*, and poems such as Cueva's 'Los amores', he treats such sources with great freedom, never allowing his imagination to be subservient to any one in particular. Ultimately, there is nothing either in their suggested sources or in the long line of classical and Renaissance handlings of the tale of Mars, Venus, and Vulcan that prepares the viewer for the scenes captured in both *La fragua* and *Marte*. Comparing the two works with such sources and handlings does not result in neat and definitive interpretations; as noted above, it underlines not similarities but differences, throwing into sharper relief the strikingly innovative nature of Velázquez's paintings of the gods and their affairs.

One of the most novel aspects of Velázquez's mythological paintings is, to repeat a convenient anachronism, their realism. Velázquez passes

---

[69] For more on the notion of pictorial conceits in the Golden Age, see e.g. Ernest B. Gilman, *The Curious Perspective: Literature and Pictorial Wit in the Seventeenth Century* (New Haven: Yale University Press, 1978); and Schwartz, 'Linguistic and Pictorial Conceits'.

classical mythology through a realist filter, placing the gods in everyday settings, minimizing their traditional attributes and features, and underlining their very humanity. This rejection of idealism is one of the hallmarks of Velázquez's work as a whole: in his representations of classical gods and philosophers, his portraits of successive generations of Spanish Habsburgs, and his studies of religious figures, the human is always accentuated at the expense of the mythological, the regal, and the divine.

The dialogue between classical mythology and everyday reality at the heart of *La fragua* and *Marte* anticipates that seen in Velázquez's two most famous mythological paintings, the enigmatic *Venus del espejo* and *Las hilanderas*. In the previous chapter we saw how the collapsing of the difference between gods and men— -between their world and our world—is a device commonly employed in seventeenth-century mythological burlesque. In Velázquez's paintings, however, the two worlds are conflated without the result tipping over into flagrant burlesque. As a result, whereas the tone of the ballads penned by Castillo Solórzano, Polo de Medina, and Barrios is easily and immediately grasped, that of the works discussed above is more open to debate.

In the *Arte de la pintura*, in a passage translated from Dolce's *Dialogo della pittura* [Dialogue on Painting] (1557), and ultimately derived from Horace, *Ars Poetica*, 361–5, Pacheco observes that the finest paintings, like the finest poems, are those that take on greater subtlety and complexity with each and every viewing:

> Este deleite no lo entiendo de aquello que agrada al vulgo, ni aun a los entendidos, a la primera vista; mas de aquello que se descubre y engrandece cuanto más se mira y se torna a mirar, como acontece en los buenos poemas, que mientras más se leen tanto más deleitan, y más acrecientan el deseo de volverlos a leer.[70]

> [I do not see this delight in works that please the masses, or even the educated, at first sight; but in works that reveal themselves and grow in stature the more they are looked at and looked at again, as happens with good poems, which give greater pleasure the more they are read, together with a stronger desire to read them again.]

La fragua and *Marte* both fall firmly into the second of these two categories. An impression of spontaneity and artlessness thinly veils works that are, at heart, much more ambiguous and much more complex than they at first seem. Detailed examination of these works—of their possible sources, origins, and meanings—leads not to straightforward and

---

[70] *Arte de la pintura*, 391.

definitive interpretation but to an appreciation of the many and varied angles from which they can be viewed. In each case, the presence of a series of ambiguous or incongruous details, the development of down-to-earth images of the pagan gods, the blending of elements found in earlier tellings of the story of Mars, Venus, and Vulcan, and the creation of conceptual difficulty all serve to problematize the quest for definitive interpretation, encouraging the viewer to devote time and intellectual effort to the very process of viewing.

Conclusion

In a well-known article on Góngora's *Polifemo*, the influential poet and critic Dámaso Alonso explains that the seventeenth-century vogue for imitation has serious implications for any understanding of originality:

> En el siglo XVII dominan netamente las fuerzas de la imitación: el valor de una obra se mide por la grandeza, la valentía y perfección en imitar. La originalidad tiene un ámbito muy reducido: casi no llega a más que a renovar el orden de elementos antiguos para engañar y halagar la imaginación de un mundo que ya se estaba ahitando. Y es inútil buscar en esta época el rabioso prurito moderno de la originalidad, que hace que una de las normas primeras para medir una obra de arte consista hoy en apreciar lo que la separa, lo que la distingue de las obras anteriores.[1]

> [The seventeenth century is clearly dominated by the forces of imitation: the value of a work is measured by the greatness, the effort, and the perfection it displays in imitating. There is little scope for originality: it is almost just a case of refreshing the order of old elements so as to deceive and flatter the imagination of a world that was already explored almost to the point of satiety. And in this period it is pointless to look for the furious modern obsession with originality, which means that one of the first rules for judging a work of art consists nowadays of understanding what separates it, what distinguishes it from previous works.]

Nothing could be further from the truth, for, as we have seen, imitation and invention go hand in hand in the Golden Age. Over 300 years earlier the Asturian historian and literary treatiser Luis Alfonso de Carvallo is closer to the mark when noting that, because *imitatio* moves one only so far, it is necessary to have *inventio*:

> No puede al fin el que imita ir muy adelante, si no tiene arte para salir algunas veces del ejemplo que ha tomado, así como no puede mucho correr el que sigue a otro sin poner los pies sino en sus pisadas.[2]

---

[1] 'La supuesta imitación por Góngora de la "Fábula de Acis y Galatea"', in *Estudios y ensayos gongorinos*, 324–70 (p. 369).

[2] Luis Alfonso de Carvallo, *Cisne de Apolo*, ed. Alberto Porqueras Mayo (Kassel: Edition Reichenberger, 1997 [1602]), 344.

[In the end he who imitates cannot go very far if he does not possess the skill to depart sometimes from the model he has taken, just as he who follows someone else cannot do much running if he has to step in their footsteps.]

The telling and retelling of classical tales represents the ultimate in imitative writing; it is only with frequent departures from, and updates to, existing models that they can continue to hold their appeal. As they are passed down through the generations, they are subject to constant change as variants are introduced and new contexts developed. In order fully to appreciate each new version, be it literary or visual, precisely what one must be able to spot and understand is 'lo que la separa, lo que la distingue de las obras anteriores', for it is in these very differences—some marked, others more subtle—that the originality of each new telling lies.

The tale of Mars, Venus, and Vulcan is an ideal case in point. In the Golden Age of Spain the story derived from Demodocus's song of Ares and Aphrodite is subject to many and varied treatments. From Garcilaso to Velázquez, each successive poet or painter demonstrates the ability to shift the focus of the tale, to make this well-known episode seem unfamiliar, unusual, or different, and to force the reader/viewer into active re-examination of what they thought they knew. The story is modified time and again, as aspects of individual classical tellings are picked up and developed, elements from competing accounts are combined and played off against one another, and new scenes or characters are added to the basic narrative. At each stage the changes introduced reveal much about the nature and purpose of a particular handling. As we have seen, significant changes include the creation of backstories detailing Mars's courtship of Venus, the fleshing out of Apollo's exchange with Vulcan, and the introduction of Momus. More subtle, yet equally significant, modifications see, for example, Mars placate Venus through the vehicle of gifts, bribes, or money, Vulcan consider wife-murder before settling on the net as a vehicle for revenge, and both gods and goddesses present as witnesses to the lovers' shaming. When deciding upon a given approach to the tale, poets and painters would have been aware of the ways in which a prospective approach both drew on and departed from previous accounts. A proper understanding of the texts and images analysed in this study—of each individual contribution to the development of representations of the tale—must, therefore, be anchored in detailed knowledge of earlier tellings, treatments, and interpretations, for it is only when armed with such knowledge that one can appreciate both what they borrow and what they add, that is, the all-important interplay between imitation and invention.

The tellings discussed above demonstrate the appeal, flexibility, and multifaceted nature of the tale of Mars, Venus, and Vulcan. The various classical accounts—which were frequently conflated by later poets, translators, mythographers, and others—already attest to its impressive capacity for renewal. As we have seen, the story that is handed down from Homer, Ovid, Lucian, and Reposianus addresses a wide range of themes, motifs, situations, and concerns prevalent in Golden Age literary and visual culture. For its cast, it brings together an old husband, a beautiful young wife, and a headstrong suitor/lover—a combination seen time and again in late sixteenth- and seventeenth-century literature (especially in the *comedia nueva*). It engages with the subject of marriage, the problems that arise from unsuitable matches, and the threat posed by adultery to a husband's honour. Venus's infidelity gives rise to both envy (what Apollo wants and cannot have) and jealousy (what Vulcan has but cannot control). 'La negra que llaman honra' [that wretched thing called honour]—the obsession of *pícaros*, wronged husbands on stage, and myriad others—provides the most obvious link with the dominant thematic concerns of the period's literature.[3] The tale of Venus's adultery with Mars and Vulcan's subsequent revenge sees a piquant twist given to the popular subject of the 'caso de la honra': whereas the majority of husbands on page and stage prescribe silence and secrecy in their attempts to protect their honour and social reputation, Vulcan deliberately publicizes his own dishonour by shaming the lovers in front of their peers. As a metaphor for an invisible, unbreakable, and inescapable trap, the net forged by Vulcan in order to carry out this revenge not only embodies the theme of *engaño*, but also allows for play on various forms of literal and figurative imprisonment associated with the traditions of Courtly Love and Petrarchan lyric: service to the *belle dame sans merci*, the topos of the *cárcel de amor* [prison of love], the figure of the galley slave shackled in Venus's *concha* [conch/pudenda], and so on. If one adds to all this other elements present in the tale—a metaphor for artistic excellence, the drama of the lovers' capture, the titillating sight of Mars and Venus caught in the act, the husband's appeal for redress to a higher authority, the witnesses' revelry in the cuckoldry and/or misfortune of others, the focus on the Deadly Sins of Lust, Envy, and Pride, and so on—then it is easy to see why the tale should have proved popular in the sixteenth and seventeenth centuries.

The changes made by each poet or painter to the basic narrative often serve to place particular emphasis on one or more of these motifs. A clear example of this is seen in Cueva's 'Los amores' and Lope's 'La rosa blanca', both of which draw out the dramatic potential inherent in the tale. Other ways of modifying and refreshing the tale include developing

---

[3] For this phrase, used by Lázaro in a solemn and portentous aside on the false god of honour, see *Lazarillo de Tormes*, ed. Francisco Rico, LH, 44 (Madrid: Cátedra, 1996), 84.

the significance of a specific moment (Apollo's message to Vulcan, the capture of the lovers, etc.); combining individual scenes or allusions to the tale with other subjects and sources of inspiration (different classical and Italianate models, specific strains of Neoplatonic thought, famous works by rival poets, etc.); shifting the tale's focus by prioritizing the perspective of one of the three protagonists—Mars (e.g. Aldana's 'Octavas en diversas materias'), Venus (e.g. Lope), or Vulcan (e.g. Hurtado de Mendoza); and adopting a range of different tones to the same subject (serious, playful, mock-epic, burlesque, ambiguous, etc.). In imitating or drawing on the Homeric and Ovidian story, each poet or painter could choose to focus on its more serious aspects, accentuate the comedy associated with its denouement, play on tension between the comic and the serious, or endeavour to resolve any innate tension between the two. Viewed from certain angles, the tale of Mars, Venus, and Vulcan is an inherently comic one. However, that fact did not preclude Golden Age poets from addressing serious questions in their treatments of the tale; indeed, it is often the tellings that appear to be the most frivolous (i.e. the flagrant burlesques of Castillo Solórzano, Polo de Medina, Barrios, and others) that, by gilding the lily and engaging the reader's intellect, convey the most forceful moral lessons.

The protagonists of the tale of Mars, Venus, and Vulcan are shown to be particularly protean. Whilst, on the one hand, the tale is about an invincible warrior, a beautiful goddess, and the archetypal artist, on the other it is about a boastful *miles gloriosus*, a crafty prostitute, and a pathetic cuckold. As we have seen, such pronounced contrasts—warrior/bravo, goddess/prostitute, artist/cuckold—are often exploited for comic effect and/or conceptual play, but there is no point of sudden transition between idealized portrayals of the gods as archetypes of positive virtues and qualities and grotesque caricatures of them as embodiments of vice and immorality. Many of the characteristics accentuated by Góngora, Quevedo, Castillo Solórzano, Polo de Medina, and others in their burlesque or satirical portraits of the three gods (and many of the devices they employ to do so) are found in embryonic form in earlier tellings. The mock-heroic poems of Cueva and Lope not only draw on commonplaces associated with the positive images of the gods but also draw out the negative characteristics central to burlesque and satirical treatments. The individual who searches frantically for his former lover in Aldana's 'Octavas', the presumptuous and arrogant warrior of Cueva's 'Los amores', and the figure who sleeps in post-coital bliss in Lope's 'La rosa blanca' are not far removed from Góngora's 'dios garañón' or Polo de Medina's Plautine braggart. The goddess who imprisons men in her *venera* in Garcilaso's *Ode*, the Celestina-like prostitute lampooned in Hurtado de Mendoza's obscene sonnet, the individual who in Aldana's 'Octavas' reclines with a satyr in a *locus amoenus*, having duped both Vulcan and Mars, and the self-assured figure of Cueva's poem who is interested only in money and gifts are all to some degree related to Polo de Medina's penny-pinching brothel madam. Finally, the smith who is subjected to unrelenting ridicule in burlesque treatments of the tale is a direct descendant of Lucian's 'marido resignado', Hurtado de Mendoza's cuckold, Cueva's anti-hero who is obsessed with his own honour, and Lope's smith who goes to comic (and ultimately futile) lengths to keep up appearances.

To make a well-known tale appear entirely new is, however, not just a question of *what* but also one of *how*. This is one of the main challenges posed by the guiding principle of imitation. Each poet or painter has to strive to find original ways of portraying the tale's protagonists and essential narrative elements. As the number of tellings of the story grows this becomes increasingly difficult. Happily, the search for ever-more erudite, recondite, or elaborate references to or descriptions of the same basic building blocks gives rise to a string of memorable devices, including subtle allusions, clever wordplays, startling metaphors, and intricate conceits. In the case of Vulcan's lameness, for example, we see a general movement away from straightforward description towards more complex forms of reference: from unambiguous adjectives such as *cojo*, to playful characterizations of Vulcan as a 'retrógrado cancro', burlesque conceits based on forms of defective poetry ('fregenal estrambote', 'sílabas diminutos', etc.), and ironic understatement in Velázquez's *La fragua*. Other elements lead, for example, to Polo de Medina's striking quatrains on links between the lovers and a sign for Cancer and between Vulcan and a scarecrow hanging in an elder. Throughout the Golden Age the challenge of saying the same things in different ways thus gave poets and painters the opportunity not only to imitate their forebears and contemporaries, but also to emulate them through the exercise of wit, humour, and *admiratio*.

The most innovative treatments of the tale of Mars, Venus, and Vulcan are marked, first and foremost, by an appeal to the intellect of the reader/viewer. The promotion of *admiratio*, the juxtaposition of the comic and the serious, the cultivation of unsettling ambiguity and incongruity, the development of conceptual difficulty, and the exercise of *agudeza*, 'don proprio de los españoles' [a talent characteristic of the Spanish], all place demands on the mind of the reader/viewer, encouraging them to dedicate time to the reading/viewing process and challenging them to engage their intellectual faculties and hone their powers of logical reasoning.[4] Many of

---

[4] For Francisco de Medina's famous description of *agudeza*, see 'El Maestro Francisco de Medina a los letores', in Herrera, *Anotaciones*, 187–203 (p. 192).

these qualities are as prominent in early sixteenth-century allusions to the tale as they are in later full-scale retellings. In addition to the subject itself, what unites the many and varied treatments discussed in this study—from Garcilaso's 'dissimulative imitation' to Cueva's theatrical *amplificatio*; from Góngora's *contrafactum* to Lope's potted biography of Venus; and from Polo de Medina's ribald burlesque to Velázquez's enigmatic portraits—is the ability to bring a well-known story back to life, to revise audiences' preconceptions of the tale and its protagonists, and to prompt astonished surprise at the creative power of the poet/painter. Finally, like those of Ronsard and Tintoretto, these works open up a world in which tales of the gods and their affairs can be appreciated as sources of both intellectual and aesthetic pleasure. Demodocus's song of Ares and Aphrodite thus blazed a trail not just through heaven but also through the Golden Age of Spain.

Bibliography

CLASSICAL AND LATE CLASSICAL PRIMARY TEXTS

Apollodorus, *The Library of Greek Mythology*, trans. Robin Hard, Oxford World's Classics (Oxford: Oxford University Press, 1997).

Apollonius Rhodius, *Argonautica*, trans. William H. Race, LCL (Cambridge, Mass.: Harvard University Press, 2008).

Aristotle, *Politics*, trans. Harris Rackham, LCL (Cambridge, Mass.: Harvard University Press, 1932).

Fulgentius, *Fulgentius the Mythographer*, trans. Leslie George Whitbread (Ohio: Ohio State University Press, 1971).

Greek Lyric, trans. David A. Campbell, LCL, 5 vols. (Cambridge, Mass.: Harvard University Press, 1982–93).

Heraclitus, *Homeric Problems*, ed. and trans. Donald A. Russell and David Konstan (Atlanta, Ga.: Society of Biblical Literature, 2005).

Hesiod, *Theogony* and *Works and Days*, trans. Martin L. West, Oxford World's Classics (Oxford: Oxford University Press, 1999).

Homer, *The Odyssey of Homer*, trans. by Alexander Pope, Elijah Fenton, and William Broome, 5 vols. (London: Bernard Lintot, 1725–6).

——— *Odyssey*, trans. Augustus T. Murray, rev. George E. Dimock, LCL, 2 vols. (Cambridge, Mass.: Harvard University Press, 1995).

——— *Iliad*, trans. Augustus T. Murray, rev. William F. Wyatt, LCL, 2 vols. (Cambridge, Mass.: Harvard University Press, 1999).

——— *Odyssey, Books VI–VIII*, ed. Alexander F. Garvie, Cambridge Greek and Latin Classics (Cambridge: Cambridge University Press, 1994).

Horace, *Odes and Epodes*, trans. Charles E. Bennett, LCL (Cambridge, Mass.: Harvard University Press, 1995).

Lucian, *Lucian*, trans. Austin M. Harmon, K. Kilburn, and M. D. MacLeod, LCL, 8 vols. (Cambridge, Mass.: Harvard University Press, 1913–67).

Lucretius, *De Rerum Natura*, trans. William H. D. Rouse, LCL (Cambridge, Mass.: Harvard University Press, 1966).

Minor Latin Poets, trans. J. Wight Duff and Arnold M. Duff, LCL (Cambridge, Mass.: Harvard University Press, 1978).

Ovid, *Metamorphoses*, trans. Frank Justus Miller, LCL, 2 vols. (Cambridge, Mass.: Harvard University Press, 1971).

——— *The Art of Love and Other Poems*, trans. John H. Mozley, rev. George P. Goold, LCL (Cambridge, Mass.: Harvard University Press, 1979).

Plato, *Republic*, trans. Robin Waterfield, Oxford World's Classics (Oxford: Oxford University Press, 1993).

Pliny, *Natural History*, trans. Harris Rackham and others, LCL, 10 vols. (Cambridge, Mass.: Harvard University Press, 1938–63).

Plutarch, *Moralia*, trans. Frank C. Babbitt and others, LCL, 16 vols. (Cambridge, Mass.: Harvard University Press, 1927–76).

Priapeos. Grafitos amatorios pompeyanos. La velada de la fiesta de Venus. El concúbito de Marte y Venus. Centón nupcial, ed. and trans. Enrique Montero Cartelle, Biblioteca Clásica Gredos, 41 (Madrid: Gredos, 1981).

Reposianus, *Concubitus Martis et Veneris,* ed. and trans. Ugo Zuccarelli, Collana di studi classici, 12 (Naples: Libreria Scientifica, 1972).

Seneca, *Epistulae Morales,* trans. Richard M. Gummere, LCL, 3 vols. (Cambridge, Mass.: Harvard University Press, 1917–25).

Virgil, *Virgil,* trans. H. Rushton Fairclough, LCL, 2 vols. (Cambridge, Mass.: Harvard University Press, 1916–18).

Xenophanes of Colophon, *Fragments,* trans. James H. Lesher (Toronto: University of Toronto Press, 1992).

MEDIEVAL AND RENAISSANCE PRIMARY TEXTS

Acuña, Hernando de, *Varias poesías,* ed. Luis F. Díaz Larios, LH, 164 (Madrid: Cátedra, 1982).

Aldana, Francisco de, *Primera parte de las obras que hasta agora se han podido hallar del Capitan Francisco de Aldana* (Milan: Paolo Gottardo da Ponte, 1589).

—— *Segunda parte de las obras que se han podido hallar del Capitan Francisco de Aldana* (Madrid: Pedro Madrigal, 1591).

—— *Poesías castellanas completas,* ed. José Lara Garrido, LH, 223 (Madrid: Cátedra, 1985).

Alemán, Mateo, *Guzmán de Alfarache,* ed. José María Micó, LH, 86–7, 2 vols. (Madrid: Cátedra, 2003).

Anguillara, Giovanni Andrea dell', *Le metamorfosi di Ovidio, ridotte da Giovanni Andrea dell' Anguillara in ottava rima con le annotazioni di messer Giuseppe Orologgi* (Venice: Francesco de' Franceschi, 1571).

An Anthology of Spanish Poetry, 1500–1700, ed. Arthur Terry, 2 vols. (Oxford: Pergamon, 1965–8).

Argensola, Lupercio Leonardo de, *Rimas de Lupercio, i del Dotor Bartolomé Leonardo de Argensola* (Zaragoza: Hospital Real, 1634).

Ariosto, Ludovico, *Orlando furioso,* trans. Guido Waldman, Oxford World's Classics (Oxford: Oxford University Press, 1998).

«Aunque entiendo poco griego . . . ». Fábulas mitológicas burlescas del Siglo de Oro, ed. Elena Cano Turrión (Córdoba: Berenice, 2007).

Barrios, Miguel de, *Flor de Apolo* (Brussels: Baltazar Vivien, 1665).

—— *Flor de Apolo,* ed. Francisco J. Sedeño Rodríguez (Kassel: Reichenberger, 2005).

Baur, Johann Wilhelm, *Dem hoch edlen unnd gestrengen Herren* (Vienna: [n. pub.], 1641).

Bernardo de Quirós, Francisco, *Obras de don Francisco Bernardo de Quiros. Alguacil propietario de la casa, y corte de su magestad. Y aventuras de don Fruela* (Madrid: Melchor Sánchez, 1656).

La Bible des poètes (Paris: Antoine Vérard, 1493).

Boccaccio, Giovanni, *Genealogie deorum gentilium libri,* ed. Vincenzo Romano, Scrittori d'Italia, 200–1, 2 vols. (Bari: Giuseppe Laterza & Figli, 1951).

Bonsignori, Giovanni, *Ovidio Metamorphoseos vulgare* (Venice: Zoane Rosso, 1497).

——— *Ovidio Metamorphoseos vulgare* (Venice: Lucantonio Giunta, 1501).

——— *Ovidio Metamorphoseos vulgare*, ed. Erminia Ardissino, Collezione di opere inedite o rare, 157 (Bologna: Commissione per i testi di lingua, 2001).

Boscán, Juan, *Las obras de Boscan y algunas de Garcilasso dela Vega repartidas en quatro libros* (Barcelona: Carles Amorós, 1543).

——— *Obra completa*, ed. Carlos Clavería, LH, 453 (Madrid: Cátedra, 1999).

Bracciolini, Francesco, *Lo scherno degli dei* (Venice: Paolo Guerrigli, 1618).

Bustamante, Jorge de, *Las Transformaciones de Ovidio en lengua española* (Antwerp: Pedro Bellero, 1595).

Butrón, Juan de, *Discursos apologeticos, en que se defiende la ingenuidad del arte de la pintura* (Madrid: Luis Sánchez, 1626).

Calderón de la Barca, Pedro, *El médico de su honra*, ed. Jesús Pérez Magallón, LH, 702 (Madrid: Cátedra, 2012).

Carducho, Vicente, *Diálogos de la pintura* (Madrid: Francisco Martínez, 1633).

Cartari, Vincenzo, *Le imagini con la spositione de i dei de gliantichi* (Venice: Francesco Marcolini, 1556).

Carvallo, Luis Alfonso de, *Cisne de Apolo*, ed. Alberto Porqueras Mayo (Kassel: Edition Reichenberger, 1997 [1602]).

Cascales, Francisco, *Tablas poéticas* (Murcia: Luis Beros, 1617).

——— *Tablas poéticas* (Madrid: Antonio de Sancha, 1779).

Castiglione, Baldassare, *Los quatro libros del cortesano, compuestos en italiano por el conde Balthasar Castellon y agora nuevamente traduzidos en lengua castellana* (Barcelona: Pedro Monpezat, 1534).

Castillo Solórzano, Alonso de, *Donayres del Parnaso. Primera Parte* (Madrid: Diego Flamenco, 1624).

Cervantes, Miguel de, *Novelas ejemplares,* ed. Harry Sieber, LH, 105–6, 2 vols. (Madrid: Cátedra, 1997).

——— *Don Quijote de la Mancha*, ed. Francisco Rico (Madrid: Alfaguara, 2004).

Cetina, Gutierre de, *Sonetos y madrigales completos*, ed. Begoña López Bueno, LH, 146 (Madrid: Cátedra, 1981).

Conti, Natale, *Mythologiae sive explicationum fabularum libri decem* (Venice: [n. pub.], 1567 [1551]).

Correas, Gonzalo, *Vocabulario de refranes y frases proverbiales*, ed. Louis Combet (Bordeaux: Institut d'études ibériques et ibéro-américaines de l'Université de Bordeaux, 1967 [1627]).

Covarrubias, Sebastián de, *Tesoro de la lengua castellana o española*, ed. Ignacio Arellano and Rafael Zafra, Biblioteca Áurea Hispánica, 21 (Madrid: Ibero-americana, 2006 [1611]).

Coypeau d'Assoucy, Charles, *L'Ovide en belle humeur* (Lyons: Nicolas Gay, 1650).

Cueva, Juan de la, *Obras de Juan de la Cueva, dirigidas al Ilustrísimo Señor don Juan Téllez Girón* (Seville: Andrea Pescioni, 1582).

——— *Primera parte de las comedias y tragedias de Juan de la Cueva dirigidas a Momo* (Seville: Andrea Pescioni, 1583).

——— *Segunda parte de las Obras de Iuan de la Cueva. Anno 1604*, BCC, Ms. 82-2-5.

Cueva, Juan de la, *Los inventores de las cosas*, ed. Beno Weiss and Louis C. Pérez (Pennsylvania: Pennsylvania State University Press, 1980).

—— *Fábulas mitológicas y épica burlesca*, ed. José Cebrián García (Madrid: Editora Nacional, 1984).

—— *Exemplar poético*, ed. José María Reyes Cano (Seville: Alfar, 1986).

Díez y Foncalda, Alberto, *Poesías varias. Primera Parte* (Zaragoza: Juan de Ibar, 1653).

Dolce, Lodovico, *Le Transformationi tratte da Ovidio* (Venice: Gabriel Giolito de' Ferrari, 1553).

Durán de Salcedo, Jerónimo, 'Venus y Marte', in *Academia que se celebró en la Universidad de Salamanca, en tres de enero de 1672, en casa del Señor Don Luis de Losada y Rivadeneyra su Rector* (Salamanca: Melchor Estévez, [n.d.]), 30–2.

Equicola, Mario, *Libro de natura de amore* (Venice: Lorenzo Lorio da Portes, 1525).

Espínola y Torres, Juan, *Transformaciones y robos de Júpiter, y celos de Juno* (Lisbon: Jorge Rodríguez, 1619).

Fennor, William, *Cornucopiae, Pasquils nightcap: or, Antidot for the head-ache* (London: Thomas Thorp, 1612).

Ficino, Marsilio, *Sopra lo amore o ver' Convito di Platone* (Florence: Neri Dortelata, 1544).

Flor de varios romances nuevos. Primera y Segunda parte (Barcelona: Iayme Cendrat, 1591).

Garcia, Francesc Vicenç, *La armonia del Parnás* (Barcelona: Rafel Figueró, 1700).

Garcilaso de la Vega, *Obras del excelente poeta Garcilaso de la Vega con anotaciones y enmiendas del Licenciado Francisco Sanchez Cathedratico de Rhetorica en Salamanca* (Salamanca: Pedro Lasso, 1574).

—— *Obras completas con comentario*, ed. Elias L. Rivers (Madrid: Castalia, 1974).

—— *Obra poética y textos en prosa*, ed. Bienvenido Morros, Clásicos y Modernos, 10 (Barcelona: Crítica, 2003).

Garcilaso de la Vega y sus comentaristas: obras completas del poeta acompañadas de los textos íntegros de los comentarios de El Brocense, Fernando de Herrera, Tamayo de Vargas y Azara, ed. Antonio Gallego Morell, 2nd rev. and exp. edn. (Madrid: Gredos, 1972).

Gómez de Tejada de los Reyes, Cosme, *León prodigioso: apología moral entretenida, y provechosa a las buenas costumbres, trato virtuoso y político* (Madrid: Francisco Martínez, 1636).

Góngora, Luis de, *Canciones y otros poemas en arte mayor*, ed. José María Micó, Clásicos Castellanos, NS 20 (Madrid: Espasa Calpe, 1990).

—— *Teatro completo*, ed. Laura Dolfi, LH, 355 (Madrid: Cátedra, 1993).

—— *Soledades*, ed. Robert Jammes, CC, 202 (Madrid: Castalia, 1994).

—— *Romances*, ed. Antonio Carreira, 4 vols. (Barcelona: Quaderns Crema, 1998).

—— *Fábula de Polifemo y Galatea*, ed. Jesús Ponce Cárdenas, LH, 658 (Madrid: Cátedra, 2010).

———— *Romances*, ed. Antonio Carreño, LH, 160 (Madrid: Cátedra, 2000).

Gracián, Baltasar, *Agudeza y arte de ingenio*, ed. Evaristo Correa Calderón, CC, 14–15, 2 vols. (Madrid: Castalia, 2001).

Guevara, Felipe de, *Comentarios de la pintura* (Madrid: viuda de Ibarra, 1588).

———— *Comentarios de la pintura*, ed. Rafael Benet (Barcelona: Selecciones Bibliófilas, 1948).

Gutiérrez de los Ríos, Gaspar, *Noticia general para la estimación de las artes* (Madrid: Pedro Madrigal, 1600).

Hebreo, León, *Diálogos de amor*, trans. Carlos Mazo del Castillo, ed. José-María Reyes Cano (Barcelona: Promociones Publicaciones Universitarias, 1986).

Hernández de Velasco, Gregorio, *La Eneida, traducción en verso del doctor Gregorio Hernández de Velasco* (Toledo: Juan de Ayala, 1555).

Herrera, Fernando de, *Poesía castellana original completa*, ed. Cristóbal Cuevas, LH, 219 (Madrid: Cátedra, 1997).

———— *Anotaciones a la poesía de Garcilaso*, ed. Inoria Pepe and José María Reyes, LH, 516 (Madrid: Cátedra, 2001).

Hita, Arcipreste de, *Libro de buen amor*, ed. Gerald B. Gybbon-Monypenny, CC, 161 (Madrid: Castalia, 1988).

Hurtado de Mendoza, Diego, *Obras del insigne cavallero Don Diego de Mendoza, embaxador del Emperador Carlos Quinto en Roma. Recopilados por Frey Ivan Diaz Hidalgo* (Madrid: Juan de la Cuesta, 1610).

———— *Poesía*, ed. Luis F. Díaz Larios and Olga Gete Carpio, LH, 328 (Madrid: Cátedra, 1990).

Lazarillo de Tormes, ed. Francisco Rico, LH, 44 (Madrid: Cátedra, 1996).

López Pinciano, Alonso, *Obras completas*, ed. José Rico Verdú, 2 vols. (Madrid: Biblioteca Castro, 1998).

Loves Schoole: Publii Ovidii Nasonis de arte amandi, Or, The Art of Loue (Amsterdam: Nicolas Jansz Visscher, [n.d.]).

Martínez, Jusepe, *Discursos practicables del nobilísimo arte de la pintura*, ed. Valentín Carderera y Solano (Madrid: Manuel Tello, 1866).

Medrano, Sebastián Francisco de, *Favores de las Musas* (Milan: Carlo Ferranti, 1631).

La Métamorphose d'Ovide figurée (Lyons: Jean de Tournes, 1557).

Metamorphoseon sive transformationum Ovidianarum libri quindecim, aeneis formis ab Antonio Tempesta florentino incisi, et in pictorum antiquitatisque studiosorum gratiam nunc primum exquisitissimis sumptibus a Petro de Iode antuerpiano in lucem editi (Amsterdam: Wilhelm Janson, 1606).

Metamorphoses, argumentis brevioribus ex Luctatio Grammatico collectis expositae: una cum vivis singularum Transformationum iconibus in aes incisis (Antwerp: Ex off. Plantiniana, Widow and Jean Moretus, 1591).

Les Métamorphoses d'Ovide traduites en prose françoise, et de nouveau soigneusement reveuës, corrigées en infinis endroits, et enrichies de figures à chacune fable. Avec XV discours contenant l'explication morale et historique (Paris: veuve Langelier, 1619).

Mey, Felipe, *Del Metamorphoseos de Ovidio en Otava rima traduzido por Felipe Mey. Siete Libros* (Tarragona: [n. pub.], 1586).

Molina, Tirso de, *La mujer que manda en casa*, ed. Dawn L. Smith (London: Tamesis, 1984).

Ovide moralisé. Poème du commencement du quatorzième siècle, ed. Cornelis de Boer, 5 vols. (Amsterdam: Johannes Müller, 1915–38).

Pacheco, Francisco, *Arte de la pintura*, ed. Bonaventura Bassegoda i Hugas (Madrid: Cátedra, 1990 [1649]).

Pérez, Gonzalo, *De la Ulyxea de Homero XIII libros, traduzidos de Griego en Romance Castellano por Gonçalo Pérez* (Salamanca: Andrea de Portonaris, 1550).

——— *La Ulyxea de Homero, traduzida de Griego en lengua Castellana por el Secretario Gonçalo Pérez* (Antwerp: Juan Steelsio, 1556).

——— *La Ulyxea de Homero, traduzida de Griego en lengua Castellana por el Secretario Gonçalo Pérez. Nuevamente por el mesmo revista y emendada* (Venice: Francesco Rampazeto, 1562).

Pérez de Moya, Juan, *Philosofía secreta. Donde debaxo de historias fabulosas se contiene mucha doctrina provechosa a todos estudios. Con el origen de los Idolos o Dioses de la Gentilidad. Es materia muy necessaria para entender Poetas y Historiadores* (Madrid: Francisco Sánchez, 1585).

——— *Philosofía secreta*, ed. Carlos Clavería, LH, 404 (Madrid: Cátedra, 1995).

Pérez Sigler, Antonio, *Los XV libros de los Metamorfoseos de el excellente Poeta Latino Ovidio* (Salamanca: Juan Perier, 1580).

Petrarca, Francesco, *Canzoniere*, ed. by Gianfranco Contini, ET classici, 104 (Turin: Einaudi, 1964).

——— *Le familiari*, trans. Ugo Dotti, 3 vols. (Rome: Archivio Guido Izzi, 1991–4).

Polo de Medina, Salvador Jacinto, *El buen humor de las musas* (Madrid: Alonso Pérez, 1630).

——— *Obras completas*, ed. José María de Cossío, Biblioteca de Autores Murcianos, 1 (Murcia: Tip. Sucesores de Nogués, 1948).

——— *Poesía. Hospital de incurables*, ed. Francisco J. Díez de Revenga, LH, 268 (Madrid: Cátedra, 1987).

Posthius, Johann, *Tetrasticha in Ovidii Metamor. lib. XV* (Frankfurt: Georg Corvinus, Sigmund Feyerabend, heirs of Wygand Galle, 1563).

Primera parte de las Flores de poetas ilustres de España, dividida en dos libros. Ordenada por Pedro Espinosa (Valladolid: Luis Sánchez, 1605).

Quevedo, Francisco de, *El Parnasso Español, monte en dos cumbres dividido, con las nueve musas castellanas* (Madrid: Pedro Coello, 1648).

——— *Obra poética*, ed. José Manuel Blecua, 4 vols. (Madrid: Castalia, 1969–81).

——— *La Hora de todos y la Fortuna con seso*, ed. Jean Bourg, Pierre Dupont, and Pierre Geneste, LH, 276 (Madrid: Cátedra, 1987).

——— *Prosa festiva completa*, ed. Celsa Carmen García-Valdés, LH, 363 (Madrid: Cátedra, 1993).

——— *Los sueños*, ed. Ignacio Arellano, LH, 335 (Madrid: Cátedra, 1999).

——— *El Buscón*, ed. Domingo Ynduráin, LH, 124 (Madrid: Cátedra, 2001).

Radcliffe, Alexander, *Ovidius exulans, or, Ovid travestie: A mock-poem on five epistles of Ovid* (London: Peter Lillicrap, 1673).

Ripa, Cesare, *Iconologia*, ed. Piero Buscaroli (Milan: TEA, 1992 [1593]).

Rojas, Fernando de, *La Celestina*, ed. Dorothy S. Severin, LH, 4 (Madrid: Cátedra, 2000).

Rojas Villandrando, Agustín de, *El viaje entretenido*, ed. Jean Pierre Ressot, CC, 44 (Madrid: Castalia, 1972).

Ronsard, Pierre de, *Les quatre premiers livres des Odes de Pierre de Ronsard* (Paris: Guillaume Cavellart, 1550).

—— *Les oeuvres de P. de Ronsard . . . Rédigées en sept tomes, Reveuës, et augmentées . . .* (Paris: Gabriel Buon, 1578).

Ruiz de Alarcón, Juan, *La verdad sospechosa*, ed. José Montero Reguera, CC, 250 (Madrid: Castalia, 1999).

Salas Barbadillo, Alonso Gerónimo de, *La estafeta del dios Momo* (Madrid: viuda de Luis Sánchez, 1627).

Sánchez de Viana, Pedro, *Las Transformaciones de Ovidio* (Valladolid: Diego Fernández de Córdoba, 1589).

—— *Anotaciones sobre los Quince libros de las Transformaciones de Ovidio* (Valladolid: Diego Fernández de Córdoba, 1589).

Scaliger, Julius Caesar, *Poetices libri septem* ([Lyons]: Antoine Vincent, 1561).

Spreng, Johannes, *Metamorphoses Ovidii* (Frankfurt: Georg Corvinus, Sigmund Feyerabend, heirs of Wygand Galle, 1563).

Textor, Ravisius, *Officinae Ioannis Ravisii Textoris epitome*, 2 vols. (Lyons: Sébastien Gryphius, 1551).

Thomas Heywood's 'Art of Love': The First Complete English Translation of Ovid's 'Ars Amatoria', ed. Michael L. Stapleton (Ann Arbor, Mich.: University of Michigan Press, 2000).

Vega, Lope de, *La Circe, con otros rimas y prosas* (Madrid: viuda de Alonso Martín, 1624).

—— *Obras poéticas*, ed. José Manuel Blecua, Clásicos Planeta, 18 (Barcelona: Planeta, 1969).

—— *La Gatomaquia*, ed. Celina Sabor de Cortázar, CC, 131 (Madrid: Castalia, 1982).

—— *Rimas*, ed. Felipe B. Pedraza Jiménez, 2 vols. ([Ciudad Real]: Universidad de Castilla-La Mancha, 1993).

—— *Rimas humanas y otros versos*, ed. Antonio Carreño, Biblioteca Clásica, 52 (Barcelona: Crítica, 1998).

—— *Arte nuevo de hacer comedias*, ed. Enrique García Santo-Tomás, LH, 585 (Madrid: Cátedra, 2006 [1609]).

La vita et Metamorfoseo d'Ovidio figurato i abbreviato in forma d'epigrammi da G. Symeoni (Lyons: Jean de Tournes, 1559).

Vitoria, Baltasar de, *Primera Parte del Teatro de los dioses de la gentilidad* (Madrid: Imprenta Real, 1657 [1620]).

—— *Segunda Parte del Teatro de los dioses de la gentilidad* (Madrid: Imprenta Real, 1657 [1623]).

SECONDARY LITERATURE

Acker, Thomas S., *The Baroque Vortex: Velázquez, Calderón, and Gracián under Philip IV*, Currents in Comparative Romance Languages and Literatures, 23 (New York: Peter Lang, 2000).

Alatorre, Antonio, 'Andanzas de Venus y Cupido en tiempos del romancero nuevo', in Beatriz Garza Cuarón and Yvette Jiménez de Báez (eds.), *Estudios de folklore y literatura dedicados a Mercedes Díaz Roig* (Mexico: El Colegio de México, 1992), 337–90.

Alden, Maureen J., 'The Resonances of the Song of Ares and Aphrodite', *Mnemosyne*, 50 (1997), 513–29.

Alfonso Fernández de Madrigal, El Tostado, ed. Roxana Recio and Antonio Cortijo Ocaña, *La corónica*, 33 (2004), 5–162.

Allen, Christopher, 'Ovid and Art', in *The Cambridge Companion to Ovid*, 336–67.

Alonso, Álvaro, *La poesía italianista* (Madrid: Laberinto, 2002).

Alonso, Dámaso, *Estudios y ensayos gongorinos*, 2nd edn. (Madrid: Gredos, 1960).

———— *Góngora y el «Polifemo»*, 6th edn., 3 vols. (Madrid: Gredos, 1974).

Alonso Hernández, José Luis, *Léxico del marginalismo del Siglo de Oro*, Acta Salmanticensia: Filosofía y Letras, 99 (Salamanca: Universidad de Salamanca, 1976).

Alonso Moreno, Guillermo, 'Otra fuente de los versos sobre Júpiter y Europa de Francisco de Aldana', in José María Maestre Maestre, Joaquín Pascual Barea, and Luis Charlo Brea (eds.), *Humanismo y pervivencia del mundo clásico. Homenaje al profesor Antonio Prieto*, 5 vols. (Madrid: CSIC, 2008–10), i. 79–89.

Alpers, Svetlana, *The Decoration of the Torre de la Parada* (London: Phaidon Press, 1971).

———— *The Vexations of Art: Velázquez and Others* (New Haven: Yale University Press, 2005).

Alpers, Svetlana, and others, *Velázquez* (Barcelona: Galaxia Gutenberg, 1999).

Alzieu, Pierre, Robert Jammes, and Yvan Lissorgues, *Poesía erótica del Siglo de Oro* (Barcelona: Crítica, 1984).

Amielle, Ghislaine, *Recherches sur des traductions françaises des Métamorphoses d'Ovide* (Paris: Jean Touzot, 1989).

Angulo Íñiguez, Diego, 'Fábulas mitológicas de Velázquez', *Goya*, 37–8 (1960), 104–19.

———— 'La fábula de Vulcano, Venus y Marte y *La Fragua* de Velázquez', *AEA* 33 (1960), 149–81.

———— *Estudios completos sobre Velázquez* (Madrid: CEEH, 2007)

———— *La mitología en el arte español: del Renacimiento a Velázquez*, ed. and intro. José Manuel Pita Andrade (Madrid: RAH, 2010).

Las 'Anotaciones' de Fernando de Herrera. Doce estudios, ed. Begoña López Bueno (Seville: Universidad de Sevilla, 1997).

Antiquity and its Interpreters, ed. Alina Payne, Ann Kuttner, and Rebekah Smick (Cambridge: Cambridge University Press, 2000).

Antonio, Trinidad de, '"La fragua de Vulcano"', in Alpers and others, *Velázquez*, 25–41.

Arce de Vázquez, Margot, 'El caso de la "Canción IV"', in *Obras completas: literatura española y literatura hispanoamericana*, ed. Matilde Albert Robatto and Edith Faría Cancel (San Juan: Universidad de Puerto Rico, 2001), 209–14.

Arellano Ayuso, Ignacio, *Poesía satírico burlesca de Quevedo. Estudio y anotación filológica de los sonetos* (Navarre: Universidad de Navarra, 1984).

—— 'Paradigmas burlescos en *Las aventuras de Don Fruela*, de Francisco Bernardo de Quirós, enciclopedia jocosa del Siglo de Oro', *Monteagudo*, NS 9 (2004), 109–26.

Arikha, Avigdor, 'Nota sobre el "Marte"', in Alpers and others, *Velázquez*, 43–55.

Arrizabalaga, Jon, John Henderson, and Roger French, *The Great Pox: The French Disease in Renaissance Europe* (New Haven: Yale University Press, 1996).

Art and Literature in Spain, 1600–1800: Studies in Honour of Nigel Glendinning, ed. Charles Davis and Paul Julian Smith, CTSA: Monografías, 148 (London: Tamesis, 1993).

Asensio, Eugenio, 'El Brocense contra Herrera y sus *Anotaciones* a Garcilaso', *El Crotalón. Anuario de Filología Española*, 1 (1984), 13–24.

Azaustre Galiana, Antonio, 'Las obras retóricas de Luciano de Samosata en la literatura española de los siglos XVI y XVII, in Ángel A. González, Juan Casas Rigall, and José Manuel González Herrán (eds.), *Homenaje a Benito Varela Jácome* (Santiago de Compostela: Universidade de Santiago de Compostela, 2001), 35–55.

Ball, Robert F., 'Góngora's Parodies of Literary Convention', unpublished doctoral thesis, Yale University (1976).

Baranda Leturio, Consolación, 'La mitología como pretexto: la *Filosofía secreta* de Pérez de Moya (1585)', *Príncipe de Viana. Anejo*, 18 (2000 = *Homenaje a Francisco Ynduráin*), 49–65.

Barceló Jiménez, Juan, *Polo de Medina: la sociedad y los tipos humanos en su obra* (Murcia: Academia Alfonso X el Sabio, 1978).

Barnard, Mary E., *The Myth of Apollo and Daphne from Ovid to Quevedo: Love, Agon, and the Grotesque* (Durham, NC: Duke University Press, 1987).

—— 'Inscribing Transgression, Siting Identity: Arguijo's Phaëthon and Ganymede in Painting and Text', in *Writing for the Eyes*, 109–29.

Beardsley, Theodore S., *Hispano-Classical Translations Printed Between 1482 and 1699* (Pittsburgh: Duquesne University Press, 1970).

Bergmann, Emilie L., *Art Inscribed: Essays on Ekphrasis in Spanish Golden Age Poetry*, Harvard Studies in Romance Languages, 35 (Cambridge, Mass.: Harvard University Press, 1979).

Bialler, Nancy Ann, *Chiaroscuro Woodcuts: Hendrick Goltzius and his Time (1558–1617)* (Amsterdam: Rijksmuseum, 1992).

Blumenfeld-Kosinski, Renate, 'The Hermeneutics of the *Ovide moralisé*', in *Reading Myth: Classical Mythology and its Interpretation in Medieval French Literature* (Stanford: Stanford University Press, 1997), 90–136.

Bohigas, Pedro, 'Más sobre la Canción IV de Garcilaso', *Ibérida*, 5 (1961), 79–90.

Bontempelli, Giulia, 'Polo de Medina, poeta gongorino', in *Venezia nella letteratura spagnola e altri studi barocchi* (Padua: University of Pisa, 1973), 85–136.

Boyd, Stephen, 'A Tale of Two Serpents: Biblical and Mythological Allusions in Cervantes's *El celoso extremeño*', in *Rewriting Classical Mythology*, 71–89.

Braswell, Bruce K., 'The Song of Ares and Aphrodite: Theme and Relevance to *Odyssey* 8', *Hermes*, 110 (1982), 129–37.

Brown, Christopher G., 'Ares, Aphrodite, and the Laughter of the Gods', *Phoenix*, 43 (1989), 283–93.

Brown, Jonathan, *Images and Ideas in Seventeenth-Century Spanish Painting* (Princeton: Princeton University Press, 1978).

—— *Velázquez: Painter and Courtier* (New Haven: Yale University Press, 1986).

—— *The Golden Age of Painting in Spain* (New Haven: Yale University Press, 1991).

—— *Kings & Connoisseurs: Collecting Art in Seventeenth-Century Europe* (New Haven: Yale University Press, 1995).

—— 'Velázquez and Italy', in *The Cambridge Companion to Velázquez*, 30–47.

—— *Collected Writings on Velázquez* (Madrid: CEEH, 2008).

—— and John H. Elliott, *A Palace for a King: The Buen Retiro and the Court of Philip IV*, 2nd edn. (New Haven: Yale University Press, 2003).

—— and Carmen Garrido, *Velázquez: The Technique of Genius* (New Haven: Yale University Press, 1998).

Bull, Malcolm, *The Mirror of the Gods: Classical Mythology in Renaissance Art* (London: Allen Lane, 2005).

Burton, David G., 'Juan de la Cueva (1543–1612)', in Mary Parker (ed.), *Spanish Dramatists of the Golden Age* (Westport, Conn.: Greenwood Press, 1998), 87–95.

Cabañas, Pablo, *El mito de Orfeo en la literatura española* (Madrid: CSIC, 1948).

Calcraft, Raymond P., 'The Lover as Icarus: Góngora's "Qué de envidiosos montes levantados"', in Salvador Bacarisse and others (eds.), *What's Past is Prologue: A Collection of Essays in Honour of L. J. Woodward* (Edinburgh: Scottish Academy Press, 1984), 10–16.

Calderón Dorda, Esteban, 'La mitología clásica en la obra poética de Juan de la Cueva', in Ricardo Escavy Zamora and others (eds.), *Amica verba: in honorem Prof. Antonio Roldán Pérez*, 2 vols. (Murcia: Servicio de Publicaciones de la Universidad de Murcia, 2005), i. 133–54.

Calonge García, Genoveva, 'El *Teatro de los dioses de la gentilidad* y sus fuentes: Bartolomé Cassaneo', *Cuadernos de Filología Clásica: Estudios Latinos*, 3 (1992), 159–70.

The Cambridge Companion to Ovid, ed. Philip Hardie (Cambridge: Cambridge University Press, 2002).

The Cambridge Companion to Velázquez, ed. Suzanne L. Stratton-Pruitt (Cambridge: Cambridge University Press, 2002).

Cammarata, Joan, *Mythological Themes in the Works of Garcilaso de la Vega* (Madrid: José Porrúa Turanzas, 1983).

Cantizano Pérez, Félix, *El erotismo en la poesía de adúlteros y cornudos en el Siglo de Oro* (Madrid: Editorial Complutense, 2007).

Carr, Dawson W., and others, *Velázquez* (London: National Gallery, 2006).

Carreño, Antonio, *El romancero lírico de Lope de Vega* (Madrid: Gredos, 1979).

———— 'De potros y asnos rucios: ludismo y parodia en Luis de Góngora', in Joaquín Roses (ed.), *Góngora Hoy*, VI: *Actas del Foro de Debate Góngora Hoy celebrado en la Diputación de Córdoba: Góngora y sus contemporáneos: de Cervantes a Quevedo del 14 al 16 de noviembre de 2002*, Colección de Estudios Gongorinos, 4 (Córdoba: Diputación de Córdoba, 2004), 59–87.

Castellani, Victor, 'Two Divine Scandals: Ovid *Met.* 2.680 ff. and 4.171 ff. and his Sources', *Transactions of the American Philological Association*, 110 (1980), 37–50.

Cebrián García, José, 'La forma poética de las fábulas mitológicas de Juan de la Cueva', *Gades*, 13 (1985), 289–306.

———— *La fábula de Marte y Venus de Juan de la Cueva. Significación y sentido* (Seville: Secretariado de Publicaciones, 1986).

———— *El mito de Adonis en la poesía de la Edad de Oro* (Barcelona: Promociones y Publicaciones Universitarias, 1988).

———— *Estudios sobre Juan de la Cueva* (Seville: Secretariado de Publicaciones, 1991).

Chamorro, María Inés, *Tesoro de Villanos. Diccionario de Germanía. Lengua de jacarandina: rufos, mandiles, galloferos, viltrotonas, zurrapas, carcaveras, murcios, floraineros y otras gentes de la carda* (Barcelona: Herder, 2002).

Checa Cremades, Fernando, *Tiziano y la monarquía hispánica. Usos y funciones de la pintura veneciana en España (siglos XVI y XVII)* (Madrid: Nerea, 1994).

Cherry, Peter, 'Velázquez y el desnudo', in *Fábulas de Velázquez*, 241–77.

Civil, Pierre, 'Erotismo y pintura mitológica en la España del Siglo de Oro', *Edad de Oro*, 9 (1990), 39–49.

Collard, Andrée, *Nueva poesía. Conceptismo, culteranismo en la crítica española* (Madrid: Castalia, 1967).

Colombier, Pierre du, 'La Forge de Vulcain au Château d'Effiat', *Gazette des Beaux-Arts*, 81 (1939), 30–8.

Colombi-Monguio, Alicia de, '"Al simple, al compuesto, al puro, al misto": la amada como microcosmos', in Keith McDuffie and Rose Minc (eds.), *Homenaje a Alfredo A. Roggiano: en este aire de América* (Pittsburgh: Instituto Internacional de Literatura Iberoamericana, 1990), 91–110.

Colomer, José Luis, '"Dar a Su Magestad algo bueno": Four Letters from Velázquez to Virgilio Malvezzi', *Burlington Magazine*, 135 (1993), 67–72.

Combet, Louis, 'Lexicographie et sémantique: quelques remarques à propos de la réédition du *Vocabulario de refranes* de Gonzalo Correas', *Bulletin Hispanique*, 71 (1969), 248–50.

A Companion to Lope de Vega, ed. Alexander Samson and Jonathan Thacker, CTSA: Monografías, 260 (Woodbridge: Tamesis, 2008).

A Companion to Ovid, ed. Peter Knox, Blackwell Companions to the Ancient World (Oxford: Blackwell, 2009).

Cornejo, Manuel, 'Lope de Vega y las fiestas de Lerma de 1617: la teatralización de «las fiestas de Castilla» en *Lo que pasa en una tarde*', *Mélanges de la Casa de Velázquez*, 37 (2007), 179–98.

Coroleu, Alejandro, 'El *Momo* de Leon Battista Alberti: una contribución al estudio de la fortuna de Luciano en España', *Cuadernos de Filología Española: Estudios Latinos*, 7 (1994), 177–83.

Correa, Gustavo, 'Garcilaso y la mitología', *HR* 45 (1977), 269–81.

Cossío, José María de, *Fábulas mitológicas en España* (Madrid: Espasa Calpe, 1952).

Cristóbal, Vicente, *Mujer y piedra. El mito de Anaxárete en la literatura española* (Huelva: Servicio de Publicaciones de la Universidad de Huelva, 2002).

Cruz, Anne J., 'La mitología como retórica poética: el mito implícito como metáfora en Garcilaso', *Romanic Review*, 77 (1986), 404–14.

Curtius, Ernst Robert, *European Literature and the Latin Middle Ages*, trans. Willard R. Trask (London: Routledge & Kegan Paul, 1953).

Dadson, Trevor J., 'Cómo se hacía un soneto en el Siglo de Oro: el caso de «Amor, la red de amor digo que es hecha»', in María Cruz García de Enterría and Alicia Cordón Mesa (eds.), *Actas del IV Congreso Internacional de la Asociación Internacional Siglo de Oro (AISO)*, 2 vols. (Alcalá de Henares: Universidad de Alcalá, 1998), i. 509–24.

Davis, Elizabeth B., *Myth and Identity in the Epic of Imperial Spain* (Columbia, Mo.: University of Missouri Press, 2000).

De Armas, Frederick A., 'Los excesos de Venus y Marte en *El gallardo español*', in Manuel Criado de Val (ed.), *Cervantes: su obra y su mundo* (Madrid: Edi-6, 1981), 249–60.

——— '*Adonis y Venus*: hacia la tragedia en Tiziano y Lope de Vega', in Frederick A. de Armas, Luciano García Lorenzo, and Enrique García Santo-Tomás (eds.), *Hacia la tragedia áurea. Lecturas para un nuevo milenio* (Madrid: Iberoamericana, 2008), 97–115.

De Jong, Irene, *A Narratological Commentary on the Odyssey* (Cambridge: Cambridge University Press, 2001).

De Jong, Jan L., 'Ovidian Fantasies: Pictorial Variations on the Story of Mars, Venus and Vulcan', in Hermann Walter and Hans-Jürgen Horn (eds.), *Die Rezeption der Metamorphosen des Ovid in der Neuzeit: Der antike Mythos in Text und Bild* (Berlin: Gebr. Mann Verlag, 1995), 161–77.

——— 'Love, Betrayal, and Corruption: *Mars and Venus* and *Danaë and Jupiter* in the Palazzi Stati-Cenci and Mattei di Paganica in Rome', *Source: Notes in the History of Art*, 19 (1999), 20–9.

De los Reyes, Antonio, and others, *Polo de Medina: tercer centenario* (Murcia: Academia Alfonso X el Sabio, 1976).

Diccionario de autoridades, Biblioteca Románica Hispánica: Diccionarios, 3, 3 vols. (Madrid: Gredos, 1979).

Díez de Revenga, Francisco Javier, *Polo de Medina, poeta del barroco* (Murcia: Real Academia Alfonso X El Sabio, 2000).

Díez Fernández, José Ignacio, 'Algunos poemas atribuidos a don Diego Hurtado de Mendoza', *Revista de Filología Románica*, 4 (1986), 181–95.

Díez Platas, Fátima, 'Tres maneras de ilustrar a Ovidio: una aproximación al estudio iconográfico de las *Metamorfosis* figuradas del XVI', in María Carmen Folgar de la Calle, Ana Goy Diz, and José Manuel López Vázquez (eds.), *Memoria Artis*.

Studia in memoriam Mª Dolores Vila Jato (Santiago de Compostela: Xunta de Galicia, 2003), 247–67.

Domínguez Ortiz, Antonio, Alfonso E. Pérez Sánchez, and Julián Gállego, *Velázquez* (New York: Metropolitan Museum of Art, 1989).

Dubois, Hélène, and Natasja Peeters, 'The Mythological Decor of the Torre de la Parada', in Joost Vander Auwera and Sabine van Sprang (eds.), *Rubens: A Genius at Work* (Tielt: Lannoo, 2007), 250–63.

Dunn, Peter N., *Castillo Solórzano and the Decline of the Spanish Novel* (Oxford: B. Blackwell, 1952).

—— 'Garcilaso's Ode *A la Flor de Gnido*: A Commentary on Some Renaissance Themes and Ideas', *Zeitschrift für Romanische Philologie*, 81 (1965), 288–309.

Ekserdjian, David, *Parmigianino* (New Haven: Yale University Press, 2006).

Elliott, John H., 'Quevedo and the Count-Duke of Olivares', in James Iffland (ed.), *Quevedo in Perspective: Eleven Essays for the Quadricentennial* (Newark: Juan de la Cuesta, 1982), 227–50.

—— *The Count-Duke of Olivares: The Statesman in an Age of Decline* (New Haven: Yale University Press, 1986).

Entwistle, William J., 'Garcilaso's Fourth Canzon and Other Matters', *MLR* 45 (1950), 225–8.

Escobar Borrego, Francisco Javier, *El mito de Psique y Cupido en la poesía española del siglo XVI*, Literatura, 65 (Seville: Universidad de Sevilla, 2002).

Fábulas de Velázquez. Mitología e historia sagrada en el Siglo de Oro, ed. Javier Portús Pérez (Madrid: Museo Nacional del Prado, 2007).

Farrell, Joseph, 'Towards a Rhetoric of (Roman?) Epic', in William J. Dominik (ed.), *Roman Eloquence: Rhetoric in Society and Literature* (New York: Routledge, 1997), 131–46.

Fasquel, Samuel, 'La enunciación paradójica y las estrategias del discurso burlesco', in *La poesía burlesca del Siglo de Oro*, 41–57.

Ferraté, Juan, *Dinámica de la poesía. Ensayos de explicación, 1952–1966* (Barcelona: Seix Barral, 1968).

Gállego, Julián, *Vision et symboles dans la peinture espagnole du Siècle d'Or* (Paris: Klincksieck, 1968).

Gallego Morell, Antonio, *El mito de Faetón en la literatura española* (Madrid: CSIC, 1961).

García Gavilán, Inmaculada, 'Notas sobre lo satírico y lo burlesco en el *Coro de las Musas* de Miguel de Barrios', in *La poesía burlesca del Siglo de Oro*, 27–40.

Gargano, Antonio, *Fonti, miti, topoi: cinque saggi su Garcilaso* (Naples: Liguori, 1988).

Garrido Pérez, Carmen, *Velázquez: técnica y evolución* (Madrid: Museo Nacional del Prado, 1992).

Ghertman, Sharon, 'Intra-Strophic Syntactic Patterning in the Extended Canzone: Garcilaso's Fourth *Canción*', in *Petrarch and Garcilaso: A Linguistic Approach to Style*, CTSA: Monografías, 44 (London: Tamesis, 1975), 76–92.

Gilman, Ernest B., *The Curious Perspective: Literature and Pictorial Wit in the Seventeenth Century* (New Haven: Yale University Press, 1978).

Glenn, Richard F., *Juan de la Cueva*, TWAS, 273 (New York: Twayne, 1973).

Gombrich, Ernst H., 'Botticelli's Mythologies: A Study of the Neoplatonic Symbolism of his Circle', *Journal of the Warburg and Courtauld Institutes*, 8 (1945), 8–60.

González Estévez, Escardiel, 'En torno a la *Fragua de Vulcano* de Velázquez. Nuevas aportaciones a la interpretación de su significado', *Laboratorio de Arte. Revista del Departamento de Historia del Arte*, 21 (2008–9), 411–26.

González Martínez, Dolores, *La poesía de Francisco de Aldana (1537–1578): introducción al estudio de la imagen*, Scriptura, 4 (Lleida: Edicions de la Universitat de Lleida, 1995).

González Palencia, Ángel, and Eugenio Mele, *Vida y obras de don Diego Hurtado de Mendoza*, 3 vols. (Madrid: Instituto de Valencia de Don Juan, 1941–3).

Green, Otis H., 'On Francisco de Aldana: Observations on Dr. Rivers' Study of "El Divino Capitán"', *HR* 26 (1958), 117–35.

Griffin, Jasper, *Homer on Life and Death* (Oxford: Clarendon Press, 1980).

Guerrieri Crocetti, Camillo, *Juan de la Cueva e le origini del teatro nazionale spagnuolo* (Turin: Giuseppe Gambino, 1936).

Guichart, Luis Arturo, 'La *Ulyxea* de Gonzalo Pérez y las traducciones latinas de Homero', in Barry Taylor and Alejandro Coroleu (ed.), *Latin and Vernacular in Renaissance Iberia, II: Translations and Adaptations*, Cañada Blanch Monographs, 8 (Manchester: MSPS, 2006), 49–72.

Guthmüller, Bodo, *Ovidio metamorphoseos vulgare. Formen und Funktionen der volkssprachlichen Wiedergabe klassischer Dichtung in der italienischen Renaissance* (Boppard am Rhein: Boldt, 1981).

Hagstrum, Jean H., *The Sister Arts: The Tradition of Literary Pictorialism and English Poetry from Dryden to Gray* (Chicago: University of Chicago Press, 1958).

Harris, Enriqueta, *Velázquez* (Oxford: Phaidon Press, 1982).

Hayes, Francis C., 'The Use of Proverbs as Titles and Motives in the *Siglo de Oro* Drama: Tirso de Molina', *HR* 7 (1939), 310–23.

Heiple, Daniel L., *Garcilaso de la Vega and the Italian Renaissance* (Pennsylvania: Pennsylvania State University Press, 1994).

Henkel, Max D., 'Illustrierte Ausgaben von Ovids Metamorphosen im XV., XVI. und XVII. Jahrhundert', in *Vorträge der Bibliothek Warburg, herausgegeben von Fritz Saxl: Vorträge 1926–27* (Leipzig: Teubner, 1930), 58–144.

Hernández Guardiola, Lorenzo, 'El Marte imprudente de Velázquez', *Ars longa: cuadernos de arte*, 1 (1990), 43–8.

Hesse, Everett W., and William C. McCrary, 'The Mars–Venus Struggle in Tirso's *El Aquiles*', *BHS* 33 (1956), 138–51.

Hobson, Anthony, *Renaissance Book Collecting: Jean Grolier and Diego Hurtado de Mendoza, their Books and Bindings* (Cambridge: Cambridge University Press, 1999).

Holmberg, Ingrid E., 'Hephaistos and Spiders' Webs', *Phoenix*, 57 (2003), 1–17.

Iffland, James, *Quevedo and the Grotesque*, CTSA: Monografías, 69 and 72, 2 vols. (London: Tamesis, 1978–82).

Images of the Pagan Gods: Papers of a Conference in Memory of Jean Seznec, ed. Rembrandt Duits and François Quiviger, Warburg Institute Colloquia, 14 (London: Warburg Institute, 2009).

Inventarios reales. Testamentaria del Rey Carlos II 1701–1703, ed. Gloria Fernández Bayton, 3 vols. (Madrid: Museo Nacional del Prado, 1975–85).

Jammes, Robert, *Études sur l'oeuvre poétique de Don Luis de Góngora y Argote*, Bibliothèque de l'École des hautes études hispaniques, 40 (Bordeaux: Féret et Fils, 1967).

Janka, Markus, *Ovid Ars Amatoria: Buch 2 Kommentar* (Heidelberg: Universitätsverlag C. Winter, 1997).

Jauralde Pou, Pablo, 'Alonso de Castillo Solórzano, *Donaires del Parnaso* y la *Fábula de Polifemo*', *Revista de Archivos, Bibliotecas y Museos*, 82 (1979), 727–66.

Justi, Carl, *Diego Velázquez and his Times*, trans. Augustus H. Keane (London: H. Grevel & Co., 1889).

Kahr, Madlyn M., *Velázquez: The Art of Painting* (New York: Harper & Row, 1976).

Lapesa, Rafael, *La trayectoria poética de Garcilaso* (Madrid: Revista de Occidente, 1948).

Larson, Donald R., *The Honor Plays of Lope de Vega* (Cambridge, Mass.: Harvard University Press, 1977).

Laskier Martín, Adrienne, *Cervantes and the Burlesque Sonnet* (Berkeley: University of California Press, 1991).

Latin and Vernacular in Renaissance Spain, III: Ovid from the Middle Ages to the Baroque, ed. Barry Taylor and Alejandro Coroleu, MSPS, 18 (Manchester: MSPS, 2008).

Latin Commentaries on Ovid from the Renaissance, ed. and trans. Ann Moss (Signal Mountain, Tenn.: Summertown, 1998).

Leeflang, Huigen, and others, *Hendrick Goltzius (1558–1617): Drawings, Prints and Paintings* (New York: Metropolitan Museum of Art, 2003).

Lieberman, Julia R., '"Jonen Dalim", auto alegórico de Miguel (Daniel Leví) de Barrios', in Yedida K. Stillman and Norman A. Stillman (eds.), *From Iberia to Diaspora: Studies in Sephardic History and Culture* (Leiden: Brill, 1999), 300–15.

Lleó Cañal, Vicente, *Nueva Roma. Mitología y humanismo en el Renacimiento sevillano* (Seville: Diputación Provincial de Sevilla, 1979).

López Gutiérrez, Luciano, '"Donaires del Parnaso" de Alonso de Castillo Solórzano: edición, estudio y notas', doctoral thesis, Universidad Complutense de Madrid (2004). Available online at <http://eprints.ucm.es/4649/>.

López-Rey, José, *Velázquez: A Catalogue Raisonné of his Oeuvre* (London: Faber & Faber, 1963).

López Torrijos, Rosa, *La mitología en la pintura española del Siglo de Oro* (Madrid: Cátedra, 1985).

Lord, Carla, 'Tintoretto and the *Roman de la Rose*', *Journal of the Warburg and Courtauld Institutes*, 33 (1970), 315–17.

Lowenthal, Anne W., *Joachim Wtewael: Mars and Venus Surprised by Vulcan*, Getty Museum Studies on Art (Malibu, Calif.: J. Paul Getty Museum, 1995).

McGaha, Michael D., 'Las comedias mitológicas de Lope de Vega', in Ángel González, Tamara Holzapfel, and Alfred Rodríguez (eds.), *Estudios sobre el Siglo de Oro en homenaje a Raymond R. MacCurdy* (Madrid: Cátedra, 1983), 67–82.

McKendrick, Melveena, *Theatre in Spain, 1490–1700* (Cambridge: Cambridge University Press, 1989).

Macrí, Oreste, 'Recensión textual de la obra de Garcilaso', in *Homenaje. Estudios de filología e historia literaria lusohispanas e iberoamericanas publicados para celebrar el tercer lustro del Instituto de Estudios Hispánicos, Portugueses e Iberoamericanos de la Universidad Estatal de Utrecht* (The Hague: Van Goor Zonen, 1966), 305–30.

Marsh, David, *Lucian and the Latins: Humor and Humanism in the Early Renaissance* (Ann Arbor, Mich.: University of Michigan Press, 1998).

Martineche, Ernest, '*La Circe* y los poemas mitológicos de Lope', *Humanidades*, 4 (1922), 59–66.

Martínez Berbel, Juan Antonio, *El mundo mitológico de Lope de Vega: siete comedias mitológicas de inspiración ovidiana* (Madrid: Fundación Universitaria Española, 2003).

Mateos Paramio, Alfredo, 'Francisco de Aldana: ¿un neoplatónico del amor humano?', in Manuel García Martín (ed.), *Estado actual de los estudios sobre el Siglo de Oro: actas del II Congreso Internacional de Hispanistas del Siglo de Oro*, Acta Salmanticensia, Estudios Filológicos, 252, 2 vols. (Salamanca: Universidad de Salamanca, 1993), ii. 657–62.

Mena Marqués, Manuela B., 'Velázquez en la Torre de la Parada', in José Alcalá-Zamora and Alfonso E. Pérez Sánchez (eds.), *Velázquez y Calderón. Dos genios de Europa* (Madrid: RAH, 2000), 101–56.

Mérimée, Henri, *Spectacles et comédiens à Valencia (1580–1630)* (Toulouse: Edouard Privat, 1913).

Micó, José María, 'La superación del petrarquismo', in *La fragua de las «Soledades». Ensayos sobre Góngora* (Barcelona: Sirmio, 1990), 59–102.

Moffitt, John F., 'Velázquez's 'Forge of Vulcan': The Cuckold, the Poets and the Painter', *Pantheon*, 41 (1968), 322–6.

Morros Mestres, Bienvenido, *Las polémicas literarias en la España del siglo XVI: a propósito de Fernando de Herrera y Garcilaso de la Vega*, Biblioteca General, 20 (Barcelona: Quaderns Crema, 1998).

—— 'La canción IV de Garcilaso como un infierno de amor: de Garci Sánchez de Badajoz y el Cariteo a Bernardo Tasso', *Criticón*, 80 (2000), 19–47.

Moya del Baño, Francisca, *El tema de Hero y Leandro en la literatura española* (Murcia: Publicaciones de la Universidad de Murcia, 1966).

Nash, Jane C., *Veiled Images: Titian's Mythological Paintings for Philip II* (Philadelphia: Art Alliance Press, 1985).

Navarrete, Ignacio, *Orphans of Petrarch: Poetry and Theory in the Spanish Renaissance*, Publications of the UCLA Center for Medieval and Renaissance Studies, 25 (Berkeley: University of California Press, 1994).

Newton, Rick M., 'Odysseus and Hephaestus in the *Odyssey*', *Classical Journal*, 83 (1987), 12–20.

Noble Wood, Oliver J., 'Mars Recontextualized in the Golden Age of Spain: Psychological and Aesthetic Readings of Velázquez's *Marte*', in *Rewriting Classical Mythology*, 139–55.

—————— 'Salvador Jacinto Polo de Medina (1603–76), "A Vulcano, Venus y Marte" (*c*.1630)', in *The Spanish Ballad*, 175–221.

—————— 'Ovid and Velázquez: Re-examining Some of the Literary Sources for Velázquez's *La Fragua de Vulcano*', in *Latin and Vernacular in Renaissance Spain*, *III*, 147–61.

—————— '«Vanitas vanitatum, et omnia vanitas»: bibliotecas y bibliofilia en la literatura del Siglo de Oro', in Oliver Noble Wood, Jeremy Roe, and Jeremy Lawrance (eds.), *Poder y saber. Bibliotecas y bibliofilia en la época del conde-duque de Olivares* (Madrid: CEEH, 2011), 277–96.

—————— '"Ensíllenme el asno rucio" (1585): Parody and Burlesque in a *Contrafactum*', in Oliver Noble Wood and Nigel Griffin (eds.), *A Poet for All Seasons: Eight Commentaries on Góngora*, Spanish Series, 156 (New York: Hispanic Seminary of Medieval Studies, 2013), 1–23.

Núñez Rivera, José Valentín, '«Y vivo solo y casi en un destierro»: Juan de la Cueva en sus epístolas poéticas', in *La epístola*, ed. Begoña López Bueno, Literatura, 42 (Seville: Universidad de Sevilla, 2000), 257–94.

—————— 'Cueva, Barahona y tal vez Cervantes. Más paradojas en la segunda mitad del XVI', in his edition of Cristóbal Mosquera de Figueroa, *Paradojas*, Textos Recuperados, 27 (Salamanca: Universidad de Salamanca, 2010), 91–109.

Orenstein, Nadine M., 'Finally Spranger: Prints and Print Designs 1586–1590', in Leeflang and others, *Hendrick Goltzius (1558–1617)*, 81–114.

Orozco Díaz, Emilio, *Lope y Góngora frente a frente* (Madrid: Gredos, 1973).

Orso, Stephen N., *Velázquez, Los Borrachos, and Painting at the Court of Philip IV* (Cambridge: Cambridge University Press, 1993).

Ortega y Gasset, José, *Velázquez*, intro. Francisco Calvo Serraller (Madrid: Espasa Calpe, 1999).

Ost, Heidrun, 'Illuminating the *Roman de la Rose* in the Time of the Debate: The Manuscript of Valencia', in Godfried Croenen and Peter Ainsworth (eds.), *Patrons, Authors and Workshops: Books and Book Production in Paris Around 1400*, Synthema, 4 (Leuven: Peeters, 2006), 405–36.

Ovid in the Age of Cervantes, ed. Frederick A. de Armas (Toronto: University of Toronto Press, 2010).

Ovid Renewed: Ovidian Influences on Literature and Art from the Middle Ages to the Twentieth Century, ed. Charles Martindale (Cambridge: Cambridge University Press, 1988).

Palomino de Castro y Velasco, Antonio, *El museo pictórico y escala óptica. Teórica de la pintura*, 3 vols. (Madrid: Imprenta de Sancha, 1795–7).

Parker, Alexander A., *The Philosophy of Love in Spanish Literature, 1480–1680*, ed. Terence O'Reilly (Edinburgh: Edinburgh University Press, 1985).

Parrack, John C., 'Mythography and the Artifice of Annotation: Sánchez de Viana's *Metamorphoses* (and Ovid)', in *Ovid in the Age of Cervantes*, 20–36.

Pedraza Jiménez, Felipe B., *El universo poético de Lope de Vega*, Colección Arcadia de las Letras, 16 (Madrid: Laberinto, 2003).

Pérez Sánchez, Alfonso E., 'Velázquez and his Art', in Domínguez Ortiz, Pérez Sánchez, and Gállego, *Velázquez*, 21–56.

Pierce, Frank, *La poesía épica del Siglo de Oro*, trans. J. C. Cayol de Bethencourt, 2nd rev. and exp. edn. (Madrid: Gredos, 1968).

La poesía burlesca del Siglo de Oro (= *Criticón*, 100), ed. Alain Bègue and Jesús Ponce Cárdenas (Toulouse: Presses Universitaires du Mirail, 2007).

Poggi, Giulia, '*Exclusus amator* e *poeta ausente*: alcune note ad una canzone gongorina', *Linguistica e letteratura*, 8 (1983), 189–222.

—— *Gli occhi del pavone. Quindici studi su Góngora* (Florence: Alinea, 2009).

Ponce Cárdenas, Jesús, «*Evaporar contempla un fuego helado*»: *género, enunciación lírica y erotismo en una canción gongorina* (Málaga: Universidad de Málaga, 2006).

Pons, Joseph-Sebastien, 'Note sur la Canción IV de Garcilaso de la Vega', *Bulletin Hispanique*, 35 (1933), 168–71.

Portús Pérez, Javier, *La Sala Reservada del Museo del Prado y el coleccionismo de pintura de desnudo en la corte española 1554–1838* (Madrid: Museo Nacional del Prado, 1998).

—— *Pintura y pensamiento en la España de Lope de Vega* (Guipúzcua: Nerea, 1999).

—— 'Nudes and Knights: A Context for Venus', in Carr and others, *Velázquez*, 56–67.

Prater, Andreas, *Venus at her Mirror: Velázquez and the Art of Nude Painting* (Munich: Prestel, 2002).

Ramos Jurado, Enrique, 'Comedia mitológica y comedia histórica: la tradición clásica en Lope de Vega', in *Cuatro estudios sobre tradición clásica en la literatura española. Lope, Blasco, Alberti y Mª Teresa León y la novela histórica* (Cadiz: Universidad de Cádiz, 2001), 11–43.

Rapetti, Rodolphe, and others, *Johann Wilhelm Baur 1607–1642: maniérisme et baroque en Europe* (Strasbourg: Musées de Strasbourg, 1998).

Rewriting Classical Mythology in the Hispanic Baroque, ed. Isabel Torres, CTSA: Monografías, 233 (London: Tamesis, 2007).

Reyes Cano, José María, *La poesía lírica de Juan de la Cueva* (Seville: Artes Gráficas Padura, 1980).

Reznicek, Emil K. J., *Hendrick Goltzius: Drawings Rediscovered 1962–1992* (New York: Master Drawings, 1993).

Rico Verdú, José, 'Dos personalidades literarias enfrentadas: comentario a dos romances de Lope y Góngora', *Hispanística*, 1 (1993), 38–53.

Ripoll, Begoña, 'Alonso de Castillo Solórzano', in *La novela barroca* (Salamanca: Universidad de Salamanca, 1991), 51–72.

Rivers, Elias L., *Francisco de Aldana, el divino capitán* (Badajoz: Institución de Servicios Culturales, 1955).

—— 'Garcilaso divorciado de Boscán', in J. Homer Herriott (ed.), *Homenaje a Antonio Rodríguez Moñino: estudios de erudición que le ofrecen sus amigos o discípulos hispanistas norteamericanos*, 2 vols. (Madrid: Castalia, 1966), i. 121–9.

Rizavi, Ali, '*Novelas a Marcia Leonarda*', in *A Companion to Lope de Vega*, 244–55.

Robbins, Jeremy, *Love Poetry of the Literary Academies in the Reigns of Philip IV and Charles II*, CTSA: Monografías, 166 (London: Tamesis, 1997).

—— *The Challenges of Uncertainty: An Introduction to Seventeenth-Century Spanish Literature* (London: Duckworth, 1998).

—— *Arts of Perception: The Epistemological Mentality of the Spanish Baroque, 1580–1720* (= *BSS* 82.8) (Abingdon: Routledge, 2005).

Robinson, Christopher, *Lucian and his Influence in Europe* (London: Duckworth, 1979).

Rodríguez-Moñino, Antonio R., *Construcción crítica y realidad histórica en la poesía española de los siglos XVI y XVII* (Madrid: Castalia, 1965).

Romojaro, Rosa, *Lope de Vega y el mito clásico* (Málaga: Universidad de Málaga, 1998).

La Rosa. Manojo de la poesía castellana, ed. Juan Pérez de Guzmán, 2 vols. (Madrid: Imprenta y Fundación de M. Tello, 1891).

Rosand, David, 'Inventing Mythologies: The Painter's Poetry', in Patricia Meilman (ed.), *The Cambridge Companion to Titian* (Cambridge: Cambridge University Press, 2004), 35–57.

Roses Lozano, Joaquín, 'La "Fábula de Adonis, Hipómenes y Atalanta" de Diego Hurtado de Mendoza: grados de la imitación renacentista', in Juan Matas Caballero and others (eds.), *Congreso Internacional sobre Humanismo y Renacimiento*, 2 vols. (León: Universidad de León, 1998), ii. 123–50.

Rossich, Albert, 'Les faules mitològiques burlesques als segles XVII–XVIII', in Roger Friedlin and Sebastian Neumeister (eds.), *Vestigia fabularum. La mitologia antiga a les literatures catalana i castellana entre l'edat mitjana i la moderna*, Textos i Estudis de Cultura Catalana, 98 (Barcelona: Publicacions de l'Abadia de Montserrat, 2004), 113–41.

Rothberg, Irving P., 'Hurtado de Mendoza and the Greek Epigrams', *HR* 26 (1958), 171–87.

—— 'Lope de Vega and the Greek Anthology', *Romanische Forschungen*, 87 (1975), 239–56.

Ruiz Pérez, Pedro, *La biblioteca de Velázquez* (Seville: Junta de Andalucía, 1999).

Ruiz Silva, Carlos, *Estudios sobre Francisco de Aldana* (Valladolid: Universidad de Valladolid, 1981).

Salamanqués Pérez, Virginia, 'El tratamiento de los dioses paganos en la obra de Baltasar de Vitoria', in José María Maestre Maestre, Joaquín Pascual Barea, and Luis Charlo Brea (eds.), *Humanismo y pervivencia del mundo clásico. Homenaje al profesor Antonio Fontán*, 5 vols (Madrid: Laberinto, 2002), iv. 1863–8.

Salinas, Pedro, 'The Idealization of Reality: Garcilaso de la Vega', in *Reality and the Poet in Spanish Poetry* (Baltimore: Johns Hopkins University Press, 1940), 65–93.

Salort Pons, Salvador, *Velázquez en Italia* (Madrid: Fundación de Apoyo a la Historia del Arte Hispánico, 2002).

Sánchez Cantón, Francisco J., 'Los libros españoles que poseyó Velázquez', in *Varia Velazqueña*, i. 640–8.

—— 'La Venus del espejo', *AEA* 33 (1960), 137–40.

Sánchez Fernández, José Luis, *Poemas mitológicos de Miguel de Barrios* (Córdoba: Instituto de Historia de Andalucía, 1981).

Sánchez Jiménez, Antonio, *Lope pintado por sí mismo: mito e imagen del autor en la poesía de Lope de Vega Carpio*, CTSA: Monografías, 229 (Woodbridge: Tamesis, 2006).

Schevill, Rudolph, *Ovid and the Renascence in Spain* (Berkeley: University of California Press, 1913).

Schneider, Luis M., 'Apuntes sobre la mitología greco-romana en Castillejo y Garcilaso', *Revista de Filología Hispánica*, 2 (1960), 295–322.

Scholberg, Kenneth R., 'Miguel de Barrios and the Amsterdam Sephardic Community', *Jewish Quarterly Review*, 53 (1962), 120–59.

Schwartz, Lía, 'Velázquez and Two Poets of the Baroque', in *Cambridge Companion to Velázquez*, 130–48.

——— 'Linguistic and Pictorial Conceits in the Baroque: Velázquez between Quevedo and Gracián', in *Writing for the Eyes*, 279–300.

Sebastián, Santiago, 'Lectura iconográfico-iconológica de *La Fragua de Vulcano*', *Traza y Baza*, 8 (1983), 20–7.

Sedeño Rodríguez, Francisco, 'El antirretrato petrarquista: metamorfosis de la poética (paradigmas en Quevedo y Barrios)', in Gregorio Cabello Porras and Javier Campos Daroca (eds.), *Poéticas de la Metamorphosis. Tradición clásica, Siglo de Oro y modernidad* (Málaga: Universidad de Málaga-Universidad de Almería, 2002), 407–46.

Sentenach y Cabañas, Narciso, *La pintura en Madrid desde sus orígenes hasta el siglo XIX* (Madrid: Administración del «Boletín de la Sociedad Española de Excursiones», 1907).

Serés, Guillermo, 'El enciclopedismo mitográfico de Baltasar de Vitoria', *La Perinola*, 7 (2003), 398–421.

——— 'Antecedentes exegéticos de la *Filosofía secreta* de Juan Pérez de Moya (1585)', in *«Por discreto y por amigo». Mélanges offerts à Jean Canavaggio*, ed. by Christophe Couderc and Benoit Pellistrandi, Collection de la Casa de Velázquez, 88 (Madrid: Casa de Velázquez, 2005), 633–48.

Seznec, Jean, *The Survival of the Pagan Gods: The Mythological Tradition and its Place in Renaissance Humanism and Art*, trans. Barbara F. Sessions, Bollingen Series, 38 (New York: Pantheon, 1953).

Shanzer, Danuta, *A Philosophical and Literary Commentary on Martianus Capella's 'De Nuptiis Philologiae et Mercurii' Book 1*, Classical Studies, 32 (Berkeley: University of California Press, 1986).

Sharratt, Peter, *Bernard Salomon: illustrateur lyonnais* (Geneva: Droz, 2005).

Shergold, Norman D., 'Juan de la Cueva and the Early Theatres of Seville', *BHS* 32 (1955), 1–7.

Sievers, Ann H., Linda D. Muehlig, and Nancy Rich, *Master Drawings from the Smith College Museum of Art* (New York: Hudson Hills, 2000).

Simms, Norman, 'Confusion and Madness: Miguel de Barrios, alias Daniel Levi', in *Masks in the Mirror: Marranism in Jewish Experience* (New York: Peter Lang, 2006), 113–31.

Simón Díaz, José, 'Libros de autores andaluces dedicados al Conde-Duque de Olivares', in *De libros a bibliotecas. Homenaje a Rocío Caracuel*, ed. Sonsoles Celestino Angulo (Seville: Universidad de Sevilla, 1995), 389–402.

—— 'Sesenta y dos libros dedicados al Conde-Duque de Olivares en los años 1621–1642', *Trabajos de la Asociación Española de Bibliografía*, 2 (1998), 143–74.

Siple, Ella S., 'A Flemish Set of Venus and Vulcan Tapestries. I: Their Origin and Design', *Burlington Magazine*, 73 (1938), 212–21.

—— 'A Flemish Set of Venus and Vulcan Tapestries. II: Their Influence on English Tapestry Design', *Burlington Magazine*, 74 (1939), 268–79.

Slatkes, Leonard J., and Wayne Franits, *The Paintings of Hendrick ter Brugghen 1588–1629: Catalogue Raisonné*, Oculi Studies in the Arts of the Low Countries, 10 (Philadelphia: John Benjamins, 2007).

Smith, Paul Julian, *Quevedo on Parnassus: Allusive Context and Literary Theory in the Love-Lyric*, MHRA Texts and Dissertations, 25 (London: MHRA, 1987).

Soons, Alan, *Alonso de Castillo Solórzano*, TWAS, 457 (Boston: Twayne, 1978).

Soria, Martin S., 'La Venus, Los Borrachos y La Coronación de Velázquez', *AEA* 26 (1953), 269–84.

Soubiran, Jean, 'Deux notes critiques au "Concubitus Martis et Veneris" de Reposianus', *Bollettino di Studi Latini*, 3 (1973), 93–5.

Southworth, Eric, 'Luis de Góngora y Argote (1561–1627), "Noble desengaño" (1584)', in *The Spanish Ballad*, 24–40.

—— 'Luis de Góngora y Argote (1561–1627), "Arrojóse el mancebito" (1589)', in *The Spanish Ballad*, 41–57.

The Spanish Ballad in the Golden Age, ed. Nigel Griffin and others, CTSA: Monografías, 264 (Woodbridge: Tamesis, 2008).

Spitzer, Leo, 'The "Ode on a Grecian Urn", or Content vs. Metagrammar', *Comparative Literature*, 7 (1955), 203–25.

Tejerina, Belén, 'El *De Genealogia Deorum gentilium* en una mitografía española del siglo XVII: el *Teatro de los dioses de la gentilidad*, de Baltasar de Vitoria', *Filología moderna*, 55 (1975), 591–601.

Terry, Arthur, *Seventeenth-Century Spanish Poetry: The Power of Artifice* (Cambridge: Cambridge University Press, 1993).

Thacker, Jonathan, *A Companion to Golden Age Theatre*, CTSA: Monografías, 235 (Woodbridge: Tamesis, 2007).

Thompson, Colin, 'Francisco de Quevedo Villegas (1580–1645), "A la Corte vas, Perico" (date unknown)', in *The Spanish Ballad*, 115–33.

Tolnay, Charles de, 'La "Venus au miroir", de Velázquez', in *Varia Velazqueña*, i. 339–43.

—— 'Las pinturas mitológicas de Velázquez', *AEA* 34 (1961), 31–45.

Torres, Isabel, 'Introduction: Con pretensión de Fénix', in *Rewriting Classical Mythology*, 1–16.

Trueblood, Alan S., *Experience and Artistic Expression in Lope de Vega: The Making of 'La Dorotea'* (Cambridge, Mass.: Harvard University Press, 1974).

Turner, John H., *The Myth of Icarus in Spanish Renaissance Poetry*, CTSA: Monografías, 56 (London: Tamesis, 1976).

Valsalobre, Pep, 'Mitologia burlesca, invenció barroca i catarsi: l'ànima frondosa de Fontanella o notes disperses a *Lo Desengany*', in Pep Valsalobre and Gabriel

Sansano (eds.), *Francesc Fontanella. Una obra, una vida, un temps* (Bellcaire d'Empordà: Edicions Vitel·la, 2006), 281–318.

Varia Velazqueña. Homenaje a Velázquez en el III centenario de su muerte 1660–1960, ed. Antonio Gallego y Burín, 2 vols. (Madrid: Ministerio de Educación Nacional, 1960).

Velasco Kindelán, Magdalena, *La novela cortesana y picaresca de Castillo Solórzano* (Valladolid: Institución Cultural Simancas, 1983).

Velázquez a Roma. Velázquez e Roma, ed. Anna Coliva (Milan: Skiva, 1999).

Velázquez in Seville, ed. Michael Clarke (Edinburgh: National Galleries of Scotland, 1996).

Veldman, Ilja M., *Maarten van Heemskerck and Dutch Humanism in the Sixteenth Century*, trans. Michael Hoyle (Maarssen: Gary Schwartz, 1977).

—— *Profit and Pleasure: Print Books by Crispijn de Passe*, trans. Michael Hoyle and Clara Klein, Studies in Prints and Printmaking, 4 (Rotterdam: Sound and Vision, 2001).

Viel, Marie-France, 'La *Bible des poètes*: une réécriture rhétorique des *Métamorphoses* d'Ovide', *Tangence*, 74 (2004), 25–44.

Vilanova, Antonio, *Las fuentes y los temas del 'Polifemo' de Góngora*, Anejos de la *Revista de Filología Española*, 66, 2 vols. (Madrid: CSIC, 1957).

Vives Coll, Antonio, *Luciano de Samosata en España (1500–1700)* (Valladolid: Sever-Cuesta, 1959).

Volk, Katharina, *Ovid*, Blackwell Introductions to the Classical World (Chichester: Wiley-Blackwell, 2010).

Vosters, Simon A., *Rubens y España. Estudio artístico-literario sobre la estética del Barroco* (Madrid: Cátedra, 1990).

Wagschal, Steven, 'Writing on the Fractured "I": Góngora's Iconographic Evocations of Vulcan, Venus, and Mars', in *Writing for the Eyes*, 130–50.

—— *The Literature of Jealousy in the Age of Cervantes* (Columbia, Mo.: University of Missouri Press, 2006).

Walters, D. Gareth, *Francisco de Quevedo, Love Poet* (Cardiff: University of Wales Press, 1985).

—— *The Poetry of Francisco de Aldana*, CTSA: Monografías, 128 (London: Tamesis, 1988).

Warnke, Martin, *Velázquez: Form & Reform* (Cologne: DuMont, 2005).

Wasyl, Anna Maria, *Genres Rediscovered: Studies in Latin Miniature Epic, Love Elegy, and Epigram of the Romano-Barbaric Age* (Krakow: Jagiellonian University Press, 2011).

Weigert, Roger-Armand, and Maxime Préaud, *Inventaire du fonds français. Graveurs du XVIIᵉ siècle*, 17 vols. (Paris: Bibliothèque nationale de France, 1939–99).

Weiss, Julian, 'Renaissance Poetry', in David T. Gies (ed.), *The Cambridge History of Spanish Literature* (Cambridge: Cambridge University Press, 2004), 159–77.

Welles, Marcia L., *Arachne's Tapestry: The Transformation of Myth in Seventeenth-Century Spain* (San Antonio, Tex.: Trinity University Press, 1986).

Wind, Edgar, *Pagan Mysteries in the Renaissance* (New Haven: Yale University Press, 1958).

Writing for the Eyes in the Spanish Golden Age, ed. Frederick A. de Armas (Lewisburg, Pa.: Bucknell University Press, 2004).

Wyss, Edith, *The Myth of Apollo and Marsyas in the Art of the Italian Renaissance: An Inquiry into the Meaning of Images* (London: Associated University Presses, 1996).

Zapata Ferrer, María de la Almudena, 'La mitología en *La rosa blanca* de Lope de Vega', in Francisca Moya del Baño (ed.), *Los humanistas españoles y el humanismo europeo (IV simposio de filología clásica)* (Murcia: Secretariado de Publicaciones, Universidad de Murcia, 1990), 261–6.

Zappala, Michael O., *Lucian of Samosata in the Two Hesperias: An Essay in Literary and Cultural Translation* (Potomac, Md.: Scripta Humanistica, 1990).

Zurli, Loriano, *Apographa Salmasiana. Sulla trasmissione di 'Anthologia Salmasiana' tra Sei e Settecento*, Spudasmata, Band 96 (Hildesheim: Georg Olms, 2004).

Index